"No other guide... a pleasure to re..."

"... Excellently .... who is looking for a mix of recreation and cultural insight."
Washington Post

★ ★ ★ ★ ★ (5-star rating) "Crisply written and remarkably personable. Cleverly organized so you can pluck out the minutest fact in a moment. Satisfyingly thorough."
Réalités

"The information they offer is up-to-date, crisply presented but far from exhaustive, the judgments knowledgeable but not opinionated." *New York Times*

"The individual volumes are compact, the prose succinct, and the coverage up-to-date and knowledgeable... The format is portable and the index admirably detailed."
John Barkham Syndicate

"... An abundance of excellent directions, diversions, and facts, including perspectives and getting-ready-to-go advice — succinct, detailed, and well organized in an easy-to-follow style." *Los Angeles Times*

"They contain an amount of information that is truly staggering, besides being surprisingly current."
Detroit News

"These guides address themselves to the needs of the modern traveler demanding precise, qualitative information ... Upbeat, slick, and well put together."
Dallas Morning News

"... Attractive to look at, refreshingly easy to read, and generously packed with information." *Miami Herald*

"These guides are as good as any published, and much better than most." *Louisville* (Kentucky) *Times*

Stephen Birnbaum Travel Guides

Acapulco
Bahamas, and Turks & Caicos
Barcelona
Bermuda
Boston
Canada
Cancun, Cozumel, & Isla Mujeres
Caribbean
Chicago
Disneyland
Eastern Europe
Europe
Europe for Business Travelers
Florence
France
Great Britain
Hawaii
Honolulu
Ireland
Italy
Ixtapa & Zihuatanejo
Las Vegas
London
Los Angeles
Mexico
Miami & Ft. Lauderdale
Montreal & Quebec City
New Orleans
New York
Paris
Portugal
Puerto Vallarta
Rome
San Francisco
South America
Spain
Toronto
United States
USA for Business Travelers
Vancouver
Venice
Walt Disney World
Washington, DC
Western Europe

CONTRIBUTING EDITORS

Gene Bourg
Sharon Donovan

SYMBOLS
Gloria McKeown

MAPS
Mark Carlson
Susan Carlson

A Stephen Birnbaum Travel Guide

Birnbaum's
NEW ORLEANS
1993

Alexandra Mayes Birnbaum
EDITOR

Lois Spritzer
EXECUTIVE EDITOR

Laura L. Brengelman
Managing Editor

Mary Callahan
Jill Kadetsky
Susan McClung
Beth Schlau
Dana Margaret Schwartz
Associate Editors

Gene Gold
Assistant Editor

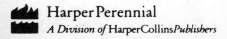

HarperPerennial
A Division of HarperCollins*Publishers*

To Stephen, who merely made all this possible.

BIRNBAUM'S NEW ORLEANS 1993. Copyright © 1993 by HarperCollins Publishers. All rights reserved. Printed in the United States of America. No part of this book may be used or reproduced in any manner whatsoever without written permission except in the case of brief quotations embodied in critical articles and reviews. For information address HarperCollins*Publishers,* 10 East 53rd Street, New York, NY 10022.

FIRST EDITION

ISSN 0749-2561 (Stephen Birnbaum Travel Guides)
ISSN 1061-5431 (New Orleans)
ISBN 0-06-278058-1 (pbk.)

93 94 95 96 97 CC/WP 10 9 8 7 6 5 4 3 2 1

Contents

ix **A Word from the Editor**

1 **How to Use This Guide**

GETTING READY TO GO

All the practical travel data you need to plan your vacation down to the final detail.

When and How to Go

9 When to Go
10 Traveling by Plane
26 On Arrival
29 Package Tours

Preparing

34 Calculating Costs
34 Planning a Trip
36 How to Use a Travel Agent
37 Insurance
41 Hints for Handicapped Travelers
47 Hints for Single Travelers
49 Hints for Older Travelers
52 Hints for Traveling with Children

On the Road

56 Credit Cards and Traveler's Checks
59 Time Zone and Business Hours
59 Mail, Telephone, and Electricity
61 Staying Healthy
65 Legal Aid
65 Drinking and Drugs
66 Tipping
67 Religion on the Road

Sources and Resources

68 Tourist Information
68 Books, Magazines, and Newsletters
70 Cameras and Equipment

vi CONTENTS

THE CITY

A thorough, qualitative guide to New Orleans. Each section offers a comprehensive report on the city's most compelling attractions and amenities, designed to be used on the spot.

73 Specific Data About New Orleans

DIVERSIONS

A selective guide to more than 15 active and/or cerebral vacation themes, including the best places to pursue them.

For the Experience

123 Quintessential New Orleans
126 New Orleans's Best Hotels
129 Big Easy's Best Eats
132 A French Quarter Shopping Spree
134 Antiques: New Orleans's Best Hunting Grounds

For the Body

136 Goin' Fishing
137 Tennis
137 Jogging
138 Bicycling
138 Big Easy Rambles
138 Sailing and Boating

For the Mind

140 All That Jazz
142 Mardi Gras Madness
145 Memorable Museums
146 Avant-Garde New Orleans
147 Historic Houses
148 A Shutterbug's New Orleans

DIRECTIONS

Nine of the best tours in and around New Orleans.

155 **Introduction**

158 The St. Charles Streetcar
165 Walk 1: The French Quarter

CONTENTS vii

174 Walk 2: Royal Street
180 Walk 3: A Literary Tour of New Orleans
188 Walk 4: The Riverfront (and Farmer's Market)
196 Walk 5: The Warehouse-Art District
202 Walk 6: The Garden District
208 Drive 1: Esplanade Avenue City Park
214 Drive 2: New Orleans Plantations

223 **Index**

A Word from the Editor

I made my first visit way down yonder in the early 1960s, and even my first view through a hazy, hot, and humid August night could not dampen my anticipation about the city that jazz musicians dubbed "The Big Easy." And the nickname tells you a lot about this unique metropolis. It's a city that understands its roots better than most other cities, a place whose leisurely past is at least as important as its very vital present.

Over the years, my husband Steve Birnbaum and I would begin a New Orleans morning with fresh–from–the–frying pan *beignets* (no, they *don't* come from the oven), accompanied by the world's best cup of chicory coffee. We agreed that even if the tourist trade had taken away some of the authenticity of Bourbon Street, the bleat of a trumpet or the syncopated sound of jazz emanating from the doors of hot spots along this street that saw the birth of the blues was (and is) guaranteed to quicken your step. For fans of grillwork, the façades of the Vieux Carré continue to attract, and the cadence of a true native accent — most especially if someone addresses you as *cher* (or *chère*) and suggests sharing a bucket of fresh-from-the-Gulf crayfish — is impossible to resist.

The fact that there no longer is a streetcar named *Desire* in no way lessens a visitor's desire to see this Southern-cum-Cajun-cum-Creole city. Big it isn't. But it is easy to love. No doubt about it, the Louisiana Purchase was one of the best buys we ever made.

My own evolution as a traveler (which happily continues) is mirrored by the evolution of our guidebook series. When we began our series of modern travel guides, we logically began with "area" books, attempting to publish guides that would include the widest possible number of attractive destinations. When the public seemed to accept our new way of delivering travel data, we added titles covering only a single country, and when these became popular we began our newest expansion phase, which centers on a group of books that deal with only a single city. Now we can not only highlight our favorite urban destinations, but really describe how to get the very most out of a visit.

Such treatment of travel information only mirrors an increasingly pervasive trend among travelers — the frequent return to a treasured travel spot. Once upon a time, even the most dedicated travelers would visit distant parts of the world no more than once in a lifetime — usually as part of some sort of Grand Tour. But greater numbers of would-be sojourners are now availing themselves of the opportunity to visit a favored part of the world over and over again.

So where once it was routine to say you'd "seen" a particular city or country after a very superficial, once-over-lightly encounter, the more perceptive travelers of today recognize that it's entirely possible to have only

x A WORD FROM THE EDITOR

skimmed the surface of a specific travel destination even after having visited that place more than a dozen times. Similarly, repeated visits to a single site permit true exploration of special interests, whether they be sporting, artistic, or intellectual.

For those of us who now have spent the last several years working out the special system under which we present information in this series, the luxury of being able to devote nearly as much space as we'd like to just a single city is as close to paradise for guide writers and editors as any of us expects to come. But clearly this is not the first guide to the glories of New Orleans — one suspects that guides of one sort or another have existed at least since the day in 1803 when Napoleon sold the city to the United States — so a traveler might logically ask why a new one is suddenly necessary.

Our answer is that the nature of travel to New Orleans — and even of the travelers who now routinely make the trip — has changed dramatically of late. For the past 200 years or so, travel to even a town within our own country was considered an elaborate undertaking, one that required extensive advance planning. But with the advent of jet air travel in the late 1950s and of increased-capacity, wide-body aircraft during the late 1960s, travel to and around once distant destinations became extremely common. Attitudes as well as costs have changed significantly in the last couple of decades.

Obviously, any new guidebook to New Orleans must keep pace with and answer the real needs of today's travelers. That's why we've tried to create a guide that's specifically organized, written, and edited for the more demanding modern traveler, one for whom qualitative information is infinitely more desirable than mere quantities of unappraised data. We think this book, along with all the other guides in our series, represents a new generation of travel guides — one that is especially responsive to modern needs and interests.

For years, dating back as far as Herr Baedeker, travel guides have tended to be encyclopedic, seemingly much more concerned with demonstrating expertise in geography and history than with a real analysis of the sorts of things that actually concern a typical modern tourist. But today, when it is hardly necessary to tell a traveler where New Orleans is (in many cases, the traveler has been there nearly as often as the guidebook editors), it becomes the responsibility of those editors to provide new perspectives and to suggest new directions in order to make the guide genuinely valuable.

That's exactly what we've tried to do in this series. I think you'll notice a different, more contemporary tone to the text, as well as an organization and focus that are distinctive and more functional. And even a random reading of what follows will demonstrate a substantial departure from the standard guidebook orientation, for we've not only attempted to provide information of a more compelling sort, but we also have tried to present the data in a format that makes it particularly accessible.

Needless to say, it's difficult to decide just what to include in a guidebook of this size — and what to omit. Early on, we realized that giving up the encyclopedic approach precluded our listing every single route and restaurant, a realization that helped define our overall editorial focus. Similarly, when we discussed the possibility of presenting certain information in other than strict geographic order, we found that the new format enabled us to

A WORD FROM THE EDITOR xi

arrange data in a way that we feel best answers the questions travelers typically ask.

Large numbers of specific questions have provided the real editorial skeleton for this book. The volume of mail we regularly receive emphasizes that modern travelers want very precise information, so we've tried to organize our material in the most responsive way possible. Readers who want to know the best restaurants or the best place to buy a porcelain mask in New Orleans will have no trouble extracting that data from this guide.

Travel guides are, understandably, reflections of personal taste, and putting one's name on a title page obviously puts one's preferences on the line. But I think I ought to amplify just what "personal" means. Like Steve, I don't believe in the sort of personal guidebook that's a palpable misrepresentation on its face. It is, for example, hardly possible for any single travel writer to visit thousands of restaurants (and nearly as many hotels) in any given year and provide accurate appraisals of each. And even if it were physically possible for one human being to survive such an itinerary, it would of necessity have to be done at a dead sprint, and the perceptions derived therefrom would probably be less valid than those of any other intelligent individual visiting the same establishments. It is, therefore, impossible (especially in a large, annually revised and updated guidebook *series* such as we offer) to have only one person provide all the data on the entire world.

I also happen to think that such individual orientation is of substantially less value to readers. Visiting a single hotel for just one night or eating one hasty meal in a random restaurant hardly equips anyone to provide appraisals that are of more than passing interest. No amount of doggedly alliterative or oppressively onomatopoeic text can camouflage a technique that is essentially specious. We have, therefore, chosen what I like to describe as the "thee and me" approach to restaurant and hotel evaluation and, to a somewhat more limited degree, to the sites and sights we have included in the other sections of our text. What this really reflects is a personal sampling tempered by intelligent counsel from informed local sources, and these additional friends-of-the-editor are almost always residents of the city and/or area about which they are consulted.

Despite the presence of several editors, writers, researchers, and local contributors, very precise editing and tailoring keep our text fiercely subjective. So what follows is the gospel according to Birnbaum, and it represents as much of our own taste and instincts as we can manage. It is probable, therefore, that if you like your cities stylish and prefer small hotels with personality to huge high-rise anonymities, we're likely to have a long and meaningful relationship. Readers with dissimilar tastes may be less enraptured.

I also should point out something about the person to whom this guidebook is directed. Above all, he or she is a "visitor." This means that such elements as restaurants have been specifically picked to provide the visitor with a representative, enlightening, stimulating, and above all pleasant experience. Since so many extraneous considerations can affect the reception and service accorded a regular restaurant patron, our choices can in no way be construed as an exhaustive guide to resident dining. We think we've listed all the best

xii A WORD FROM THE EDITOR

places, in various price ranges, but they were chosen with a visitor's enjoyment in mind.

Other evidence of how we've tried to tailor our text to reflect modern travel habits is most apparent in the section we call DIVERSIONS. Where once it was common for travelers to spend an urban visit in a determinedly passive state, the emphasis is far more active today. So we've organized every activity we could reasonably evaluate and arranged the material in a way that is especially accessible to activists of either athletic or cerebral bent. It is no longer necessary, therefore, to wade through a pound or two of superfluous prose just to find the very best creole cooking or the quaintest neighborhood within the city limits.

If there is a single thing that best characterizes the revolution in and evolution of current holiday habits, it is that most travelers now consider travel a right rather than a privilege. No longer is a family trip to the far corners of the world necessarily a once-in-a-lifetime thing; nor is the idea of visiting exotic, faraway places in the least worrisome. Travel today translates as the enthusiastic desire to sample all of the world's opportunities, to find that elusive quality of experience that is not only enriching but comfortable. For that reason, we've tried to make what follows not only helpful and enlightening, but the sort of welcome companion of which every traveler dreams.

Finally, I also should point out that every good travel guide is a living enterprise; that is, no part of this text is carved in stone. In our annual revisions, we refine, expand, and further hone all our material to serve your travel needs better. To this end, no contribution is of greater value to us than your personal reaction to what we have written, as well as information reflecting your own experiences while using the book. We earnestly and enthusiastically solicit your comments about this guide *and* your opinions and perceptions about places you have recently visited. In this way, we will be able to provide the most current information — including the actual experiences of recent travelers — and to make those experiences more readily available to others. Please write to us at 10 E. 53rd St., New York, NY 10022.

We sincerely hope to hear from you.

ALEXANDRA MAYES BIRNBAUM

How to Use This Guide

A great deal of care has gone into the special organization of this guidebook, and we believe it represents a real breakthrough in the presentation of travel material. Our aim is to create a new, more modern generation of travel books, and to make this guide the most useful and practical travel tool available today.

Our text is divided into four basic sections in order to present information in the best way on every possible aspect of a vacation to New Orleans. This organization itself should alert you to the vast and varied opportunities available, as well as indicate all the specific data necessary to plan a successful visit. You won't find much of the conventional "swaying palms and shimmering sand" text here; we've chosen instead to deliver more useful and practical information. Prospective itineraries tend to speak for themselves, and with so many diverse travel opportunities, we feel our main job is to highlight what's where and to provide basic information — how, when, where, how much, and what's best — to assist you in making the most intelligent choices possible.

Here is a brief summary of the four basic sections of this book, and what you can expect to find in each. We believe that you will find both your travel planning and en route enjoyment enhanced by having this book at your side.

GETTING READY TO GO

This mini-encyclopedia of practical travel facts is a sort of know-it-all companion with all the precise information necessary to create a successful trip to New Orleans. There are entries on about two dozen separate topics, including how to get where you're going, what preparations to make before leaving, what to expect, what your trip is likely to cost, and how to avoid prospective problems. The individual entries are specific, realistic, and where appropriate, cost-oriented.

We expect you to use this section most in the course of planning your trip, for its ideas and suggestions are intended to simplify this often confusing period. Entries are intentionally concise, in an effort to get to the meat of the matter with the least extraneous prose. These entries are augmented by extensive lists of specific sources from which to obtain even more specialized data, plus some suggestions for obtaining travel information on your own.

THE CITY

The individual report on New Orleans has been created with the assistance of researchers, contributors, professional journalists, and experts who live in the city. Although useful at the planning stage, THE CITY is really designed to be taken along and used on the spot. The reports offer a short-stay guide,

2 HOW TO USE THIS GUIDE

including an essay introducing the city as a historic entity and as a contemporary place to visit. *At-a-Glance* material is actually a site-by-site survey of the most important, interesting, and sometimes most eclectic sights to see, and things to do. *Sources and Resources* is a concise listing of pertinent tourist information meant to answer myriad potentially pressing questions as they arise — from simple things such as the address of the local tourism office, how to get around, which sightseeing tours to take, and when special events occur to something more difficult, like where to find the best nightspot or hail a taxi, which are the chic places to shop, and where the jazz clubs and theaters are to be found. *Best in Town* lists our collection of cost-and-quality choices of the best places to eat and sleep on a variety of budgets.

DIVERSIONS

This section is designed to help travelers find the best places in which to engage in a wide range of physical and cerebral activities, without having to wade through endless pages of unrelated text. This very selective guide lists the broadest possible range of activities, including all the best places to pursue them.

We start with a list of special places to stay and eat, move to activities that require some perspiration — sports preferences and other rigorous pursuits — and go on to report on a number of more spiritual vacation opportunities. In every case, our suggestions of a particular location — and often our recommendation of a specific hotel — is intended to guide you to that special place where the quality of experience is likely to be highest. Whether you seek a historic hotel or museum or the best place to shop or sail, each category is the equivalent of a comprehensive checklist of the absolute best in New Orleans.

DIRECTIONS

Here are six walks, two drives, and a streetcar ride that cover the city, along its main thoroughfares and side streets, past its most charming neighborhoods and historic quarters. This is the only section of the book that is organized geographically; itineraries can be "connected" for longer sojourns or used individually for short, intensive explorations.

Although each of the book's sections has a distinct format and a special function, they have all been designed to be used together to provide a complete inventory of travel information. To use this book to full advantage, take a few minutes to read the table of contents and random entries in each section to get a firsthand feel for how it all fits together.

Pick and choose needed information. Assume, for example, that you have always wanted to visit New Orleans and partake of its spectacular Cajun dinners — but you never really knew how to organize it or where to go. Choose specific restaurants from the selections offered in "Eating Out" in THE CITY, add some of those noted in each walking tour in DIRECTIONS, and cross-reference with those in the roundup of the best in the city in the *Big Easy's Best Eats* section in DIVERSIONS.

HOW TO USE THIS GUIDE 3

In other words, the sections of this book are building blocks designed to help you put together the best possible trip. Use them selectively as a tool, a source of ideas, a reference work for accurate facts, and a guidebook to the best buys, the most exciting sights, the most pleasant accommodations, the tastiest food — *the best travel experience* that you can possibly have.

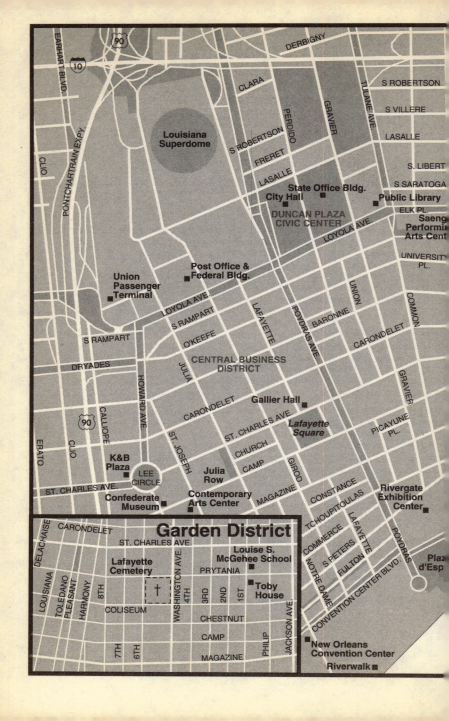

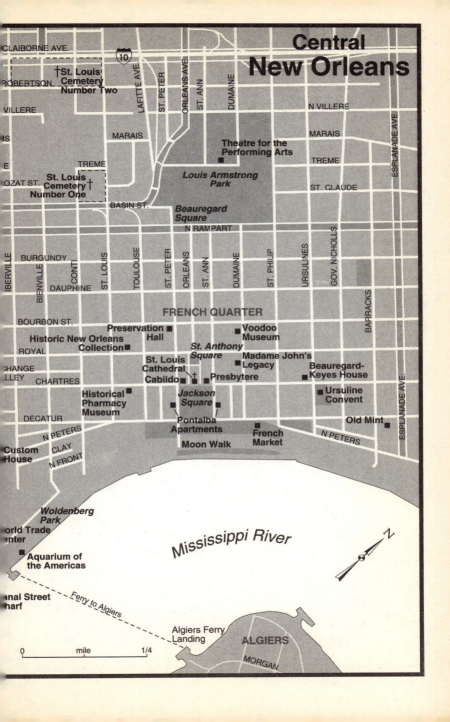

GETTING READY TO GO

When and How to Go

When to Go

While there isn't really a best time to visit New Orleans, summer can be hot and sticky, while late winter and early spring are temperate but the time of the most popular festivals, making for crowds — happy ones, but still crowds. Fall offers the opportunity for the most sunshine at lower relative humidity. The city's climate is subtropical, with average summer temperatures in the mid-80s, rising up to the 90s, and the winter temperatures averaging in the high 50s, rarely dropping to freezing. Summers are humid and rainy, so be prepared with rain gear if you are visiting during that season.

There are good reasons for visiting New Orleans any time of the year. There are no real off-season periods when attractions are closed, so you aren't risking the disappointment of arriving at an attraction and finding the gates locked. However, you can benefit from lower room rates if you visit during the less busy periods — summer (June through August) or in December.

■ **Note:** When planning the timing of your visit, there is one period during which you must be careful. During the week of *Mardi Gras* (which is on February 23 this year), hotels are packed and most bargains disappear. During this period, make your bookings extra early — preferably 2, 3, or more months ahead.

WEATHER: Travelers can get current readings and extended forecasts through the *Weather Channel Connection,* the worldwide weather report center of the *Weather Channel,* a cable TV station. By dialing 900-WEATHER and punching in either the first four letters of the city name or the area code (NEWO or 504 for New Orleans) for over 600 cities in the US (including Puerto Rico and the US Virgin Islands), an up-to-date recording will provide such information as current temperature, barometric pressure, relative humidity, and wind speed, as well as a general 2-day forecast. Beach, boating, and highway reports are also provided for some locations. This 24-hour service can be accessed from any touch-tone phone in the US, and costs 95¢ per minute. The charge will show up on your phone bill. For additional information, contact the *Weather Channel Connection,* 2600 Cumberland Pkwy., Atlanta, GA 30339 (phone: 404-434-6800).

CULTURAL EVENTS: While New Orleans has the traditional cultural events — alternating productions of the *New Orleans Opera Association* and the *New Orleans City Ballet* from fall to spring at the *Theatre for the Performing Arts,* and performances by the new *Louisiana Philharmonic* in the *Saenger Performing Arts Center* — jazz is the preeminent art form in New Orleans and *Preservation Hall* is its most famous venue. For the stage, there are several theaters providing regional and touring theater and *Le Petit Théâtre du Vieux Carré,* the oldest continuously operating community theater in the nation, and host of the annual *Tennessee Williams Literary Festival* in March.

The museum presence is headed by the *New Orleans Museum of Art,* in the midst

10 GETTING READY / Traveling by Plane

of a major renovation and expansion due to be completed early this year, and home to a fine and varied collection. The *Old Mint,* part of the *Louisiana State Museum,* contains *Mardi Gras* and jazz exhibits, while the *Historic New Orleans Collection* is a scholarly archive in a preserved French Quarter residence. Other notable New Orleans museums include the *Voodoo Museum,* the *Confederate Museum,* and the *Contemporary Arts Center.*

FESTIVALS: Special events, of course, are headed by New Orleans' famed, frenetic, joyous *Mardi Gras,* this year on February 23. The *Black Heritage Festival* takes place in March, while the family-oriented *French Quarter Festival* in April celebrates food and jazz. The *New Orleans Jazz and Heritage Festival,* held for 2 weeks each April and May, presents the top names in jazz throughout the city. In August the city celebrates with the hot sounds of the *Latino Festival.* Another food-oriented event, in June, is the *Great French Market Tomato Festival,* followed by the area's largest Hispanic celebration, *Carnaval Latino.* Later in the summer, *La Fête,* a festival of food and cookery, continues the emphasis on fine dining, as does the *Gumbo Festival* in October. A *Creole Christmas* ends the year with caroling by candlelight and open houses at historic homes.

Traveling by Plane

Flying is the quickest, most convenient means of travel between different parts of the country. It *sounds* expensive to travel across the US by air, but when all costs are taken into account for traveling any substantial distance, plane travel usually is less expensive per mile than traveling by car. It also is the most economical way to go in terms of time. Although touring by car, bus, or train certainly is a more scenic way to travel, air travel is far faster and more direct — and the less time spent in transit, the more time spent in New Orleans.

SCHEDULED FLIGHTS: Numerous airlines offer regularly scheduled flights to New Orleans International Airport, which is located 12 miles west of the city center and handles international and domestic traffic.

Listed below are the major national air carriers serving New Orleans and their toll-free telephone numbers:

American and *American Eagle:* 800-433-7300.
Continental: 800-525-0280.
Delta and *Delta Connection:* 800-221-1212.
Northwest and *NW Airlink:* 800-225-2525.
Southwest: 800-531-5601.
TWA: 800-221-2000.
United: 800-241-6522.
USAir and *USAir Express:* 800-428-4322.

Among the international carriers that serve New Orleans are *Aeroméxico, Aviateca, LACSA,* and *TACA.*

Tickets – A full-fare ticket provides maximum flexibility for travel on regularly scheduled flights. There are no advance booking or other ticketing requirements — except seat availability — although cancellation restrictions vary. It pays to check *before* booking your flight. It also is advisable to reserve well in advance during popular vacation periods and around holiday times.

Fares – Full-fare tickets continue to change so rapidly that even the experts find it difficult to keep up with them. This ever-changing situation is due to a number of

GETTING READY / Traveling by Plane 11

factors, including airline deregulation, volatile labor relations, increasing fuel costs, and vastly increased competition.

Perhaps the most common misconception about fares on scheduled airlines is that the cost of the ticket determines how much service will be provided on the flight. This is true only to a certain extent. A far more realistic rule of thumb is that the less you pay for your ticket, the more restrictions and qualifications are likely to come into play before you board the plane (as well as after you get off). These qualifying aspects relate to the months (and the days of the week) during which you must travel, how far in advance you must purchase your ticket, the minimum and maximum amount of time you may or must remain away, your willingness to decide on a return date at the time of booking — and your ability to stick to that decision. It is not uncommon for passengers sitting side by side on the same wide-body jet to have paid fares varying by hundreds of dollars, and all too often the traveler paying more would have been equally willing (and able) to accept the terms of the far less expensive ticket.

In general, domestic airfares break down to four basic categories — first class, business class, coach (also called economy or tourist class), and excursion or discount fares. In addition, Advance Purchase Excursion (APEX) fares offer savings under certain conditions.

A **first class** ticket admits you to the special section of the aircraft with larger seats, more legroom, better (or, at least, more elaborately served) food, free drinks, free headsets for movies and music channels, and above all, personal attention. First class fares cost about twice those of full-fare (often called "regular") economy.

Behind first class often lies **business class**, usually a separate cabin or cabins. While standards of comfort and service are not as high as in first class, they represent a considerable improvement over conditions in the rear of the plane, with roomier seats, more leg and shoulder space between passengers, and fewer seats abreast. Free liquor and headsets, a choice of meal entrées, and a separate counter for speedier check-in are other inducements. Note that airlines often have their own names for their business class service — such as Ambassador Class on *TWA* and Medallion Class on *Delta*.

The terms of the **coach** or **economy** fare may vary slightly from airline to airline, and in fact from time to time airlines may be selling more than one type of economy fare. Coach or economy passengers sit more snugly, as many as 10 in a single row on a wide-body jet, behind the first class and business class sections. Normally, alcoholic drinks are not free, nor are the headsets.

In first, business class, and regular economy, passengers are entitled to reserve seats and are sold tickets on an open reservation system. They may travel on any scheduled flight they wish, buy a one-way or round-trip ticket, and have the ticket remain valid for a year. There are no requirements for a minimum or maximum stay or for advance booking and (often) no cancellation penalties — but beware, the rules regarding cancellation vary from carrier to carrier. The fare also allows free stopover privileges, although these can be limited in economy.

Excursion and other **discount** fares are the airlines' equivalent of a special sale and usually apply to round-trip bookings only. These fares generally differ according to the season and the number of travel days permitted. They are only a bit less flexible than full-fare economy tickets, and are, therefore, often useful for both business and holiday travelers. Most round-trip excursion tickets include strict minimum and maximum stay requirements and reservations and can be changed only within the specified time limits. So don't count on extending a ticket beyond the specified time of return or staying less time than required. Different airlines may have different regulations concerning the number of stopovers permitted, and sometimes excursion fares are less expensive during midweek. The availability of these reduced-rate seats is most limited at busy times such as holidays. Discount or excursion fare ticket holders sit with the coach passengers and, for all intents and purposes, are indistinguishable from them. They receive all the same

12   GETTING READY / Traveling by Plane

basic services, even though they may have paid anywhere between 30% and 55% less for the trip. Obviously, it's wise to make plans early enough to qualify for this less expensive transportation if possible.

These discount or excursion fares may masquerade under a variety of names and invariably have strings attached. A common requirement is that the ticket be purchased a certain number of days — usually between 7 and 21 days — in advance of departure, though it may be booked weeks or months in advance (it has to be "ticketed," or paid for, shortly after booking, however). The return reservation usually has to be made at the time of the original ticketing and often cannot be changed later than a certain number of days (again, usually 7 to 21 days) before the return flight. If events force a change in the return reservation after the date allowed, the passenger may have to pay the difference between the round-trip excursion rate and the round-trip coach rate, although some carriers permit such scheduling changes for a nominal fee. In addition, some airlines may allow passengers to use their discounted fares by standing by for an empty seat, even if the carrier doesn't otherwise have standby fares. Another common condition is the minimum and maximum stay requirement; for example, 1 to 6 days or 6 to 14 days (but including at least a Saturday night). Last, cancellation penalties of up to 50% of the full price of the ticket have been assessed — if a refund is offered at all — so check the specific penalty in effect when you purchase your discount/excursion ticket.

On some airlines, the ticket bearing the lowest price of all the current discount fares is the ticket where no change at all in departure and/or return flights is permitted, and where the ticket price is totally nonrefundable. If you do buy such a nonrefundable ticket, you should be aware of a policy followed by some airlines that may make it easier to change your plans if necessary. For a fee — set by each airline and payable at the airport when checking in — you *may* be able to change the time or date of a return flight on a nonrefundable ticket. However, if the nonrefundable ticket price for the replacement flight is higher than that of the original (as often is the case when trading in a weekday for a weekend flight), you also will have to pay the difference. Any such change must be made a certain number of days in advance — in some cases as little as 2 days — of either the original or the replacement flight, whichever is earlier; restrictions are set by the individual carrier. (Travelers holding a nonrefundable or other restricted ticket who must change their plans due to a family emergency should know that some carriers may make special allowances in such situations.)

■ **Note:** Due to recent changes in many US airlines' policies, nonrefundable tickets are now available that carry none of the above restrictions. Although passengers still may *not* be able to obtain a refund for the price paid, the time or date of a departing or return flight may be changed at any time (assuming seats are available) for a nominal service charge.

There also is a newer, often less expensive, type of excursion fare, the **APEX**, or **Advanced Purchase Excursion**, fare. As with traditional excursion fares, passengers paying an APEX fare sit with and receive the same basic services as any other coach or economy passengers, even though they may have paid 50% less for their seats. In return, they are subject to certain restrictions. In the case of domestic flights, the ticket usually is good for a minimum of 1 to 3 days away (including a Saturday) and a maximum, currently, of 1 to 6 months (depending on the airline and the destination); and as its name implies, it must be "ticketed," or paid for in its entirety, a certain period of time before departure — usually 21 days.

The drawback to some APEX fares is that they penalize travelers who change their minds — and travel plans. Usually, the return reservation must be made at the time of the original ticketing, and if for some reason you change your schedule, you will have to pay a penalty of $100 or 10% of the ticket value, whichever is greater, as long as

GETTING READY / Traveling by Plane   13

you travel within the validity period of your ticket. More flexible APEX fares recently have been introduced, which allow travelers to make changes in the date or time of their flights for a nominal charge (as low as $25).

With either type of APEX fare, if you change your return to a date less than the minimum stay or more than the maximum stay, the difference between the round-trip APEX fare and the full round-trip coach rate will have to be paid. There also is a penalty of anywhere from $50 to $125 or more for canceling or changing a reservation *before* travel begins — check the specific penalty in effect when you purchase your ticket. No stopovers are allowed on an APEX ticket, but it is possible to create an open-jaw effect by buying an APEX on a split-ticket basis. Depending on the destination, domestic APEX tickets may be sold at basic and peak rates (the peak season will vary) and may include surcharges for weekend flights.

Standby fares, at one time the rock-bottom price at which a traveler could fly to different parts of the US, have become elusive. At the time of this writing, most major scheduled airlines did not regularly offer standby fares on US domestic flights. Because airline fares and their conditions constantly change, however, bargain hunters should not hesitate to ask if such a fare exists at the time they plan to travel.

Something else to check is the possibility of qualifying for a **GIT** (Group Inclusive Travel) fare, which requires that a specific dollar amount of ground arrangements be purchased, in advance, along with the ticket. The requirements vary as to the number of travel days and stopovers permitted, and the minimum number of passengers required for a group. The actual fares also vary, but the cost will be spelled out in brochures distributed by the tour operators handling the ground arrangements. In the past, GIT fares were among the least expensive available from the established carriers, but the prevalence of discount fares has caused group fares to all but disappear from some air routes. Travelers reading brochures on group package tours to New Orleans will find that, in almost all cases, the applicable airfare given as a sample (to be added to the price of the land package to obtain the total tour price) is an APEX fare, the same discount fare available to the independent traveler.

The major airlines serving US domestic routes also may offer individual fare excursion rates similar to GIT fares, which are sold in conjunction with ground accommodation packages. Previously called ITX, and sometimes referred to as individual tour-basing fares, these fares generally are offered as part of "air/hotel/car/transfer packages," and can reduce the cost of an economy fare by more than a third. The packages are booked for a specific amount of time, with return dates specified; rescheduling and cancellation restrictions and penalties vary from carrier to carrier. At the time of this writing, these fares were offered by *American, Delta, Northwest, TWA,* and *USAir.* Note that their offerings may or may not represent substantial savings over standard economy fares, so check at the time you plan to travel. (For further information on package options, see *Package Tours,* in this section.)

Travelers looking for the least expensive possible airfares should, finally, scan the pages of their hometown newspapers (especially the Sunday travel section) for announcements of special promotional fares. Most airlines offer their most attractive special fares to encourage travel during slow seasons and to inaugurate and publicize new routes. Even if none of these factors applies, prospective passengers can be fairly sure that the number of discount seats per flight at the lowest price is strictly limited, or that the fare offering includes a set expiration date — which means it's absolutely necessary to move fast to enjoy the lowest possible price.

Among other special airline promotional deals for which you should be on the lookout are discount or upgrade coupons sometimes offered by the major carriers and found in mail-order merchandise catalogues. For instance, airlines sometimes issue coupons that typically cost around $25 each and are good for a percentage discount or an upgrade on a domestic airline ticket. The only requirement beyond the fee

14 GETTING READY / Traveling by Plane

generally is that a coupon purchaser must buy at least one item from the catalogue. There usually are some minimum airfare restrictions before the coupon is redeemable, but in general these are worthwhile offers. Restrictions often include certain blackout days (when the coupon cannot be used at all), usually imposed during peak travel periods. These coupons are particularly valuable to business travelers who tend to buy full-fare tickets, and while the coupons are issued in the buyer's name, they can be used by others who are traveling on the same itinerary.

It's always wise to ask about discount or promotional fares and about any conditions that might restrict booking, payment, cancellation, and changes in plans. Check the prices from neighboring cities. A special rate may be offered in a nearby city but not in yours, and it may be enough of a bargain to warrant your leaving from that city. Ask if there is a difference in price for midweek versus weekend travel, or if there is a further discount for traveling early in the morning or late at night. Also be sure to investigate package deals, which are offered by virtually every airline. These may include car rental, accommodations, and dining and/or sightseeing features, in addition to the basic airfare, and the combined cost of packaged elements usually is considerably less than the cost of the exact same elements when purchased separately.

If in the course of your research you come across a deal that seems too good to be true, keep in mind that logic may not be a component of deeply discounted airfares — there's not always any sane relationship between miles to be flown and the price to get there. More often than not, the level of competition on a given route dictates the degree of discount, so don't be dissuaded from accepting an offer that sounds irresistible just because it also sounds illogical. Better to buy that inexpensive fare while it's being offered and worry about the sense — or absence thereof — while you're flying to your desired destination.

When you're satisfied that you've found the lowest price for which you can conveniently qualify (you may have to call the airline more than once, because different airline reservations clerks have been known to quote different prices), make your booking. Then, to protect yourself against fare increases, purchase and pay for your ticket as soon as possible after you've received a confirmed reservation. Airlines generally will honor their tickets, even if the price at the time of your flight is higher than the price you paid. If fares go up between the time you *reserve* a flight and the time you *pay* for it, however, you likely will be out of luck. Finally, with excursion or discount fares, it is important to remember that when a reservations clerk says that you must purchase a ticket by a specific date, this is an absolute deadline. Miss the deadline and the airline usually will automatically cancel your reservation without telling you.

■**Note:** Another wrinkle in the airfare scene is that if the fares go *down* after you purchase your ticket, you *may* be entitled to a refund of the difference. However, this is only possible in certain situations — availability and advance purchase restrictions pertaining to the lower rate are set by the airline. If you suspect that you may be able to qualify for such a refund, check with your travel agent or the airline.

Frequent Flyers – Most of the leading carriers serving New Orleans — including *American, Delta, Northwest, United,* and *USAir* — offer a bonus system to frequent travelers. After the first 10,000 miles, for example, a passenger might be eligible for a first class seat for the coach fare; after another 10,000 miles, he or she might receive a discount on his or her next ticket purchase. The value of the bonuses continues to increase as more miles are logged.

Bonus miles also may be earned by patronizing affiliated car rental companies or hotel chains, or by using one of the credit cards that now offer this reward. In deciding whether to accept such a credit card from one of the issuing organizations that tempt you with frequent flyer mileage bonuses on a specific airline, first determine whether

GETTING READY / Traveling by Plane   15

the interest rate charged on the unpaid balance is the same as (or less than) possible alternate credit cards, and whether the annual "membership" fee also is equal or lower. If these charges are slightly higher than those of competing cards, weigh the difference against the potential value in airfare savings. Also ask about any bonus miles awarded just for signing up — 1,000 is common, 5,000 generally the maximum.

For the most up-to-date information on frequent flyer bonus options, you may want to send for the monthly newsletter *Frequent.* Issued by Frequent Publications, it provides current information about frequent flyer plans in general, as well as specific data about promotions, awards, and combination deals to help you keep track of the profusion — and confusion — of current and upcoming availabilities. For a year's subscription, send $33 to Frequent Publications, 4715-C Town Center Dr., Colorado Springs, CO 80916 (phone: 800-333-5937).

There also is a monthly magazine called *Frequent Flyer,* but unlike the newsletter mentioned above, its focus is primarily on newsy articles of interest to business travelers and other frequent flyers. Published by Official Airline Guides (PO Box 58543, Boulder, CO 80322-8543; phone: 800-323-3537), *Frequent Flyer* is available for $24 for a 1-year subscription.

Low-Fare Airlines – Increasingly, the stimulus for special fares is the appearance of airlines associated with bargain rates. On these airlines, all seats on any given flight generally sell for the same price, which tends to be somewhat below the lowest discount fare offered by the larger, more established airlines. It is important to note that tickets offered by these smaller companies frequently are not subject to the same restrictions as some of the discounted fares offered by the more established carriers. They may not require advance purchase or minimum and maximum stays, may involve no cancellation penalties, and may be available one way or round trip. A disadvantage to some low-fare airlines, however, is that when something goes wrong, such as delayed baggage or a flight cancellation due to equipment breakdown, their smaller fleets and fewer flights mean that passengers may have to wait longer for a solution than they would on one of the equipment-rich major carriers.

Taxes and Other Fees – Travelers who have shopped for the best possible flight at the lowest possible price should be warned that a number of extras will be added to that price and collected by the airline or travel agent who issues the ticket. The 10% federal US Transportation Tax applies to travel within the US or US territories. Another fee is charged by some airlines to cover more stringent security procedures, prompted by recent terrorist incidents. Note that these taxes *usually* (but not always) are included in advertised fares and in the prices quoted by airlines reservations clerks.

Reservations – For those who don't have the time or patience to investigate personally all possible air departures and connections for a proposed trip, a travel agent can be of inestimable help. A good agent should have all the information on which flights go where and when, and which categories of tickets are available on each. Most have computerized reservation links with the major carriers, so that a seat can be reserved and confirmed in minutes. An increasing number of agents also possess fare-comparison computer programs, so they often are very reliable sources of detailed competitive price data. (For more information, see *How to Use a Travel Agent,* in this section.)

When making plane reservations through a travel agent, ask the agent to give the airline your home phone number, as well as your daytime business phone number. All too often the agent uses his or her agency's number as the official contact for changes in flight plans. Especially during the winter, weather conditions hundreds or even thousands of miles away can wreak havoc with flight schedules. Aircraft are constantly in use, and a plane delayed in the Orient or on the West Coast can miss its scheduled flight from the East Coast the next morning. The airlines are fairly reliable about getting this sort of information to passengers if they can reach them; diligence does little good at 10 PM if the airline has only the agency's or an office number.

16 GETTING READY / Traveling by Plane

Reconfirmation is not generally required on domestic flights. However, it always is wise to call ahead to make sure that the airline did not slip up in entering your original reservation, or in registering any changes you may have made since, and that it has your seat reservation and/or special meal request in the computer. If you look at the printed information on your ticket, you'll see the airline's reconfirmation policy stated explicitly. Don't be lulled into a false sense of security by the "OK" on your ticket next to the number and time of the flight. This only means that a reservation has been entered; a reconfirmation still may be necessary. If in doubt — call.

If you plan not to take a flight on which you hold a confirmed reservation, by all means inform the airline. Because the problem of "no-shows" is a constant expense for airlines, they are allowed to overbook flights, a practice that often contributes to the threat of denied boarding for a certain number of passengers (see "Getting Bumped," below).

Seating – For most types of tickets, airline seats usually are assigned on a first-come, first-served basis at check-in, although some airlines make it possible to reserve a seat at the time of ticket purchase. Always check in early for your flight, even with advance seat assignments. A good rule of thumb for domestic flights is to arrive at the airport *at least* 1 hour before the scheduled departure to give yourself plenty of time in case there are long lines.

Most airlines furnish seating charts, which make choosing a seat much easier, but there are a few basics to consider. You must decide whether you prefer a window, aisle, or middle seat. On those few domestic flights where smoking is permitted (see "Smoking," below), you also should indicate if you prefer the smoking or nonsmoking section.

The amount of legroom provided (as well as chest room, especially when the seat in front of you is in a reclining position) is determined by something called "pitch," a measure of the distance between the back of the seat in front of you and the front of the back of your seat. The amount of pitch is a matter of airline policy, not the type of plane you fly. First class and business class seats have the greatest pitch, a fact that figures prominently in airline advertising. In economy class or coach, the standard pitch ranges from 33 to as little as 31 inches — downright cramped.

The number of seats abreast, another factor determining comfort, depends on a combination of airline policy and airplane dimensions. First class and business class have the fewest seats per row. Economy generally has 9 seats per row on a DC-10 or an L-1011, making either one slightly more comfortable than a 747, on which there normally are 10 seats per row. A 727 has 6 seats per row.

Airline representatives claim that most aircraft are more stable toward the front and midsection, while the seats farthest from the engines are quietest. Passengers who have long legs and are traveling on a wide-body aircraft might request a seat directly behind a door or emergency exit, since these seats often have greater than average pitch, or a seat in the first row of a given section, which offers extra legroom — although these seats are increasingly being reserved for passengers who are willing (and able) to perform certain tasks in the event of emergency evacuation. It often is impossible, however, to see the movie from seats that are directly behind the plane's exits. Be aware that the first row of the economy section (called a "bulkhead" seat) on a conventional aircraft (not a widebody) does *not* offer extra legroom, since the fixed partition will not permit passengers to slide their feet under it, and that watching a movie from this first-row seat also can be difficult and uncomfortable. These bulkhead seats do, however, provide ample room to use a bassinet or safety seat and often are reserved for families traveling with small children.

A window seat protects you from aisle traffic and clumsy serving carts and also provides a view, while an aisle seat enables you to get up and stretch your legs without disturbing your fellow travelers. Middle seats are the least desirable, and seats in the last row are the worst of all, since they seldom recline fully. If you wish to avoid

GETTING READY / Traveling by Plane 17

children on your flight or if you find that you are sitting in an especially noisy section, you usually are free to move to any unoccupied seat — if there is one.

If you are large, you may face the prospect of a long flight with special trepidation. Center seats in the alignments of wide-body 747s, L-1011s, and DC-10s are about 1½ inches wider than those on either side, so larger travelers tend to be more comfortable there.

Despite all these rules of thumb, finding out which specific rows are near emergency exits or at the front of a wide-body cabin can be difficult because seating arrangements on any two identical planes usually vary from airline to airline. There is, however, a quarterly publication called the *Airline Seating Guide* that publishes seating charts for most major US airlines and many foreign carriers as well. Your travel agent should have a copy, or you can buy the US edition for $39.95 per year. Order from Carlson Publishing Co., Box 888, Los Alamitos, CA 90720 (phone: 800-728-4877 or 310-493-4877).

Simply reserving an airline seat in advance, however, actually may guarantee very little. Most airlines require that passengers arrive at the departure gate at least 45 minutes (sometimes more) ahead of time to hold a seat reservation. Some carriers may cancel seat assignments and may not honor reservations of passengers who have not checked in some periods of time — usually around 30 minutes, depending on the airport — before the scheduled departure time, and they ask travelers to check in at least 1 hour before all domestic flights. It pays to read the fine print on your ticket carefully and follow its requirements.

A far better strategy is to visit an airline ticket office (or one of a select group of travel agents) to secure an actual boarding pass for your specific flight. Once this has been issued, airline computers show you as checked in, and you effectively own the seat you have selected (although some carriers may not honor boarding passes of passengers arriving at the gate less than 10 minutes before departure). This also is good — but not foolproof — insurance against getting bumped from an overbooked flight and is, therefore, an especially valuable tactic at peak travel times.

Smoking – One decision regarding choosing a seat has been taken out of the hands of most domestic travelers who smoke. Effective February 25, 1990, the US government imposed a ban that prohibits smoking on all flights scheduled for 6 hours or less within the US and its territories. The new regulation applies to both domestic and international carriers serving these routes.

Only flights with a *continuous* flying time of over 6 hours between stops in the US or its territories are exempt. Even if the total flying time is longer, smoking is not permitted on segments of domestic flights where the time between US landings is under 6 hours — for instance, flights that include a stopover (even with no change of plane), or connecting flights. To further complicate the situation, several individual carriers ban smoking altogether on certain routes.

On those flights that do permit smoking, the US Department of Transportation has determined that nonsmoking sections must be enlarged to accommodate all passengers who wish to sit in one. The airline does not, however, have to shift seating to accommodate nonsmokers who arrive late for a flight or travelers flying standby. Cigar and pipe smoking are prohibited on all flights, even in the smoking sections.

For a wallet-size guide that notes in detail the rights of nonsmokers according to these regulations, send a self-addressed, stamped envelope to *ASH (Action on Smoking and Health),* Airline Card, 2013 H St. NW, Washington, DC 20006 (phone: 202-659-4310).

Meals – If you have specific dietary requirements, be sure to let the airline know well before departure time. The available meals include vegetarian, seafood, kosher, Muslim, Hindu, high-protein, low-calorie, low-cholesterol, low-fat, low-sodium, diabetic, bland, and children's menus (not all of these may be available on every carrier). There

18 GETTING READY / Traveling by Plane

is no extra charge for this option. It usually is necessary to request special meals when you make your reservations — check-in time is too late. It's also wise to reconfirm that your request for a special meal has made its way into the airline's computer — the time to do this is 24 hours before departure. (Note that special meals generally are not available on shorter domestic flights, particularly on small local carriers. If this poses a problem, try to eat before you board, or bring a snack with you.)

Baggage – Though airline baggage allowances vary slightly, in general, all passengers are allowed to carry on board, without charge, one piece of luggage that will fit easily under a seat of the plane or in an overhead bin, and whose combined dimensions (length, width, and depth) do not exceed 45 inches. A reasonable amount of reading material, camera equipment, and a handbag also are allowed. In addition, all passengers are allowed to check two bags in the cargo hold: one usually not to exceed 62 inches when length, width, and depth are combined, the other not to exceed 55 inches in combined dimensions. Generally no single bag may weigh more than 70 pounds.

Charges for additional, oversize, or overweight bags usually are made at a flat rate; the actual dollar amount varies from carrier to carrier. If you plan to travel with any special equipment or sporting gear, be sure to check with the airline beforehand. Most have specific procedures for handling such baggage, and you may have to pay for transport regardless of how much other baggage you have checked. Golf clubs and skis may be checked through as luggage (most airlines are accustomed to handling them), but tennis rackets should be carried onto the plane.

To reduce the chances of your luggage going astray, remove all airline tags from previous trips, and label each bag inside and out — with your business address, rather than your home address, on the outside, to prevent thieves from knowing whose house might be unguarded. Lock everything and double-check the tag that the airline attaches to make sure that it is correctly coded MSY for New Orleans International.

If your bags are not in the baggage claim area after your flight or if they're damaged, report the problem to airline personnel immediately. Keep in mind that policies regarding the specific time limit within which you have to make your claim vary from carrier to carrier. Fill out a report form on your lost or damaged luggage and keep a copy of it and your original baggage claim check. If you must surrender the check to claim a damaged bag, get a receipt for it to prove that you did, indeed, check your baggage on the flight. If luggage is missing, be sure to give the airline your destination and/or a telephone number where you can be reached. Also take the name and number of the person in charge of recovering lost luggage.

Most airlines have emergency funds for passengers stranded away from home without their luggage, but if it turns out that your bags are truly lost and not simply delayed, do not then and there sign any paper indicating you'll accept an offered settlement. Since the airline is responsible for the value of your bags within certain statutory limits ($1,250 per passenger for lost baggage on a US domestic flight) you should take the time to assess the extent of your loss (see *Insurance,* in this section). It's a good idea to keep records indicating the value of the contents of your luggage. A wise alternative is to take a Polaroid picture of the most valuable of your packed items just after putting them in your suitcase.

Considering the increased incidence of damage to baggage, now more than ever it's advisable to keep the sales slips that confirm how much you paid for your bags. These are invaluable in establishing the value of damaged luggage and eliminate any arguments. A better way to protect your precious gear from the luggage-eating conveyers is to try to carry it on board whenever possible.

Airline Clubs – US carriers often have clubs for travelers who pay for membership. These clubs are not solely for first class passengers, although a first class ticket *may* entitle a passenger to lounge privileges. Membership entitles the traveler use of the private lounges at airports along their route, to refreshments served in those lounges, and to check-cashing privileges at most of their counters. Extras include special tele-

GETTING READY / Traveling by Plane 19

phone numbers for individual reservations, embossed luggage tags, and a membership card for identification. Airlines serving New Orleans that offer membership in such clubs include the following:

American: The *Admiral's Club.* Single yearly membership $225 for the first year; $125 yearly thereafter; spouse an additional $70 per year.

Delta: The *Crown Club.* Single yearly membership $150; spouse an additional $50 per year; 3-year and lifetime memberships also available.

Northwest: The *World Club.* Single yearly membership $140 (plus a onetime $50 initiation fee); spouse an additional $50 per year; 3-year and lifetime memberships also available.

TWA: The *Ambassador Club.* Single yearly membership $150; spouse an additional $25 per year; 3-year and lifetime memberships also available.

United: The *Red Carpet Club.* Single yearly membership $125 (plus a onetime $100 initiation fee); spouse an additional $70; 3-year and lifetime memberships also available.

USAir: The *USAir Club.* Single yearly membership $125; spouse an additional $25 per year; 3-year and lifetime memberships also available.

Note that the companies above do not have club facilities in all airports. Other airlines also may offer a variety of special services in many airports.

Getting Bumped – A special air travel problem is the possibility that an airline will accept more reservations (and sell more tickets) than there are seats on a given flight. This is entirely legal and is done to make up for "no-shows," passengers who don't show up for a flight for which they have made reservations and bought tickets. If the airline has oversold the flight and everyone does show up, there simply aren't enough seats. When this happens, the airline is subject to stringent rules designed to protect travelers.

In such cases, the airline first seeks ticket holders willing to give up their seats voluntarily in return for a negotiable sum of money or some other inducement, such as an offer of upgraded seating on the next flight or a voucher for a free trip at some other time. If there are not enough volunteers, the airline may bump passengers against their wishes.

Anyone inconvenienced in this way, however, is entitled to an explanation of the criteria used to determine who does and does not get on the flight, as well as compensation if the resulting delay exceeds certain limits. If the airline can put the bumped passengers on an alternate flight that is *scheduled to arrive* at their original destination within 1 hour of their originally scheduled arrival time, no compensation is owed. If the delay is more than 1 hour but less than 2 hours on a domestic US flight, they must be paid denied-boarding compensation equivalent to the one-way fare to their destination (but not more than $200). If the delay is more than 2 hours after the original arrival time on a domestic flight, the compensation must be doubled (not more than $400). The airline also may offer bumped travelers a voucher for a free flight instead of the denied-boarding compensation. The passenger may be given the choice of either the money or the voucher, the dollar value of which may be no less than the monetary compensation to which the passenger would be entitled. The voucher is not a substitute for the bumped passenger's original ticket; the airline continues to honor that as well. Keep in mind that the above regulations and policies are for US flights only.

To protect yourself as best you can against getting bumped, arrive at the airport early, allowing plenty of time to check in and get to the gate. If the flight is oversold, ask immediately for the written statement explaining the airline's policy on denied-boarding compensation and its boarding priorities. If the airline refuses to give you this information, or if you feel they have not handled the situation properly, file a complaint with both the airline and the appropriate government agency (see "Consumer Protection," below).

Delays and Cancellations – The above compensation rules also do not apply if the

20 GETTING READY / Traveling by Plane

flight is canceled or delayed, or if a smaller aircraft is substituted due to mechanical problems. Each airline has its own policy for assisting passengers whose flights are delayed or canceled or who must wait for another flight because their original one was overbooked. Most airline personnel will make new travel arrangements if necessary. If the delay is longer than 4 hours, the airline may pay for a phone call or telegram, a meal, and in some cases, a hotel room and transportation to it.

■ **Caution:** If you are bumped or miss a flight, be sure to ask the airline to notify other airlines on which you have reservations or connecting flights. When your name is taken off the passenger list of your initial flight, the computer usually cancels all of your reservations automatically, unless *you* take steps to preserve them.

CHARTER FLIGHTS: By booking a block of seats on a specially arranged flight, charter tour operators offer travelers air transportation for a substantial reduction over the full coach or economy fare. These operators may offer air-only charters (selling transportation alone) or charter packages (the flight plus a combination of land arrangements such as accommodations, meals, tours, or car rentals). Charters are especially attractive to people living in smaller cities or out-of-the-way places, because they frequently leave from nearby airports, saving travelers the inconvenience and expense of getting to a major gateway.

From the consumer's standpoint, charters differ from scheduled airlines in two main respects: You generally need to book and pay in advance, and you can't change the itinerary or the departure and return dates once you've booked the flight. In practice, however, these restrictions don't always apply. Today, although most charter flights still require advance reservations, some permit last-minute bookings (when there are unsold seats available), and some even offer seats on a standby basis. Though charters almost always are round-trip, and it is unlikely that you would be sold a one-way seat on a round-trip flight, on rare occasions one-way tickets on charters are offered.

Things to keep in mind about the charter game:

1. It cannot be repeated often enough that if you are forced to cancel your trip, you can lose much (and possibly all) of your money unless you have cancellation insurance, which is a *must* (see *Insurance,* in this section). Frequently, if the cancellation occurs far enough in advance (often 6 weeks or more), you may forfeit only a $25 or $50 penalty. If you cancel only 2 or 3 weeks before the flight, there may be no refund at all unless you or the operator can provide a substitute passenger.
2. Charter flights may be canceled by the operator up to 10 days before departure for any reason, usually underbooking. Your money is returned in this event, but there may be too little time for you to make new arrangements.
3. Most charters have little of the flexibility of some regularly scheduled flights regarding refunds and the changing of flight dates; if you book a return flight, you must be on it or lose your money.
4. Charter operators are permitted to assess a surcharge, if fuel or other costs warrant it, of up to 10% of the airfare up to 10 days before departure.
5. Because of the economics of charter flights, your plane almost always will be full, so you will be crowded, though not necessarily uncomfortable. (There is, however, a new movement among charter airlines to provide flight accommodations that are more comfort-oriented, so this situation may change in the near future.)

To avoid problems, *always* choose charter flights with care. When you consider a charter, ask your travel agent who runs it and carefully check the company. The Better Business Bureau in the company's home city can report on how many complaints, if any, have been lodged against it in the past. Protect yourself with trip cancellation and

GETTING READY / Traveling by Plane 21

interruption insurance, which can help safeguard your investment if you, or a traveling companion, are unable to make the trip and must cancel too late to receive a full refund from the company providing your travel services. (This is advisable whether you're buying a charter flight alone or a tour package for which the airfare is provided by charter or scheduled flight.)

Bookings – If you do fly on a charter, read the contract's fine print carefully and pay particular attention to the following:

Instructions concerning the payment of the deposit and its balance and to whom the check is to be made payable. Ordinarily, checks are made out to an escrow account, which means the charter company can't spend your money until your flight has safely returned. This provides some protection for you. To ensure the safe handling of your money, make out your check to the escrow account, the number of which must appear by law on the brochure, though all too often it is on the back in fine print. Write the details of the charter, including the destination and dates, on the face of the check; on the back, print "For Deposit Only." Your travel agent may prefer that you make out your check to the agency, saying that it will then pay the tour operator the fee minus commission. It is perfectly legal to write the check as we suggest, however, and if your agent objects too vociferously (he or she should trust the tour operator to send the proper commission), consider taking your business elsewhere. If you don't make your check out to the escrow account, you lose the protection of that escrow should the trip be canceled. Furthermore, recent bankruptcies in the travel industry have served to point out that even the protection of escrow may not be enough to safeguard a traveler's investment. More and more, insurance is becoming a necessity. The charter company should be bonded (usually by an insurance company), and if you want to file a claim against it, the claim should be sent to the bonding agent. The contract will set a time limit within which a claim must be filed.

Specific stipulations and penalties for cancellations. Most charters allow you to cancel up to 45 days in advance without major penalty, but some cancellation dates are 50 to 60 days before departure.

Stipulations regarding cancellation and major changes made by the charterer. US rules say that charter flights may not be canceled within 10 days of departure except when circumstances — such as natural disasters or political upheavals — make it physically impossible to fly. Charterers may make "major changes," however, such as in the date or place of departure or return, but you are entitled to cancel and receive a full refund if you don't wish to accept these changes. A price increase of more than 10% at any time up to 10 days before departure is considered a major change; no price increase at all is allowed during the last 10 days immediately before departure.

The following companies regularly offer charter flights within the US. Although at the time of this writing none of the companies were offering flights to New Orleans, it might be worthwhile to call when planning your trip for more current information. As indicated, some of these companies sell charter flights directly to clients, while others are wholesalers and must be contacted through a travel agent.

Amber Tours (7337 W. Washington St., Indianapolis, IN 46251; phone: 800-225-9920). Retails to the general public.

Apple Vacations East (7 Campus Blvd., Newtown Sq., PA 19073; phone: 800-727-3400). This agency is a wholesaler, so use a travel agent.

Funway Holidays/Funjet (PO Box 1460, Milwaukee, WI 53201-1460; phone: 800-558-3050). This agency is a wholesaler, so use a travel agent.

MLT Vacations (5130 Hwy. 101, Minnetonka, MN 55345; phone: 800-328-0025). This agency is a wholesaler, so use a travel agent.

Morris Air Service (260 E. Morris Ave., Salt Lake City, UT 84115-3200; phone: 800-444-5660). Retails to the general public.

MTI Vacations (1220 Kensington, Oak Brook, IL 60521; phone: 800-323-7285). This agency is a wholesaler, so use a travel agent.

22   GETTING READY / Traveling by Plane

Suntrips (2350 Paragon Dr., San Jose, CA 95131; phone: 800-SUNTRIP in California; 408-432-0700 elsewhere in the US). Retails to the general public.

You also may want to subscribe to the travel newsletter *Jax Fax*, which regularly features a list of charter companies and packagers offering seats on US charter flights. For a year's subscription send a check or money order for $12 to *Jax Fax*, 397 Post Rd., Darien, CT 06820 (phone: 203-655-8746).

DISCOUNTS ON SCHEDULED FLIGHTS: Promotional fares often are called discount fares because they cost less than what used to be the standard airline fare — full-fare economy. Nevertheless, they cost the traveler the same whether they are bought through a travel agent or directly from the airline. Tickets that cost less if bought from some outlet other than the airline do exist, however. While it is likely that the vast majority of travelers flying within the US in the near future will be doing so on a promotional fare or charter rather than on a "discount" air ticket of this sort, it still is a good idea for cost-conscious consumers to be aware of the latest developments in the budget airfare scene. Note that the following discussion makes clear-cut distinctions among the types of discounts available based on how they reach the consumer; in actual practice, the distinctions are not nearly so precise.

Net Fare Sources – The newest notion for reducing the costs of travel services comes from travel agents who offer individual travelers "net" fares. Defined simply, a net fare is the bare minimum amount at which an airline or tour operator will carry a prospective traveler. It doesn't include the amount that normally would be paid to the travel agent as a commission. Traditionally, such commissions amount to about 10% on domestic fares — not counting significant additions to these commission levels that are paid retroactively when agents sell more than a specific volume of tickets or trips for a single supplier. At press time, at least one travel agency in the US was offering travelers the opportunity to purchase tickets and/or tours for a net price. Instead of earning its income from individual commissions, this agency assesses a fixed fee that may or may not provide a bargain for travelers; it requires a little arithmetic to determine whether to use the services of a net travel agent or those of one who accepts conventional commissions. One of the potential drawbacks of buying from agencies selling travel services at net fares is that some airlines refuse to do business with them, thus possibly limiting your flight options.

Travel Avenue is a fee-based agency that rebates its ordinary agency commission to the customer. For domestic flights, they will find the lowest retail fare, then rebate 7% to 10% (depending on the airline selected) of that price, minus a $25 ticket-writing charge. If the ticket includes more than eight separate flights, an additional $10 fee is charged. Customers using free flight coupons pay the ticket-writing charge, plus an additional $5 coupon-processing fee.

Travel Avenue will rebate its commissions on all tickets, including heavily discounted fares and senior citizen passes. Available 7 days a week, reservations should be made far enough in advance to allow the tickets to be sent by first class mail, since extra charges accrue for special handling. It's possible to economize further by making your own airline reservation, then asking *Travel Avenue* only to write/issue your ticket. For travelers outside the Chicago area, business may be transacted by phone and purchases charged to a credit card. For information, contact *Travel Avenue* at 641 W. Lake St., Suite 201, Chicago, IL 60606-1012 (phone: 312-876-1116 in Illinois; 800-333-3335 elsewhere in the US).

Consolidators and Bucket Shops – Other vendors of travel services can afford to sell tickets to their customers at an even greater discount because the airline has sold the tickets to them at a substantial discount (usually accomplished by sharply increasing commissions to that vendor), a practice in which many airlines indulge, albeit discreetly, preferring that the general public not know they are undercutting their own

GETTING READY / Traveling by Plane 23

"list" prices. Airlines anticipating a slow period on a particular route sometimes sell off a certain portion of their capacity at a very great discount to a wholesaler, or consolidator. The wholesaler sometimes is a charter operator who resells the seats to the public as though they were charter seats, which is why prospective travelers perusing the brochures of charter operators with large programs frequently see a number of flights designated as "scheduled service." As often as not, however, the consolidator, in turn, sells the seats to a travel agency specializing in discounting. Airlines also can sell seats directly to such an agency, which thus acts as its own consolidator. The airline offers the seats either at a net wholesale price, but without the volume-purchase requirement that would be difficult for a modest retail travel agency to fulfill, or at the standard price, but with a commission override large enough (as high as 50%) to allow both a profit and a price reduction to the public.

Travel agencies specializing in discounting sometimes are called "bucket shops," a term once fraught with connotations of unreliability in this country. But in today's highly competitive travel marketplace, more and more conventional travel agencies are selling consolidator-supplied tickets, and the old bucket shops' image is becoming respectable. Agencies that specialize in discounted tickets exist in most large cities, and usually can be found by studying the smaller ads in the travel sections of local Sunday newspapers.

Before buying a discounted ticket, whether from a bucket shop or a conventional, full-service travel agency, keep the following considerations in mind: To be in a position to judge how much you'll be saving, first find out the "list" prices of tickets to your destination. Then do some comparison shopping among agencies. Also bear in mind that a ticket that may not differ much in price from one available directly from the airline may, however, allow the circumvention of such things as the advance-purchase requirement. If your plans are less than final, be sure to find out about any other restrictions, such as penalties for canceling a flight or changing a reservation. Most discount tickets are non-endorsable, meaning that they can be used only on the airline that issued them, and they usually are marked "nonrefundable" to prevent their being cashed in for a list-price refund.

A great many bucket shops are small businesses operating on a thin margin, so it's a good idea to check the local Better Business Bureau for any complaints registered against the one with which you're dealing — before parting with any money. If you still do not feel reassured, consider buying discounted tickets only through a conventional travel agency, which can be expected to have found its own reliable source of consolidator tickets — some of the largest consolidators, in fact, sell only to travel agencies.

A few bucket shops require payment in cash or by certified check or money order, but if credit cards are accepted, use that option. Note, however, if buying from a charter operator selling both scheduled and charter flights, that the scheduled seats are not protected by the regulations — including the use of escrow accounts — governing the charter seats. Well-established charter operators, nevertheless, may extend the same protections to their scheduled flights, and, when this is the case, consumers should be sure that the payment option selected directs their money into the escrow account.

Listed below are some of the consolidators frequently offering discounted domestic fares:

> *Bargain Air* (655 Deep Valley Dr., Suite 355, Rolling Hills, CA 90274; phone: 800-347-2345 or 213-377-2919).
> *Maharaja/Consumer Wholesale Travel* (34 W. 33rd St., Suite 1014, New York, NY 10016; phone: 212-213-2020 in New York; 800-223-6862 elsewhere in the US).
> *TFI Tours International* (34 W. 32nd St., 12th Floor, New York, NY 10001; phone: 212-736-1140 in New York State; 800-825-3834 elsewhere in the US).

24   GETTING READY / Traveling by Plane

25 West Tours (2490 Coral Way, Miami, FL 33145; phone: 305-856-0810 in Florida; 800-925-0250 elsewhere in the US).

Unitravel (1177 N. Warson Rd., St. Louis, MO 63132; phone: 314-569-0900 in Missouri; 800-325-2222 elsewhere in the US).

Check with your travel agent for other sources of consolidator-supplied tickets.

■**Note:** Although rebating and discounting are becoming increasingly common, there is some legal ambiguity concerning them. Strictly speaking, it is legal to discount domestic tickets but not international tickets. On the other hand, the law that prohibits discounting, the Federal Aviation Act of 1958, is consistently ignored these days, in part because consumers benefit from the practice and in part because many illegal arrangements are indistinguishable from legal ones. Since the line separating the two is so fine that even the authorities can't always tell the difference, it is unlikely that most consumers would be able to do so, and in fact it is not illegal to *buy* a discounted ticket. If the issue of legality bothers you, ask the agency whether any ticket you're about to buy would be permissible under the above-mentioned act.

Last-Minute Travel Clubs – Still another way to take advantage of bargain airfares is open to those who have a flexible schedule. A number of organizations, usually set up as last-minute travel clubs and functioning on a membership basis, routinely keep in touch with travel suppliers to help them dispose of unsold inventory at discounts of between 15% and 60%. A great deal of the inventory consists of complete package tours and cruises, but some clubs offer air-only charter seats and, occasionally, seats on scheduled flights.

Members generally pay an annual fee and receive a toll-free hotline telephone number to call for information on imminent trips. In some cases, they also receive periodic mailings with information on bargain travel opportunities for which there is more advance notice. Despite the suggestive names of the clubs providing these services, last-minute travel does not necessarily mean that you cannot make plans until literally the last minute. Trips can be announced as little as a few days or as much as 2 months before departure, but the average is from 1 to 4 weeks' notice.

Among the organizations regularly offering such discounted travel opportunities in the US are the following:

Discount Travel International (152 W. 72nd St., Suite 223, New York, NY 10023; phone: 212-362-3636). Annual fee: $45 per household.

Encore/Short Notice (4501 Forbes Blvd., Lanham, MD 20706; phone: 301-459-8020; 800-638-0930 for customer service). Annual fee: $36 per family for *Encore* (main discount travel program), $48 per family for *Short Notice* program.

Last Minute Travel (1249 Boylston St., Boston, MA 02215; phone: 800-LAST-MIN or 617-267-9800). No fee.

Moment's Notice (425 Madison Ave., New York, NY 10017; phone: 212-486-0503). Annual fee: $45 per family.

Traveler's Advantage (3033 S. Parker Rd., Suite 1000, Aurora, CO 80014; phone: 800-548-1116). Annual fee: $49 per family.

Vacations to Go (2411 Fountain View, Suite 201, Houston, TX 77057; phone: 800-338-4962). Annual fee: $19.95 per family.

Worldwide Discount Travel Club (1674 Meridian Ave., Miami Beach, FL 33139; phone: 305-534-2082). Annual fee: $40 per person; $50 per family.

■**Note:** For additional information on last-minute travel discounts, a new "900" number telephone service called *Last Minute Travel Connection* (phone: 900-446-

GETTING READY / Traveling by Plane 25

8292) provides recorded advertisements (including contact information) for discount offerings on airfares, package tours, cruises, and other travel opportunities. Since companies update their advertisements as often as every hour, listings are current. This 24-hour service is available to callers using touch-tone phones; the cost is $1 per minute (the charge will show up on your phone bill). For more information, contact *La Onda, Ltd.,* 601 Skokie Blvd., Suite 224, Northbrook, IL 60062 (phone: 708-498-9216).

Generic Air Travel – Organizations that apply the same flexible-schedule idea to air travel only and arrange for flights at literally the last minute also exist. Their service sometimes is known as "generic" air travel, and it operates somewhat like an ordinary airline standby service except that the organizations running it do not guarantee flights to a specific destination, but only to a general region, and offer seats on not one but several scheduled and charter airlines.

One pioneer of generic flights is *Airhitch* (2790 Broadway, Suite 100, New York, NY 10025; phone: 212-864-2000). Prospective travelers stipulate a range of at least 5 consecutive departure dates and their desired destination, along with alternate choices, and pay the fare in advance. They are then sent a voucher good for travel *on a space-available basis* on flights to their destination region (i.e., not necessarily the specific destination requested) during this time period. The week before this range of departure dates begins, travelers must contact *Airhitch* for specific information about flights on which seats may be available and instructions on how to proceed for check-in. (Return fights are arranged in the same manner as the outbound flights — a specified period of travel is decided upon, and a few days before this date range begins, prospective passengers contact *Airhitch* for details about flights that may be available.) If the client does not accept any of the suggested flights or cancels his or her travel plans after selecting a flight, the amount paid may be applied toward a future fare or the flight arrangements can be transferred to another individual (although, in both cases, an additional fee may be charged). No refunds are offered unless the prospective passenger does not ultimately get on any flight in the specified date range; in such a case, the full fare is refunded. (Note that *Airhitch*'s slightly more expensive Target program, which provides confirmed reservations on specific dates to specific destinations, offers passengers greater — but not guaranteed — certainty regarding destinations and other flight arrangements.) At press time, *Airhitch* did not fly to the southern US, but it might be worthwhile to call when planning a trip to see if it has expanded its service.

Bartered Travel Sources – Suppose a hotel buys advertising space in a newspaper. As payment, the hotel gives the publishing company the use of a number of hotel rooms in lieu of cash. This is barter, a common means of exchange among hotels, airlines, car rental companies, cruise lines, tour operators, restaurants, and other travel service companies. When a bartering company finds itself with empty airline seats (or excess hotel rooms, or cruise ship cabin space, and so on) and offers them to the public, considerable savings can be enjoyed.

Bartered travel clubs often offer can give discounts of up to 50% to members, who pay an annual fee (approximately $50 at press time), which entitles them to select from the flights, cruises, hotel rooms, or other travel services that the club obtained by barter. Members usually present a voucher, club credit card, or scrip (a dollar-denomination voucher negotiable only for the bartered product) to the hotel, which in turn subtracts the dollar amount from the bartering company's account.

Selling bartered travel is a perfectly legitimate means of retailing. One advantage to club members is that they don't have to wait until the last minute to obtain flight or room reservations.

Among the companies specializing in bartered travel, those that frequently offer members travel services throughout the US include the following:

Travel Guild (18210 Redmond Way, Redmond, WA 98052; phone: 206-861-1900). Annual fee: $48 per family.

Travel World Leisure Club (225 W. 34th St., Suite 2203, New York, NY 10122; phone: 800-444-TWLC or 212-239-4855). Annual fee: $50 per person; $20 for each additional member of a family.

OTHER DISCOUNT TRAVEL SOURCES: An excellent source of information on economical travel opportunities is the *Consumer Reports Travel Letter,* published monthly by Consumers Union. It keeps abreast of the scene on a wide variety of fronts, including package tours, rental cars, insurance, and more, but it is especially helpful for its comprehensive coverage of airfares, offering guidance on all the options, from scheduled flights on major or low-fare airlines to charters and discount sources. For a year's subscription, send $37 ($57 for 2 years) to *Consumer Reports Travel Letter* (PO Box 53629, Boulder, CO 80322-3629; phone: 800-999-7959). For information on other travel newsletters, see *Books, Magazines, and Newsletters,* in this section.

CONSUMER PROTECTION: Consumers who feel that they have not been dealt with fairly by an airline should make their complaints known. Begin with the customer service representative at the airport where the problem occurred. If your complaint cannot be resolved there to your satisfaction, write to the airline's consumer office. In a businesslike, typed letter, explain what reservations you held, what happened, the names of the employees involved, and what you expect the airline to do to remedy the situation. Send copies (never the originals) of the tickets, receipts, and other documents that back your claims. Ideally, all correspondence should be sent via certified mail, return receipt requested. This provides proof that your complaint was received.

Passengers with consumer complaints — lost baggage, compensation for getting bumped, violation of smoking and nonsmoking rules, deceptive practices by an airline — who are not satisfied with the airline's response should contact the Department of Transportation (DOT), Consumer Affairs Division (400 7th St. SW, Room 10405, Washington, DC 20590; phone: 202-366-2220). DOT personnel stress, however, that consumers initially should direct their complaints to the airline that provoked them.

Remember, too, that the federal Fair Credit Billing Act permits purchasers to refuse to pay for credit card charges for services that have not been delivered, so the onus of dealing with the receiver for a bankrupt airline, for example, falls on the credit card company. Do not rely on another airline to honor any ticket you're holding from a failed airline, since the days when virtually all major carriers subscribed to a default protection program that bound them to do so are long gone. Some airlines may voluntarily step forward to accommodate the stranded passengers of a fellow carrier, but this is now an entirely altruistic act.

The deregulation of US airlines has meant that travelers must find out for themselves what they are entitled to receive. The Department of Transportation's informative consumer booklet *Fly Rights* is a good place to start. To receive a copy, send $1 to the Superintendent of Documents (US Government Printing Office, Washington, DC 20402-9325; phone: 202-783-3238). Specify its stock number, 050-000-00513-5, and allow 3 to 4 weeks for delivery.

On Arrival

FROM THE AIRPORT TO THE CITY: New Orleans International Airport is located 12 miles west of the city center. The ride from the airport to downtown usually takes from 20 to 45 minutes, depending on traffic and time of day. The taxi fare is set at $21 for up to 3 people.

The *Louisiana Transit Co.* (phone: 504-737-9611) runs an *Airport-Downtown Express*

GETTING READY / On Arrival 27

bus on a 10- to 25-minute schedule from downtown at the corner of Elks Place and Tulane Avenue for a fare of $1.10. *Airport Shuttle* (phone: 504-942-5000) provides services between the airport and downtown and French Quarter hotels, with passenger vans departing every 20 minutes at a fare of $17.

Car Rental – Unless planning to drive round trip from home, most travelers who want to drive while on vacation simply rent a car. They can rent a car through a travel agent or national rental firm before leaving home, or from a local company once they arrive in New Orleans. Another possibility, also arranged before departure, is to rent the car as part of a larger travel package.

It's tempting to wait until arrival to scout out the lowest-priced rental from the company located the farthest from the airport high-rent district and offering no pick-up services. But if your arrival coincides with a holiday or a peak travel period, you may be disappointed to find that even the most expensive car in the city was reserved months ago. Whenever possible, it is best to reserve in advance, anywhere from a few days ahead in slack periods to a month or more during the busier seasons.

Often, the easiest place to rent (or at least pick up) the car is at the airport on arrival. The majority of the national car rental companies have locations at New Orleans International Airport, where shuttle buses from each company pick up clients and take them to the car rental locations. Travel agents can arrange rentals for clients, but it is just as easy to call and rent a car yourself. Listed below are the nationwide, toll-free telephone numbers of the major national rental companies that have locations in New Orleans:

Alamo: 800-327-9633.
American International Rent-A-Car: 800-527-0202.
Avis: 800-331-1212.
Budget Rent-A-Car: 800-527-0700.
Dollar Rent A Car: 800-800-4000.
Hertz: 800-654-3131.
National Car Rental: 800-CAR-RENT.
Sears Rent-A-Car: 800-527-0770.
Thrifty Rent-A-Car: 800-367-2277.

Often, less expensive car rentals may be obtained from the lesser-known national and regional chains that in many cases limit their advertising to the yellow pages. These companies frequently do most of their business in insurance replacement but are happy to accommodate any tourists that come their way. Following is a list of such firms with their nationwide 800 numbers:

Agency Rent-A-Car: 800-321-1972.
Airways Rent A Car: 800-952-9200.
Automate Car Rental: 800-633-2824.
Enterprise Rent-A-Car: 800-325-8007.
General Rent-A-Car: 800-327-7607.
Payless Car Rental: 800-PAYLESS.
Reserve Rent-A-Car: 800-346-6556.

If you decide to wait until after you arrive, you'll often find a surprising number of small companies listed in the local yellow pages. (All of the following companies are in the 504 area code.) One such company is *Spinato Rent-a-Car* (2300 Canal St.; phone: 504-822-4400). *Auto Rent International,* near the French Quarter (740 Baronne St.; phone: 504-524-4645), sends courtesy cars to hotels in the area. Another company is *Rainbow Rent-A-Car* with 5 locations, one 3 blocks from the airport (1711 Airline Hwy., Kenner; phone: 504-468-2990) and another downtown (227 N. Broad; phone: 504-821-2248). The Kenner location will make airport pick-ups.

To economize on a car rental, also consider one of the firms that rents 3- to 5-year-old

28 GETTING READY / On Arrival

cars that are well worn but (presumably) mechanically sound; one such company is *Cheapie Rent-A-Car* (3215 Dublin; phone: 504-486-0961), near the *Super Dome*.

Requirements – Whether you decide to rent a car in advance from a large national rental company or wait to rent from a local company, you should know that renting a car is rarely as simple as signing on the dotted line and roaring off into the night. If you are renting for personal use, you must have a valid driver's license and will have to convince the renting agency that (1) you are personally creditworthy, and (2) you will bring the car back at the stated time. This will be easy if you have a major credit card; most rental companies accept credit cards in lieu of a cash deposit, as well as for payment of your final bill. If you prefer to pay in cash, leave your credit card imprint as a "deposit," then pay your bill in cash when you return the car.

Note that *Avis, Budget, Hertz,* and other national companies usually *will* rent to travelers paying in cash and leaving either a credit card imprint or a substantial amount of cash as a deposit. This is not necessarily standard policy, however, as other national chains and a number of local companies will *not* rent to an individual who doesn't have a valid credit card. In this case, you may have to call around to find a company that accepts cash.

Also keep in mind that although the minimum age to drive in most states is 16, the minimum age to rent a car is set by the rental company. (Restrictions vary from company to company, as well as at different locations.) Many firms have a minimum age requirement of 21 years, some raise that to between 23 and 25 years, and for some models of cars it rises to 30 years. The upper limit at many companies is between 69 and 75; others have no upper limit or may make drivers above a certain age subject to special conditions.

Costs – Finding the most economical car rental will require some telephone shopping on your part. As a *general* rule, expect to hear lower prices quoted by the smaller, strictly local companies than by the well-known international names.

Comparison shopping always is advisable, however. Even the international giants offer discount plans whose conditions are easy for most travelers to fulfill. For instance, *Budget* and *National* sometimes offer discounts of anywhere from 10% to 30% off their usual rates (according to the size of the car and the duration of the rental), provided that the car is reserved a certain number of days before departure (usually 7 to 14 days, but it can be less), is rented for a minimum period (5 days or, more often, a week), is paid for at the time of booking, and, in most cases, is returned to the same location that supplied it or to another in the same area. Similar discount plans include *Hertz*'s Leisure Rates and *Avis*'s Supervalue Rates.

If driving short distances for only a day or two, the best deal may be a per-day, per-mile rate: You pay a flat fee for each day you keep the car, plus a per-mile charge. An increasingly common alternative is to be granted a certain number of free miles each day and then be charged on a per-mile basis over that number.

Most companies also offer a flat per-day rate with unlimited free mileage; this certainly is the most economical rate if you plan to drive over 100 miles. Make sure that the low, flat daily rate that catches your eye, however, is indeed a per-day rate: Often the lowest price advertised by a company turns out to be available only with a minimum 3-day rental — fine if you want the car that long, but not the bargain it appears if you really intend to use it no more than 24 hours. Flat weekly rates also are available, as are some flat monthly rates that represent a further saving over the daily rate.

Another factor influencing the cost is the type of car you rent. Rentals are based on a tiered price system, with different sizes of cars — variations of budget, economy, regular, and luxury — often listed as A (the smallest and least expensive) through F, G, or H, and sometimes even higher. Charges may increase by only a few dollars a day through several categories of subcompact and compact cars — where most of the competition is — then increase by great leaps through the remaining classes of full-size and luxury cars and passenger vans. The larger the car, the more it costs to rent and the more gas it consumes, but for some people the greater comfort and extra luggage space of a larger car (in which bags and sporting gear can be safely locked out of sight) may make it worth the additional expense. Also more expensive are sleek sports cars, but again, for some people the thrill of driving such a car — for a week or a day — may be worth it.

Electing to pay for collision damage waiver (CDW) protection will add considerably to the cost of renting a car. (Some companies, such as *Hertz* and *Avis,* call the option a loss damage waiver, or LDW.) You may be responsible for the *full value* of the vehicle being rented if it is damaged or stolen, but you can dispense with all of the possible liability by buying the offered waiver at a cost of around $10 to $13 a day (although in some states, it may cost as little as $5). Before making any decisions about optional collision damage waivers, however, check with your own insurance agent and determine whether your personal automobile insurance policy covers rented vehicles; if it does, you probably won't need to pay for the waiver. Be aware, too, that increasing numbers of credit cards automatically provide CDW coverage if the car rental is charged to the appropriate credit card. However, the specific terms of such credit card coverage differ sharply among individual card companies, so check with the credit card company for information on the nature and amount of coverage provided. Business travelers also should be aware that, at the time of this writing, *American Express* had withdrawn its automatic CDW coverage from some corporate *Green* card accounts and limited the length of coverage — watch for similar cutbacks by other credit card companies.

When inquiring about CDW or LDW coverage and costs, be aware that a number of car rental companies now are automatically including the cost of this waiver in their quoted prices. This does not mean that they are absorbing this cost and you are receiving free coverage — in many cases total rental prices have increased to include the former CDW charge. The disadvantage of this inclusion is that you probably will not have the option to refuse this coverage, and will end up paying the added charge — even if you already are adequately covered by your own insurance policy or through a credit card company.

Additional costs to be added to the price tag include drop-off charges or one-way service fees. The lowest price quoted by any given company may apply only to a car that is returned to the same location from which it was rented. A slightly higher rate may be charged if the car is to be returned to a different location (even within the same city).

Also, don't forget to factor in the price of gas. Rental cars usually are delivered with a full tank of gas. (This is not always the case, however, so check the gas gauge when picking up the car, and have the amount of gas noted on your rental agreement if the tank is not full.) Remember to fill the tank before you return the car or you will have to pay to refill it, and gasoline at the car rental company's pump always is much more expensive than at a service station. This policy may vary for smaller local and regional companies; ask when picking up the vehicle. Before leaving the lot, also check that the rental car has a spare tire and jack in the trunk.

Package Tours

If the mere thought of buying a package for your visit to New Orleans conjures up visions of a trip spent marching in lockstep through the city's attractions with a horde of frazzled fellow travelers, remember that packages have come a long way. For one thing, not all packages necessarily are escorted tours, and the one you buy does not have to include any organized touring

30 GETTING READY / Package Tours

at all — nor will it necessarily include traveling companions. If it does, however, you'll find that people of all sorts — many just like yourself — are taking advantage of packages today because they are economical and convenient and save an immense amount of planning time. Given the high cost of travel these days, packages have emerged as a particularly wise buy.

In essence, a package is just an amalgam of travel services that can be purchased in a single transaction. A package (tour or otherwise) may include any or all of the following: round-trip transportation, local transportation (and/or car rentals), accommodations, some or all meals, sightseeing, entertainment, transfers to and from the hotel, taxes, tips, escort service, and a variety of incidental features that might be offered as options at additional cost. In other words, a package can be any combination of travel elements, from a fully escorted tour offered at an all-inclusive price to a simple fly/drive booking that allows you to move about totally on your own. Its principal advantage is that it saves money: The cost of the combined arrangements invariably is well below the price of all of the same elements if bought separately, and, particularly if transportation is provided by discount flight, the whole package could cost less than just a round-trip economy airline ticket on a regularly scheduled flight. A package provides more than economy and convenience: It releases the traveler from having to make individual arrangements for each separate element of a trip.

Tour programs generally can be divided into two categories — "escorted" (or locally hosted) and "independent." An escorted tour means that a guide will accompany the group from the beginning of the tour through to the return flight; a locally hosted tour means that the group will be met upon arrival at each location by a different local host. On independent tours, there generally is a choice of hotels, meal plans, and sightseeing trips, as well as a variety of special excursions. The independent plan is for travelers who do not want a totally set itinerary, but who do prefer confirmed hotel reservations. Whether choosing an escorted or an independent tour, always bring along complete contact information for your tour operator in case a problem arises, although tour operators often have local affiliates who can give additional assistance or make other arrangements on the spot.

To determine whether a package — or more specifically, *which* package — fits your travel plans, start by evaluating your interests and needs, deciding how much and what you want to spend, see, and do. Gather brochures on New Orleans tours. Be sure that you take the time to read each brochure *carefully* to determine precisely what is included. Keep in mind that they are written to entice you into signing up for a package tour. Often the language is deceptive and devious. For example, a brochure may quote the lowest prices for a package tour based on facilities that are unavailable during the off-season, undesirable at any season, or just plain nonexistent. Information such as "breakfast included" or "plus tax" (which can add up) should be taken into account. Note, too, that the prices quoted in brochures almost always are based on double occupancy: The rate listed is for each of two people sharing a double room, and if you travel alone, the supplement for single accommodations can raise the price considerably (see *Hints for Single Travelers,* in this section).

In this age of erratic airfares, the brochure most often will *not* include the price of an airline ticket in the price of the package, though sample fares from various gateway cities usually will be listed separately, as extras to be added to the price of the ground arrangements. Before figuring your actual costs, check the latest fares with the airlines, because the samples invariably are out of date by the time you read them. If the brochure gives more than one category of sample fares per gateway city — such as an individual tour-basing fare, a group fare, an excursion, APEX, or other discount ticket — your travel agent or airline tour desk will be able to tell you which one applies to the package you choose, depending on when you travel, how far in advance you book, and other factors. (An individual tour-basing fare is a fare computed as part of a

GETTING READY / Package Tours 31

package that includes land arrangements, thereby entitling a carrier to reduce the air portion almost to the absolute minimum. Though it always represents a saving over full-fare coach or economy, lately the individual tour-basing fare has not been as inexpensive as the excursion and other discount fares that also are available to individuals. The group fare usually is the least expensive fare, and it is the tour operator, not you, who makes up the group.) When the brochure does include round-trip transportation in the package price, don't forget to add the cost of round-trip transportation from your home to the departure city to come up with the total cost of the package.

Finally, read the general information regarding terms and conditions and the responsibility clause (usually in fine print at the end of the descriptive literature) to determine the precise elements for which the tour operator is — and is not — liable. Here the tour operator frequently expresses the right to change services or schedules as long as equivalent arrangements are offered. This clause also absolves the operator of responsibility for circumstances beyond human control, such as avalanches, earthquakes, or floods, or injury to you or your property. While reading, ask the following questions:

1. Does the tour include airfare or other transportation, sightseeing, meals, transfers, taxes, baggage handling, tips, or any other services? Do you want all these services?
2. If the brochure indicates that "some meals" are included, does this mean a welcoming and farewell dinner, two breakfasts, or every evening meal?
3. What classes of hotels are offered? If you will be traveling alone, what is the single supplement?
4. Does the tour itinerary or price vary according to the season?
5. Are the prices guaranteed; that is, if costs increase between the time you book and the time you depart, can surcharges unilaterally be added?
6. Do you get a full refund if you cancel? If not, be sure to obtain cancellation insurance.
7. Can the operator cancel if too few people join? At what point?

One of the consumer's biggest problems is finding enough information to judge the reliability of a tour packager, since individual travelers seldom have direct contact with the firm putting the package together. Usually, a retail travel agent is interposed between customer and tour operator, and much depends on his or her candor and cooperation. So ask a number of questions about the tour you are considering. For example:

- Has the travel agent ever used a package provided by this tour operator?
- How long has the tour operator been in business? Check the Better Business Bureau in the area where the tour operator is based to see if any complaints have been filed against it.
- Is the tour operator a member of the *United States Tour Operators Association* (*USTOA;* 211 E. 51st St., Suite 12B, New York, NY 10022; phone: 212-944-5727)? *USTOA* will provide a list of its members on request; it also offers a useful brochure called *How to Select a Package Tour.*
- How many and which companies are involved in the package?

■ **A word of advice:** Purchasers of vacation packages who feel they're not getting their money's worth are more likely to get a refund if they complain in writing to the operator — and bail out of the whole package immediately. Alert the tour operator to the fact that you are dissatisfied, that you will be leaving for home as soon as transportation can be arranged, and that you expect a refund. They may have forms to fill out detailing your complaint; otherwise, state your case in a letter. Even if difficulty in arranging immediate transportation home detains you, your dated, written complaint should help in procuring a refund from the operator.

32 GETTING READY / Package Tours

SAMPLE PACKAGES: Following is a list of some of the major tour operators that offer New Orleans packages. Most companies offer several departure dates, depending on the length of the tour and subject matter. Some operators offer flexible city stays that start with 1 night in a hotel, with a choice of locations and prices available, to which may be added more nights and a wide variety of options, such as sightseeing, transfers, car rental, and, in some cases, dine-around plans. As indicated, some operators are wholesalers only, and will deal only with a travel agent.

ABA Tours and Travel (300 Bourbon St., New Orleans, LA 70130; phone: 800-375-8585 or 504-569-1590). Features flexible multi-option plans beginning at 2 nights.

Adventure Tours (9818 Liberty Rd., Randallstown, MD 21133; phone: 301-922-7000 in Baltimore; 800-638-9040 elsewhere in the US). Offers flexible city stays. This company is a wholesaler; consult a travel agent.

American Express Travel Related Services (offices throughout the US; phone: 800-241-1700 for information and local branch offices). Offers flexible city stays in New Orleans as well as independent and escorted tours throughout the US. The tour operator is a wholesaler, so use a travel agent.

Collette Tours (162 Middle St., Pawtucket, RI 02860; phone: 800-832-4656 or 800-752-2655 in New England). Operates escorted 5-day program to New Orleans.

Corliss Tours (436 W. Foothill Blvd., Monrovia, CA 91016; phone: 818-359-5358). Offers 8-day Stay Put escorted program featuring the city and its environs. This company is a wholesaler, so consult a travel agent.

Dan Dipert Tours (PO Box 580, Arlington, TX 76004-0580; phone: 817-543-3710). Offers 5-day tour to New Orleans.

Destination Management (2 Canal St., Suite 1415, New Orleans, LA 70130; phone: 800-366-8882 or 504-592-0500). Features hotel packages on land-only basis or including air.

Domenico Tours (751 Broadway, PO Box 144, Bayonne, NJ 07002; phone: 201-823-8687, 212-757-8687, or 800-554-8687). Offers 5-day air-plus-motorcoach packages to New Orleans.

Experience America Tours (3723 Sunshine Ranch, San Antonio, TX 78228; phone: 800-324-2380 or 512-732-2380). Operates unusual programs focusing on New Orleans as the locals live it.

GoGo Tours (69 Spring St., Ramsey, NJ 07446-0507; phone: 201-934-3500, or call any of the 75 local *GoGo* offices). Operates hotel-and-sightseeing programs.

Jefferson Tours (1206 Currie Ave., Minneapolis, MN 55403; phone: 800-767-7433 or 612-338-4174). Offers escorted 11-day New Orleans and Cajun Country motorcoach trip from Minneapolis and Des Moines.

Le'Obs Tours (4635 Touro St., New Orleans, LA 70122-3933; phone: 504-288-3478). Operates 1- to 3-day tours emphasizing the city's history and black culture.

Maupintour (PO Box 807, Lawrence, KS 66044; phone: 800-255-4266). Offers 1-week Mardi Gras program. The tour operator is a wholesaler, so use a travel agent.

Mayflower Tours (1225 Warren Ave., PO Box 490, Downers Grove, IL 60515; phone: 800-323-7604 outside Illinois, or 708-960-3430). Operates 6-day motorcoach tour to New Orleans from Chicago area.

SuperCities (Radisson Reservations Center, 11340 Blondo St., Omaha, NE 68164; phone: 800-333-1234). Offers highly flexible mix-and-match city packages. This tour operator is a wholesaler, so use a travel agent.

Tours by Andrea (2838 Touro St., New Orleans, LA 70122; phone: 800-535-2732

GETTING READY / Package Tours 33

or 504-942-5708). Features 2- and 3-night programs, including Gourmet Delight focusing on restaurants, and special-event packages.

Travel New Orleans (434 Dauphine St., New Orleans, LA 70112; phone: 800-535-8747 or 504-561-8747). One of the city's largest tour operators offering a wide variety of packages at all levels plus many special-event programs, including ones designed around *Mardi Gras,* the *New Orleans Jazz and Heritage Festival,* and sporting events such as the *Super Bowl.*

Travel Tours International (250 W. 49th St., Suite 600, New York, NY 10019; phone: 800-767-8777 or 212-262-0700). Offers air-inclusive and land-only city packages. It is a wholesaler, so contact your travel agent.

Many of the major air carriers maintain their own tour departments or subsidiaries to stimulate vacation travel to the cities they serve. In all cases, the arrangements may be booked through a travel agent or directly with the company. Air/hotel New Orleans packages are offered by the following tour operations of airlines serving the city:

American Airlines FlyAAway Vacations (Southern Reservation Center, Mail Drop 1000, Box 619619, Dallas/Ft. Worth Airport, TX 75261-9619; phone: 800-321-2121).

Continental's Grand Destinations (PO Box 1460, Milwaukee, WI 53201-1460; phone: 800-634-5555).

Delta's Dream Vacations (PO Box 1525, Ft. Lauderdale, FL 33302; phone: 800-872-7786).

Whether visiting New Orleans independently or through one of the above packages, if you would like to include some organized touring, *Travel New Orleans* (see above under "Sample Packages") offers various half- and 1-day tours of major city attractions. A smaller company that offers a more personalized approach and groups never larger than 13 persons is *Tours by Isabelle* (PO Box 740972, New Orleans, LA 70174; phone: 504-367-3963).

■ **Note:** Frequently, the best city packages are offered by the hotels, which are trying to attract guests during the weekends, when business travel drops off, and during other off periods. These packages are sometimes advertised in local newspapers and in the Sunday travel sections of major metropolitan papers, such as *The New York Times,* which has a national edition available in most parts of the US. It's worth asking about packages, especially family and special-occasion offerings, when you call to make a hotel reservation. Calling several hotels can garner you a variety of options from which to choose.

Preparing

Calculating Costs

DETERMINING A BUDGET: A realistic appraisal of travel expenses is the most crucial bit of planning before any trip. It also is, unfortunately, one for which it is most difficult to give precise practical advice.

Estimating travel expenses for New Orleans depends on the mode of transportation you choose and how long you will stay, as well as the kind of trip you are planning.

When calculating costs, start with the basics, the major expenses being transportation, accommodations, and food. For New Orleans that will mean $110 or more a night for a double at an expensive hotel, $75 to $95 for a moderate property, and somewhat under $70 for an inexpensive one. Dinner for two runs to over $80 at an expensive restaurant, $50 to $80 at a moderate one, and under $50 at an inexpensive one. Then there are breakfast and lunch to consider.

Don't forget such extras as local transportation, shopping, and such miscellaneous items as laundry and tips. The reasonable cost of these items often is a positive surprise to your budget. And ask about discount passes on local transportation. For example, the *Regional Transit Authority* (101 Dauphine; phone: 504-569-2600) offers a *VisiTour Pass* entitling the bearer to unlimited travel on all streetcar and bus lines for $4 a day or $8 for 3 days.

Other expenses, such as the cost of local sightseeing tours and other excursions, should be included. Tourist information offices and most of the better hotels will have someone at the front desk to provide a rundown on the cost of local tours and full-day excursions in and out of New Orleans. Travel agents also can provide this information.

In planning any travel budget, it also is wise to allow a realistic amount for both entertainment and recreation. Are you planning to spend time sightseeing and visiting local tourist attractions? Is tennis or golf a part of your plan? Are you traveling with children who want to visit every site? Finally, allow for the extra cost of nightlife, if such is your pleasure. This one item alone can add a great deal to your daily expenditures.

If at any point in the planning process it appears impossible to estimate expenses, consider this suggestion: The easiest way to put a ceiling on the price of all these elements is to buy a package tour with transportation, rooms, meals, sightseeing, local travel, tips, and a dinner show or two included and prepaid. This provides a pretty exact total of what the trip will cost beforehand, and the only surprise will be the one you spring on yourself by succumbing to some irresistible souvenir.

Planning a Trip

Travelers fall into two categories: those who make lists and those who do not. Some people prefer to plot the course of their trip to the finest detail, with contingency plans and alternatives at the ready. For others, the joy of a voyage is its spontaneity; exhaustive planning only lessens the thrill of anticipation and the sense of freedom.

GETTING READY / Planning a Trip   35

For most travelers, however, a week-plus trip can be too expensive for an "I'll take my chances" attitude. Even perennial gypsies and anarchistic wanderers have to take into account the time-consuming logistics of getting around and, even with minimal baggage, they need to think about packing. Hence, at least some planning is critical.

This is not to suggest that you work out your itinerary in minute detail before you go, but it's still wise to decide certain basics at the very start; where to go, what to do, and how much to spend. These decisions require a certain amount of consideration. So before rigorously planning specific details, you might want to establish your general travel objectives:

1. How much time will you have for the entire trip, and how much of it are you willing to spend getting where you're going?
2. What interests and/or activities do you want to pursue while on vacation?
3. At what time of year do you want to go?
4. Do you want peace and privacy or lots of activity and company?
5. How much money can you afford to spend for the entire vacation?

You now can make almost all of your own travel arrangements if you have time to follow through with hotels, airlines, tour operators, and so on. But you'll probably save considerable time and energy if you have a travel agent make arrangements for you. The agent also should be able to advise you of alternative arrangements of which you may not be aware. Only rarely will a travel agent's services cost a traveler any money, and they may even save you some (see *How to Use a Travel Agent,* below).

Pay particular attention to the dates when off-season rates go into effect. In major resort areas, accommodations may cost less during the off-season (and the weather often is perfectly acceptable at this time). Off-season rates frequently are lower for other facilities, too, although don't expect to save much on car rental costs during any season. In general, it is a good idea to beware of holiday weeks, as rates at hotels generally are higher during these periods and rooms normally are heavily booked.

Make plans early. During festival months and holidays, make hotel reservations at least a month in advance. If you are flying at these times and want to benefit from savings offered through discount fares, purchase tickets as far ahead as possible. The less flexible your schedule requirements, the earlier you should book. Many hotels require deposits before they will guarantee reservations, and this most often is the case during peak travel periods. (Be sure to get a receipt for any deposit or, better yet, charge the deposit to a credit card.)

When packing, make a list of any valuable items you are carrying with you, including credit card numbers and the serial numbers of your traveler's checks. Put copies in your purse or pocket, and leave other copies at home. Put a label with your name and home address on the inside of your luggage for identification in case of loss. Put your name and business address — *never your home address* — on a label on the outside of your luggage. (Those who run businesses from home should use the office address of a friend or relative.)

Review your travel documents. If you are traveling by air, check that your ticket has been filled in correctly. The left side of the ticket should have a list of each stop you will make (even if you are stopping only to change planes), beginning with your departure point. Be sure that the list is correct, and count the number of copies to see that you have one for each plane you will take. If you have confirmed reservations, be sure that the column marked "status" says "OK" beside each flight. Have in hand vouchers or proof of payment for any reservation for which you've paid in advance; this includes hotels, transfers to and from the airport, sightseeing tours, car rentals, and tickets to special events.

Although policies vary from carrier to carrier, it's still smart to reconfirm your flight 48 to 72 hours before departure, both going and returning. If you are traveling by car,

36 GETTING READY / How to Use a Travel Agent

bring your driver's license, car registration, and proof of insurance, as well as gasoline credit cards and auto service card (if you have them).

Finally, you always should bear in mind that despite the most careful plans, things do not always occur on schedule. If you maintain a flexible attitude and try to accept minor disruptions as less than cataclysmic, you will enjoy yourself a lot more.

How to Use a Travel Agent

A reliable travel agent remains the best source of service and information for planning a trip, whether you have a specific itinerary and require an agent only to make reservations or you need extensive help in sorting through the maze of airfares, tour offerings, hotel packages, and the scores of other arrangements that may be involved in your trip.

Know what you want from a travel agent so that you can evaluate what you are getting. It is perfectly reasonable to expect your travel agent to be a thoroughly knowledgeable travel specialist, with information about your destination and, even more crucial, a command of current airfares, ground arrangements, and other wrinkles in the travel scene.

Most travel agents work through computer reservations systems (CRS). These are used to assess the availability and cost of flights, hotels, and car rentals, and through them they can book reservations. Despite reports of "computer bias," in which a computer may favor one airline over another, the CRS should provide agents with the entire spectrum of flights available to a given destination and the complete range of fares in considerably less time than it takes to telephone the airlines individually — and at no extra cost to the client.

Make the most intelligent use of a travel agent's time and expertise; understand the economics of the industry. As a client, traditionally you pay nothing for the agent's services; with few exceptions it's all free, from hotel bookings to advice on package tours. Any money the travel agent makes on the time spent arranging your itinerary — booking hotels, resorts, or flights, or suggesting activities — comes from commissions paid by the suppliers of these services — the airlines, hotels, and so on. These commissions generally run from 10% to 15% of the total cost of the service, although suppliers often reward agencies that sell their services in volume with an increased commission called an override.

A travel agent sometimes may charge a fee for special services. These chargeable items may include long-distance telephone costs incurred in making a booking, for reserving a room in a place that does not pay a commission (such as a small, out-of-the-way hotel), or for a special attention such as planning a highly personalized itinerary. A fee also may be assessed in instances of deeply discounted airfares.

Choose a travel agent with the same care with which you would choose a doctor or lawyer. You will be spending a good deal of money on the basis of the agent's judgment, so you have a right to expect that judgment to be mature, informed, and interested. At the moment, unfortunately, there aren't many standards within the travel agent industry to help you gauge competence, and the quality of individual agents varies enormously.

At present, only nine states have registration, licensing, or other forms of travel agent–related legislation on their books. Rhode Island licenses travel agents; Florida, Hawaii, Iowa, and Ohio register them; and California, Illinois, Oregon, and Washington have laws governing the sale of transportation or related services. While state licensing of agents cannot absolutely guarantee competence, it can at least ensure that an agent has met some minimum requirements.

Perhaps the best-prepared agents are those who have completed the CTC Travel Management program offered by the *Institute of Certified Travel Agents (ICTA)* and carry the initials CTC (Certified Travel Counselor) after their names. This indicates a relatively high level of expertise. For a free listing of CTCs in your area, send a self-addressed, stamped, #10 envelope to *ICTA,* 148 Linden St., Box 56, Wellesley, MA 02181 (phone: 617-237-0280 in Massachusetts; 800-542-4282 elsewhere in the US).

An agent's membership in the *American Society of Travel Agents (ASTA)* can be a useful guideline in making a selection. But keep in mind that *ASTA* is an industry organization, requiring only that its members be licensed in those states where required; be accredited to represent the suppliers whose products they sell, including airline and cruise tickets; and adhere to its Principles of Professional Conduct and Ethics code. *ASTA* does not guarantee the competence, ethics, or financial soundness of its members, but it does offer some recourse if you feel you have been dealt with unfairly. Complaints may be registered with *ASTA* (Consumer Affairs Dept., 1101 King St., Alexandria, VA 22314; phone: 703-739-2782). First try to resolve the complaint directly with the supplier. For a list of *ASTA* members in your area, send a self-addressed, stamped, #10 envelope to *ASTA* (Public Relations Dept.) at the address above.

There also is the *Association of Retail Travel Agents (ARTA),* a smaller but highly respected trade organization similar to *ASTA.* Its member agencies and agents similarly agree to abide by a code of ethics, and complaints about a member can be made to *ARTA*'s Grievance Committee, 1745 Jefferson Davis Hwy., Suite 300, Arlington, VA 22202-3402 (phone: 800-969-6069 or 703-553-7777).

Perhaps the best way to find a travel agent is by word of mouth. If the agent (or agency) has done a good job for your friends over a period of time, it probably indicates a certain level of commitment and competence. Always ask for the name of the company *and* for the name of the specific agent with whom your friends dealt, for it is that individual who will serve you, and quality can vary widely within a single agency.

Insurance

It is unfortunate that most decisions to buy travel insurance are impulsive and usually are made without any real consideration of the traveler's existing policies. Therefore, the first person with whom you should discuss travel insurance is your own insurance broker, not a travel agent or the clerk behind the airport insurance counter. You may discover that the insurance you already carry — homeowner's policies and/or accident, health, and life insurance — protects you adequately while you travel and that your real needs are in the more mundane areas of excess value insurance for baggage or trip cancellation insurance.

TYPES OF INSURANCE: To make insurance decisions intelligently, however, you first should understand the basic categories of travel insurance and what they cover. Then you can decide what you should have in the broader context of your personal insurance needs, and you can choose the most economical way of getting the desired protection: through riders on existing policies; with onetime, short-term policies; through a special program put together for the frequent traveler; through coverage that's part of a travel club's benefits; or with a combination policy sold by insurance companies through brokers, automobile clubs, tour operators, and travel agents.

There are seven basic categories of travel insurance:

1. Baggage and personal effects insurance
2. Personal accident and sickness insurance
3. Trip cancellation and interruption insurance
4. Default and/or bankruptcy insurance

38 GETTING READY / Insurance

5. Flight insurance (to cover injury or death)
6. Automobile insurance (for driving your own or a rented car)
7. Combination policies

Baggage and Personal Effects Insurance – Ask your insurance agent if baggage and personal effects are included in your current homeowner's policy, or if you will need a special floater to cover you for the duration of a trip. The object is to protect your bags and their contents in case of damage or theft anytime during your travels, not just while you're in flight, where only limited protection is provided by the airline. Baggage liability varies from carrier to carrier, but generally speaking, on domestic flights, luggage usually is insured to $1,250 — that's per passenger, not per bag. This limit should be specified on your airline ticket, but to be awarded any amount, you'll have to provide an itemized list of lost property, and if you're including new and/or expensive items, be prepared for a request that you back up your claim with sales receipts or other proof of purchase.

If you are carrying goods worth more than the maximum protection offered by the airlines, consider excess value insurance. Additional coverage is available from airlines at an average, currently, of $1 to $2 per $100 worth of coverage, up to a maximum of $5,000. This insurance can be purchased at the airline counter when you check in, though you should arrive early to fill out the necessary forms and to avoid holding up other passengers.

Major credit card companies also provide coverage for lost or delayed baggage — and this coverage often is over and above what the airline will pay. The basic coverage usually is automatic for all cardholders who use the credit card to purchase tickets, but to qualify for additional coverage, cardholders generally must enroll.

American Express: Provides $500 coverage for checked baggage; $1,250 for carry-on baggage; and $250 for valuables, such as cameras and jewelry.

Carte Blanche and *Diners Club:* Provide $1,250 free insurance for checked or carry-on baggage that's lost or damaged.

Discover Card: Offers $500 insurance for checked baggage and $1,250 for carry-on baggage — but to qualify for this coverage cardholders first must purchase additional flight insurance (see "Flight Insurance," below).

MasterCard and *Visa:* Baggage insurance coverage set by the issuing institution.

Additional baggage and personal effects insurance also is included in certain of the combination travel insurance policies discussed below.

■ **A note of warning:** Be sure to read the fine print of any excess value insurance policy; there often are specific exclusions, such as cash, tickets, furs, gold and silver objects, art, and antiques. Insurance companies ordinarily will pay only the depreciated value of the goods rather than their replacement value. The best way to protect your property is to take photos of your valuables, and keep a record of the serial numbers of such items as cameras, typewriters, laptop computers, radios, and so on. This will establish that you do, indeed, own the objects. If your luggage disappears en route or is damaged, deal with the situation immediately. If an airline loses your luggage, you will be asked to fill out a Property Irregularity Report before you leave the airport. Also report the loss to the police (since the insurance company will check with the police when processing the claim).

Personal Accident and Sickness Insurance – This covers you in case of illness during your trip or death in an accident. Most policies insure you for hospital and doctors' expenses, lost income, and so on. In most cases, it is a standard part of existing health insurance policies (especially where domestic travel is concerned), though you should check with your insurance broker to be sure of the conditions for which your

GETTING READY / Insurance 39

policy will pay. If your coverage is insufficient, take out a separate vacation accident policy or an entire vacation insurance policy that includes health and life coverage.

One example of such comprehensive health and life insurance coverage is the travel insurance packages offered by *Wallach & Co.* This insurance package, which can be purchased for periods of 10 to 180 days, is offered for two age groups: Men and women up to age 75 receive $25,000 medical insurance and a $50,000 death benefit; those from age 75 to 84 are eligible for $12,500 medical insurance and a $25,000 death benefit. For either policy, the cost for a 10-day period is $25, with decreasing rates up to 75 days, after which the rate is $1.50 per day. This basic program also may be bought in combination with trip cancellation and baggage insurance at extra cost. For further information, write to *Wallach & Co.*, 107 W. Federal St., Box 480, Middleburg, VA 22117-0480 (phone: 703-687-3166 in Virginia; 800-237-6615 elsewhere in the US).

Trip Cancellation and Interruption Insurance – Most package tour passengers pay for their travel well before departure. The disappointment of having to miss a vacation because of illness or any other reason pales before the awful prospect that not all (and sometimes none) of the money paid in advance might be returned. So cancellation insurance for any package tour is a must.

Although cancellation penalties vary (they are listed in the fine print of every tour brochure, and before you purchase a package tour you should know exactly what they are), rarely will a passenger get more than 50% of this money back if forced to cancel within a few weeks of scheduled departure. Therefore, if you book a package tour, you should have trip cancellation insurance to guarantee full reimbursement or refund should you, a traveling companion, or a member of your immediate family get sick, forcing you to cancel your trip or *return home early.*

The key here is *not* to buy just enough insurance to guarantee full reimbursement for the cost of the package in case of cancellation. The proper amount of coverage should include reimbursement for the cost of having to catch up with a tour after its departure or having to travel home at the full economy airfare if you have to forgo the return flight tied to the package. There usually is quite a discrepancy between an excursion or other special airfare and the amount charged to travel the same distance on a regularly scheduled flight at full economy fare.

Trip cancellation insurance is available from travel agents and tour operators in two forms: as part of a short-term, all-purpose travel insurance package (sold by the travel agent); or as specific cancellation insurance designed by the operator for a specific tour. Generally, tour operators' policies are less expensive, but also less inclusive. Cancellation insurance also is available directly from insurance companies or their agents as part of a short-term, all-inclusive travel insurance policy.

Before you decide on a policy, read each one carefully. (Either type can be purchased from a travel agent when you book the package tour.) Be sure to check the fine print for stipulations concerning "family members" and "pre-existing medical conditions," as well as allowances for living expenses if you must delay your return due to injury or illness.

Default and/or Bankruptcy Insurance – Although trip cancellation insurance usually protects you if *you* are unable to complete — or begin — your trip, a fairly recent innovation is coverage in the event of default and/or bankruptcy on the part of the tour operator, airline, or other travel supplier. In some travel insurance packages, this contingency is included in the trip cancellation portion of the coverage; in others, it is a separate feature. Either way, it is becoming increasingly important. Whereas sophisticated travelers have long known to beware of the possibility of default or bankruptcy when buying a tour package, in recent years more than a few respected airlines have unexpectedly revealed their shaky financial condition, sometimes leaving hordes of stranded ticket holders in their wake. While default/bankruptcy insurance will not ordinarily result in reimbursement in time to pay for new arrangements, it can

40 GETTING READY / Insurance

ensure that you will get your money back, and even independent travelers buying no more than an airplane ticket may want to consider it.

Flight Insurance – US airlines' liability for injury or death to passengers on domestic flights currently is determined on a case-by-case basis in court — this means potentially unlimited liability. But remember, this liability is not the same thing as an insurance policy; every penny that an airline eventually pays in the case of death or injury likely will be subject to a legal battle.

But before you buy last-minute flight insurance from an airport vending machine, consider the purchase in light of your total existing insurance coverage. A careful review of your current policies may reveal that you already are amply covered for accidental death. Be aware that airport insurance, the kind typically bought at a counter or from a vending machine, is among the most expensive forms of life insurance coverage, and that even within a single airport, rates for approximately the same coverage vary widely.

If you buy your plane ticket with a major credit card, you generally receive automatic insurance coverage at no extra cost. Additional coverage usually can be obtained at extremely reasonable prices, but a cardholder must sign up for it in advance.

Automobile Insurance – If you have an accident in a state that has "no fault" insurance, each party's insurance company pays his or her expenses up to certain specified limits. When you rent a car, the rental company is required to provide you with collision protection.

In your car rental contract, you'll see that for about $5 to $13 a day, you may buy optional collision damage waiver (CDW) protection. Some companies, such as *Hertz* and *Avis,* now call the option a loss damage waiver (LDW). (If partial coverage with a deductible is included in the rental contract, the CDW will cover the deductible in the event of an accident, and can cost as much as $25 per day.)

If you do not accept the CDW coverage, you may be liable for as much as the full retail value of the rental car if it is damaged or stolen; by paying for the CDW, you are relieved of all responsibility for any damage to the car. Before agreeing to this coverage, however, check with your own broker about your own existing personal automobile insurance policy. It very well may cover your entire liability exposure without any additional cost, or you automatically may be covered by the credit card company to which you are charging the cost of your rental. To find out the amount of rental car insurance provided by major credit cards, contact the issuing institutions.

You also should know that an increasing number of the major US car rental companies automatically are including the cost of the CDW in their basic rates. Car rental prices have increased to include this coverage, although rental company ad campaigns may promote this as a new, improved rental package feature. The disadvantage of this inclusion is that you may not have the option to turn down the CDW — even if you already are adequately covered by your own insurance policy or through a credit card company.

Combination Policies – Short-term insurance policies, which may include a combination of all of the types of insurance discussed above, are available through retail insurance agencies, automobile clubs, and many travel agents. These combination policies are designed to cover you for the duration of a single trip.

The following companies provide such coverage for the insurance needs discussed above:

> *Access America International:* A subsidiary of the Blue Cross/Blue Shield plans of New York and Washington, DC, now available nationwide. Contact *Access America,* PO Box 90310, Richmond, VA 23230 (phone: 800-284-8300 or 804-285-3300).

GETTING READY / Hints for Handicapped Travelers 41

Carefree: Underwritten by The Hartford. Contact *Carefree Travel Insurance,* Arm Coverage, PO Box 310, Mineola, NY 11501 (phone: 800-645-2424 or 516-294-0220).

NEAR Services: In addition to a full range of travel services, this organization offers a comprehensive travel insurance package. An added feature is coverage for lost or stolen airline tickets. Contact *NEAR Services,* 450 Prairie Ave., Suite 101, Calumet City, IL 60409 (phone: 708-868-6700 in the Chicago area; 800-654-6700 elsewhere in the US and Canada).

Tele-Trip: Underwritten by the Mutual of Omaha Companies. Contact *Tele-Trip Co.,* 3201 Farnam St., Omaha, NE 68131 (phone: 402-345-2400 in Nebraska; 800-228-9792 elsewhere in the US).

Travel Assistance International: Provided by Europ Assistance Worldwide Services, and underwritten by Transamerica Occidental Life Insurance. Contact *Travel Assistance International,* 1133 15th St. NW, Suite 400, Washington, DC 20005 (phone: 202-331-1609 in Washington, DC; 800-821-2828 elsewhere in the US).

Travel Guard International: Underwritten by the Insurance Company of North America, it is available through authorized travel agents; or contact *Travel Guard International,* 1145 Clark St., Stevens Point, WI 54481 (phone: 715-345-0505 in Wisconsin; 800-826-1300 elsewhere in the US).

Travel Insurance PAK: Underwritten by The Travelers. Contact *The Travelers Companies,* Ticket and Travel Plans, One Tower Sq., Hartford, CT 06183-5040 (phone: 203-277-2319 in Connecticut; 800-243-3174 elsewhere in the US).

Hints for Handicapped Travelers

From 40 to 50 million people in the US alone have some sort of disability, and over half this number are physically handicapped. Like everyone else today, they — and the uncounted disabled millions around the world — are on the move. More than ever before, they are demanding facilities they can use comfortably, and they are being heard. With the 1990 passage of the Americans with Disabilities Act, the physically handicapped increasingly will be finding better access to places and services throughout the US. The provisions of the act relating to public accommodations and transportation, which took effect in January 1992, mandate that means of access be provided except where the cost would be prohibitive, and creative alternatives are being encouraged. As the impact of the law spreads across the country, previous barriers to travel in the US should be somewhat ameliorated.

PLANNING: Make your travel arrangements well in advance and specify to services involved the exact nature of your condition or restricted mobility, as your trip will be much more comfortable if you know that there are accommodations and facilities to suit your needs. The best way to find out if your intended destination can accommodate a handicapped traveler is to write or call the local tourist authority or hotel and ask specific questions. If you require a corridor of a certain width to maneuver a wheelchair or if you need handles on the bathroom walls for support, ask the hotel manager. A travel agent or the local chapter or national office of the organization that deals with your particular disability — for example, the *American Foundation for the Blind* or the *American Heart Association* — will supply the most up-to-date information on the subject. Another source of information on facilities for the disabled in New Orleans is the *Advocacy Center for the Elderly and Disabled* (210 O'Keefe Ave., Suite 700, New Orleans, LA 70112; phone: 504-522-2337), which publishes an 82-page booklet, *Rollin'*

42 GETTING READY / Hints for Handicapped Travelers

by the River, for hotels, restaurants, tourist attractions, and other commercial establishments in the French Quarter, the central business district, and other tourist areas. It is available from the center for $2.25 by mail, or for $1 if it is picked up in person.

The following organizations also offer general information on access:

ACCENT on Living (PO Box 700, Bloomington, IL 61702; phone: 309-378-2961). This information service for persons with disabilities provides a free list of travel agencies specializing in arranging trips for the disabled; for a copy send a self-addressed, stamped envelope. It also offers a wide range of publications, including a quarterly magazine ($10 per year; $17.50 for 2 years) for persons with disabilities.

Direct Link (PO Box 1036, Solvang, CA 93463; phone: 805-688-1603). This company provides an on-line computer service and links the disabled and their families with a wide range of information, including accessibility, attendant care, transportation, and travel necessities.

Disabled Individuals Assistance Line (*DIAL;* 100 W. Randolph St., Suite 8-100, Chicago, IL 60601; 800-233-DIAL, both voice and TDD — telecommunications device for the deaf). This toll-free hotline provides information about public and private resources available to people with disabilities.

Information Center for Individuals with Disabilities (Ft. Point Pl., 1st Floor, 27-43 Wormwood St., Boston, MA 02210; phone: 800-462-5015 in Massachusetts; 617-727-5540/1 elsewhere in the US; both numbers provide voice and TDD). The center offers information and referral services on disability-related issues, publishes fact sheets on travel agents, tour operators, and other travel resources, and can help you research your trip.

Mobility International USA (*MIUSA;* PO Box 3551, Eugene, OR 97403; phone: 503-343-1284, both voice and TDD). This US branch of *Mobility International* (the main office is at 228 Borough High St., London SE1 1JX, England; phone: 011-44-71-403-5688), a nonprofit British organization with affiliates worldwide, offers members advice and assistance — including information on accommodations and other travel services, and publications applicable to the traveler's disability. *Mobility International* also offers a quarterly newsletter and a comprehensive sourcebook, *A World of Options for the 90s: A Guide to International Education Exchange, Community Service and Travel for Persons with Disabilities* ($14 for members; $16 for non-members). Membership includes the newsletter and is $20 a year; subscription to the newsletter alone is $10 annually.

National Rehabilitation Information Center (8455 Colesville Rd., Suite 935, Silver Spring, MD 20910; phone: 301-588-9284). A general information, resource, research, and referral service.

Paralyzed Veterans of America (*PVA;* PVA/ATTS Program, 801 18th St. NW, Washington, DC 20006; phone: 202-416-7708 in Washington, DC; 800-424-8200 elsewhere in the US). The members of this national service organization all are veterans who have suffered spinal cord injuries, but it offers advocacy services and information to all persons with a disability. *PVA* also sponsors *Access to the Skies* (*ATTS*), a program that coordinates the efforts of the national and international air travel industry in providing airport and airplane access for the disabled. Members receive several helpful publications, as well as regular notification of conferences that address subjects of interest to the disabled traveler.

Society for the Advancement of Travel for the Handicapped (*SATH;* 347 Fifth Ave., Suite 610, New York, NY 10016; phone: 212-447-7284). To keep abreast of developments in travel for the handicapped as they occur, you may want to join *SATH,* a nonprofit organization whose members include consumers, as well as travel service professionals who have experience (or an interest) in travel for the handicapped. For an annual fee of $45 ($25 for students and travelers who

GETTING READY / Hints for Handicapped Travelers   43

are 65 and older), members receive a quarterly newsletter and have access to extensive information and referral services. *SATH* also offers two useful publications: *Travel Tips for the Handicapped* (a series of informative fact sheets) and *The United States Welcomes Handicapped Visitors* (a 48-page guide covering domestic transportation and accommodations, as well as useful hints for travelers with disabilities); to order, send a self-addressed, #10 envelope and $1 per title for postage.

Travel Information Service (Moss Rehabilitation Hospital, 1200 W. Tabor Rd., Philadelphia, PA 19141-3099; phone: 215-456-9600 for voice; 215-456-9602 for TDD). This service assists physically handicapped people in planning trips and supplies detailed information on accessibility, for a nominal fee.

Blind travelers should contact the *American Foundation for the Blind* (15 W. 16th St., New York, NY 10011; phone: 800-829-0500 or 212-620-2147) and *The Seeing Eye* (Box 375, Morristown, NJ 07963-0375; phone: 201-539-4425); both provide useful information on resources for the visually impaired. The *American Society for the Prevention of Cruelty to Animals* (*ASPCA*, Education Dept., 441 E. 92nd St., New York, NY 10128; phone: 212-876-7700) offers a useful booklet, *Traveling With Your Pet*, which lists inoculation and other requirements by state. It is available for $5 (including postage and handling).

In addition, there are a number of publications — from travel guides to magazines — of interest to handicapped travelers. Among these are the following:

Access to the World, by Louise Weiss, offers sound tips for the disabled traveler. Published by Facts on File (460 Park Ave. S., New York, NY 10016; phone: 212-683-2244 in New York State; 800-322-8755 elsewhere in the US; 800-443-8323 in Canada), it costs $16.95. Check with your local bookstore; it also can be ordered from the publisher by phone with a credit card.

The Diabetic Traveler (PO Box 8223 RW, Stamford, CT 06905; phone: 203-327-5832) is a useful quarterly newsletter for travelers with diabetes. Each issue highlights a single destination or type of travel and includes information on general resources and hints for diabetics. A 1-year subscription costs $18.95. When subscribing, ask for the free fact sheet including an index of special articles; back issues are available for $4 each.

Guide to Traveling with Arthritis, a free brochure available by writing to the Upjohn Company (PO Box 307-B, Coventry, CT 06238), provides lots of good, commonsense tips on planning your trip and how to be as comfortable as possible when traveling by car, bus, train, cruise ship, or plane.

The Handicapped Driver's Mobility Guide, compiled by the *AAA*, lists over 1,100 sources of equipment and services for the handicapped, including manufacturers and retailers of special adaptive devices for automobiles. This guide also provides listings of car rental companies that can fit cars with hand controls, as well as information on accessibility of hotels and public transportation to the handicapped. Available for $5.95, plus shipping and handling, from the *AAA* chapter in your area or from the national office, 1000 AAA Dr., Heathrow, FL 32746 (phone: 407-444-7000).

Handicapped Travel Newsletter is regarded as one of the best sources of information for the disabled traveler. It is edited by wheelchair-bound Vietnam veteran Michael Quigley, who has traveled to 93 countries around the world. Issued every 2 months (plus special issues), a subscription is $10 per year. Write to *Handicapped Travel Newsletter*, PO Box 269, Athens, TX 75751 (phone: 903-677-1260).

Handi-Travel: A Resource Book for Disabled and Elderly Travellers, by Cinnie Noble, is a comprehensive travel guide full of practical tips for those with disabilities affecting mobility, hearing, or sight. To order this book, send $12.95,

44 GETTING READY / Hints for Handicapped Travelers

plus shipping and handling, to the *Canadian Rehabilitation Council for the Disabled,* 45 Sheppard Ave. E., Suite 801, Toronto, Ontario M2N 5W9, Canada (phone: 416-250-7490; both voice and TDD).

The Itinerary (PO Box 2012, Bayonne, NJ 07002-2012; phone: 201-858-3400). This quarterly travel magazine for people with disabilities includes information on accessibility, listings of tours, news of adaptive devices, travel aids, and special services, as well as numerous general travel hints. A subscription costs $10 a year.

The Physically Disabled Traveler's Guide, by Rod W. Durgin and Norene Lindsay, rates accessibility of a number of travel services and includes a list of organizations specializing in travel for the disabled. It is available for $9.95, plus shipping and handling, from Resource Directories, 3361 Executive Pkwy., Suite 302, Toledo, OH 43606 (phone: 419-536-5353 in the Toledo area; 800-274-8515 elsewhere in the US).

Ticket to Safe Travel offers useful information for travelers with diabetes. A reprint of this article is available free from local chapters of the *American Diabetes Association.* For the nearest branch, contact the central office at 1660 Duke St., Alexandria, VA 22314 (phone: 703-549-1500 in Virginia; 800-232-3472 elsewhere in the US).

Travel for the Patient with Chronic Obstructive Pulmonary Disease, a publication of the George Washington University Medical Center, provides some sound practical suggestions for those with emphysema, chronic bronchitis, asthma, or other lung ailments. To order, send $2 to Dr. Harold Silver, 1601 18th St. NW, Washington, DC 20009 (phone: 202-667-0134).

Traveling Like Everybody Else: A Practical Guide for Disabled Travelers, by Jacqueline Freedman and Susan Gersten, offers the disabled tips on traveling by car, cruise ship, and plane, as well as lists of accessible accommodations, tour operators specializing in tours for disabled travelers, and other resources. It is available for $11.95, plus postage and handling, from Modan Publishing, PO Box 1202, Bellmore, NY 11710 (phone: 516-679-1380).

Travel Tips for Hearing-Impaired People, a free pamphlet for deaf and hearing-impaired travelers, is available from the *American Academy of Otolaryngology* (One Prince St., Alexandria, VA 22314; phone: 703-836-4444). For a copy, send a self-addressed, stamped, business-size envelope to the academy.

Travel Tips for People with Arthritis, a 31-page booklet published by the *Arthritis Foundation,* provides helpful information regarding travel by car, bus, train, cruise ship, or plane, planning your trip, medical considerations, and ways to conserve your energy while traveling. It also includes listings of helpful resources, such as associations and travel agencies that operate tours for disabled travelers. For a copy, contact your local *Arthritis Foundation* chapter, send $1 to the national office, PO Box 19000, Atlanta, GA 30326 (phone: 404-872-7100).

The Wheelchair Traveler, by Douglass R. Annand, lists accessible hotels, motels, restaurants, and other sites by state throughout the US. This valuable resource is available directly from the author. For the price of the most recent edition, contact Douglass R. Annand, 123 Ball Hill Rd., Milford, NH 03055 (phone: 603-673-4539).

A few more basic resources to look for are *Travel for the Disabled,* by Helen Hecker ($19.95), and by the same author, *Directory of Travel Agencies for the Disabled* ($19.95). *Wheelchair Vagabond,* by John G. Nelson, is another useful guide for travelers confined to a wheelchair (hardcover, $14.95; paperback, $9.95). All three titles are published by Twin Peaks Press, PO Box 129, Vancouver, WA 98666 (phone: 800-637-CALM or 206-694-2462). The publisher also offers a catalogue of 26 other books on travel for the disabled for $2.

GETTING READY / Hints for Handicapped Travelers   45

PLANE: The US Department of Transportation (DOT) has ruled that US airlines must accept all passengers with disabilities. As a matter of course, US airlines were pretty good about accommodating handicapped passengers even before the ruling, although each airline has somewhat different procedures. Ask for specifics when you book your flight.

Disabled passengers should always make reservations well in advance and should provide the airline with all relevant details of their conditions. These details include information on mobility and equipment that you will need the airline to supply — such as a wheelchair for boarding or portable oxygen for in-flight use. Be sure that the person to whom you speak fully understands the degree of your disability — the more details provided, the more effective help the airline can give you.

On the day before the flight, call back to make sure that all arrangements have been prepared, and arrive early on the day of the flight so that you can board before the rest of the passengers. It's a good idea to bring a medical certificate with you, stating your specific disability or the need to carry particular medicine.

Because most airports have jetways (corridors connecting the terminal with the door of the plane), a disabled passenger usually can be taken as far as the plane, and sometimes right onto it, in a wheelchair. If not, a narrow boarding chair may be used to take you to your seat. Your own wheelchair, which will be folded and put in the baggage compartment, should be tagged as escort luggage to assure that it's available at planeside upon landing rather than in the baggage claim area. Travel is not quite as simple if your wheelchair is battery-operated: Unless it has non-spillable batteries, it might not be accepted on board, and you will have to check with the airline ahead of time to find out how the batteries and the chair should be packaged for the flight. Usually people in wheelchairs are asked to wait until other passengers have disembarked. If you are making a tight connection, be sure to tell the attendant.

Passengers who use oxygen may not use their personal supply in the cabin, though it may be carried on the plane as cargo when properly packed (the tank must be empty) and labeled. If you will need oxygen during the flight, the airline will supply it to you (there is a charge), provided you have given advance notice — 24 hours to a few days, depending on the carrier.

The free booklet *Air Transportation of Handicapped Persons* explains the general guidelines that govern air carrier policies. For a copy, write to the US Department of Transportation (Distribution Unit, Publications Section, M-443-2, Washington, DC 20590) and ask for "Free Advisory Circular #AC-120-32." *Access Travel: A Guide to the Accessibility of Airport Terminals,* a free publication of the *Airport Operators Council International,* provides information on more than 500 airports worldwide and offers ratings of 70 features, such as accessibility to bathrooms, corridor width, and parking spaces. For a copy, contact the Consumer Information Center (Dept. 563W, Pueblo, CO 81009; phone: 719-948-3334).

The following airlines serving New Orleans have TDD toll-free lines in the US for the hearing-impaired:

American: 800-582-1573 in Ohio; 800-543-1586 elsewhere in the US.
America West: 800-526-8077.
Continental: 800-343-9195.
Delta: 800-831-4488.
Northwest: 800-328-2298.
TWA: 800-252-0622 in California; 800-421-8480 elsewhere in the US.
United: 800-942-8819 in Illinois; 800-323-0170 elsewhere in the US.
USAir: 800-242-1713 in Pennsylvania; 800-245-2966 elsewhere in the US.

GROUND TRANSPORTATION: Perhaps the simplest solution to getting around is to travel with an able-bodied companion who can drive. If you are accustomed to

46 GETTING READY / Hints for Handicapped Travelers

driving your own hand-controlled car and want to rent one, you are in luck. Some rental companies will fit cars with hand controls. *Avis* (phone: 800-331-1212) can convert a car to hand controls with as little as 24 hours' notice, though it's a good idea to arrange for one further in advance. *Hertz* (phone: 800-654-3131) requires a minimum of 4 days to install the controls, and makes the additional stipulation that the car be returned to the office from which it was rented. Most companies do not charge extra for hand controls, but *Budget* (phone: 800-527-0700) requires an additional $50 deposit (refunded when the car is returned). *Alamo* (phone: 800-327-9633) and *Avis* will fit them only on a full-size cars — which tend to be among the most expensive models to rent. In addition, companies may request that you bring your handicapped driver's permit with you. Hand controls often are installed only at some locations of a given company, and there usually are a limited number of these devices available, so make arrangements as early as possible.

A relatively new company, *Wheelchair Getaways,* rents vans accommodating one or two wheelchairs and up to five passengers. Each vehicle has 4-point straps to secure wheelchairs, air conditioning, and stereo. The renter provides the driver. The Pennsylvania-based company (PO Box 819, Newtown, PA 18940; phone: 800-642-2042 or 215-579-9120) has franchises in a number of US cities, although at press time, nothing in the New Orleans area. It would be worthwhile, however, to call the headquarters when making travel plans to find out if the company has extended service to the New Orleans area.

TOURS: Programs designed for the physically impaired are run by specialists who have researched hotels, restaurants, and sites to be sure they present no insurmountable obstacles. The following travel agencies and tour operators specialize in making group and individual arrangements for travelers to New Orleans with physical or other disabilities:

Access: The Foundation for Accessibility by the Disabled (PO Box 356, Malverne, NY 11565; phone: 516-887-5798). A travelers' referral service that acts as an intermediary with tour operators and agents worldwide, and provides information on accessibility at various locations.

Accessible Journeys (412 S. 45th St., Philadelphia, PA 19104; phone: 215-747-0171). Arranges for medical-professional traveling companions — registered or licensed practical nurses, therapists, or doctors (all are experienced travelers). Several prospective companions' profiles and photos are sent to the client for perusal, and if one is acceptable, the "match" is made. The client usually pays all travel expenses for the companion, plus a certain amount in "earnings" to replace wages the companion would be making at his or her usual job.

Accessible Tours/Directions Unlimited (720 N. Bedford Rd., Bedford Hills, NY 10507; phone: 914-241-1700 in New York State; 800-533-5343 elsewhere in the continental US). Arranges group or individual tours for disabled persons traveling in the company of able-bodied friends or family members. Accepts the unaccompanied traveler if completely self-sufficient.

Beehive Business and Leisure Travel (1130 W. Center St., N. Salt Lake, UT 84054; phone: 800-777-5727 or 801-292-4445). John Warner runs Dialysis in Wonderland, a guided tour program for dialysis patients, which includes arrangements for treatment en route. Among destinations offered last year was Hawaii.

Dahl Good Neighbor Travel Service (124 S. Main St., Viroqua, WI 54665; phone: 608-637-2128; and 535 N. St. Mary's Rd., Libertyville, IL 60048; phone: 708-362-0129). This agency can supply a full range of services and provide necessities to travelers with any special needs, mental or physical.

Evergreen Travel Service (4114 198th St. SW, Suite 13, Lynnwood, WA 98036-6742; phone: 800-435-2288 or 206-776-1184 throughout the continental US and Canada). Offers tours for the disabled (Wings on Wheels Tours), sight im-

GETTING READY / Hints for Single Travelers 47

paired/blind (White Cane Tours), and hearing impaired/deaf (Flying Fingers Tours). Most programs are first class or deluxe, and include a trained escort. It also offers programs for people who are not disabled but who want a slower pace (Lazybones Tours), and arranges special programs for people who need dialysis.

Flying Wheels Travel (143 W. Bridge St., Box 382, Owatonna, MN 55060; phone: 800-535-6790 or 507-451-5005). Handles both tours and individual arrangements.

The Guided Tour (613 W. Cheltenham Ave., Suite 200, Melrose Park, PA 19126-2414; phone: 215-782-1370). Arranges tours, including to New Orleans, for people with developmental and learning disabilities and sponsors separate tours for members of the same population who also are physically disabled or who simply need a slower pace.

Hinsdale Travel (201 E. Ogden Ave., Hinsdale, IL 60521; phone: 708-325-1335 or 708-469-7349). Janice Perkins takes groups of handicapped travelers on the road, making arrangements to meet their special needs.

Prestige World Travel (5710X High Point Rd., Greensboro, NC 27407; phone: 800-476-7737 or 919-292-6690). Owner Kay Jones arranges for the handicapped, including the wheelchair-bound, to travel on her regular tour programs; and also designs independent travel programs.

USTS Travel Horizons (11 E. 44th St., New York, NY 10017; phone: 800-487-8787 or 212-687-5121). Travel agent and registered nurse Mary Ann Hamm designs trips for individual travelers requiring all types of kidney dialysis and handles arrangements for the dialysis.

Weston Travel Agency (134 N. Cass Ave., PO Box 1050, Westmont, IL 60559; phone: 800-633-3725 outside of Illinois, or 708-968-2513). It specializes in travel services for people with cerebral palsy and those who are wheelchair-bound.

Travelers who would benefit from being accompanied by a nurse or physical therapist also can hire a companion through *Traveling Nurses' Network,* a service provided by Twin Peaks Press (PO Box 129, Vancouver, WA 98666; phone: 800-637-CALM or 206-694-2462). For a $10 fee, clients receive the names of three nurses, whom they can then contact directly; for a $125 fee, the agency will make all the hiring arrangements for the client. Travel arrangements also may be made in some cases — the fee for this further service is determined on an individual basis.

A similar service is offered by *MedEscort International* (ABE International Airport, PO Box 8766, Allentown, PA 18105; phone: 800-255-7182 in the continental US; elsewhere, call 215-791-3111). Clients can arrange to be accompanied by a nurse, paramedic, respiratory therapist, or physician through *MedEscort*. The fees are based on the disabled traveler's needs. This service also can assist in making travel arrangements.

Hints for Single Travelers

Just about the last trip in human history on which the participants were neatly paired was the voyage of Noah's Ark. Ever since, passenger lists and tour groups have reflected the same kind of asymmetry that occurs in real life, as countless individuals set forth to see the world unaccompanied (or unencumbered, depending on your outlook) by spouse, lover, friend, companion, or relative. Unfortunately, traveling alone can turn a traveler into a second class citizen. The truth is that the travel industry is not very fair to people who vacation by

48 GETTING READY / Hints for Single Travelers

themselves. People traveling alone almost invariably end up paying more than individuals traveling in pairs. Most travel bargains, including package tours, accommodations, resort packages, and cruises, are based on *double occupancy* rates. This means that the per-person price is offered on the basis of two people traveling together and sharing a double room (which means they each will spend a good deal more on meals and extras). The single traveler will have to pay a surcharge, called a single supplement, for exactly the same package. In extreme cases, this can add as much as 35% — and sometimes more — to the basic per-person rate.

Don't despair, however. Throughout the US, there are scores of smaller hotels and other hostelries where, in addition to a cozier atmosphere, prices still are quite reasonable for the single traveler.

The obvious, most effective alternative is to find a traveling companion. Even special "singles' tours" that promise no supplements usually are based on people sharing double rooms. Perhaps the most recent innovation along these lines is the creation of organizations that "introduce" the single traveler to other single travelers. Some charge fees, while others are free, but the basic service offered is the same: to match an unattached person with a compatible travel mate. Among such organizations are the following:

Jane's International (2603 Bath Ave., Brooklyn, NY 11214; phone: 718-266-2045). This service puts potential traveling companions in touch with one another. It has started a new organization, *Sophisticated Women Travelers,* to create groups for single women to travel together. No age limit, no fee for either.

Odyssey Network (118 Cedar St., Wellesley, MA 02181; phone: 617-237-2400). Originally founded to match single women travelers, this company now includes men in its enrollment. Odyssey offers a quarterly newsletter for members who are seeking a travel companion, and occasionally organizes small group tours. A newsletter subscription is $50.

Partners-in-Travel (PO Box 491145, Los Angeles, CA 90049; phone: 213-476-4869). Members receive a list of singles seeking traveling companions; prospective companions make contact through the agency. The membership fee is $40 per year and includes a chatty newsletter (6 issues per year).

Travel Companion Exchange (PO Box 833, Amityville, NY 11701; phone: 516-454-0880). This group publishes a newsletter for singles and a directory of individuals looking for travel companions. On joining, members fill out a lengthy questionnaire and write a small listing (much like an ad in a personal column). Based on these listings, members can request copies of profiles and contact prospective traveling companions. It is wise to join well in advance of your planned vacation so that there's enough time to determine compatibility and plan a joint trip. Membership fees, including the newsletter, are $30 for 6 months or $60 a year for a single-sex listing; $66 and $120, respectively, for a complete listing. Subscription to the newsletter alone costs $24 for 6 months or $36 per year.

In addition, a number of tour packagers cater to single travelers. These companies offer packages designed for individuals interested in vacationing with a group of single travelers or in being matched with a traveling companion. Among the better established of these agencies are the following:

Gallivanting (515 E. 79th St., Suite 20 F, New York, NY 10021; phone: 800-933-9699 or 212-988-0617). Offers matching service for singles ages 25 through 55 willing to share accommodations in order to avoid paying single supplement charges, with the agency guaranteeing this arrangement if bookings are paid for at least 75 days in advance.

Marion Smith Singles (611 Prescott Pl., N. Woodmere, NY 11581; phone: 516-

GETTING READY / Hints for Older Travelers 49

791-4852, 516-791-4865, or 212-944-2112). Specializes in tours for singles ages 20 to 50, who can choose to share accommodations to avoid paying single supplement charges.

Saga International Holidays (222 Berkeley St., Boston MA 02116; phone: 800-343-0273 or 617-451-6808). A subsidiary of a British company specializing in older travelers, many of them single, *Saga* offers a broad selection of packages for people age 60 and over or those 50 to 59 traveling with someone 60 or older. Although anyone can book a *Saga* trip, a club membership (no fee) includes a subscription to their newsletter, as well as other publications and travel services — such as a matching service for single travelers.

Singles in Motion (545 W. 236th St., Suite 1D, Riverdale, NY 10463; phone: 718-884-4464). Has a scheduled program.

Travel in Two's (239 N. Broadway, Suite 3, N. Tarrytown, NY 10591; phone: 914-631-8409). For city programs, this company matches up solo travelers and then customizes programs for them. The firm also puts out a quarterly *Singles Vacation Newsletter,* which costs $7.50 per issue or $20 per year.

A good book for single travelers is *Traveling On Your Own,* by Eleanor Berman, which offers tips on traveling solo and includes information on trips for singles. Available in bookstores, it also can be ordered by sending $12.95, plus postage and handling, to Random House, Order Dept., 400 Hahn Rd., Westminster, MD 21157 (phone: 800-733-3000).

Single travelers also may want to subscribe to *Going Solo,* a newsletter that offers helpful information on going on your own. Issued eight times a year, a subscription costs $36. Contact Doerfer Communications, PO Box 1035, Cambridge, MA 02238 (phone: 617-876-2764).

Those interested in a particularly cozy type of accommodation should consider going the bed and breakfast route. Though a single person will likely pay more than half of the rate quoted for a couple even at a bed and breakfast establishment, the prices still are quite reasonable, and the homey atmosphere will make you feel less conspicuously alone.

Another possibility is the *United States Servas Committee* (11 John St., Room 407, New York, NY 10038; phone: 212-267-0252), which maintains a list of hosts around the world, including New Orleans, who are willing to take visitors into their homes as guests. *Servas* will send an application form and a list of interviewers at the nearest locations for you to contact. After the interview, if you are accepted as a *Servas* traveler, you'll receive a membership certificate. The membership fee is $45 per year for an individual, with a $15 deposit to receive the host list, refunded upon its return.

Hints for Older Travelers

Special discounts and more free time are just two factors that have given Americans over age 65 a chance to see the world at affordable prices. Senior citizens make up an ever-growing segment of the travel population, and the trend among them is to travel more frequently and for longer periods of time.

PLANNING: When planning a vacation, prepare your itinerary with one eye on your own physical condition and the other on your interests. One important factor to keep in mind is not to overdo anything and to be aware of the effects that the weather may have on your capabilities.

Older travelers may find the following publications of interest:

50   GETTING READY / Hints for Older Travelers

Discount Guide for Travelers Over 55, by Caroline and Walter Weintz, is an excellent book for budget-conscious older travelers. Published by Penguin USA, it is currently out of print; check your local library.

International Health Guide for Senior Citizen Travelers, by Dr. W. Robert Lange, covers such topics as trip preparations, food and water precautions, adjusting to weather and climate conditions, finding a doctor, motion sickness, jet lag, and so on. Also includes a list of resource organizations that provide medical assistance for travelers. It is available for $4.95 postpaid from Pilot Books, 103 Cooper St., Babylon, NY 11702 (phone: 516-422-2225).

Mature Traveler is a monthly newsletter that provides information on travel discounts, places of interest, useful tips, and other topics of interest for travelers 49 and up. To subscribe, send $24.95 to GEM Publishing Group, PO Box 50820, Reno, NV 89513 (phone: 702-786-7419).

Senior Citizen's Guide to Budget Travel in the US and Canada, by Paige Palmer, provides specific information on economical travel options for senior citizens. To order, send $4.95, plus $1 for postage and handling, to Pilot Books (address above).

Take a Camel to Lunch and Other Adventures for Mature Travelers, by Nancy O'Connell, offers offbeat and unusual adventures for travelers over 50. Available at bookstores or directly from Bristol Publishing Enterprises (PO Box 1737, San Leandro, CA 94577; phone: 800-346-4889 or 510-895-4461) for $8.95, plus shipping and handling.

Travel Easy: The Practical Guide for People Over 50, by Rosalind Massow, discusses a wide range of subjects — from trip planning, transportation options, and preparing for departure to avoiding and handling medical problems en route. The book is out of print, so check your local library.

Unbelievably Good Deals & Great Adventures That You Absolutely Can't Get Unless You're Over 50, by Joan Rattner Heilman, offers travel tips for older travelers, including discounts on accommodations and transportation, as well as a list of organizations for seniors. It is available for $7.95, plus shipping and handling, from Contemporary Books, 180 N. Michigan Ave., Chicago, IL 60601 (phone: 312-782-9181).

HEALTH: Pre-trip medical and dental checkups are strongly recommended. In addition, be sure to take along any prescription medication you need, enough to last *without a new prescription* for the duration of your trip; pack all medications with a note from your doctor for the benefit of airport authorities. If you have specific medical problems, bring prescriptions and a "medical file" composed of the following:

1. A summary of your medical history and current diagnosis.
2. A list of drugs to which you are allergic.
3. Your most recent electrocardiogram, if you have heart problems.
4. Your doctor's name, address, and telephone number.

DISCOUNTS AND PACKAGES: Since guidelines change from place to place, it is a good idea to inquire in advance about discounts on transportation, hotels, concerts, movies, museums, and other activities. For instance, the National Park Service has a Golden Age Passport, which entitles people over 62 (and those in the car with them) to free entrance to all national parks and monuments (available by showing a Medicare card or driver's license as proof of age at any national park).

Many hotel chains, airlines, cruise lines, bus companies, car rental companies, and other travel suppliers offer discounts to older travelers. For instance, *United* offers senior citizen coupon books — with either four or eight coupons each — that can be exchanged for tickets on domestic flights of up to 2,000 miles. These coupons are good 7 days a week for travel in all 50 states, although some peak travel periods are omitted.

GETTING READY / Hints for Older Travelers 51

Other airlines also offer discounts for passengers age 60 (or 62) and over, which may be applicable to one traveling companion per senior. Among the airlines that often offer such discounted airfares are *America West, Continental,* and *TWA.* Given the continuing changes in the airline industry, however, these discounted fares may not be available when you purchase your tickets. For information on current prices and applicable restrictions, contact the individual carriers.

Some discounts, however, are extended only to bona fide members of certain senior citizens organizations. Because the same organizations frequently offer package tours to both domestic and international destinations, the benefits of membership are twofold: Those who join can take advantage of discounts as individual travelers and also reap the savings that group travel affords. In addition, because the age requirements for some of these organizations are quite low (or nonexistent), the benefits can begin to accrue early.

In order to take advantage of these discounts, you should carry proof of your age (or eligibility). A driver's license, membership card in a recognized senior citizens organization, or a Medicare card should be adequate. Among the organizations dedicated to helping older travelers see the world are the following:

American Association of Retired Persons (AARP; 601 E St. NW, Washington, DC 20049; phone: 202-434-2277). The largest and best known of these organizations. Membership is open to anyone 50 or over, whether retired or not; dues are $8 a year, $20 for 3 years, or $45 for 10 years, and include spouse. The *AARP* Travel Experience Worldwide program, available through *American Express Travel Related Services,* offers members tours and other travel programs designed exclusively for older travelers. For example, it offers an independent New Orleans city program. Members can book these services by calling *American Express* at 800-927-0111 for land and air travel.

Golden Companions (PO Box 754, Pullman, WA 99163-0754; phone: 509-334-9351). This club assists members in finding suitable traveling companions. Its Travel Companion Network includes a mail exchange service and bimonthly newsletter for those age 45 and over. Other services include vacation home exchanges, discounts on hotels and package tours, and group trips and cruises, some of which are sponsored by the club.

Mature Outlook (Customer Service Center, 6001 N. Clark St., Chicago, IL 60660; phone: 800-336-6330). Through its *Travel Alert,* tours, cruises, and other vacation packages are available to members at special savings. Hotel and car rental discounts and travel accident insurance also are available. Membership is open to anyone 50 years of age or older, costs $9.95 a year, and includes a bimonthly newsletter and magazine, as well as information on package tours.

National Council of Senior Citizens (1331 F St. NW, Washington, DC 20005; phone: 202-347-8800). Here, too, the emphasis is on keeping costs low. This nonprofit organization offers members a different roster of package tours each year, as well as individual arrangements through its affiliated travel agency *(Vantage Travel Service).* Although most members are over 50, membership is open to anyone (regardless of age) for an annual fee of $12 per person or couple. Lifetime membership costs $150.

Certain travel agencies and tour operators offer special trips geared to older travelers. Among them are the following:

Evergreen Travel Service (4114 198th St. SW, Suite 13, Lynnwood, WA 98036-6742; phone: 800-435-2288 or 206-776-1184 throughout the continental US and Canada). This specialist in trips for persons with disabilities recently introduced Lazybones Tours, a program offering leisurely tours for older travelers. Most programs are first class or deluxe, and include an escort.

Gadabout Tours (700 E. Tahquitz Canyon Way, Palm Springs, CA 92262; phone:

800-521-7309 or 619-325-5556 in California; 800-952-5068 elsewhere in the US). Offers escorted tours and cruises to a number of destinations, including New Orleans.

Grandtravel (6900 Wisconsin Ave., Suite 706, Chevy Chase, MD 20815; phone: 800-247-7651 or 301-986-0790). This agency specializes in trips for grandparents and their grandchildren (aunts and uncles are welcome, too), bringing the generations together through travel. Several itineraries coincide with school vacations and emphasize historic and natural sites. Transportation, accommodations, and activities are throughtfully arranged to meet the needs of the young and the young-at-heart.

Saga International Holidays (120 Boylston St., Boston MA 02116; phone: 800-343-0273 or 617-451-6808). A subsidiary of a British company catering to older travelers, *Saga* offers a broad selection of packages for people age 60 and over or those 50 to 59 traveling with someone 60 or older. Although anyone can book a *Saga* trip, a $15 club membership includes a subscription to their newsletter, as well as other publications and travel services.

Many travel agencies, particularly the larger ones, are delighted to make presentations to help a group of senior citizens select destinations. A local chamber of commerce should be able to provide the names of such agencies. Once a time and place are determined, an organization member or travel agent can obtain group quotations for transportation, accommodations, meal plans, and sightseeing. Larger groups usually get the best breaks.

Hints for Traveling with Children

What better way to encounter New Orleans's historic past than in the company of the young, wide-eyed members of your family? Their presence does not have to be a burden or an excessive expense. The current generation of discounts for children and family package deals can make a trip together quite reasonable.

A family trip to New Orleans will be an investment in your children's future, making geography and the history of the early years of our country come alive to them, and leaving a sure memory that will be among the fondest you will share with them someday. Their insights will be refreshing to you; their impulses may take you to unexpected places with unexpected dividends. The experience will be invaluable to them at any age.

PLANNING: Here are several hints for making a trip with children easy and fun:

1. Children, like everyone else, will derive more pleasure from a trip if they know something about their destination before they arrive. Begin their education about a month before you leave. Using maps, travel magazines, and books, give children a clear idea of where you are going and how far away it is.

2. Children should help to plan the itinerary, and where you go and what you do should reflect some of their ideas. If they already know something about the city and the sites they will visit, they will have the excitement of recognition when they arrive.

3. Give children specific responsibilities: The job of carrying their own flight bags and looking after their personal things, along with some other light chores, will give them a stake in the journey.

4. Give each child a travel diary or scrapbook to take along.

GETTING READY / Hints for Traveling with Children   53

Children's books about New Orleans and its place in the history of our country provide an excellent introduction and can be found at children's bookstores (see *Books, Magazines, and Newsletters*), many general bookstores, and in libraries.

And for parents, *Travel With Your Children* (*TWYCH*; 80 Eighth Ave., New York, NY 10011; phone: 212-206-0688) publishes a newsletter, *Family Travel Times*, that focuses on families with young travelers and offers helpful hints. An annual subscription (10 issues) is $35 and includes a copy of the "Airline Guide" issue (updated every other year), which focuses on the subject of flying with children. This special issue is available separately for $10.

Another newsletter devoted to family travel is *Getaways*. This quarterly publication provides reviews of family-oriented literature, activities, and useful travel tips. To subscribe, send $25 to *Getaways*, Att. Ms. Brooke Kane, PO Box 8282, McLean, VA 22107 (phone: 703-534-8747).

Also of interest to parents traveling with their children is *How to Take Great Trips With Your Kids*, by psychologist Sanford Portnoy and his wife, Joan Flynn Portnoy. The book includes helpful tips from fellow family travelers, tips on economical accommodations and touring by car, as well as over 50 games to play with your children en route. It is available for $8.95, plus shipping and handling, from Harvard Common Press, 535 Albany St., Boston, MA 02118 (phone: 617-423-5803). Another title worth looking for is *Great Vacations with Your Kids*, by Dorothy Jordan (Dutton, $12.95).

Another book on family travel, *Travel with Children*, by Maureen Wheeler, offers a wide range of practical tips on traveling with children. It is available for $10.95, plus shipping and handling, from Lonely Planet Publications, Embarcadero W., 112 Linden St., Oakland, CA 94607 (phone: 510-893-8555).

Finally, parents arranging a trip with their children may want to deal with an agency specializing in family travel such as *Let's Take the Kids* (1268 Devon Ave., Los Angeles, CA 90024; phone: 800-726-4349 or 213-274-7088). In addition to arranging and booking trips for individual families, this group occasionally organizes trips for single-parent families traveling together. They also offer a parent travel network, whereby parents who have been to a particular destination can evaluate it for others.

PLANE: Begin early to investigate all available family discount flights, as well as any package deals and special rates offered by the major airlines. Booking is sometimes required up to 2 months in advance. You may well find that charter companies offer no reductions for children, or not enough to offset the risk of last-minute delays or other inconveniences to which charters are subject. Some of the major scheduled airlines, on the other hand, do provide hefty discounts for children. When using local transportation such as a bus, train, or subway, ask about lower fares for children or family rates.

When you make your reservation, tell the airline that you are traveling with a child. Where discounts are offered, children ages 2 through 11 generally travel at about 80% of the adult fare on domestic flights. As a general rule, children under 2 fly free if they sit on an adult's lap. A second infant without a second adult would pay the fare applicable to children ages 2 through 11.

Although some airlines will, on request, supply bassinets for infants, most carriers encourage parents to bring their own safety seat on board, which then is strapped into the airline seat with a regular seat belt. This is much safer — and certainly more comfortable — than holding the child in your lap. If you do not purchase a seat for your baby, you have the option of bringing the infant restraint along on the off chance that there might be an empty seat next to yours — in which case some airlines will let you use that seat at no charge for your baby and infant seat. However, if there is no empty seat available, the infant seat no doubt will have to be checked as baggage (and you may have to pay an additional charge), since it generally does not fit under the airplane seats or in the overhead racks. The safest bet is to pay for a seat.

54 GETTING READY / Hints for Traveling with Children

Be forewarned: Some safety seats designed primarily for use in cars do not fit into plane seats properly. Although nearly all seats manufactured since 1985 carry labels indicating whether they meet federal standards for use aboard planes, actual seat sizes may vary from carrier to carrier. At the time of this writing, the FAA was in the process of reviewing and revising the federal regulations regarding infant travel and safety devices — it was still to be determined if children should be *required* to sit in safety seats and whether the airlines will have to provide them.

If using one of these infant restraints, you should try to get bulkhead seats, which will provide extra room to care for your child during the flight. You also should request a bulkhead seat when using a bassinet — again, this is not as safe as strapping the child in. On some planes the bassinet hooks into a bulkhead wall; on others they are placed on the floor in front of you. (Note that bulkhead seats often are reserved for families traveling with small children.) As a general rule, babies should be held during takeoff and landing.

Request seats on the aisle if you have a toddler or if you think you will need to use the bathroom frequently. Carry onto the plane all you will need to care for and occupy your children during the flight — formula, diapers, a sweater, books, favorite stuffed animals, and so on. Dress your baby simply, with a minimum of buttons and snaps, because the only place you may have to change a diaper is at your seat or in a small lavatory.

On most US carriers, you also can ask for a hot dog, hamburger, or even a fruit plate instead of the airline's regular lunch or dinner if you give at least 24 hours' notice. Some, but not all, airlines have baby food aboard, and the flight attendant can warm a bottle for you. While you should bring along toys from home, also ask about children's diversions. Some carriers have terrific free packages of games, coloring books, and puzzles.

When the plane takes off and lands, make sure your baby is nursing or has a bottle, pacifier, or thumb in its mouth. This sucking will make the child swallow and help to clear stopped ears. A piece of hard candy will do the same for an older child.

Parents traveling by plane with toddlers, children, or teenagers may want to consult *When Kids Fly,* a free booklet published by Massport (Public Affairs Dept., 10 Park Plaza, Boston, MA 02116-3971; phone: 617-973-5600), which includes helpful information on airfares for children, infant seats, what to do in the event of overbooked or canceled flights, and so on.

■ **Note:** Newborn babies, whose lungs may not be able to adjust to the altitude, should not be taken aboard an airplane. And some airlines may refuse to allow a pregnant woman in her eighth or ninth month to fly. Check with the airline ahead of time, and carry a letter from your doctor stating that you are fit to travel — and indicating the estimated date of birth.

ACCOMMODATIONS: Often a cot for a child will be placed in a hotel room at little or no extra charge. If you wish to sleep in separate rooms, special rates sometimes are available for families; some places do not charge for children under a certain age. In many of the larger chain hotels, the staffs are more used to children. These hotels also are likely to have swimming pools or gamerooms — both popular with most youngsters. Many large resorts also have recreation centers for children.

At mealtime, don't deny yourself or your children the delights of a new style of cooking. Encourage them to try new foods. Children like to know what kind of food to expect, so it will be interesting to look up regional specialties. And don't forget about picnics.

Things to Remember
1. If you are visiting many sites, pace the days with children in mind. Break the trip into half-day segments, with running around or "doing" time built in.

GETTING READY / Hints for Traveling with Children 55

2. Don't forget that a child's attention span is far shorter than an adult's. Children don't have to see every sight or all of any sight to learn something from their trip; watching, playing with, and talking to other children can be equally enlightening.
3. Let your children lead the way sometimes; their perspective is different from yours, and they may lead you to things you would never have noticed on your own.
4. Remember the places that children love to visit: aquariums, zoos, amusement parks, beaches, nature trails, and so on. Among the activities that may pique their interest are bicycling, boat trips, visiting planetariums and children's museums, and viewing natural habitat exhibits. The perennial New Orleans attractions for children are the *Audubon Zoological Gardens,* the *Aquarium of the Americas,* and the riverboats that ply the harbor and the bayou.

On the Road

Credit Cards and Traveler's Checks

 It may seem hard to believe, but one of the greatest (and least understood) costs of travel is money itself. Your one single objective in relation to the care and retention of your travel funds is to make them stretch as far as possible. When you do spend money, it should be on things that expand and enhance your travel experience, with no buying power lost due to carelessness or lack of knowledge. This requires more than merely ferreting out the best airfare or the most charming budget hotel. It means being canny about the management of money itself. Herewith, a primer on making money go as far as possible while traveling.

TRAVELER'S CHECKS: It's wise to carry traveler's checks while on the road instead of (or in addition to) cash, since it's possible to replace them if they are stolen or lost; in the US, you usually can receive partial or full replacement funds the same day if you have your purchase receipt and proper identification. Issued in various denominations, with adequate proof of identification (credit cards, driver's license, passport), traveler's checks are as good as cash in most hotels, restaurants, stores, and banks. Don't assume, however, that restaurants, small shops, and other establishments are going to be able to change checks of large denominations. More and more establishments are beginning to restrict the face amount of traveler's checks they will accept or cash, so it is wise to purchase at least some of your checks in small denominations — say, $10 and $20.

Every type of traveler's check is legal tender in banks around the world, and each company guarantees full replacement if checks are lost or stolen. After that the similarity ends. Some charge a fee for purchase, while others are free; you can buy traveler's checks at almost any bank, and some are available by mail. Most important, each traveler's check issuer differs slightly in its refund policy — the amount refunded immediately, the accessibility of refund locations, the availability of a 24-hour refund service, and the time it will take you to receive replacement checks. For instance, *American Express* offers a 3-hour replacement of lost or stolen traveler's checks at any *American Express* office — other companies may not be as prompt. (Note that *American Express*'s 3-hour policy is based on the traveler's being able to provide the serial numbers of the lost checks. Without these numbers, refunds can take much longer. The *American Express* office in New Orleans is located at 158 Baronne (phone: 504-586-8201).

We cannot overemphasize the importance of knowing how to replace lost or stolen checks. All of the traveler's check companies have agents throughout the US, both in their own name and at associated agencies (usually, but not necessarily, banks), where refunds can be obtained during business hours. Most of them also have 24-hour toll-free telephone lines, and some even will provide emergency funds to tide you over on a Sunday.

Be sure to make a photocopy of the refund instructions that will be given to you by the issuing institution at the time of purchase. To avoid complications should you need to redeem lost checks (and to speed up the replacement process), keep the purchase

GETTING READY / Credit Cards, Traveler's Checks 57

receipt and an accurate list, by serial number, of the checks that have been spent or cashed. You may want to incorporate this information in an "emergency packet," also including the numbers of the credit cards you are carrying, and any other bits of information you shouldn't be without. Always keep these records separate from the checks and the original records themselves (you may want to give them to a traveling companion to hold).

Several of the major traveler's check companies charge 1% for the acquisition of their checks; others don't. To receive fee-free traveler's checks you may have to meet certain qualifications — for instance, *Thomas Cook*'s checks issued in US currency are free if you make your travel arrangements through its travel agency. *American Express* traveler's checks are available without charge to members of the *American Automobile Association (AAA)*. Holders of some credit cards (such as the *American Express Platinum* card) also may be entitled to free traveler's checks. The issuing institution (e.g., the particular bank at which you purchase them) may itself charge a fee. If you purchase traveler's checks at a bank in which you or your company maintains significant accounts (especially commercial accounts of some size), the bank may absorb the 1% fee as a courtesy.

American Express, Bank of America, Citicorp, MasterCard, Thomas Cook, and *Visa* all offer traveler's checks. Here is a list of the major companies issuing traveler's checks and the numbers to call to report lost or stolen checks throughout the US:

American Express: 800-221-7282.
Bank of America: 800-227-3460.
Citicorp: 800-645-6556.
MasterCard: Note that *Thomas Cook MasterCard* is now handling all *MasterCard* traveler's check inquiries and refunds.
Thomas Cook MasterCard: 800-223-7373.
Visa: 800-227-6811.

CREDIT CARDS: Some establishments you may encounter during the course of your travels may not honor any credit cards and some may not honor all cards, so there is a practical reason to carry more than one. The following is a list of credit cards that enjoy wide domestic and international acceptance:

American Express: Cardholders can cash personal checks for traveler's checks and cash at *American Express* or its representatives' offices in the US up to the following limits (within any single 21-day period): $1,000 for *Green* and *Optima* cardholders; $5,000 for *Gold* cardholders; and $10,000 for *Platinum* cardholders. Check cashing also is available to cardholders who are guests at participating hotels (up to $250), and for holders of airline tickets at participating airlines (up to $50). Free travel accident, baggage, and car rental insurance is provided if the ticket or rental is charged to the card; additional insurance also is available for additional cost. For further information or to report a lost or stolen *American Express* card, call 800-528-4800 throughout the continental US.

Carte Blanche: Free travel accident, baggage, and car rental insurance if ticket or rental is charged to card; additional insurance also is available at additional cost. For medical, legal, and travel assistance, call 800-356-3448 throughout the US. For further information or to report a lost or stolen *Carte Blanche* card, call 800-525-9135 throughout the US.

Diners Club: Emergency personal check cashing for cardholders staying at participating hotels and motels (up to $250 per stay). Free travel accident, baggage, and car rental insurance if ticket or rental is charged to card; additional insurance also is available for an additional fee. For medical, legal, and travel assistance worldwide, call 800-356-3448 throughout the US. For further information

58 GETTING READY / Credit Cards, Traveler's Checks

or to report a lost or stolen *Diners Club* card, call 800-525-9135 throughout the US.

Discover Card: Offered by a subsidiary of Sears, Roebuck & Co., it provides cardholders with cash advances at numerous automatic teller machines and *Sears* stores throughout the US. For further information or to report a lost or stolen *Discover* card, call 800-DISCOVER throughout the US.

MasterCard: Cash advances are available at participating banks worldwide. Check with your issuing bank for information. *MasterCard* also offers a 24-hour emergency lost card service; call 800-826-2181 throughout the US.

Visa: Cash advances are available at participating banks worldwide. Check with your issuing bank for information. *Visa* also offers a 24-hour emergency lost card service; call 800-336-8472 throughout the US.

SENDING MONEY: If you have used up your traveler's checks, cashed as many emergency personal checks as your credit card allows, drawn on your cash advance line to the fullest extent, and still need money, have it sent to you via one of the following services:

American Express (phone: 800-543-4080). Offers a service called "Moneygram," completing money transfers in as little as 15 minutes. The sender can go to any *American Express* office in the US and transfer money by presenting cash, a personal check, money order, or credit card — *Discover, MasterCard, Visa,* or *American Express Optima* (no other *American Express* or other credit cards are accepted). *American Express Optima* cardholders also can arrange for this transfer over the phone. The minimum transfer charge is $12, which rises with the amount of the transaction; the sender can forward funds of up to $10,000 per transaction (credit card users are limited to the amount of their pre-established credit line). To collect at the other end, the receiver must show identification (driver's license or other picture ID) at an *American Express* branch office. The company's office in New Orleans is listed above in the "Traveler's Checks" section.

Western Union Telegraph Company (phone: 800-325-4176 throughout the US). A friend or relative can go, cash in hand, to any *Western Union* office in the US, where, for a *minimum* charge of $13 (it rises with the amount of the transaction), the funds will be transferred to a centralized *Western Union* account. When the transaction is fully processed — generally within 30 minutes — you can go to any *Western Union* branch office to pick up the transferred funds; for an additional fee of $2.95 you will be notified by phone when the money is available. For a higher fee, the sender may call *Western Union* with a *MasterCard* or *Visa* number to send up to $2,000, although larger transfers will be sent to a predesignated location. One convenient location is 701 Royal St. (phone: 504-523-1353).

CASH MACHINES: Automatic teller machines (ATMs) are increasingly common throughout the US. If your bank participates in one of the international ATM networks (most do), the bank will issue you a "cash card" along with a personal identification code or number (also called a PIC or PIN). You can use this card at any ATM in the same electronic network to check your account balances, transfer monies between checking and savings accounts, and — most important for a traveler — withdraw cash instantly. Network ATMs generally are located in banks, commercial and transportation centers, and near major tourist attractions.

Some financial institutions offer exclusive automatic teller machines for their own customers only at bank branches. At the time of this writing, ATMs that *are* connected generally belong to one of the following two international networks:

GETTING READY / Mail, Telephone, and Electricity 59

CIRRUS: Has over 70,000 ATMs in more than 45 countries, including over 65,000 locations in the US — about 25 in New Orleans proper, not counting the suburbs. *MasterCard* holders also may use their cards to draw cash against their credit lines. For further information on the *CIRRUS* network, call 800-4-CIRRUS.

PLUS: Has over 70,000 automatic teller machines worldwide, including over 50,000 locations in the US — around 35 of them in New Orleans. *MasterCard* and *Visa* cardholders also may use their cards to draw cash against their credit lines. For further information on the *PLUS* network, call 800-THE-PLUS.

Information about the *CIRRUS* and *PLUS* systems also is available at member bank branches, where you can obtain free booklets listing the locations worldwide. Note that a recent change in banking regulations permits financial institutions to subscribe to *both* the *CIRRUS* and *PLUS* systems, allowing users of either network to withraw funds from ATMs at participating banks.

Time Zone and Business Hours

TIME ZONE: New Orleans is in the central time zone and observes daylight saving time beginning on the first Sunday in April and continuing until the last Sunday in October.

BUSINESS HOURS: New Orleans maintains business hours that are fairly standard throughout the country: 9 AM to 5 PM, Mondays through Fridays.

Banks generally are open weekdays from 9 AM to 3 PM, and 24-hour "automatic tellers" or "cash machines" are increasingly common (for information on national networks, see *Credit Cards and Traveler's Checks,* in this section).

Retail stores usually are open from 9:30 or 10 AM to 5:30 or 6 PM, Mondays through Saturdays. Some of the larger stores are open until 9 PM Wednesdays through Saturdays in warm weather, with Thursday being the most common late-closing night in winter. Many retail establishments also remain open on Sundays until 5 PM or so.

Mail, Telephone, and Electricity

MAIL: Most major post offices are open 24 hours a day, with at least a self-service section for weighing packages and buying stamps, as is the case at the main New Orleans post office (701 Loyola Ave.; phone: 504-589-1111), which has counter hours from 8:30 AM to 4:30 PM on weekdays and until noon on Saturdays. Another post office convenient for visitors is at 3923 Carondelet (phone: 504-891-2816) and opens from 7 AM to 5 PM Mondays through Fridays and until noon on Saturdays.

Stamps also are available at most hotel desks. There are vending machines for stamps in drugstores, transportation terminals, and other public places. Stamps cost more from these machines than they do at the post office.

There are several places that will receive and hold mail for travelers. Mail sent to you at a hotel and clearly marked "Guest Mail, Hold for Arrival" is one safe approach. Post offices will extend this service to you if the mail is sent to you in care of General Delivery in the city or town you will visit. This will direct it to the main post office in any large city. Ask the sender to put "Hold for 30 Days" (the maximum period of time that the US Postal Service will hold correspondence), as well as a return address

60 GETTING READY / Mail, Telephone, and Electricity

on the envelope so that the post office can return it if you are unable to pick it up. To claim this mail, go to the main post office in New Orleans (see above for address), ask for General Delivery, and present identification (driver's license, credit cards, birth certificate, or passport). Mail must be collected in person.

If you are an *American Express* customer (a cardholder, a carrier of *American Express* traveler's checks, or traveling on an *American Express Travel Related Services* tour) you can have mail sent to its New Orleans office. Letters are held free of charge — registered mail and packages are not accepted. You must be able to show an *American Express* card, traveler's checks, or a voucher proving you are on one of the company's tours to qualify. Those who aren't clients cannot use the service. Mail should be addressed to you, care of *American Express,* and should be marked "Client Mail Service." Additional information on its mail service and the addresses of American Express offices throughout the US are listed in the pamphlet *American Express Travelers' Companion,* available from any American Express branch office.

Members of the *American Automobile Association (AAA)* also can have mail held free of charge at any *AAA* office in the US. Instruct the sender to mark the envelope "Hold for Arrival." For more information regarding *AAA*'s mail service and branch locations, contact your local chapter or the national office, 1000 AAA Dr., Heathrow, FL 32745-5063 (phone: 407-444-8544).

For rapid, overnight delivery to other cities, *Federal Express* can be useful. The phone number to call for pick-up in New Orleans is 800-238-5355, while a convenient drop-off address is 701 Poydras. The pick-up number for another such service, *DHL Worldwide Courier Express,* is 504-733-9717.

TELEPHONE: Public telephones are available just about everywhere — including transportation terminals, hotel lobbies, restaurants, drugstores, libraries, post offices, and other municipal buildings, as well as major tourist centers.

The New Orleans area code is 504.

Although you can use a telephone company credit card number on any phone, pay phones that take major credit cards (*American Express, MasterCard, Visa,* and so on) are increasingly common, particularly in transportation and tourism centers. Also now available is the "affinity card," a combined telephone calling card/bank credit card that can be used for domestic and international calls. Cards of this type include the following:

AT&T/Universal (phone: 800-662-7759).
Executive Telecard International (phone: 800-950-3800).

Similarly, *MCI VisaPhone* (phone: 800-866-0099) can add phone card privileges to the services available through your existing *Visa* card. This service allows you to use your *Visa* account number, plus an additional code, to charge calls on any touch-tone phone.

You must first dial 1 to indicate that you are making a long-distance call. The nationwide number for information is 555-1212. If you need a number in another area code, dial 1 + the area code + 555-1212. (If you don't know the area code, simply dial 0 for an operator who will tell you.)

Long-distance rates are charged according to when the call is placed: weekday daytime; weekday evenings; and nights, weekends, and holidays. Least expensive are the calls you dial yourself from a private phone at night and on weekends and major holidays. It generally is more expensive to call from a pay phone than it is to call from a private phone, and you must pay for a minimum 3-minute call. If the operator assists you, calls are more expensive. This includes credit card, bill-to-a-third-number, collect, and time-and-charge calls, as well as person-to-person calls, which are the most expen-

GETTING READY / Staying Healthy 61

sive. Rates are fully explained in the front of the white pages of every telephone directory.

Hotel Surcharges – Before calling from your hotel room, inquire about any surcharges the hotel may impose. These can be excessive, but are avoidable by calling collect, using a telephone credit card (see above), or calling from a public pay phone. (Note that when calling from your hotel room, even if the call is made collect or charged to a credit card number, some establishments still may add on a nominal line usage charge — so ask before you call.)

Emergency Number – As in most US cities, 911 is the number to dial in the event of an emergency in New Orleans. Operators at this number will get you the help you need from the police, fire department, or ambulance service. It is, however, a number that should be used for real emergencies only.

Other Resources – Particularly useful for planning a trip is *AT&T's Toll-Free 800 Directory,* which lists thousands of companies with 800 numbers, both alphabetically (white pages) and by category (yellow pages), including a wide range of travel services — from travel agents to transportation and accommodations. Issued in a consumer edition for $9.95 and a business edition for $14.95, both are available from *AT&T Phone Centers* or by calling 800-426-8686. Other useful directories for use before you leave and on the road include the *Toll-Free Travel & Vacation Information Directory* ($4.95 postpaid from Pilot Books, 103 Cooper St., Babylon, NY 11702; phone: 516-422-2225) and *The Phone Booklet,* which lists the nationwide, toll-free (800) numbers of travel information sources and suppliers — such as major airlines, hotel and motel chains, car rental companies, and tourist information offices (send $2 to *Scott American Corporation,* Box 88, W. Redding, CT 06896).

ELECTRICITY: All 50 US states have the same electrical current system: 110 volts, 60 cycles, alternating current (AC). Appliances running on standard current can be used throughout the US without adapters or converters.

Staying Healthy

The surest way to return home in good health is to be prepared for medical problems that might occur en route. Below, we've outlined everything about which you need to think before you go.

BEFORE YOU GO: Older travelers or anyone suffering from a chronic medical condition, such as diabetes, high blood pressure, cardiopulmonary disease, asthma, or ear, eye, or sinus trouble, should consult a physician before leaving home. Those with conditions requiring special consideration when traveling should consider seeing, in addition to their regular physician, a specialist in travel medicine. For a referral in a particular community, contact the nearest medical school or ask a local doctor to recommend such a specialist. Dr. Leonard Marcus, a member of the *American Committee on Clinical Tropical Medicine and Travelers' Health,* provides a directory of more than 100 travel doctors across the country. For a copy, send a 9- by 12-inch, addressed, stamped envelope to Dr. Marcus at 148 Highland Ave., Newton, MA 02165 (phone: 617-527-4003).

Also be sure to check with your insurance company ahead of time about the applicability of your hospitalization and major medical policies while you're away. If your medical policy does not protect you while you're traveling, there are comprehensive combination policies specifically designed to fill the gap. (For a discussion of medical insurance and a list of inclusive combination policies, see *Insurance,* in this section.)

62 GETTING READY / Staying Healthy

First Aid – Put together a compact, personal medical kit including Band-Aids, first-aid cream, antiseptic, nose drops, insect repellent, aspirin or non-aspirin pain reliever, an extra pair of prescription glasses or contact lenses (and a copy of your prescription for glasses or contact lenses), sunglasses, over-the-counter remedies for diarrhea, indigestion, and motion sickness, a thermometer, and a supply of those prescription medicines you take regularly.

In a corner of your kit, keep a list of all the drugs you have brought and their purpose, as well as duplicate copies of your doctor's prescriptions (or a note from your doctor). As brand names may vary in different parts of the US, it's a good idea to ask your doctor for the generic name of any drugs you use so that you can ask for their equivalent should you need a refill. It also is a good idea to ask your doctor to prepare a medical identification card that includes such information as your blood type, your social security number, any allergies or chronic health problems you have, and your medical insurance information. Considering the essential contents of your medical kit, keep it with you, rather than in your checked luggage.

MINIMIZING THE RISKS: In the US, travelers do not face many of the health risks encountered in visits to many destinations around the world (such as Mexico or South America). Certainly travel always entails *some* possibility of injury or illness, but neither is inevitable and, with some basic precautions, your trip should proceed untroubled by ill health.

Food and Water – The tap water in the US is thoroughly purified, so feel free to drink it; fruit, vegetables, and dairy products are likewise safe. However, you should avoid swimming in or drinking water from freshwater streams, rivers, or pools, as they may be contaminated with *Leptospira,* a bacterium that causes a disease called leptospirosis (its symptoms resemble influenza).

Sunburn – The burning power of the sun can quickly cause severe sunburn or sunstroke. To protect yourself against these ills, wear sunglasses, take along a broad-brimmed hat and cover-up, and, most important, use a sunscreen lotion.

Following these precautions will not guarantee an illness-free trip, but should minimize the risk. For more information regarding preventive health care for travelers, contact the *International Association for Medical Assistance to Travelers* (*IAMAT;* 417 Center St., Lewiston, NY 14092; phone: 716-754-4883). This organization also assists travelers in obtaining emergency medical assistance around the world.

MEDICAL ASSISTANCE IN NEW ORLEANS: Nothing ruins a vacation or business trip more effectively than sudden injury or illness. Fortunately, should you need medical attention, competent health professionals perfectly equipped to handle any medical problem can be found in New Orleans. Most towns and cities of any size have a hospital in the area, and generally, even the smallest of areas has at least a medical clinic or private physician nearby. All hospitals are prepared for emergency cases — although the sophistication of facilities may vary — and many hospitals also have walk-in clinics to serve people who do not really need emergency service, but who have no place to go for immediate medical attention. The level of medical care in the US, especially in the larger cities, generally is excellent, providing all the basic specialties and services.

Emergency Treatment – You will find, in the event of an emergency, that most tourist facilities — transportation companies, hotels, theme parks, and resorts — are equipped to handle the situation quickly and efficiently. If a bona fide emergency occurs, dial 911, the emergency number, and immediately state the nature of your problem and your location. If you are able to, another alternative is to go directly to the emergency room of the nearest hospital. In New Orleans, *Tulane Medical Center* (1415 Tulane Ave.; phone: 504-588-5711) provides first-rate emergency service. *Charity Hospital* (1532 Tulane Ave.; phone: 504-568-2311) also has a 24-hour emergency room. Other major medical institutions are *Hotel Dieu* (2021 Perdido; phone: 504-588-3000);

GETTING READY / Staying Healthy 63

Touro Infirmary (1401 Foucher St., phone: 504-897-8250); *Mercy Hospital* (301 N. Jefferson Davis Pkwy.; phone: 504-483-5777).

Non-Emergency Care – If a doctor is needed for something less than an emergency, there are several ways to find one. If you are staying in a hotel, ask for help in reaching a doctor or other emergency services, or for the house physician, who may visit you in your room or ask you to visit an office. When you check in at a hotel, it's not a bad idea to include your home address and telephone number; this will facilitate the process of notifying friends, relatives, or your own doctor in case of an emergency.

Pharmacies and Prescriptions – For other medical emergencies, 24-hour pharmacies such as *Eckerd Drug Store* at 3400 Canal St. (phone: 504-488-6661). In addition, there is *Walgreen's Drug Store* at two convenient locations, 900 Canal St. (phone: 504-523-7201), which is open 7 AM to 9 PM weekdays and until 7 PM on Sundays, and 134 Royal St. (phone: 504-522-2736), which is open from 8 AM to 10 PM weekdays and 9 AM to 9 PM on Sundays.

If you need to refill a prescription from your own doctor, you should be aware that in some states pharmacists only will fill prescriptions made out by a doctor licensed to practice in that state, so you may have to have a local doctor rewrite a prescription. Even in an emergency — such as a diabetic needing insulin — a traveler more than likely will be given only enough of a drug to last until a local prescription can be obtained. Generally a hospital emergency room or walk-in clinic can provide a refill from its pharmaceutical department or a prescription that can be filled at a nearby pharmacy.

ADDITIONAL RESOURCES: Information and medical assistance also is available from various organizations, some of which offer programs designed to assist travelers who have chronic ailments or whose illness requires them to return home. Among these are the following:

International Association for Medical Assistance to Travelers (IAMAT; 417 Center St., Lewiston, NY 14092; phone: 716-754-4883). Entitles members to the services of participating doctors around the world, as well as clinics and hospitals in various locations. Participating physicians agree to adhere to a basic charge of around $50 to see a patient referred by *IAMAT.* To join, simply write to *IAMAT;* in about 3 weeks you will receive a membership card, the booklet of members, and an inoculation chart. A nonprofit organization, *IAMAT* appreciates donations; with a donation of $25 or more, you will receive a set of worldwide climate charts detailing weather and sanitary conditions. (Delivery can take up to 5 weeks, so plan ahead.)

International Health Care Service (New York Hospital–Cornell Medical Center, 525 E. 68th St., Box 210, New York, NY 10021; phone: 212-746-1601). This service provides a variety of travel-related health services, including a complete range of immunizations at moderate per-shot rates. A pre-travel counseling and immunization package costs $255 for the first family member and $195 for each additional member; a post-travel consultation is $175 to $275, plus lab work. Consultations are by appointment only, from 4 to 8 PM Mondays through Thursdays, although 24-hour coverage is available for urgent travel-related problems. In addition, sending $4.50 (with a self-addressed envelope) to the address above will procure the service's publication, *International Health Care Travelers Guide,* a compendium of facts and advice on health care and diseases around the world.

International SOS Assistance (PO Box 11568, Philadelphia, PA 19116; phone: 800-523-8930 or 215-244-1500). Subscribers are provided with telephone access — 24 hours a day, 365 days a year — to a worldwide, monitored, multilin-

64 GETTING READY / Staying Healthy

gual network of medical centers. A phone call brings assistance ranging from a telephone consultation to transportation home by ambulance or aircraft, or, in some cases, transportation of a family member to wherever you are hospitalized. Individual rates are $35 for 2 weeks of coverage ($3.50 for each additional day), $70 for 1 month, or $240 for 1 year; couple and family rates also are available.

Medic Alert Foundation (2323 N. Colorado, Turlock, CA 95380; phone: 800-ID-ALERT or 209-668-3333). If you have a health condition that may not be readily perceptible to the casual observer — one that might result in a tragic error in an emergency situation — this organization offers identification emblems specifying such conditions. The foundation also maintains a computerized central file from which your complete medical history is available 24 hours a day by phone (the telephone number is clearly inscribed on the emblem). The onetime membership fee (between $35 and $50) is based on the type of metal from which the emblem is made — the choices range from stainless steel to 10K gold-filled.

TravMed (PO Box 10623, Baltimore, MD 21204; phone: 800-732-5309 or 410-296-5225). For $3 per day, subscribers receive comprehensive medical assistance while abroad. Major medical expenses are covered up to $100,000, and special transportation home or of a family member to wherever you are hospitalized is provided at no additional cost.

Helpful Publications – Practically every phase of health care — before, during, and after a trip — is covered in *The New Traveler's Health Guide,* by Drs. Patrick J. Doyle and James E. Banta. It is available for $4.95, plus postage and handling, from Acropolis Books Ltd., 13950 Park Center Rd., Herndon, VA 22071 (phone: 800-451-7771 or 703-709-0006).

The *Traveling Healthy Newsletter,* which is published six times a year, also is brimming with health-related travel tips. For a year's subscription, which costs $24, contact Dr. Karl Neumann (108-48 70th Rd., Forest Hills, NY 11375; phone: 718-268-7290). A sample issue is available for $4. Dr. Neumann also is the editor of the useful free booklet *Traveling Healthy,* which is available by writing to the *Travel Healthy Program* (Clark O'Neill, 1 Broad Ave., Fairview, NJ 07022; phone: 201-947-3400).

For more information regarding preventive health care for travelers, contact the *International Association for Medical Assistance to Travelers* (*IAMAT;* 417 Center St., Lewiston, NY 14092; phone: 716-754-4883). The Centers for Disease Control also publishes an interesting booklet, *Health Information for International Travel.* To order send a check or money order for $5 to the Superintendent of Documents (US Government Printing Office, Washington, DC 20402), or charge it to your credit card by calling 202-783-3238. For information on vaccination requirements, disease outbreaks, and other health information pertaining to traveling abroad, you also can call the Centers for Disease Control's 24-hour International Health Requirements and Recommendations Information Hotline: 404-332-4559.

■ **Note:** Those who are unable to take a reserved flight due to personal illness or who must fly home unexpectedly due to a family emergency should be aware that airlines may offer a discounted airfare (or arrange a partial refund) if the traveler can demonstrate that his or her situation is indeed a legitimate emergency. Your inability to fly or the illness or death of an immediate family member usually must be substantiated by a doctor's note or the name, relationship, and funeral home from which the deceased will be buried. In such cases, airlines often will waive certain advance purchase restrictions or you may receive a refund check or voucher for future travel at a later date. Be aware, however, that this bereavement

GETTING READY / Drinking and Drugs   65

fare may not necessarily be the least expensive fare available and, if possible, it is best to have a travel agent check all possible flights through a computer reservations system (CRS).

Legal Aid

The best way to begin looking for legal aid in an unfamiliar area is to call your own lawyer. If you don't have, or cannot reach, your own attorney, most cities offer legal referral services (sometimes called attorney referral services) maintained by county bar associations. Such referral services see that anyone in need of legal representation gets it. (Attorneys also are listed in the yellow pages.) The *New Orleans Bar Association* offers such a service (phone: 504-561-8828). They can match you up with an attorney and set up an appointment for you. If your case goes to court, you are entitled to court-appointed representation if you can't get a lawyer or can't afford one.

In the case of minor traffic accidents (such as a fender bender), it often is most expedient to settle the matter before the police get involved. If you get a traffic or parking ticket, pay it. For most violations, you will receive a citation at most, and be required to appear in court on a specified date.

Drinking and Drugs

DRINKING: As in all 50 states, the legal drinking age in New Orleans is 21. There are no legal mandates for controlling the hours that liquor may be served, and some bars stay open 24 hours a day, 7 days a week.

For retail purchases, liquor, wine, and beer are sold at package stores, supermarkets, drugstores, or any other establishment that cares to stock them.

DRUGS: Despite the US government's intensified and concerted effort to stamp out drugs, illegal narcotics still are prevalent in the US, as elsewhere. Enforcement of drug laws is becoming increasingly strict throughout the nation, however, and local narcotics officers are renowned for their absence of understanding and lack of a sense of humor.

Opiates and barbiturates, and other increasingly popular drugs — "white powder" substances like heroin, cocaine, and "crack" (the cocaine derivative) and ICE (a crystallized amphetamine) — continue to be of major concern to narcotics officials. **Warning:** Authorities warn those traveling with children that ICE is virtually indistinguishable from rock salt and rock candy, so it is particularly important to stress to children not to accept anything from strangers.

In New Orleans, possession of marijuana is a misdemeanor or a felony depending on the amount and the charged individual's previous record. For stronger illegal drugs, such as crack or cocaine, the penalty again depends on the amount and whether there was evidence of intent to sell, with sentences ranging from 5 years to life. There is a mandatory life sentence for possession of heroin. The best advice we can offer is this: Don't carry, use, buy, or sell illegal drugs.

To avoid difficulties during spot luggage inspections at the airport, those who carry medicines that contain a controlled drug such as codeine should be sure to have a current doctor's prescription with them.

■**Be Forewarned:** US narcotics agents warn travelers of the incresingly common ploy of drug dealers asking travelers to transport a "gift" or other package for them. In other words, do not, under any circumstances, agree to take anything with you for a stranger.

Tipping

While tipping is at the discretion of the person receiving the service, 50¢ is the rock-bottom tip for anything, and $1 is the current customary minimum for small services. In restaurants, tip between 10% and 20% of the bill. For average service in an average restaurant, a 15% tip to the waiter is reasonable, although one should never hesitate to penalize poor service or reward excellent and efficient attention by leaving less or more.

Although it's not necessary to tip the maître d' of most restaurants — unless he has been especially helpful in arranging a special party or providing a table (slipping the maitre d' something in a crowded restaurant *may,* however, get you seated sooner or procure a preferred table) — when tipping is desirable or appropriate, the least amount should be $5. In the finest restaurants, where a multiplicity of servers are present, plan to tip 5% to the captain in addition to the gratuity left for the waiter. The sommelier (wine waiter) is tipped approximately 10% of the price of the bottle of wine.

In allocating gratuities at a restaurant, pay particular attention to what has become the standard credit card charge form, which now includes separate places for gratuities for waiters and/or captains. If these separate boxes are not on the charge slip, simply ask the waiter or captain how these separate tips should be indicated. In some establishments, tips indicated on credit card receipts may not be given to the help, so you may want to leave tips in cash.

In a large hotel, where it is difficult to determine just who out of a horde of attendants actually performed particular services, it is perfectly proper for guests to ask to have an extra 10% to 15% added to their bill. For those who prefer to distribute tips themselves, a chambermaid generally is tipped at the rate of around $1 a day. Tip the concierge or hall porter for specific services only, with the amount of such gratuities dependent on the level of service provided. For any special service you receive in a hotel, a tip is expected — $1 being the minimum for a small service.

Bellhops, doormen, and porters at hotels and transportation centers generally are tipped at the rate of $1 per piece of luggage, along with a small additional amount if a doorman helps with a cab or car. Taxi drivers should get about 15% of the total fare.

Miscellaneous tips: Sightseeing tour guides should be tipped. If you are traveling in a group, decide together what you want to give the guide and present it from the group at the end of the tour ($1 per person is a reasonable tip). If you have been individually escorted, the amount paid should depend on the degree of your satisfaction, but it should not be less than 10% of the tour price. Museum and monument guides also are usually tipped a few dollars.

In barbershops and beauty parlors, tips also are expected, but the percentages vary according to the type of establishment — 10% in the most expensive salons; 15% to 20% in less expensive establishments. (As a general rule, the person who washes your hair should get a small additional tip.) Washroom attendants should get a small tip — they usually set out a little plate with a coin (or coins) already on it indicating the suggested denomination. Coat checks are worth about 50¢ to $1 a coat. And don't forget service station attendants, for whom a tip of around 50¢ for cleaning the windshield or other attention is not unusual.

Tipping always is a matter of personal preference. In the situations covered above, as well as in any others that arise where you feel a tip is expected or due, feel free to express your pleasure or displeasure. Again, never hesitate to reward excellent and efficient attention or to penalize poor service. Give an extra gratuity and a word of thanks when someone has gone out of his or her way for you. Either way, the more personal the act of tipping, the more appropriate it seems. And if you didn't like the service — or the attitude — don't tip.

Religion on the Road

The surest source of information on religious services in an unfamiliar community is the desk clerk of the hotel or resort in which you are staying; the local tourist information office or a church of another religious affiliation also may be able to provide this information. For a full range of options, joint religious councils often provide circulars with the addresses and times of services of other houses of worship in the area. These often are printed as part of general tourist guides provided by the local tourist and convention center, or as part of a "what's going on" guide to the city. Many newspapers also offer a listing of religious services in their area in weekend editions.

You may want to use your vacation to broaden your religious experience by joining an unfamiliar faith in its service. This can be a moving experience, especially if the service is held in a church, synagogue, or temple that is historically significant or architecturally notable. You almost always will find yourself made welcome and comfortable.

Sources and Resources

Tourist Information

The Louisiana Office of Tourism can be reached by writing PO Box 94291, Baton Rouge, LA 70804-9291 (phone: 800-33-GUMBO or 504-342-8119). The Greater New Orleans Tourist and Convention Commission is at 1520 Sugar Bowl Dr., New Orleans, LA 70112 (phone: 504-566-5011). For other local tourist information, see *Sources and Resources* in THE CITY.

Books, Magazines, and Newsletters

BOOKS: The variety and scope of books and other travel information in and on the United States today is astounding. Every city and region are represented, so before you leave on your journey you can prepare by perusing books relevant to your special travel interests. These can usually be found in bookshops devoted to travel, among them the following:

Book Passage (51 Tamal Vista Blvd., Corte Madera, CA 94925; phone: 415-927-0960 in California; 800-321-9785 elsewhere in the US). Travel guides and maps to all areas of the world. A free catalogue is available.

The Complete Traveller (199 Madison Ave., New York, NY 10016; phone: 212-685-9007). Travel guides and maps. A catalogue is available for $2.

Forsyth Travel Library (PO Box 2975, Shawnee Mission, KS 66201-1375; phone: 800-367-7984 or 913-384-3440). Travel guides and maps, old and new, to all parts of the world. Ask for the "Worldwide Travel Books and Maps" catalogue.

Globe Corner (1 School St., Boston, MA 02180; phone: 617-523-6658). Travel guides, maps, and histories.

Phileas Fogg's Books and Maps (87 Stanford Shopping Center, Palo Alto, CA 94304; phone: 800-533-FOGG or 415-327-1754). Travel guides and maps.

Powell's Travel Store (Pioneer Courthouse Sq., 701 SW 6th Ave., Portland, OR 97204; phone: 503-228-1108). A wealth of travel-related books (over 15,000 titles) and reference materials (globes, an extensive selection of maps, and so on), as well as luggage and travel accessories (travel irons and the like). There is even a travel agency on the premises.

The Reader's Catalog (250 W. 57th St., New York, NY 10107; phone: 800-733-BOOK or 212-262-7198). This general mail-order catalogue business will make recommendations on travel — and other — books, and ship them anywhere in the world.

Tattered Cover (2955 E. First Ave., Denver, CO 80206; phone: 800-833-9327 or 303-322-7727). The travel department alone of this enormous bookstore carries

GETTING READY / Books, Magazines, and Newsletters   69

over 7,000 books, as well as maps and atlases. No catalogue is offered (the list is too extensive), but a newsletter, issued three times a year, is available on request.

Thomas Brothers Maps & Travel Books (603 W. Seventh St., Los Angeles, CA 90017; phone: 213-627-4018). Maps (including road atlases, street guides, and wall maps), guidebooks, and travel accessories.

Traveldays Book Shop (317 *Columbus City Center,* Columbus, OH 43215; phone: 614-221-0506). Maps, guidebooks, and travel videos.

Traveller's Bookstore (22 W. 52nd St., New York, NY 10019; phone: 212-664-0995). Travel guides, maps, literature, and accessories. A catalogue is available for $2.

MAGAZINES: As sampling the regional fare is likely to be one of the highlights of any visit, you will find reading about local edibles worthwhile before you go or after you return. *Gourmet,* a magazine specializing in food, frequently features mouth-watering articles on food and restaurants in the US, although its scope is much broader than domestic fare alone. It is available at newsstands nationwide for $2.50 an issue or for $18 a year from *Gourmet,* PO Box 53780, Boulder, CO 80322 (phone: 800-365-2454).

There are numerous additional magazines for every special interest available; check at your library information desk for a directory of such publications, or look over the selection offered at a well-stocked newsstand.

NEWSLETTERS: One of the very best sources of detailed travel information is *Consumer Reports Travel Letter.* Published monthly by Consumers Union (PO Box 53629, Boulder, CO 80322-3629; phone: 800-999-7959), it offers comprehensive coverage of the travel scene on a wide variety of fronts. A year's subscription costs $37; 2 years, $57.

In addition, the following travel newsletters provide useful up-to-date information on travel services and bargains:

Entree (PO Box 5148, Santa Barbara, CA 93150; phone: 805-969-5848). Monthly; a year's subscription costs $59. Subscribers also have access to a 24-hour hotline providing information on restaurants and accommodations around the world. This newsletter caters to a sophisticated, discriminating traveler with the means to explore the places mentioned.

The Hideaway Report (Harper Associates, Subscription Office: PO Box 300, Whitefish, MO 59937; phone: 406-862-3480). This monthly source highlights retreats — including domestic idylls — for sophisticated travelers. A year's subscription costs $90.

Romantic Hideaways (217 E. 86th St., Suite 258, New York, NY 10028; phone: 212-969-8682). This newsletter leans toward those special places made for those traveling in twos. A year's subscription to this monthly publication costs $65.

Travel Smart (Communications House, 40 Beechdale Rd., Dobbs Ferry, NY 10522; phone: 914-693-8300 in New York; 800-327-3633 elsewhere in the US). This monthly newsletter covers a wide variety of trips and travel discounts. A year's subscription costs $44.

COMPUTER SERVICES: Anyone who owns a personal computer and a modem can subscribe to a database service providing everything from airline schedules and fares to restaurant listings. Two such services to try:

CompuServe (5000 Arlington Center Blvd., Columbus, OH 43220; phone: 800-848-8199 or 614-457-8600). It costs $39.95 to join, plus hourly usage fees of $6 to $12.50.

Prodigy Services (445 Hamilton Ave., White Plains, NY 10601; phone: 800-822-6922 or 914-993-8000). A month's subscription costs $12.95, plus variable phone charges.

- **Note:** Before using any computer bulletin-board services, be sure to take precautions to prevent downloading of a computer "virus." First install one of the programs designed to screen out such nuisances.

Cameras and Equipment

Vacations (and even some business trips) are everybody's favorite time for taking pictures and home movies. After all, most of us want to remember the places we visit — and to show them off to others. Here are a few suggestions to help you get the best results from your travel photography or videography.

BEFORE THE TRIP

If you're taking your camera or camcorder out after a long period in mothballs, or have just bought a new one, check it thoroughly before you leave to prevent unexpected breakdowns or disappointing pictures.

1. Still cameras should be cleaned carefully and thoroughly, inside and out. If using a camcorder, run a head cleaner through it. You also may want to have your camcorder professionally serviced (opening the casing yourself will violate the manufacturer's warranty). Always use filters to protect your lens while traveling.
2. Check the batteries for your camera's light meter and flash, and take along extras just in case yours wear out during the trip. For camcorders, bring along extra Nickel-Cadmium (Ni-Cad) batteries; if you use rechargeable batteries, a recharger will cut down on the extras.
3. Using all the settings and features, shoot at least one test roll of film or one videocassette, using the type you plan to take along with you.

EQUIPMENT TO TAKE ALONG

Keep your gear light and compact. Items that are too heavy or bulky to be carried comfortably on a full-day excursion will likely remain in your hotel room.

1. Invest in a broad camera or camcorder strap if you now have a thin one. It will make carrying the camera much more comfortable.
2. A sturdy canvas, vinyl, or leather camera or camcorder bag, preferably with padded pockets (not an airline bag), will keep your equipment organized and easy to find. If you will be doing much shooting around the water, a waterproof case is best.
3. For cleaning, bring along a camel's hair brush that retracts into a rubber squeeze bulb. Also take plenty of lens tissue, soft cloths, and plastic bags to protect equipment from dust and moisture.

FILM AND TAPES: If you are concerned about airport security X-rays damaging rolls of undeveloped still film (X-rays do not affect processed film) or tapes, store them in one of the lead-lined bags sold in camera shops. This possibility is not as much of a threat as it used to be, however. In the US, incidents of X-ray damage to unprocessed film (exposed or unexposed) are few because low-dosage X-ray equipment is used virtually everywhere. If you're traveling without a protective bag, you may want to ask

GETTING READY / Cameras and Equipment 71

to have your photo equipment inspected by hand. One type of film that should never be subjected to X-rays is the very high speed ASA 1000 film; there are lead-lined bags made especially for it — and, in the event that you are refused a hand inspection, this is the only way to save your film. The walk-through metal detector devices at airports do not affect film, though the film cartridges may set them off.

You should have no problem finding film or tapes in New Orleans. When buying film, tapes, or photo accessories the best rule of thumb is to stick to name brands with which you are familiar. The availability of film processing labs and equipment repair shops will vary.

For tips on some of New Orleans's most photogenic spots, see *A Shutterbug's New Orleans* in DIVERSIONS.

THE CITY

NEW ORLEANS

In New Orleans, food for both body and soul drives the urban psyche. And if anyone can convey a feeling for the city, it is its cooks who conjure up its soul-satisfying food and its jazz musicians — they call the city the Big Easy — who syncopate its rhythms with soul-stirring hot licks or lyrical wails. Some of these renowned chefs have never seen a recipe and some artists can't even read music — but they all can call on their seemingly inbred intuition and improvise; and in New Orleans, that's what it's all about.

The past has been a double-edged sword for New Orleans. Not even its port on the Mississippi — once second only to New York City in cargo tonnage — has shaken it out of a certain Old South torpor. The city (with a metropolitan population of about 1,200,000) lacks manufacturing and heavy industry, although it has been throughout its long history a center of trade and source of great wealth for some. It has maintained a European, 18th-century air and for the rich, it always has been a sophisticated, cultured haven; for the poor — many of whom are black — it has offered little hope of betterment over the years. The poverty just seems to roll along like the river; and little has appeared to change it. But at the same time, this languor has managed to preserve the city's old-fashioned charms, where in a different place they might have fallen long ago before the trumpet of civic progress.

Initially, New Orleans was something of a hot property, traded back and forth between governments. First, the French were attracted in the early 1700s by the area's deep, swift harbor. They named the city for Philippe, Duc d'Orleans, the Regent of France, and it served as the capital of the French territories in America from 1723 to 1763, when a Bourbon family pact transferred it to Spanish rule. It was then ceded back to France in 1800. Two important things developed from all this swapping and ceding: the creole culture, unique to North America, created by the French, Spanish, and Africans; and one of the greatest bargains of the century. In 1803 Napoleon sold New Orleans and the entire Louisiana Territory — extending from the Gulf of Mexico up the Mississippi Valley to the Canadian border — to the United States for $15 million, doubling the size of the country's territory. In 1815, to protect this wily investment, General Andrew Jackson and his Kentucky militiamen teamed with anyone and everyone — including the pirate Jean Lafitte, the Choctaw Indians, numerous Creoles, and some black slaves — to defeat the British in the Battle of New Orleans. The War of 1812, unfortunately, had ended about 2 weeks earlier, somewhat dampening the victors' spirits. (News of the peace treaty had not yet reached the combatants.) Jackson secured the Mississippi River for America, and New Orleans began to grow as a major port for the cotton, sugarcane, and indigo crops grown on the surrounding plantations, and as a kind of Old World cosmopolitan center in the midst of the deep South. The terrain is basically flat plains

76 NEW ORLEANS

of the river delta — the Mississippi flows to the south, and the bay-size Lake Pontchartrain borders the city on the north.

Today, the Vieux Carré, or French Quarter, the main area of interest in New Orleans, reflects and preserves the New Orleans style, even though the T-shirt shops and glitzy souvenir boutiques seem to multiply. The powerful Vieux Carré Commission, a state-constituted agency, regulates construction and modification of the district's buildings, as well as their commercial or residential usage. A ferocious fire at the end of the 18th century, during the Spanish colonial period, destroyed all but a handful of the French colonial structures; the Spaniards' renovation replaced the simple, classical French architecture with "iron lace" balconies and courtyards. The city's architects of the early 19th century borrowed from both cultures to create the creole hybrid found today on almost every block of the French Quarter. Fine examples of the mixture of cultures and styles are the *Cabildo,* once the headquarters of Spanish colonial rule, and the *Presbytere.* Both buildings (now museums) date to the 1790s and flank St. Louis Cathedral at Jackson Square. (The *Cabildo*'s top floor was gutted by fire in 1988 and, as we went to press, it was still closed for reconstruction; there are plans to reopen this fall.) Each of these buildings features wide Spanish arches and French mansard roofs. Completing the Jackson Square quadrangle are the Pontalba Apartments, twin structures with French-inspired, red brick façades and elegant wrought-iron balconies. And there is a lot more. The *French Market*'s origins date to the pre-colonial era, when the site was used by the local Indians as a trading post. It still has a colorful atmosphere and some of the best café au lait on either side of the Atlantic. The best way to see the French Quarter is the old-fashioned way — simply by strolling down its pedestrian malls and sidewalks. Royal Street is closed to traffic from approximately late morning to late afternoon; Bourbon Street is car-free from 7 PM to about 3 or 4 in the morning; and Jackson Square never has any traffic. This city is the sort of place where you can relax and take it easy — and just let its charms surround you.

The Mississippi, once New Orleans's major source of sustenance, still helps to shape the city's persona. Until just a few years ago, a series of wharves formed a barrier between the river and the city. These have been removed, and the Mississippi is once more a vital part of New Orleans life. Only this time the reason is tourism rather than shipping. The entire riverfront area has been completely renovated; on the riverbank, where Canal Street ends, there is the *Aquarium of the Americas;* beautiful Plaza d'España, with its spectacular central fountain and geometric tiles; *Riverwalk Mall,* filled with shops and casual restaurants; and the picturesque Warehouse District, where handsome turn-of-the-century brick structures have been converted into trendy apartment buildings, restaurants, and shops. Across Canal Street and parallel to the French Quarter is Poydras Avenue, whose high-rises now form the core of the city's business district.

Far from the bustle of the city center, the Uptown section reveals another aspect of New Orleans's multifaceted personality. The Garden District, a quaint, beautifully preserved late-19th-century neighborhood, boasts graceful, pristine mansions that were built by prosperous American merchants and

NEW ORLEANS 77

shippers to rival the creole townhouses found in the once more affluent French Quarter.

To the north, in the direction of Lake Pontchartrain, is City Park — which contains an enormous oak grove — the point where tranquil Bayou Street begins, leading to the lake itself.

In New Orleans, though, you don't just see and feel the city, you must also taste what it has to offer. The indigenous cuisine is creole, which includes a variety of styles — from homey and hearty to elegant. Creole cookery is, like everything else from the city's polyglot past, a blend of the French, Spanish, African, American Indian, and Caribbean. The results are so good that they say down in New Orleans that when a Creole goes to heaven, the first thing he asks Saint Peter is where he can find the jambalaya (a rice dish that's a relative of Spain's paella) or filé gumbo (which falls somewhere between a stew and a soup and contains seemingly infinite combinations of seafood, poultry, game, and charcuterie — sausage). Other key dishes include rémoulade, a thick, peppery vinaigrette usually ladled onto cool and spicy shrimp; and bread pudding, often drenched in a custard sauce spiked with rum or bourbon.

And then there is the *Carnival* season — an extravagant blowout that begins shortly after *Christmas* and builds up steam till *Mardi Gras* (Fat Tuesday), preceding *Ash Wednesday*. The tradition of *Mardi Gras* in New Orleans began more than 150 years ago with spontaneous street parades at the approach of the *Lenten* season. In 1857, a group of locals banded together to form the first *Carnival* parading organization, the *Mystick Krewe of Comus.* Other private clubs picked up the idea, which started the tradition of elaborate balls and parades that continues today. The balls are still major social events for all socio-economic classes of New Orleans, and with rare exceptions are by-invitation-only affairs. "Kings" and "queens" are chosen from among the *krewe* membership, and in some *krewes,* or carnival clubs, the balls serve as formal "coming-out" parties for debutantes. But the parades are decidedly public; about 50 of them — they vary widely in size and complexity — are held in the city and its suburbs during the 2 weeks preceding *Fat Tuesday* itself. In addition to the traditional float parades, there are marching jazz bands and decorated flatbed trucks. Souvenir doubloons, cups, and beaded necklaces are tossed to onlookers. Beginning on the Friday before *Fat Tuesday,* the parade routes along St. Charles Avenue and Canal Street are jammed with revelers, and the French Quarter is closed to vehicular traffic to accommodate the crowds. *Fat Tuesday*'s royal personages are Rex, King of Carnival, and a black *krewe* led by King Zulu, who shares some of the spotlight with the Big Shot of Africa. Zulu meanders through downtown New Orleans throwing painted coconuts, doubloons, and beads. In the French Quarter, there is the annual costume competition for transvestites that colorfully jams the corner of Burgundy and St. Ann Streets, while less competitive maskers in all kinds of outrageous attire roam around. Suburban *krewes* also hold parades on *Fat Tuesday;* the principal one is *Argus* in Metairie.

Another special event that's beginning to rival the *Carnival* season is the *Jazz and Heritage Festival,* usually held during the last 2 weeks of April at the *New Orleans Fair Grounds* racetrack. Dozens of top local and national

78 NEW ORLEANS

performers, such as Fats Domino, Lionel Hampton, and Carmen MacRae, and New Orleans native Harry Connick, Jr., to name a few, hold forth in the open air and in tents.

Mardi Gras and the *Jazz and Heritage Festival* are the best and the worst of times to visit New Orleans. The spontaneous fun reaches great heights, but so, too, do the hotel prices and the frenetic pace. Don't expect the more popular restaurants to operate at their best during these periods. There are other festivals which offer New Orleans in a different mood, without the crowds of *Mardi Gras* or the *Jazz Festival* (see *Special Events*).

At any time of year, however, the place that started off such great jazzmen as Louis Armstrong, Buddy Bolden, Joe "King" Oliver, Kid Ory, and Jelly Roll Morton still swings. The *Old Mint,* which has been renovated, is the permanent home of excellent exhibitions on how it all began with a merging of African-American and European rhythms. At *Preservation Hall,* Dixieland jazz is played every night; and in countless honky-tonks on Bourbon Street the beat goes on.

New Orleans's legendary jazz funerals still are held occasionally, but they're increasingly rare. The traditional "celebration" includes a marching band that accompanies the procession from the church to the cemetery, playing solemn marches and hymns. As soon as the burial takes place, the rhythm picks up and the theme changes to something like "Didn't He Ramble" or "I'll Be Glad When You're Dead, You Rascal You." The mourners begin prancing and cavorting behind the band, picking up others who join the "Second Line," though they probably don't even know who died. But it doesn't really matter because when you leave the Big Easy, New Orleans folk act as if you are on your way to the Bigger Easy, and send you off easily. Regardless of where you go afterward, though, while you're here, it's hard not to join in. And why not? As they say in New Orleans, "If you ain't gonna shake it, what did you bring it for?"

Another New Orleans tradition that has become more mythical than real is the exotic cult known as voodoo. Based partly on African tribal rites and partly on Catholic ritual, voodoo is believed to have been brought to New Orleans by slaves from the West Indies — Santo Domingo, in particular — in the early 18th century. Voodoo as a functioning religion disappeared from the city long ago, and the occasional report of a "Black Mass" or other bizarre rite always turns out to be something other than the real thing. In *Fabulous New Orleans,* published in 1928, writer Lyle Saxon, a specialist in local color, recounted witnessing a voodoo ceremony. But even in the 1920s, such events were rare. In any case, no tangible evidence of voodoo seems to exist in present-day New Orleans, although 19th-century "voodoo queen" Marie Laveau is purportedly interred in St. Louis Cemetery Number One (see *Special Places*). One spot in the city with tenuous voodoo connections is Congo Square, across North Rampart Street near the French Quarter, where slaves once gathered to socialize. It may have been used for voodoo rites — there's no way of knowing — but it is now a lush public park.

But myth and folklore are part of this city's charm, as vital to its sense of itself as its carefully preserved creole architecture and the mighty Mississippi that rolls right by it — a tasty gumbo of Old South elegance and rowdy rockin' and rollin' good times set to the beat of its legendary musicians and fed by its transcendent chefs. There is an inspired cross-fertilization of cultures and memories here, added to the simple desire just to have fun. It's an attitude toward life that visitors find when they come here and that can best be summed up in the phrase that has become a kind of axiom: *"Laissez les bon temps roulez!"* — "Let the good times roll!"

NEW ORLEANS AT-A-GLANCE

SEEING THE CITY: The best bird's-eye view of New Orleans is from the *Top of the Mart,* a revolving bar on the 33rd floor of the World Trade Center, where Canal Street meets the Mississippi River. It's open from mid-morning to midnight (phone: 522-9795). There also is an observation deck on the same floor (open 9 AM to 5 PM; admission charge). There is a grand view of the French Quarter and the river from the 11th floor of the *Westin–Canal Place* hotel (100 Iberville St.; phone: 566-7006).

Bus Tours – A variety of itineraries is offered by numerous companies operating bus tours of the French Quarter, Garden District, Lakefront, and major points of interest outside the city proper. Cost is usually $15 to $20 for adults; $8 to $10 for children under 12. Among the companies are *Gray Line* (phone: 587-0861), *New Orleans Tours* (phone: 592-1991), *Tours by Isabelle* (phone: 367-3963), *American-Acadian* (phone: 467-1734), and *Machu Picchu Tours* (phone: 392-5118).

Carriage Rides – Mule-drawn carriages, most with fringed tops and holding as many as ten passengers, may be hired by the hour from early morning to nighttime on the Decatur Street side of Jackson Square. The carriages roll around the streets of the French Quarter as drivers comment on points of interest. Be aware that while carriages are supposedly licensed by the city, they are de facto unregulated, and practices — and prices — can vary. Many of the drivers have been known to deliver "historical" commentary that is more fancy than fact. (Do not believe, for instance, that Napoleon died in the *Napoleon House* bar, or that Elvis Presley once lived at the *Cornstalk* hotel.) Also, some drivers may attempt to give you a subtle sales pitch for some shops or restaurants along the way. *Charbonnet Transportation* (1615 St. Philip St.; phone: 581-4411) rents carriages that hold eight to ten passengers for $75 per hour plus a 15% tip for the driver; *Gay Nineties Carriage Tours* (1824 N. Rampart St.; phone: 943-8820) charges $8 per adult and $4 per child under 12 years old for a half-hour tour.

River Tours – On the Canal Street ferry, operating daily from 6 AM to 9 PM, you can ride back and forth across the river to Algiers free (phone: 362-2981). The large sternwheeler *Steamboat Natchez* departs the Toulouse Street Wharf (behind *Jax Brewery*) several times a day on 2-hour runs up and down the river. The *Bayou Jean Lafitte* excursion boat departs the Toulouse Street Wharf for the bayou country, to Bayou Barataria, home of the famous pirate. A small paddle wheeler, the *Cotton Blossom,* makes three runs daily from the Canal Street docks to the Audubon Zoo. A high-speed catamaran, the *Audubon Express,* makes six trips daily between the *Aquarium of the Americas* and the Audubon Zoo. (For information on these excursions, call 586-8777). The motorized, 3-decker *Cajun Queen* and the sternwheeler *Creole Queen* offer both daytime and dinner cruises, which depart from behind the *Riverwalk Mall* (phone: 524-0814). The *Voyageur,* a sightseeing craft, cruises from Canal Street to the bayou country, with a stop at Chalmette Battlefield (phone: 523-5555).

Streetcar Tours – Four vintage streetcars travel the 1.5-mile stretch alongside the

Mississippi River while guides answer your questions. Fare is 35¢ (phone: 569-2899).

Guided Walks – The *Friends of the Cabildo* provides walking tours of the French Quarter, beginning at Jackson Square; the price includes admission to two nearby state museums (phone: 523-3939). The *National Park Service* conducts free walking tours of the French Quarter, St. Louis Cemetery Number One, and the Garden District, and occasionally offers specialized tours on subjects that range from the story of pirate Jean Lafitte to the history of the Louisiana legal system (phone: 589-2636). The walks offered by *Heritage Tours* focus on the French Quarter's literary history, with commentary on the places where such writers as Tennessee Williams and William Faulkner lived and worked (phone: 949-9805).

Voodoo Tours – Voodoo, the ancient African religion that filtered into Louisiana in the early 1700s, still exists in New Orleans. When the government refused to recognize it as a religion and suppressed voodoo rites, practitioners went underground and voodoo became a cult. Today, there's a Voodoo Walking Tour of the French Quarter and the *Voodoo Museum;* a tour that lets you witness a voodoo ceremony; a Voodoo Ritual Swamp Tour; and other tours that wind through mysterious bayous, historic plantations, gardens, villages, Indian burial grounds, and fascinating swamp scenery and wildlife. Tours range from 2½ to 10 hours, and prices run from $15 to $55 (phone: 523-7685).

SPECIAL PLACES: Nestled between the Mississippi River and Lake Pontchartrain, New Orleans's natural crescent shape can be confusing. North, south, east, and west mean very little here. Residents keep life simple by using terms such as "lakeside" or "riverside" and "uptown" or "downtown" for directions.

FRENCH QUARTER (VIEUX CARRÉ)

Many have wondered why French explorer Jean Baptiste le Moyne, Sieur de Bienville, chose this muggy, low-lying spot to establish a colony in 1718. The reasons are that it was the nearest habitable spot north of the mouth of the Mississippi River and one of the few places for miles around that lay above sea level. The terrain to the south was, at the time, little more than muck, subject to frequent flooding. To this day, when New Orleans and its environs are hit by one of its monsoon-like rains, the French Quarter sits high and dry, while several inches or more cover the lower sections of the area. The street plan of the Vieux Carré (a term that translates roughly from the French as "old squared area") has not changed since it was first laid out in the 1720s. Most of the streets retain their original names, too.

Jackson Square – This stately square, originally the Place d'Armes, was the town square of the original French colonial settlement and the scene of most of New Orleans's history — from hangings to the transfer ceremony commemorating the Louisiana Purchase. It is also where early French settlers worshiped, peddled their wares, and conducted governmental and military ceremonies. Rebuilt in the 1850s with the equestrian statue of General Andrew Jackson, the hero of the Battle of New Orleans, placed at its center, today it's a pleasant place from which to watch the passing scene against a backdrop of charming cast-iron and brick buildings, or to browse through shops. Heads no longer roll here, but occasional open-air jazz concerts do, and the only hangings are on the iron fence bounding the area, where local artists display their work. Since the early 1970s, this area has been a pedestrian mall. 700 Chartres (pronounced *Chart*-ers) St., bordered by St. Ann, St. Peter, and Decatur Sts.

St. Louis Cathedral – While the present cathedral was built in the 1850s, there has been a church of some kind at this site on Jackson Square since the city's first settlement in the early 18th century. This beautiful Spanish building boasts towers, painted ceilings, an altar imported from Belgium, and a bell and clock in the central spire that has marked the hours for the city's inhabitants for many centuries. Today it is the seat of

NEW ORLEANS / At-a-Glance   81

the Roman Catholic Archdiocese of New Orleans, and masses, weddings, and other rites are still held here regularly. The interior was completely refurbished in the early 1980s. Markers in French, Spanish, Latin, and English identify those buried in the sanctuary. Tours given daily except Sundays. Donations requested. 700 Chartres St., on Jackson Square (phone: 525-9585).

The Cabildo and Presbytere – The twin, classically proportioned buildings flanking St. Louis Cathedral are now the city's most important historical museums. They were erected in the late 18th century by the Spanish colonial governors, and the mansard-style roofs were added in the 1850s. The *Cabildo,* on Jackson Square's St. Peter Street side, was the seat of the colonial government, and it was here in 1803 that the Louisiana Purchase was signed, transferring the vast Louisiana Territory from France to the United States. A major fire occurred in the building's attic in 1988; it was still being repaired as we went to press, but is expected to open later this year. Meanwhile, the *Presbytere,* the *Cabildo*'s twin on the St. Ann Street side of the square — originally used as both the seat of church government and as a courthouse — contains permanent and temporary exhibitions relating to Louisiana history, culture, and art (phone: 568-6968).

Pontalba Apartments – Extending along the two sides of Jackson Square perpendicular to the Mississippi River are these twin, block-long, red brick buildings, said to be the first true apartment houses constructed in the United States. They were built in 1850 by prominent local architect James Gallier, Sr. for the Spanish Baroness Micaela Almonester y Pontalba. (Her family names, Almonester and Pontalba, are preserved in the "AP" monogram set into the original cast-iron balcony railings.) Today, the buildings' upper floors are still apartments for some lucky New Orleans residents, while the arcades below are lined with ice cream parlors, boutiques, and cafés. Jackson Square at St. Ann and St. Peter Sts.

Moon Walk – The name of this promenade alongside the Mississippi River may be a bit misleading: It is politically rather than celestially motivated, since it was named for former Mayor Moon Landrieu, whose administration in the early 1970s oversaw numerous physical improvements to the French Quarter's public spaces, including this one. The steps along Decatur Street lead to a landscaped terrace that offers superb views of the river and Jackson Square. Go to the grass-lined walkway right near the river — to the left is the first of many bends the river takes on its way to the Gulf of Mexico; to the right are fine views of the New Orleans skyline and river bridges. Across the levee from Decatur St. at St. Ann and St. Peter Sts.

French Market – A farmer's market for 2 centuries (even before the first Europeans arrived, the Choctaws and other local Indians traded on this site), the *French Market* still has a colorful atmosphere with stalls, beneath large stone colonnades, offering a variety of local produce (try the Louisiana oranges, creole tomatoes, mirlitons (the pale-green, pear-shape squash known in Mexico as *chayote*), sugarcane, and sweet midget bananas), meat, and fish, including live crab, turtle, shrimp, catfish, and trout. There are boutiques, cafés, and a large flea market. At Jackson Square and St. Ann Street is the *Café du Monde,* a bustling New Orleans coffeehouse serving authentic café au lait (half coffee with chicory, half hot milk) and *beignets,* square fried crullers dusted with powdered sugar (813 Decatur; phone: 581-2914). The café never closes, and the market itself is open daily. On Decatur St. extending from St. Ann to Barracks Sts.

Ursuline Convent – Constructed around 1750 in French Provincial style, this is the oldest building in Louisiana, and the only one to survive the two devastating fires that swept through the city during the 18th century. Originally the home of the city's Ursuline nuns — who came from France in 1727 to care for the sick and orphaned and to teach the slaves, Indians, and the colonists' children — today the structure, topped by a mansard roof and surrounded by a brick stucco wall, contains archives of the Archdiocese of New Orleans. Not open to the public. Chartres and Ursuline Sts.

Beauregard-Keyes House – Although George Washington never slept here, almost

82   NEW ORLEANS / At-a-Glance

everyone else lived in this neo-classical residence, including the legendary chess champion Paul Morphy, Confederate General Pierre G.T. Beauregard, and, in the 1940s, novelist Frances Parkinson Keyes, whose will designated it for use as a museum. It was also where a local wine maker was shot by a member of the Sicilian Black Hand, a secret organization that operated in the Quarter during the 1920s. Its rooms today are handsomely furnished, with a cozy, un-museum-like atmosphere, and Mrs. Keyes's antique-doll collection is on view. The adjoining formal garden, enclosed by a brick wall and lined with boxwoods, jasmine, and tropical flora, is one of the French Quarter's prettiest. It's across the street from the Ursuline Convent. Closed Sundays. Admission charge. 1113 Chartres St. (phone: 523-7257).

Madame John's Legacy – This ancient frame cottage is believed to be one of the oldest buildings in the Mississippi Valley, constructed in 1726 by Jean Pascal, a sea captain from Provence who received the site from La Compagnie des Indes, which controlled the Louisiana colony for the King of France. The brick and stucco building, with its sloping roof and colonnaded gallery, survived the two major fires that all but destroyed New Orleans during the late 1700s. Inhabited until 1925, the name of the house comes from the title of a romance novel by 19th-century author George W. Cable in which the house plays a central part in the story. Although it is one of the *Louisiana State Museum*'s properties and has major historical value, it is not open to the public. 632 Dumaine St.

Royal Street – There really was a streetcar named *Desire* that used to run along Royal Street to Canal from the late 19th century to the 1950s. Though the streetcar is gone, along this street the desire for the past continues, and a stroll down here will yield views of some of the Quarter's finest examples of cast- and wrought-iron balconies and some of New Orlean's most distinctive architecture. The city's finest antiques shops still dominate the blocks between Bienville and St. Peter Streets, although T-shirt and inexpensive souvenir outlets have proliferated in recent years. The street is a pedestrian mall closed to traffic from late morning to late afternoon every day.

Historic New Orleans Collection – This preserved French Quarter residence houses a gift shop, scholarly archives, and historic exhibitions. Closed Sundays and Mondays. No admission charge. 533 Royal St. (phone: 523-4662).

Old Mint – Opened in 1982 and part of the *Louisiana State Museum,* the Mint contains a *Mardi Gras* exhibition, a jazz display, and state archives. Jazz lovers will find souvenirs of the patron saints of jazz — Louis Armstrong's first horn, Bix Beiderbecke's cuff links, and instruments played by members of the *Original Dixieland Jazz Band.* Fine exhibits trace the development of jazz from its African-American rhythms and European brass band tradition. This stately mid-19th-century Federalist building was where silver dollars and other US coins, as well as Confederate currency, was produced from 1835 to 1909. Later, it was used as a prison and then as offices of the US Coast Guard. Closed Mondays. Admission charge. 400 Esplanade Ave. (phone: 568-6968).

Preservation Hall – What's recorded in the jazz collection at the Mint still happens live before an audience every night at *Preservation Hall.* In this ramshackle old creole building at the French Quarter's heart, the New Orleans jazz renaissance — begun in the 1960s — continues to this day as small Dixieland bands hold forth nightly with classic renditions of "St. James Infirmary Blues," "Rampart Street Parade," and "When the Saints Go Marchin' In." Sparse surroundings, but this is the real thing. Open daily. Admission charge. 726 St. Peter St. (phone: 522-2841).

Bourbon Street – Though the street was named for the illustrious French royal family, it actually has a lot more in common with the liquor, which, along with anything else potable, can be found here in abundance (and New Orleans establishments have added many drinks to the bartender's list, with such wicked liquids as the Hurricane and the absinthe frappé). Round-the-clock honky-tonks offer live jazz, which

NEW ORLEANS / At-a-Glance 83

can get wild in the wee hours, and live booze, which can get wicked the morning after. (It's legal to drink on the streets as long as metal or glass containers are not used; plastic "to-go" cups are offered everywhere). The 7 blocks extending from Iberville to Dumaine Streets are filled with a hodgepodge of creole restaurants of varying quality, tacky corn-dog stands, elegant hotels, sleazy strip joints, jazz clubs, porno shops, and every sort of carny attraction. Often rowdy and raunchy, Bourbon Street has been a hot strip since the postwar years; this is where everybody heads to let it all hang out during the *Carnival* season or after a game in the *Superdome*. The area has a lot of strip joints and peep shows, where, even if you stay outside, you'll get more of an eyeful than a peep as the hawkers swing the doors open to lure customers. Among the hot spots are Al Hirt's club, *Jelly Roll's* (501 Bourbon; phone: 568-0501), and the *Famous Door* (339 Bourbon; phone: 522-7626).

St. Louis Cemetery Number One – About a block from North Rampart Street at the edge of the Vieux Carré, this old New Orleans cemetery with its tombs designed by earlier architects is literally a diminutive necropolis. The marshy ground dictated aboveground burial, and monuments are interesting for their structure, inscriptions, and number of remains inside (to solve overcrowding, tombs are opened, and the remaining bones are moved deeper into the vault to accommodate new arrivals). If you are interested, the caretaker will give you a tour. Dating back to the early 18th century, among the illustrious occupants are Marie Laveau (née Glapion), who used her charms and spells as a voodoo queen in the 1900s; the two wives of Louisiana's first governor, W. C. C. Claiborne; Jean Etienne de Boré, father of the Louisiana sugar industry and first Mayor of New Orleans; and Louisiana historian Charles Gayarre. Many of the brick-and-stucco tombs have crumbled to near-ruin. The earliest decipherable epitaph is that of Nannette F. de Bailly, dated Sept. 24, 1800. Because of the cemetery's isolation, visitors are strongly advised to visit only in daytime, and in large groups. Open daily. No admission charge to the cemetery, but a small charge for guided tours. 400 Basin St.

RIVERFRONT/WAREHOUSE DISTRICT

It has only been within the last 2 decades that the Mississippi River has been reunited with the city it spawned. During the rehabilitation of the waterfront area, huge wharves and sheds were torn down to make way for parks, bandstands, walkways, excursion-boat docks, plazas, hotels, a shopping mall, and public spaces. Stretching from the French Quarter to the Warehouse District, the riverfront has become a favorite spot to relax and stroll for locals and tourists alike. *Riverwalk,* a vast, 2-level mall of trendy shops and eating spots, with exterior walkways and sweeping views of the Mississippi, is a remnant of the New Orleans *1984 World's Fair.* Another beneficial legacy of the otherwise ill-fated fair was that it motivated city planners to rehabilitate many sturdy, handsome old warehouses, stores, and office buildings in the port area. Fashioned mostly of iron, brick, and wood beams, these highly practical, well-made — and often beautifully proportioned — buildings are getting a new lease on life. Their restoration revitalized the entire area, luring apartment dwellers, lawyers, architects, shop owners, and restaurateurs. Bounded by Canal and Poydras Sts. and Convention Center Blvd.

Aquarium of the Americas – Opened in August 1990 on the bank of the Mississippi, there are more than 7,500 specimens of marine life on view here. The main attractions are the Gulf of Mexico exhibit, a half-million-gallon tank holding hundreds of species found in the deep waters of the gulf; the walk-through Amazon Rain Forest, which re-creates the hot, humid environment of the subtropics with indigenous birds, butterflies, and flora; the Caribbean Reef display, visible from a see-through, tunnel-shaped walkway; and the Mississippi River Delta Habitat, featuring the freshwater reptiles and fish inhabiting inland Southern waters. Open daily. Admission charge. 1 Canal St. (phone: 861-2537).

84 NEW ORLEANS / At-a-Glance

Woldenberg Park – Fourteen acres of walkways and park areas bring an oasis-like serenity to the French Quarter riverfront area. Contemporary works by local sculptors are exhibited throughout the park, which also contains benches and a bandstand that is used primarily during festivals. Off Conti St. near the riverfront.

Plaza d'España – The dramatic fountain and intricately patterned tiles that form this huge pavilion along the Mississippi were a gift from the Spanish government in recognition of New Orleans's strong historical Hispanic ties. Since it was completed in the early 1980s, it has become a favorite spot for small festivals and band concerts.

New Orleans Convention Center – This is the city's primary convention facility, and with more than 700,000 square feet of meeting and exhibition space, it is one of the largest facilities of its kind in the country. Completed in 1985, and recently enlarged, it accommodates conventions and trade shows as various as the National Association of Television Producers and Executives and the American Library Association. The center's development has spurred a commercial renaissance in the Warehouse District, which each year sees the addition of new apartment and office complexes, restaurants, nightclubs, and shops. 900 Convention Center Blvd. (phone: 582-3000).

Contemporary Arts Center – This colorful, lively complex of exhibition and performance spaces is home to the avant-garde — local and regional artists, playwrights, dance groups, composers, and filmmakers. The strikingly contemporary spaces, refashioned from an early-20th-century drugstore and office building, contain no permanent collections, but the galleries are always filled with interesting new works, many by emerging artists. Closed Mondays and Tuesdays. Admission charge. 900 Camp St. (phone: 523-1216).

Julia Row – Built in 1830–32 to accommodate newly arrived immigrants, this handsome set of 13 row houses is the Warehouse District's most important architectural setpiece. These elegant red brick buildings — once the homes of some of New Orleans's most well-to-do and socially prominent families — have graceful cast-iron balconies, ornamented entrances, fanlights, and sidelights, considered an architectural innovation at the time. After decades of neighborhood deterioration, the row houses were restored by local preservationists in the 1970s. Today, the street-level spaces hold offices and shops. Along the 600 block of Julia St., west of Poydras and just south of St. Charles Ave.

At 604 Julia Street, the nonprofit *Preservation Resource Center* offers information and interesting exhibitions concerning the district. Open only on weekdays, the center also provides architectural tours of various neighborhoods (phone: 581-7032).

K&B Plaza – One of New Orleans's first examples of the sleek, modern "international style" of architecture, this creation of the Skidmore Owings Merrill architectural firm is now the headquarters of a regional drugstore chain. On the surrounding terrace are works by such noted late-20th-century sculptors as George Segal, George Rickey, and Isamu Noguchi. The ground-floor lobby also houses one of the South's most important privately owned collections of contemporary paintings and sculpture. Open Mondays through Fridays, 8 AM to 5 PM. No admission charge. 1055 St. Charles Ave. at Lee Circle (phone: 586-1234).

CANAL STREET AND THE CENTRAL BUSINESS DISTRICT

Today's commercial hub of New Orleans, bounded roughly by Canal Street, the Mississippi River, Poydras Street, and South Claiborne Avenue, was where the city's English-speaking population first established roots in the mid- to late 19th century. This is where cotton brokers traded, department stores flourished, and movie theaters first took hold. The blocks of Canal Street nearest to the French Quarter formed the city's primary shopping district for generations, and still contain many structures dating back 100 years or more. Poydras Street, about 5 blocks from Canal Street in the business

NEW ORLEANS / At-a-Glance 85

district, is the densest concentration of financial, governmental, and legal offices in the city. Several major hotels and a dozen or more new office towers — including the city's tallest building, the 50-story One Shell Square — overlook the street's leafy median. At one end is the *Louisiana Superdome,* and at the other end, the Mississippi Riverfront area.

Canal Street – For most of the 19th century, this broad, tree-lined avenue formed the dividing line between the French sector of New Orleans and the newer, Anglo-Saxon part of town. The origin of its name is uncertain, since no canal ever existed here (although there were half-serious plans in the 19th century to dig one). In the 1800s, Canal Street boasted a couple of opera houses and a number of tony residences. Two private men's clubs — the *Pickwick Club* on the corner of St. Charles Avenue and the *Boston Club* at 824 Canal — are among the last vestiges of the street's aristocratic past. From the late 19th to the mid-20th century, Canal Street was New Orleans's shopping hub. While such long-established department stores as *Maison Blanche* and *Krauss* and a few other specialty merchants still operate, other buildings have either been boarded up or turned into office buildings. In recent decades, the river end of Canal has been the site of continuing development, with construction of the *Canal Place* office building and shopping mall, the *Rivergate* exhibition center, major hotels, and the *Aquarium of the Americas.*

Custom House – Canal Street's most historic structure, the old US Custom House — which takes up the entire block bounded by Canal, Decatur, Iberville, and N. Peters Streets — is the city's handsomest example of Federalist architecture. A fine example of Greek Revival style is the majestic Marble Hall (in the center of the building on the second floor), with its 14 columns of pure white marble that rise to a ceiling of huge iron and ground-glass plates. Begun in 1849, the building was still under construction in 1862, at the peak of the Civil War, and was never completed according to the original plans. The Custom House is still home to various offices of the US Customs Service. Open Mondays through Fridays, 8 AM to 4 PM. No admission charge. 423 Canal St. (phone: 589-4532).

Louisiana Superdome – Completed in 1975, this awesome piece of architectural engineering has been described as the largest freestanding room in the world. Twenty-seven stories tall, with a seating capacity of 100,000 people, it is large enough to accommodate all of Rome's St. Peter's Cathedral. The 1988 Republican National Convention, several *Super Bowls,* and many rock concerts have taken place here. Primarily a football stadium, it is home to the NFL's New Orleans *Saints* as well as to dozens of local high school and college sports teams. Daily tours are offered when it's not in use. One Sugar Bowl Dr. at Poydras St. (phone: 587-3810).

Gallier Hall – Considered by many to be the best example of Greek Revival public architecture in New Orleans, the hall was designed by James Gallier, Sr., and dedicated in 1853 as City Hall; it served in this capacity until the late 1950s. The granite and white marble building has been restored over the years, and the classically proportioned rooms, separated by a 12-foot-wide central hall, are now used mostly for official receptions. It faces Lafayette Square, which contains a touching monument to John McDonogh, the 19th-century philanthropist who was the principal benefactor of the city's public school system. Open Mondays through Fridays, 8 AM to 4 PM. No admission charge. 543 St. Charles Ave. (phone: 565-7457).

GARDEN DISTRICT

The 65 square blocks that comprise the Garden District began as a plantation; in the 1850s it became a residential community of newly arrived Anglo-Saxon entrepreneurs; and since the turn of the century, its image as an urban expression of Old Southern refinement has remained intact. The houses, in a seemingly riotous conglomeration of architectural styles, and the gardens, lush with tropical greenery and shaded by im-

86   NEW ORLEANS / At-a-Glance

mense oak trees, blend to create a harmonious and unique neighborhood. Most of the Greek Revival mansions of the Lower Garden District, extending roughly from Lee Circle to Jackson Avenue, have succumbed to the demands of creeping commercialism; the buildings have mostly been converted to shops, restaurants, and galleries, but some are still private homes. Happily, the section beyond Jackson Avenue has retained its timeless air of grace and tranquillity. The best strolling is along and off Prytania Street, between 1st Street and Washington Avenue.

Coliseum Square – When city planners laid out this rectangular park in the Lower Garden District in the 1830s, they designed it as the campus of a university to be called the Prytaneum. Appropriately, they named the nearby streets for the seven Greek muses — Melpomene, Erato, Terpsichore, Clio, Euterpe, Thalia, and Calliope. The university was never built. Instead, the park became the catalyst for a tony neighborhood of Greek Revival residences, most of which remain today. While the square has lost its aristocratic veneer, many of the old homes have been restored. The Prytaneum survives only in the name of nearby Prytania Street.

Toby House – This imposing residence, a raised frame cottage with a façade of square, white columns, dates to the 1830s. Typical of the period, it was built by Thomas Toby, a Philadelphian who established a large plantation on the site (it once dominated the area that was eventually to become the Garden District). Enclosed within the white picket fence is a garden filled with such typical New Orleans flora as palm and magnolia. Visible from the street is one of the city's finest oak trees, located at the rear of the house. Not open to the public. 2340 Prytania St.

Louise S. McGehee School – "Free Renaissance" was the term used to describe the heavily decorative architectural style of this huge old residence, completed in 1870 and now a private school for girls. Pairs of fluted Corinthian columns define the wide porch at the front of the house. The building contains a fully finished basement, a rarity in New Orleans because of the city's watery substratum. The building is open only for groups of 50 or more. 2343 Prytania St. (phone: 561-1224).

1300 Block of First Street – Many a knowledgeable New Orleanian identifies this as the most beautiful residential block in the city, filled as it is with majestic examples of the Greek Revival style of the mid- to late 19th century. Two especially impressive houses are the residences at No. 1331, with its fancy stucco work, dental molding, and ironwork, and at No. 1315, a stately Greek Revival mansion that has been faithfully preserved in a condition close to the original.

Lafayette Cemetery – Fans of New Orleans novelist Anne Rice will find this an especially interesting spot, since it figures prominently in her *Vampire Chronicles.* Before the Garden District became part of New Orleans, it was a suburban town called Lafayette. The community's cemetery, dating from the mid-1850s, was the first one in the area laid out on a grid of symmetrical lanes and driveways. Most of the aboveground tombs hold the remains of prosperous businessmen and traders who inhabited the fancy residences nearby. The gates are open weekdays from 7:30 AM to 2 PM and on Saturdays from 7:30 AM to noon. Visiting the cemetery alone at any time is not advised. For a fee, guided tours are given by *Save Our Cemeteries,* a preservationist organization, on Mondays, Wednesdays, and Fridays. Washington Ave. between Prytania and Coliseum Sts. (phone: 589-2636).

UPTOWN — UNIVERSITY SECTION

Audubon Zoological Gardens – Once a neglected, foul-smelling place, the Audubon Zoo has been transformed since the mid-1970s into one of the country's best. An exotic white tiger is just one of the 1,500 species housed here in habitats that approximate natural conditions. Some fascinating special exhibits re-create in-the-wild environments: Not to be missed is the Louisiana Swamp, with alligators and other indigenous creatures slithering and hopping through marshy terrain. Dozens of tropical and

NEW ORLEANS / At-a-Glance 87

shore birds from Louisiana and around the world flit around the trees and shrubs of the huge, walk-through aviary. The Asian Domain, Grasslands of the World, and a large pool of frisky sea lions are other favorites. For children, there is a petting zoo, wildlife theater with live animals, and a hands-on natural history museum. Open daily, 9:30 AM to 5:30 PM. Admission charge. 6500 Magazine St. (phone: 861-2537).

Audubon Park – Under the leafy umbrella of Audubon Park's immense oaks, joggers now tread ground that was, in the late 18th century, a sugarcane plantation. Occupying the 340 acres extending from St. Charles Avenue to the Mississippi River, the park was named for naturalist John James Audubon, who had lived briefly in New Orleans. In 1884–85, it was the site of the *World's Industrial and Cotton Exposition,* commemorating the 100th anniversary of the shipment of Louisiana cotton to a foreign port. Today it's a haven, not only for joggers, but for picnickers, golfers, tennis players, and bicyclists. While the park's tranquil lagoons are no longer stocked with fish, they form, along with the graceful oaks, a pleasant backdrop for a morning stroll. Main entrances on the 6400 block of St. Charles Ave. and 6500 block of Magazine St.

Audubon Place – If New Orleans has a millionaire's row, it is this short, private parkway lined with 28 understated but sumptuous residences, announced by an arched gate on St. Charles Avenue. It was developed early in the 20th century by a Texas real estate speculator, and all but a few of the homes flanking the elaborately landscaped median date from that period. The immense, white-columned manse to the left of the entry gate is the Zemurray House, the traditional residence of the President of Tulane University. 6900 St. Charles Ave.

Academy of the Sacred Heart – In 1889 the nuns of the Order of the Sacred Heart opened this school to educate the daughters of prominent Creole families, and French conversation and grammar remain a major part of its curriculum to this day. Elementary and secondary students attend classes in the three buildings that overlook a large, pleasant garden near St. Charles Avenue. The red brick façade, with tiers of arched, shuttered windows, columns, and balconies, is one of the most graceful architectural spaces in the city's Uptown section. 4521 St. Charles Ave.

Orleans Club – One of the very few buildings on St. Charles inspired by the creole architecture of the French Quarter, the *Orleans Club* was built in 1868 as a private residence. Since 1925 it's been the headquarters of a local social-cultural women's group, which has carefully preserved the structure's elegant stucco façade, handsome iron lace balconies, and pleasantly manicured gardens. Not open to the public. 5005 St. Charles Ave.

Milton H. Latter Memorial Library – None of St. Charles Avenue's mansions exceeds this one for lavishness. Built in 1907 in the Beaux Arts style and occupying an entire block, it was the home in the 1920s of silent-screen star Marguerite Clarke and her husband, aviator Harry Williams; their Jazz Age parties were the talk of the town. In 1948, the house was acquired by a couple who donated it to the New Orleans Public Library in memory of their son, a casualty of World War II. Many of the original mantels, murals, and ceiling paintings remain, making this branch of the city's library the most beautiful of all. Open daily. 5120 St. Charles Ave. (phone: 596-2625).

"Tara" – As far as we know, Vivien Leigh and Clark Gable never set foot in this plantation-style residence, but Scarlett and Rhett would have felt right at home here. The house was constructed during the 1940s according to the antebellum descriptions of Tara in *Gone With The Wind.* And everything is here, from the lofty columns of partially exposed, whitewashed brick to the elegant arched doorway inset with a fan-shaped window. Not open to the public. 5705 St. Charles Ave.

THE LAKEFRONT

City Park extends almost to Lake Pontchartrain and, along with Bayou St. John, serves as a kind of gateway to the northern section known as The Lakefront. Technically, Lake

88 NEW ORLEANS / At-a-Glance

Pontchartrain, the body of water forming New Orleans's northern boundary, is a bay rather than a lake. In any case, this comparatively shallow, brackish basin has served the city in countless ways: In winter, the chill of a north wind is warmed considerably as it skims southward; in fair weather, it becomes an ideal playground for picnickers and boaters (although pollution from sewage and industrial sources has made swimming a serious health hazard on the southern, New Orleans side). The northern area of the lake, however, has always been a prime source of trout, crab, and shrimp almost any time of year. Named for Louis XIV's naval minister, Lake Pontchartrain connects with the Gulf of Mexico via narrow straits that have been fertile fishing grounds since before the Europeans arrived.

City Park – Dozens of graceful ancient oaks and quiet lagoons make City Park's 1,500 or so acres an ideal environment for jogging, tennis, fishing, biking and any number of participatory sports and games. Its occasional sculptures and formal gardens, especially the Botanical Garden and conservatory, offer a pleasant respite from the city. From late November to early January each year, a large section near City Park Avenue is transformed into a magical place, with hundreds of thousands of lights and holiday decorations strung along the gigantic oaks. For children, there are all sorts of amusements, including pony and buggy rides, a puppet show, a vintage carousel, a miniature train, paddleboats, and the *Storyland* theme park. In the late 18th and early 19th centuries, when the park was part of the Allard Plantation, Creole gentlemen defended their honor here, dueling with swords or pistols under the lacy Spanish moss. Main entrance at Esplanade Ave. and Bayou St. John (phone: 482-4888).

New Orleans Museum of Art – This is the city's major art museum, and inside the neo-classical building is one of the southeastern US's most important collections of paintings, sculpture, photographs, and objets d'art. The collection ranges from antiquities to works from the major movements of the late 20th century. Temporary exhibitions, including major international ones, are held year-round, and lectures and other educational programs are presented frequently in the comfortable auditorium. A gift shop and a restaurant are on site. Closed Mondays. Admission charge. In City Park (phone: 488-2631).

Bayou St. John – This gently flowing stream extending from City Park to Lake Pontchartrain once connected the heart of the Old City with the lake via canals that have long since been filled in or covered over. The local Indians and early settlers used the bayou to transport their wares into town. The bayou's banks have long been a favorite place for outings. A number of family-style resort hotels once dotted the area near the lake known as Old Spanish Fort; it is now the site of seafood restaurants, apartment buildings, and the city's largest marina. Along much of the bayou's length are some of the city's oldest residences, including the Caribbean-style Pitot House (see below), home of New Orleans's first mayor.

Pitot House – In the late 1700s, a well-heeled Spanish colonial built this gracefully designed, West Indies–style cottage as a retreat from the busy town. In 1810 it was bought by James Pitot, Mayor of New Orleans from 1804 to 1805. The small house, with its unpretentious columns and wraparound verandah, is completely in its element along Bayou St. John's quiet waters. The rooms have been restored and furnished in the style of the early 19th century. Open Wednesdays through Saturdays. Admission charge. 1440 Moss St. (phone: 482-0312).

Tavern on the Park – This handsome 2-story structure — dating to 1860 — was built 10 years after New Orleans's city government acquired the City Park tract for public use. Originally designed as a restaurant, it faces two massive trees, known as the Dueling Oaks, across the avenue. The place gained considerable notoriety early in the century as a boxing arena, a speakeasy, and, at one point in its history, a bordello. In the late 1980s, the building was extensively restored to its present state. Currently, it is home to *Tavern on the Park,* a steak and seafood restaurant (phone: 486-3333). 900 City Park Ave.

NEW ORLEANS / At-a-Glance 89

Lakeshore Drive – The parkway that extends along much of Lake Pontchartrain's southern shore begins in the west with the Orleans Marina, where dozens of sailboats and pleasure craft are berthed when they're not plying the lake's gentle waters. Farther along the breezy landscaped roadway are the old *Southern Yacht Club,* and just past Marconi Drive, the *Mardi Gras* Fountains (memorializing the *krewes* who make the tradition of the pre-*Lenten Carnival* possible), the campus of the University of New Orleans, and the municipal airport, now used mostly for private aircraft. On holiday weekends, the miles of grassy strips between Lakeshore Drive and the lake seawall are often filled with picnickers.

Lake Pontchartrain Causeway – Stretching more than 24 miles from the Jefferson Parish shoreline to Mandeville, the roadbed — sitting just a few yards above the lake — is advertised as the world's longest bridge. At midpoint, neither shore is visible, but the occasional spectacular sunset or thunderstorm offers respite from the rather monotonous drive. Entrance at the north end of Causeway Blvd. in Metairie. There's a $1 toll each way for passenger cars.

OTHER SPECIAL PLACES

Jean Lafitte National Historical Park, Barataria Unit – If a trip to the Cajun country of southwest Louisiana is not practical, this beautiful slice of Louisiana wetlands, maintained by the US Interior Department's National Park Service, is an excellent alternative. Less than an hour's drive from the French Quarter via the Mississippi River Bridge, the park contains most of the marshy flora that flourish on the Louisiana coastline. There are a couple of pretty bayous surrounded by moss-draped cypress; one of the bayous is carpeted with beautiful water lilies. Wooden walkways lead from the parking area through rows of palmetto, oak, and cypress. Guided tours by park rangers, on foot or by canoe, are available. No admission charge. 7400 La. Hwy. 45, in Marrero (phone: 589-2330).

Metairie Cemetery – A necropolis in the truest sense of the word, this aboveground underworld of towering tombs and memorials pays tribute to some of New Orleans's most illustrious dead, mostly successful business and professional figures of the late 19th and early 20th centuries. The architectural styles of the elaborate stone tombs range from Egyptian to rococo; much of the statuary is monumental. Some bizarre examples of funerary art await at almost every turn along the alleys and walkways through the manicured grounds. A free tape-recorded tour is available at the *Lake Lawn Metairie Funeral Home,* 5100 Pontchartrain Blvd. (phone: 486-6331).

Longue Vue House and Gardens – Although built in the mid-20th century, this handsome estate in the elegant, old suburb of Metairie evokes the grandeur of Edwardian England. It was the residence of the late philanthropists Edgar B. and Edith Stern. Beyond the imposing neo-classical entrance, exquisitely decorated rooms contain a trove of treasures — from rare English furniture and porcelain to paintings by major contemporary artists. Inspiration for the design of the fountains and 8 acres of gardens came from Mrs. Stern's frequent trips to Europe. Each of the meticulously maintained flower beds, shrubs, and trees is labeled. Open daily; Sundays, afternoons only. Admission charge. 7 Bamboo Rd., near Metairie Rd. (phone: 488-5488).

■**EXTRA SPECIAL:** Somewhere out there in Louisiana country was once the heart of the Old South, and it still beats faintly along the banks of the Mississippi. A little over 100 years ago sugarcane was king in Louisiana, and large plantations established commercial empires, as well as an entire social system, around it. A few of these plantations have been restored and are open to visitors who want to see what the period was like, at least for the people on top. And the life that the Southern gentry created for themselves really is something to see. Just a short drive north of New Orleans, these elegant relics have survived not only the Civil War but 150 years of hurricanes, humidity, and countless other perils. Among the most impressive are Oak Alley (on the west bank of the river at Vacherie), fronted by twin rows of 28 gnarled oaks that form a vast, majestic umbrella; San Francisco Plantation (on the river's east bank, north of LaPlace), a combination of mid-Victorian and Steamboat Gothic ornamentation second to none in the state; Houmas House (on the east bank near Burnside), with its magnificent setting and charming auxiliary buildings; and Destrehan Plantation (on the east bank in Destrehan), said to be the oldest building left intact in the Mississippi Valley. Detailed maps and brochures are available at hotels and the New Orleans Tourist Information Center in the French Quarter (529 St. Ann St.; phone: 568-5661). Most of the city's tour companies also offer bus tours of the plantation houses. (See *Drive #1: New Orleans Plantations* in DIRECTIONS.)

SOURCES AND RESOURCES

TOURIST INFORMATION: The New Orleans Tourist Information Center, in the French Quarter, provides a wealth of information on the city's attractions, including maps, brochures, and personal help (529 St. Ann St., New Orleans, LA 70116; phone: 568-5661). The Greater New Orleans Tourist and Convention Commission (1520 Sugar Bowl Dr., New Orleans, LA 70112; phone: 566-5011) has information about the outlying areas. Contact the Louisiana state hotline (phone: 800-33-GUMBO) for maps, calendars of events, health updates, and travel advisories.

For up-to-date information about arts, cultural, or historical events, call the New Orleans Hospitality Hotline (phone: 522-9200) between 10 AM and 6 PM daily.

Frenchmen, Desire, Goodchildren by John C. Chase (Robert L. Crager, $12.95) is an entertaining and informative guide to New Orleans's geography and history. Other recommended reading: *The French Quarter,* by Herbert Asbury (Mockingbird Books, $3.50) and *Voodoo in New Orleans,* by Robert Tallant (Pelican, $3.95).

Local Coverage – The city's daily, *Times-Picayune,* with a special Friday edition that includes "Lagniappe," an arts-and-entertainment section with a comprehensive list of musical, art, theatrical, film, cultural, historical, and recreational activities; *Gambit,* a free arts-oriented weekly found in local shops and restaurants; *New Orleans,* a general-interest monthly. Two other monthlies, *Tourist News* and *Where,* distributed free in hotels, list restaurants, shops, and hotels.

Television Stations – WWL Channel 4–CBS; WDSU Channel 6–NBC; WVUE Channel 8–ABC; WNOL Channel 38–Fox; WYES Channel 12, and WLAE Channel 32–both PBS.

Radio Stations – AM: WWL 870 (CBS, ABC Information, talk/news); WNOE 1060 (talk, news). FM: WWNO 89.9 (classical, National Public Radio); WWOZ 90.7 (jazz and folk); WRNO 99.5 (rock); WLTS 106.3 (pop and light rock).

Food – Check *The New Orleans Eat Book* by Tom Fitzmorris (New Orleans Big Band and Pacific Co., $6.95); and the Eating Out column in the Lagniappe tabloid section of the Friday edition of the *Times-Picayune.*

TELEPHONE: The area code for New Orleans is 504.

NEW ORLEANS / Sources and Resources 91

SALES TAX: State and city sales taxes total 9.5%.

GETTING AROUND: Buses, Streetcars – The city's *Regional Transit Authority* operates throughout the city. The *St. Charles Avenue Streetcar* offers a scenic ride through the Central Business District and Uptown. Board at Canal and Carondelet Streets, or at St. Charles Avenue and Common Street. Special lines include the *Easy Rider*, which circuits the Central Business District and Riverfront; the *French Quarter Minibus*, operating between Elysian Fields Avenue and Poydras Street; and the *Riverfront Streetcar*, which runs along the Mississippi River from Esplanade Avenue to Julia Street. Complete information is available at the *Regional Transit Authority* office in the *Maison Blanche* building (101 Dauphine St., a few steps from Canal St.; phone 569-2600), or by calling *RideLine* at 569-2700.

Car Rental – For *Carnival* or the *Jazz and Heritage Festival*, be sure to reserve wheels well in advance. All of the major national car rental companies have offices in New Orleans. For information on renting a car, see *On Arrival* in GETTING READY TO GO.

Taxis – Radio cabs can be ordered by telephone without a surcharge, hailed in the streets, or picked up at stands in front of hotels, restaurants, and transportation terminals. Major taxi companies are *United* (phone: 522-9771), *White Fleet* (phone: 948-6605), and *Yellow-Checker* (phone: 525-3311).

LOCAL SERVICES: For additional information about local services that are not listed below, call the Chamber of Commerce of New Orleans and the River Region at 527-6900.

Audiovisual Equipment – *AV Communications* (210 Decatur St.; phone: 522-9769); *Jasper Ewing & Sons Inc.* (1904 Poydras St.; phone: 525-5257).

Computer Rental – *Audubon Computer Rentals* (1036 Annunciation St.; phone: 522-0348); *New Orleans Computer Rental* (58 Westbank Expwy., Gretna; phone: 394-1324).

Dry Cleaner/Tailor – *Alessi Cleaners* (837 Gravier St.; phone: 586-9632); *Gonzales Tailoring* (1015 Common St.; phone: 524-2802).

Limousine – *London Livery Ltd.* (phone: 944-1984); *A Touch of Class Limousine Service Inc.* (phone: 522-7565); *A Confidential Limousine* (phone: 833-9999).

Mechanic – *MasterCare Car Service* (800 Camp St.; phone: 525-2241); *Western Battery and Electric Co.* (524 S. Claiborne Ave.; phone: 523-8225).

Medical Emergency – *Tulane Medical Center* (1415 Tulane Ave.; phone: 588-5711); *Touro Infirmary* (1401 Foucher St.; phone: 897-8250); *Mercy Hospital* (301 N. Jefferson Davis Pkwy.; phone: 483-5777); *Charity Hospital* (1532 Tulane Ave.; phone: 568-2311); *Hotel Dieu* (2021 Peridido; phone: 588-3000)

Messenger Services – *United Cabs* offers 24-hour service (1627 Polymnia St.; phone: 524-9606); *Controlled Business Deliveries* (401 Carondelet St.; phone: 525-9917).

National/International Courier – *Federal Express*, drop-off at 701 Poydras St. (phone: 523-6001).

Pharmacy – *Walgreen's Drug Store* (900 Canal St.; phone: 523-7201; and 134 Royal St.; phone: 522-2736); *Eckerd Drugs*, open 24 hours daily (3400 Canal St.; phone: 488-6661).

Photocopies – *Kinko's Copies* has many locations, including 762 St. Charles Ave.

(phone: 581-2541). In the French Quarter, try *Longstreet & Co.* (734 Orleans St.; phone: 523-6350).

Post Office – The downtown post is at 1022 Iberville St. (phone: 589-1287). The French Quarter branch is at 940 Royal St. (phone: 525-6651).

Professional Photographer – *Mitchell L. Osborne Photography* (920 Frenchmen St.; phone: 949-1366); *Commercial and Industrial Photographers* (613 Fielding Ave., Gretna; phone: 368-6089) is on call 24 hours daily.

Secretary/Stenographer – *Dictation Inc.,* 24-hour service (phone: 895-8637); *Workload Inc.* (225 Baronne St.; phone: 522-7171).

Teleconference Facilities – The *New Orleans Hilton* (2 Poydras St.; phone: 561-0500); *Inter-Continental* (444 St. Charles Ave.; phone: 525-5566); *Meridien* (614 Canal St.; phone: 525-6500); *Westin–Canal Place* (100 Iberville St.; phone: 566-7006); and *Omni Royal Orleans* (621 St. Louis St.; phone: 529-5333) hotels have teleconferencing facilities.

Translator – *Professional Translators and Interpreters Inc.,* World Trade Center (phone: 581-3122).

Typewriter Rental – *Office Machine Rental,* 605 S. Jefferson Davis Pkwy. (phone: 482-4408).

Western Union/Telex – Among the many *Western Union* locations is one at 334 Carondelet St. downtown (phone: 529-5971).

Other – *H.Q. Headquarters Company,* word processing, telex, fax machines, conference rooms, One Canal Pl. (phone: 525-1175).

SPECIAL EVENTS: The *Sugar Bowl Classic,* one of football's oldest college bowl games, is held *New Year's Day* in the *Louisiana Superdome.* Every year New Orleans celebrates its famous pre-*Lenten Carnival* during the 2 weeks or so preceding the final blowout on *Fat Tuesday.* Since *Mardi Gras* is 40 days before *Easter,* the date varies from year to year; this year it is February 23. A score or more of street parades and dozens of costume balls (mostly private) are held, and the French Quarter, especially Bourbon Street, fills with revelers. Another huge annual outdoor event is the *New Orleans Jazz and Heritage Festival,* featuring dozens of bands, vocalists, and gospel groups from nearby and around the world (including New Orleans native Harry Connick, Jr., who regularly sings and plays piano here), as well as food and crafts stalls. It takes place mornings to late afternoons in late April and early May on the grassy expanse inside the racetrack at the *New Orleans Fair Grounds.* Nighttime concerts are held during the music festival's 2 weeks on riverboats and in nightclubs and concert halls. Admission charges (phone: 522-4786). On a weekend in early April, the *French Quarter Festival* fills the Quarter's streets with parades, food vendors, artists, musical groups, and other performers (phone: 522-5730). Also in early April is the *Spring Fiesta,* highlighted by tours of private French Quarter patios by daylight or candlelight (admission charge) and a nighttime parade (phone: 581-1367).

Ethnic festivals reflect the city's many subcultures: The *Black Heritage Festival* in early March includes food booths, jazz and church music, and art exhibits (phone: 861-2537). The city's Irish Americans celebrate *St. Patrick's Day* (March 17) with a huge street party Uptown in the old Irish Channel and parades in several parts of the city and suburbs. A tradition that dates back to the turn of the century is the *St. Joseph's Day* parade, held on the weekend night nearest the March 19 feast day of the patron saint of Sicily. Italian-American men of all ages, dressed in tuxedos and carrying canes festooned with red, white, and green carnations, file through the French Quarter's streets amid floats, marching bands, and statues of the saint and the Virgin Mary. Greece has its day in late May, when traditional foods, crafts, and music fill the Hellenic Cultural Center near Bayou St. John for a *Greek Festival* (phone: 282-0259). In July the city celebrates *Carnaval Latino* and in August brings the *Latino Festival* to Canal

Street (phone: 524-0427). A few weeks later, in early September, is the *Fiesta Latina* in the Audubon Zoo (phone: 861-2537). Italian-Americans are in the spotlight again in October, when the *Festa d'Italia* takes over the downtown Piazza d'Italia with traditional food, music, and exhibits (phone: 891-1904). Food is the focus for the *Great French Market Tomato Festival,* held inside the colonnades of the *French Market*'s complex of food and gift shops in the French Quarter, usually the first full weekend in June (phone: 522-2621 on weekdays only). During the summer is *La Fête,* a festival of food and cookery, and in October it's hard to resist the *Gumbo Festival.* Christmas is observed with *Celebration in the Oaks* from late November to early January. The shrubbery and huge oaks filling many acres of City Park are festooned with spectacular electrical ornaments. Admission charge. Another month-long holiday event is *Creole Christmas,* when the French Quarter's historic homes are decorated in 19th-century creole style and restaurants offer special menus replicating the traditional French-creole *reveillon* holiday meal.

MUSEUMS AND HISTORIC HOUSES: In addition to those described in *Special Places,* other notable New Orleans museums include the following:

Confederate Museum – Louisiana's oldest, this small, red stone museum, just off Lee Circle, dates from 1891. Civil War buffs will find a trove of weapons, uniforms, maps, records, flags, and other memorabilia. Open Mondays through Saturdays from 10 AM to 4 PM. Admission charge. 929 Camp St. (phone: 523-4522).

1850 House – This townhouse, one of the row houses that comprise the Pontalba Apartments flanking Jackson Square, has been furnished and decorated as a typical home of prosperous Creoles in the mid-19th century, when the Baroness Pontalba had the twin apartment buildings constructed. A lack of ostentation is the principal asset of the furnishings. Closed Mondays and Tuesdays. Admission charge. 523 St. Ann St. (phone: 524-9118).

Gallier House Museum – Upper class New Orleans in the Victorian era is mirrored in the elaborate appointments of this meticulously restored mansion in a quiet section of the French Quarter. Designed by architect James Gallier as his family's residence, the wall coverings, fabrics, rugs, and fixtures authentically re-create the lifestyle of 1857. The small, simple garden contains a facsimile of the house's cistern, and a carriage sits ready in the carriageway separating the residence from the gift shop. After each tour, coffee is served on the balcony overlooking an especially picturesque block of Royal Street. Open Mondays through Saturdays, 10 AM to 4:30 PM. Admission charge. 1118-1132 Royal St. (phone: 523-6722).

Hermann-Grima House – A small army of historians, botanists, and social scientists took part in restoring this aristocratic, red brick residence to its original state. Built in 1831 by a wealthy merchant at the outset of New Orleans's "golden age" (1830 to 1860), its floor plan, with rooms flanking a central hall, is a departure from typical creole design of the era. The details are remarkably authentic, from the cast-iron pots of the creole-style kitchen to the harnesses in the stables and the aromatic plants in the garden. The appointments in the living quarters also are true to the period. Open Mondays through Saturdays, 10 AM to 4 PM. Admission charge. 820 St. Louis St. (phone: 525-5661).

Historical Pharmacy Museum – More quaint than scientific, this little shop in the 1820s was the apothecary of Louis J. Dufilho, said to have been the first licensed pharmacist in the US. Today, the displays of 19th-century jars and equipment may not be as interesting as the old rooms and the charming interior herbal and botanical garden. Closed Mondays. Admission charge. 514 Chartres St. (phone: 524-9077).

Louisiana Children's Museum – More play-school than museum, this cleverly designed spot features all kinds of hands-on fun for kids under 12. It contains a little coffee factory, numerous games and educational exhibits, and miniature versions of a supermarket, TV studio, and hospital. Closed Mondays. Admission charge. 428 Julia St. (phone: 523-1357).

Louisiana Nature and Science Center – Several of the natural sciences are spotlighted in this small museum that is also connected to nature trails on the city's eastern edge. The planetarium offers a number of astronomical programs (usually on weekends) as well as laser rock shows. Raised wooden walkways winding through the surrounding woods afford visitors a short, pleasant hike. Closed Mondays. Admission charge. Joe Brown Park; enter at Read Blvd. and Nature Center Dr. (phone: 246-5672).

Musée Conti Wax Museum – Voodoo, *Mardi Gras,* and the pirate Jean Lafitte are represented in the numerous tableaux here, filled with life-size wax mannequins in elaborate stage settings. Major events and personages of New Orleans's colorful history are the focus. Printed or tape-recorded commentary. Open daily from 10 AM to 5:30 PM. Admission charge. 917 Conti St. (phone: 525-2605).

Rivertown – There are several small museums contained in these nostalgically designed buildings situated on the Mississippi River in the New Orleans suburb of Kenner. The *Freeport-McMoRan Daily Living Science Center* has a planetarium and observatory (409 Williams Blvd.; phone: 468-7229). Six working layouts of toy trains, trolleys, and a toy carousel are on display in the *Louisiana Toy Train Museum* (519 Williams Blvd.; phone: 468-7223). The *Louisiana Wildlife and Fisheries Museum* features an aquarium and preserved wildlife specimens and displays (303 Williams Blvd.; phone: 468-7232). And the *Saints Hall of Fame Museum* contains memorabilia of New Orleans's pro football team (409 Williams Blvd.; phone: 468-6617). All are open Tuesdays through Saturdays from 9 AM to 5 PM; Sundays, 1 to 5 PM. Admission charge.

Voodoo Museum – African masks, voodoo dolls, and other exhibits are on display; although the authenticity of the items is in question, it can give you a taste of voodoo's mystique and history, especially in relation to New Orleans. Open daily from 10 AM to 7 PM; admission charge. 724 Dumaine St. (phone: 523-7685).

Williams Residence – Accessible to the *Historic New Orleans Collection* research center, this French Quarter townhouse has been restored to reflect the elegant lifestyle of the late L. Kemper Williams, who endowed the center. Although the rooms were furnished by the Williamses in the 1940s, they are filled with examples of fine Louisiana antiques and objets d'art. Three tours daily except Sundays and Mondays. Admission charge. 533 Royal St. (phone: 523-4662).

MAJOR COLLEGES AND UNIVERSITIES: Tulane University (6400 St. Charles Ave.; phone: 865-5000) is one of the South's leading private universities. A bequest by philanthropist Paul Tulane in 1883 allowed an expansion that resulted in today's 93-acre campus. Gibson Hall, the Romanesque stone building facing St. Charles Avenue, was built in 1894, and now contains the College of Arts and Sciences and major administrative offices. Tulane's sister institution, the Sophie H. Newcomb College for Women, adjoins Tulane's central campus but has a separate dean and faculty. The university's School of Medicine and teaching hospital are in the Central Business District (6823 St. Charles Ave.; phone: 588-5187). Loyola University (6363 St. Charles Ave.; phone: 865-2011) is New Orleans's largest Catholic university, founded by the Society of Jesus in 1911. Adjacent to the Tulane University campus. The open quadrangle facing St. Charles Avenue contains red brick buildings in the Tudor-Gothic style, which also inspired the design of the richly furnished Holy Name of Jesus Church, to the left of the quadrangle. Loyola maintains a College of Music, a School of Law, and departments of philosophy, theater, and English. The University of New Orleans (Elysian Fields near Lakeshore Dr.; phone: 286-6000) was once a branch campus of Louisiana State University in Baton Rouge, and given its independence in the 1960s.

NEW ORLEANS / Sources and Resources 95

SHOPPING: Although the largest shopping centers are found in the surrounding suburbs, downtown New Orleans also contains several major malls offering an immense variety of merchandise, as well as hundreds of specialty shops. The principal malls are the *New Orleans Centre* (just steps away from the *Louisiana Superdome* on Poydras St.), where *Macy's* and *Lord & Taylor* are the main tenants; *Canal Place* (at 333 Canal St. near the Mississippi River), with a 3-level branch of *Saks Fifth Avenue* and a large *Brooks Brothers;* and *Riverwalk,* extending along the riverfront near Canal Street with 2 levels of restaurants and shops that include *Banana Republic* (casual clothing), *Abercrombie & Fitch* (sportswear and gifts), *Sharper Image* (electronic gadgets), and *Brookstone* (household products). Canal Street itself still contains a few department stores harking back to its years as the city's shopping artery; the two major ones are the upscale *Maison Blanche* (901 Canal St.; phone: 566-1000) and *Krauss* (1201 Canal St., phone: 523-3311). Each is a full-scale emporium. Antiques hunters should focus their attention on the French Quarter, especially Royal and Chartres Streets, which contain all sorts of antiques shops and art galleries, and, farther out from the city center, Magazine Street, which contains dozens of stores offering moderate to expensive antique furniture, rugs, bric-a-brac, and artworks, from regional to European. Below is a list of New Orleans's favorite shopping places. (Also see *A French Quarter Shopping Spree* in DIVERSIONS.)

The Acorn – Glittering malachite pillboxes, Oriental textiles, and unusual jewelry are among the items displayed in this little boutique. 736 Royal St. (phone: 525-7110).

Adler's – A large selection of jewelry, porcelain, gifts, and bibelots fills the 2 floors of this plush establishment, now being operated by the third generation of the Adler family. 723 Canal St. (phone: 523-5292).

Alfredo's Cameras – Expert advice and a wide range of cameras and photographic equipment. 916 Gravier St. (phone: 523-2421).

Arthur Roger Gallery – Top contemporary artists from New Orleans and other parts of the country show their paintings and sculpture in this spacious, elegantly designed gallery in the Warehouse District. 432 Julia St. (phone: 522-1990).

B. Dalton Bookseller – A good place to seek out local guides, it also specializes in professional, technical, and other practical books. 714 Canal St. (phone: 529-2705).

Ballin's – Women's and children's clothes, from the frilly to the very up-to-date, are the specialty here, with many well-known designer labels on the racks. 721 Dante St. (phone: 866-4367). *New Orleans Centre,* 1400 Poydras St. (phone: 561-1100).

Benetton – A wide array of colors is their fashionable trademark. *Jackson Brewery Millhouse,* 600 Decatur St. (phone: 581-3020).

Bep's Antiques – Modest treasures — you just might discover that indispensable objet d'art among the hundreds of old bottles, homey Victorian washstands, and charming little side tables. 2051 Magazine St. (phone: 525-7726).

Bergeron's – Dozens of styles by top designers are the stock-in-trade at the city's preeminent source of fine-quality women's shoes. Unusual handbags are another specialty. *Canal Place,* 333 Canal St. (phone: 525-2195).

Bookstar – Two very large floors filled with every type of publication. A good selection of audiotapes, magazines, and maps, too. 414 N. Peters St. (phone: 523-6411).

Brass Menagerie – If it's brass, this place almost certainly stocks it — everything from faucets to coat hooks. 524 St. Louis St. (phone: 524-0921).

Central Grocery Co. – Known for its muffuletta sandwiches and a huge array of Italian food specialties, this is also a good source for a wide variety of non-perishable groceries from around the world. 923 Decatur St. (phone: 523-1620).

Coghlan Gallery – This shop features odds and ends to decorate your garden or terrace, including hand-crafted copper fountains and other ornaments. 710 Toulouse St. (phone: 525-8550).

96 NEW ORLEANS / Sources and Resources

Cuisine Classique – Along with the vast array of cooking tools offered here, there is also a wide selection of local cookbooks. 439 Decatur St. (phone: 524-0068).

Dansk Factory Outlet – All kinds of Scandinavian-designed dishes, glasses, pots, and other household items are offered at a deep discount. 541 Royal St. (phone: 522-0482).

DeVille Books & Prints – This is the place to check for hard-to-find authors and unusual literary works. The art, architecture, and photography sections are especially well stocked. Three locations: One Shell Sq., St. Charles at Poydras St. (phone: 525-1846); *Jackson Brewery,* 620 Decatur (phone: 525-4508); and *Riverwalk Mall,* Poydras St. at the Mississippi River (phone: 595-8916).

Ditto 19th Century Antiques – Specializes in clocks, cut-glass, and above-average bric-a-brac. 4838 Magazine St. (phone: 891-4845).

Esprit – Moderate prices and chic casual styles for children and teens. 901 St. Charles Ave. (phone: 561-5050).

French Market – This famous market sells a wide variety of items — souvenirs, confectioneries, toys, candles, pralines, spices, and funky clothes, just to name a few. Vendors' stalls set up along the street offer a cornucopia of fresh fruits and vegetables, as well as old books and records, tropical plants, and a hodgepodge of creole and Cajun spices. Decatur St., between St. Ann and Barracks Sts.

Galerie Simonne Stern – Aficionados of abstract expressionism and other schools of the American vanguard should find this prestigious gallery worth a visit. Emerging local, regional, and national artists are featured in the ever-changing exhibitions. 518 Julia St. (phone: 529-1118) and 305 Royal St. (phone: 524-9757).

A Gallery for Fine Photography – The work of the world's best-known photographers, from Matthew Brady to Irving Penn, are represented in this vast collection of fine works, shown on 2 floors. Also look for rare and unusual photographs relating to New Orleans, especially its musicians. 322 Royal (phone: 568-1313).

Gasperi Gallery – Contemporary folk art and works that have strong ethnic connections. 320 Julia St. (phone: 524-9373).

Hayes Antiques – A remarkably good selection of early-20th-century prints, photographs, and trinkets can be found in this quaint shop. 828 Chartres St. (phone: 529-4221).

Henry Stern Antiques – A long-established dealer in fine English furniture and paintings from the late 18th and early 19th centuries. 329-331 Royal St. (phone: 522-8687).

Hove Parfumeur – Perfumes, colognes, and soaps are produced on the premises of this charming, family-owned boutique, and dried aromatic herbs such as vetiver are also available. 824 Royal St. (phone: 525-7827).

The Idea Factory – Hand-crafted wooden creations — whimsical creatures as well as marquetry boxes and other practical items — can be found here; all are made in a workshop out back. 838 Chartres St. (phone: 524-5195).

Jacqueline Vance Oriental Rugs – The reliable quality of the merchandise and the expertise of the owner make this New Orleans's number one source of antique and modern oriental rugs. Appraisals and repairs are also offered. 3944 Magazine St. (phone: 891-3304).

Joan Vass New Orleans – Fans of Joan Vass, one of America's top designers of women's knitwear, will find this handsomely done shop a prime outlet for her creations, from the practical to the luxurious. *Martha and Me,* the affiliated shop in the same building, specializes in tailored wovens from other respected designers. 1100 Sixth St. (phone: 891-4502).

Jon Antiques – Among the better purveyors of 18th- and 19th-century furniture, china, and objets d'art. 4605 Magazine St. (phone: 899-4482).

NEW ORLEANS / Sources and Resources 97

K&B Camera Center – Whether you're a point-and-shooter or a professional, this is a handy source of camera equipment, film, and accessories; it also operates its own custom-processing laboratory. 227 Dauphine St. (phone: 524-2266).

Kite Shop – All kinds of kites, from the whimsical to the artistic, crowd the ceiling and walls of this colorful and fascinating little store on Jackson Square. 542 St. Peter St. (phone: 524-0028).

Krauss – Local homemakers find this one of their best sources of practical, reasonably priced fabrics, linen, and housewares. The sales staff is congenial and helpful. 1201 Canal St. (phone: 523-3311).

Lucullus – Crowded with antique French and English dining room furniture, crystal, porcelain, and decorative objects relating to food and wine. 610 Chartres St. (phone: 528-9620).

Maison Blanche – The 3 floors of this fine regionally owned department store at the heart of downtown are very well organized, with a multitude of nationally known brands, as well as designer clothing. 901 Canal St. (phone: 566-1000).

Maple Street Book Shop – If New Orleans has a literary heart, it is this unpretentious uptown cottage crammed with a very selective collection of novels, anthologies, and biographies, from the latest best sellers to the most obscure Southern writers. A bookworm's paradise. 7523 Maple St. (phone: 866-4916). The branch at 2727 Prytania St. (phone: 895-2266) is interesting, too.

Merrill B. Domas American Indian Art – The work of the best weavers, potters, and painters from the Southwest is sold here, as well as jewelry in silver and gemstones by some of Santa Fe's leading artisans. 824 Chartres St. (phone: 586-0479).

Mignon Faget Ltd. – Much of this New Orleans jewelry designer's inspiration comes from nature, and her exquisite ornaments can be found on the city's most sophisticated women. *Canal Place,* 333 Canal St. (phone: 524-2973), 710 Dublin St. (phone: 865-7361), and 8220 Maple St. (phone: 865-1107).

Morton M. Goldberg Auction Galleries – A virtual warehouse filled with every sort of antique, it is worth a visit if only for browsing among the trove of American, European, and Oriental objects. Estate auctions are a specialty, and good values are there for the cognoscenti. 547 Baronne St. (phone: 592-2300).

M.S. Rau – Two large floors packed to the rafters with antiques — everything from art glass to music boxes, and more crystal and porcelain than you may have thought existed. 630 Royal St. (phone: 523-5660).

Old Town Praline Shop – Charmingly old-fashioned, it turns out pecan-studded sugar patties with that traditional creole taste, wrapped in the same little waxed-paper bags they've used for decades. They'll pack and ship, as well. 627 Royal St. (phone: 525-1413).

Perlis – Conservative men's clothing with a dash of élan. Fashion headquarters for many of the city's lawyers and stockbrokers, the styles range from Duck's Head khaki pants to Southwick and Ralph Lauren suits. Boy's and women's clothes are sold, too. 6070 Magazine St. (phone: 895-8661).

Le Petit Soldier Shoppe – Collector or not, you're apt to be charmed by the exquisite lead soldiers sold in this museum-cum-shop. 528 Royal St. (phone: 523-7741).

Progress Grocery Co. – It's part delicatessen, part fancy grocery store, with a muffuletta sandwich take-out counter and a huge variety of exotic edibles on the shelves, including the proprietor's own herbed olive oils. Imported pasta and unusual dried legumes are also available. 915 Decatur St. (phone: 525-6627).

Rapp's Luggage and Gifts – Whether you're looking for a plastic carry-on or a briefcase of fine leather, you'll probably find it here; also all sorts of handy travel gear. Minor luggage repairs, too. 604 Canal St. (phone: 568-1953).

Record Ron's Good & Plenty Records – Everything from Bing Crosby to heavy metal to the baroque, with a specialty in rarities and the offbeat, fills the seemingly endless bins of LPs. 1129 Decatur St. (phone: 524-9444), 407 Decatur St. (phone: 525-2852), and 7605 Maple St. (phone: 866-1388).

Rubenstein Bros. – The fashion-conscious man looking for top American and European designers will find them here. So will the follower of the latest trends in casual wear. The choices, from haberdashery to topcoats, are many and varied. 102 St. Charles Ave. (phone: 581-6666).

Serendipitous – A wide variety of brightly colored masks can be found here. 831 Decatur St. (phone: 522-9158).

Stan Levy Imports – A good source not only of European pieces but also Southern armoires, 19th-century Louisiana furniture, and more recent objects from the region — affordable, too. 1028 Louisiana Ave., near Magazine St. (phone: 899-6384).

Still-Zinsel Contemporary Fine Art – New painters and photographers working in a variety of styles are often introduced here. 328 Julia St. (phone: 588-9999).

Tower Records – *The* place to find the CD or cassette you want. The classical section on the second floor is remarkably complete. 408 N. Peters St. (phone: 529-4411).

Victoria's Designer Discount Shoes – From simple pumps to glittery evening shoes, much of the footwear is made by the leading names in fashion — and they're priced to sell. 532 Chartres St. (phone: 568-9990).

Waldenbooks – Mysteries and a good selection of paperbacks are the forte in the Canal Street outlet of the national chain. 739 Canal St. (phone: 522-8418). Other locations in several major shopping malls.

Waldhorn – An antiques dealer for connoisseurs of English and French furniture. 343 Royal St. (phone: 581-6379).

Wehmeier's Belt Shop – The large inventory of men's and women's leather goods includes shoes and handbags; emergency repairs are made on the premises. 719 Toulouse (phone: 525-2758).

William Norris Ltd. – Antique and contemporary cast-iron ornaments are shown in this one-of-a-kind shop. The glass-topped tables, side chairs, and beds are all strikingly original. 1029 Royal St. (phone: 524-1010).

F. W. Woolworth – The old five-and-dime is alive and well at two centrally located stores. 737 Canal St. (phone: 522-6426); 1041 Canal St. (phone: 522-7461); and in several other parts of the city.

SPORTS AND FITNESS: Bicycling – Bicycles can be rented at *Bicycle Michael's* (618 Frenchmen St., a few blocks from the French Quarter; phone: 945-9505). City Park rents bikes at Dreyfous Avenue (phone: 483-9371). (Also see *Bicycling* in DIVERSIONS.)

Boating – At City Park, you can rent canoes, paddleboats, and skiffs to cruise on the lagoons (phone: 483-9371). (Also see *Sailing and Boating* in DIVERSIONS.)

Fishing – Non-residents are required to purchase temporary state licenses for all fishing, crabbing, and shrimping in either fresh or salt water. Licenses are available from the Louisiana Department of Wildlife and Fisheries (400 Chartres St., in the French Quarter; phone: 568-5636). City Park regularly stocks its lagoons, and provides daily and annual fishing permits at the Casino Building (phone: 483-9371). Individuals and groups of up to a dozen or more can charter piloted boats for fresh- or salt-water fishing in the coastal wetlands and the Gulf of Mexico at the Venice Marina, about 80 miles from New Orleans near the mouth of the Mississippi River (phone: 534-9357). (Also see *Goin' Fishing* in DIVERSIONS.)

Fitness Centers – The *New Orleans Athletic Club* has a 60-foot indoor lap pool, exercise equipment and classes, a boxing ring, racquetball and basketball courts, and indoor and outdoor tracks (222 N. Rampart St.; phone: 525-2375). *Racquetball One Fitness Centers* offers 5 racquetball courts, aerobics programs, free weights, stair climbers, and exercise cycles (One Shell Sq., 13th Floor, Poydras St. and St. Charles Ave.; phone: 522-2956; and *Canal Place,* Suite 380, 333 Canal St.; phone: 525-2956). Several hotels also allow non-guests to use their centers for a fee, usually about $10 a session. The *Rivercenter Racquet and Health Club* in the *New Orleans Hilton* has a jogging track, weight training, saunas, and basketball, racquetball, tennis, and squash courts (Poydras St. at the Mississippi River; phone: 587-7242). *Eurovita Spa* offers a fitness room with weights, sauna, steamroom, whirlpool bath, and tanning rooms, as well as therapeutic massages (*Avenue Plaza Suite Hotel,* 2111 St. Charles Ave.; phone: 566-1212). *Le Meridien Sports Center* has an outdoor heated pool, Nautilus equipment, Lifecycles, an aerobics program, yoga classes, a sauna, and massage therapists (*Meridien Hotel,* 614 Canal St.; phone: 527-6750).

Football – The New Orleans *Saints* play in the *Louisiana Superdome* on Poydras St. (phone: 522-2600).

Golf – Several public 18-hole courses, all open daily with greens fees at $10 or less, are short distances from the city center. *City Park* has four courses (phone: 483-9396). *Audubon Park* (in the Uptown section; phone: 861-9511) has its own course. Also check out the *Joe Bartholomew* golf course (in eastern New Orleans's Pontchartrain Park; phone: 288-0928); *Brechtel Park* (on the west bank of the Mississippi River; phone: 362-4761); and *Plantation* golf course (1001 Behrman Hwy.; phone: 392-3363).

Horseback Riding – *Cascade Stables*' 2-mile trail is shaded by Audubon Park's huge oaks. From 9 AM to 4 PM daily, horses and ponies are available for adults and youngsters (phone: 891-2246).

Horse Racing – Two thoroughbred-racing tracks operate from *Thanksgiving* to mid-April. The *Fair Grounds,* one of the country's oldest thoroughbred-racing tracks, is a 15-minute taxi ride from the city center (1751 Gentilly Blvd.; phone: 944-5515). Near the airport, in suburban Kenner, is *Jefferson Downs* (1300 Sunset Blvd.; phone: 466-8521).

Jogging – Good routes are in City Park at the end of Esplanade Avenue, Audubon Park in the Uptown section, Woldenberg Park on the French Quarter's edge, and along the Mississippi River levee along Leake Avenue in the Carrollton section.

Sailing – For skimming along Lake Pontchartrain, hourly or daily rentals of sailboats, from 9 to 36 feet, are offered by *Sailboats South,* 300 Sapphire St. (phone: 288-7245). (Also see *Sailing and Boating,* DIVERSIONS.)

Tennis – The 39 lighted courts at the *Wisner Tennis Center* in City Park are open from 7 AM to past sunset, and the pro shop provides racquet repairs (phone: 483-9383). Audubon Park's 10 courts, near the Mississippi River Uptown, are open at 8 AM (phone: 895-1042). The *Rivercenter Racquet and Health Club* has 8 indoor and 3 outdoor courts atop the Hilton hotel's garage (2 Poydras St.; phone: 587-7242). (Also see *Tennis* in DIVERSIONS.)

THEATER: National touring companies of Broadway shows perform regularly in the fall and spring at the *Saenger Performing Arts Center* (143 N. Rampart St. at Canal St.; phone: 524-2490). For those seeking something more daring, contemporary American plays, many of them by local writers and most of them avant-garde, are presented regularly in the arena theater of the *Contemporary Arts Center* (900 Camp St.; phone: 523-1216). In the French Quarter's community theater, the picturesque *Le Petit Théâtre du Vieux Carré* presents modern musical comedies and dramas from Broadway's past, and original plays for children (616 St. Peter St.; phone: 522-2081). The several productions put on each year by the *Southern Repertory Theater* spotlight regional themes and works of playwrights such as Tennessee Williams (1437 S. Carrollton Ave.; phone: 861-2254). Respectable amateur productions, from the spirited *Dashiki Theatre* group to original spoofs of old Hollywood musicals, are put on in the tiny *NORD Theater* space on the ground floor of Gallier Hall (543 St. Charles Ave.; phone: 949-0493). Original dramas, some experimental, are the forte at the little *Theater Marigny* (616 Frenchmen St.; phone: 944-2653). Campy satires and musical revues are the specialty at the *Toulouse Theatre* in the French Quarter (615 Toulouse St.; phone: 523-4207). Meatier works, from 19th-century classics to contemporary plays, are presented by the drama departments of Tulane University (*Dixon Performing Arts Center* on the Newcomb College campus; phone: 865-5106), Loyola University's *Lower Depths Theatre* (on the St. Charles Ave. campus; phone: 865-3824), and the *University of New Orleans Performing Arts Center* (near the Lakefront; phone: 834-9774). The closest New Orleans gets to summer stock is Tulane's semi-professional *Summer Lyric Theater,* which presents several Broadway musicals from June through August at the *Dixon Center* (phone: 865-5269). Lighter fare, in the form of contemporary Broadway comedies and revues, is the stock-in-trade at the city's numerous dinner-theaters. The main ones are *Bayou Cabaret Theater* (4040 Tulane Ave.; phone: 486-4545) and *New Rose Dinner Playhouse* (201 Robert St., Gretna; phone: 367-5400).

CINEMA: If you want to see a particular first-run Hollywood production, you may have to head for a multi-screen theater in the suburbs (Metairie or the West Bank). But a couple of in-town cinemas also show current general-interest films. *Canal Place Cinema* (*Canal Place,* 5th Floor, 333 Canal St.; phone: 581-5400) has four screens and shows top American and foreign films. Uptown near St. Charles Avenue, the *Prytania* (5339 Prytania St.; phone: 895-4513) focuses on more serious fare — art films and occasionally something from the underground.

MUSIC AND DANCE: The demise of the *New Orleans Symphony Orchestra* in early 1990 left the city without a major orchestra of its own for the first time since the 1930s. Late in the year, however, a core group of musicians launched a grass-roots movement that resulted in the creation of the *Louisiana Philharmonic Orchestra,* with a limited season in the spring and fall and a roster of guest conductors. The group's concerts are given in the *Saenger Performing Arts Center* (143 N. Rampart St. at Canal St.; phone: 523-6530). Aficionados of chamber music should check the schedule of the *Friends of Music,* a group that sponsors several concerts each year by local and nationally known professionals (usually held at Tulane University's *Dixon Performing Arts Center;* phone: 895-0690). Loyola University and Sophie Newcomb College at Tulane University sponsor occasional recitals and concerts by students, faculty, and visiting performers at Loyola's *Roussel Performance Hall* on the university campus (7214 St. Charles Ave.; phone: 865-2492) and at Tulane/Newcomb's *Dixon Hall* or Rogers Memorial Chapel (phone: 865-5269). New Orleans was the first American city to build an opera house, in the early 19th century. The musical tradition continues with several productions yearly by the *New Orleans Opera Association,* featuring internationally known performers offering classical European repertories. They're presented at the *Theatre for the Performing Arts* (N. Rampart St. near the corner of Dumaine St.; phone: 529-2278). Also, the Department of Music at Xavier University occasionally stages student productions (7325 Palmetto St.; phone: 486-7411). Several years ago the *New Orleans City Ballet* merged with the *Cincinnati Ballet,* and the company stages several major productions annually in the *Theatre for the Performing Arts* (phone: 522-0996).

The biggest pop and rock stars regularly perform at the *Saenger Performing Arts Center* downtown (143 N. Rampart St.; phone: 523-6530), the *Kiefer UNO Lakefront Arena* (on the University of New Orleans campus; phone: 286-7222), the *Louisiana Superdome* (on Poydras St.; phone: 587-3800), and at private halls and clubs around town.

■ **ALL THAT JAZZ:** Jazz and Cajun musicians have brought New Orleans its international regard as a musical center. New Orleans is a port city, and nowhere is this more apparent than in the flamboyant overlapping of musical influences which have produced the distinctively syncopated swagger and improvisational fire of this city's music. The music is a rich gumbo created from the cross-fertilization of Caribbean music, African, the blues tradition, and zydeco, the local Cajun tradition. Today, New Orleans has exported its music around the globe and has garnered an enthusiastic international following. Some of the current stars of this musical seedbed include the *Neville Brothers, Dr. John,* the *Dirty Dozen Brass Band,* and such zydeco groups as *Buckwheat Zydeco* and *Rockin' Dopsie and the Zydeco Twisters.* At the same time, never forget that Louis Armstrong, Jelly Roll Morton, Sidney Bechet, and other jazz immortals were the New Orleans musicians who brought jazz to a new plateau of improvisational genius, making a major impact on the evolution of this quintessentially American sound. New Orleanians take quite justifiable pride in their unique musical heritage and no other city in the country has a beat quite like the Big Easy.

NIGHTCLUBS AND NIGHTLIFE: No fan of New Orleans jazz should miss the authentic music and incomparable atmosphere of *Preservation Hall,* where 60- and 70-year veterans of the city's jazz scene perform nightly for an audience sitting hip-to-haunch on backless benches in a ramshackle double parlor. The experience is unforgettable (726 St. Peter St.; phone: 522-2841). More comfortable, and just as much the real thing musically, is the *Palm Court Jazz Café,* a spacious restaurant in an old French Quarter building where young and old traditionalists hold forth nightly (1204 Decatur St.; phone: 525-0200). A cushy spot to enjoy traditional New Orleans music is the *Louis Armstrong Foundation Jazz Club* in the *Meridien Hotel*'s vast ground-floor lobby, where *Jacques Gauthé's Yerba Buena Creole Rice Jazz Band* regularly holds forth on weekends (614 Canal St.; phone: 525-6500).

Two of the city's most celebrated Dixieland musicians, clarinetist Pete Fountain and trumpeter Al Hirt, have their own clubs, and the seats are always filled when the masters themselves are onstage. Fountain's headquarters is *Pete Fountain's* in the *New Orleans Hilton* (phone: 523-4374), and Hirt holds forth from time to time at *Jelly Roll's* in the French Quarter (501 Bourbon St.; phone: 568-0501). Good-quality local bands perform in their absence; if you're interested only in the stars themselves, call ahead. At *Chris Owens* in the French Quarter, the club's namesake is the sole performer, and if her maraca shaking and fancy footwork aren't the most advanced in town, her showmanship usually fills the place to the rafters (502 Bourbon St.; phone: 523-6400).

The music of southwest Louisiana's bayous has an international following and it is certainly not neglected in New Orleans's clubs. Authentic Cajun bands, including groups performing in the even earthier and folksier zydeco style, stomp and fiddle every night at *Mulate's* in the Warehouse District, which also has a dance floor and a kitchen dispensing spicy Louisiana dishes (201 Julia St.; phone: 522-1492). Another good Cajun dance hall–restaurant is *Michaul's,* on the Warehouse District's fringe (701 Magazine St.; phone: 522-5517). A smaller Cajun music venue is *Cajun Cabin* (501 Bourbon St.; phone: 529-4256).

The most durable comedy-and-music club in town is *The Mint,* a large, laid-back bar where homegrown talent performs on Friday through Sunday nights. The humor usually has lots of local connotations, but out-of-towners seem to catch on quickly (504 Esplanade Ave.; phone: 525-2000). An earthier atmosphere pervades *Tipitina's,* deep in the heart of the Uptown waterfront, where the music is down-and-dirty and the crowd never stops moving — on or off the dance floor (501 Napoleon Ave. at

Tchoupitoulas St.; phone: 895-8477). *Snug Harbor* (626 Frenchmen St.; phone: 949-0696), a couple of blocks from the French Quarter, is the place to listen to the "New Orleans Sound," performed by such masters as singers Charmaine Neville and Germaine Bazzle. For authentic New Orleans jazz in more elegant surroundings, there's the *Louis Armstrong Foundation Jazz Club* in the lofty lobby bar of the *Meridien* hotel, with body-hugging chairs, well-made cocktails, and live band music inspired by New Orleans's steamboat days (614 Canal St.; phone: 525-6500). At *Benny's,* a funky club featuring New Orleans rhythm and blues, the real action doesn't get going until after midnight (938 Valence St.; phone: 895-9405). Recent passage of a bill legalizing casino gambling in Louisiana has spurred plans for construction of a casino in New Orleans; as we went to press, the location was scheduled to be the Rivergate convention hall downtown.

BEST IN TOWN

CHECKING IN: Hotels in New Orleans usually are more than just places to stay after spending a day (and half the night) seeing the city. Many of the hotels reflect the influence of French, Spanish, and/or Louisiana colonial architecture and often a full measure of charm. No matter where you stay or what you pay, make reservations well in advance, particularly during *Sugar Bowl Week* (approximately December 30 to January 2) preceding the annual football classic on *New Year's Day, Carnival* season (in February or early March), and the *New Orleans Jazz and Heritage Festival* (in late April). Expect rates to increase by about 25% during these periods of high demand. (Many hotels have 3- or 4-day minimums during *Carnival.*) In general, however, the spate of hotel building that coincided with New Orleans's ill-fated *1984 World's Fair* has tended to keep the hotel business very competitive and rather reasonable — especially on weekends, when special promotional packages are frequently offered by the large chain hotels. Expect to pay $110 to $160 a night for a double room — and much higher, especially for suites — in the expensive range; $75 to $95 in the moderate category; and $50 to $70 in the inexpensive category.

For bed and breakfast accommodations, contact *Bed & Breakfast Inc.* (1360 Moss St., Box 52257, New Orleans, LA 70152; phone: 525-4640 or 800-228-9711); *Bed & Breakfast of New Orleans* (671 Rosa Ave., Metairie; phone: 838-0071); or the Greater New Orleans Tourist and Convention Commission (1520 Sugar Bowl Dr., New Orleans, LA 70112; phone: 566-5011). All telephone numbers are in the 504 area code unless otherwise indicated.

Fairmont – They say that New Orleanians wept when its predecessor, the legendary *Roosevelt,* was sold to Fairmont interests. But they weep no more. With its wedding-cake façade, a block-long lobby illuminated by massive chandeliers, and luxurious public spaces, the hotel is a delightful blending of the best in San Francisco style and New Orleans charm. The 750 rooms that made up the original hotel and more recent annex are efficiently maintained (but ask for one in the newer wing). Its location, just a half block from Canal Street and a few blocks from the heart of the French Quarter, make it convenient for shopping and dining. The *Sazerac,* a luxury, ground-floor restaurant, is frilly and romantic (see *Eating Out*), and the more casual *Bailey's,* open 24 hours, is a satisfactory place for everything from snacks to good creole fare. There is a heated pool, and 2 tennis courts. Business conveniences include 30 meeting rooms, a concierge desk, A/V equipment, photocopiers, computers, CNN, and express checkout. University Pl. (phone: 529-7111 or 800-527-4727; fax: 522-2303). Expensive.

NEW ORLEANS / Best in Town 103

Hyatt Regency – Situated just a stone's throw from the *Superdome* and connected to the *New Orleans Centre* shopping mall, this 1,200-room link in the Hyatt chain has an atrium-style lobby, an inner courtyard fountain, lots of greenery, and numerous multilevel public spaces. The hotel is undergoing a $16-million renovation of its lobby, restaurants, and guestrooms that is scheduled to be completed by this spring. There are rooms with private patios and balconies, some overlooking the heated outdoor swimming pool. The grand view of the city from the *Top of the Dome* restaurant is a plus, and *Hyttops,* the sports bar on the mezzanine level, is always lively, especially during big *Superdome* sports events. CNN, room service, and well-equipped convention facilities are available. 500 Poydras Plaza (phone: 561-1234 or 800-233-1234). Expensive.

Inter-Continental New Orleans – An imposing presence in the business district, it has 482 comfortable guestrooms and luxury suites that are tempered in their modern design by some antique appointments. The lavishly decorated *Veranda* restaurant, featuring creole-continental food, has period dining rooms as well as a huge atrium filled with exotic plants (see *Eating Out*). Only minutes away from the *New Orleans Convention Center, Riverwalk* shopping mall, and the *Louisiana Superdome,* the hotel is especially lively during *Carnival,* when many parades file by along St. Charles Avenue. The 20 meeting rooms include a vast ballroom on the top floor that has excellent views of Poydras Street. Twenty-four-hour room service is available, as are CNN, a concierge desk, secretarial services, and complete electronic facilities for business conferences. 444 St. Charles Ave. (phone: 525-5566, 800-332-4246, or 800-327-0200; fax: 523-7310). Expensive.

Maison de Ville – This fine small inn in the French Quarter is actually a variety of accommodations: the main house, on a lively block between Royal and Bourbon Streets, with handsome rooms in wonderfully restored former slave quarters; and a few blocks away, the *Audubon Cottages* (named for the naturalist, who lived and painted in this city a century ago), each of which has a patio with access to a small swimming pool. The cottages get our nod for the best of French Quarter ambience. The spaces at the main house aren't large, but they're quite adequate, and the antique furniture, rich fabrics, and interesting color schemes give the rooms a pleasant homey feel. The hotel's tiny restaurant next door, the *Bistro,* is a favorite of locals for its sophisticated menu and simple but chic decor (see *Eating Out*). Room service is available for lunch and dinner only. CNN. Also see *New Orleans's Best Hotels,* DIVERSIONS. 727 Toulouse St. (phone: 561-5858 or 800-634-1600). Expensive.

Melrose – A lushly renovated Victorian house with polished wood floors and beautiful antiques that make this luxury bed and breakfast establishment cozy yet elegant. Fresh flowers and down pillows are found in each room. While this property is convenient to the Faubourg Marigny, it isn't within easy walking distance of the French Quarter's heart, so plan on using taxis fairly regularly if you're without a car. A definite plus is the limo that greets guests at the airport. Located on the northern edge of the French Quarter at 937 Esplanade Ave. (phone: 944-2255). Expensive.

Meridien – This 497-room, sleekly designed hotel in the business district is directly along the *Mardi Gras* parade routes. Contemporary-style rooms are elegantly decorated in muted tones. The French atmosphere is palpable, especially in the casual *La Gauloise* restaurant, with its extensive but moderately priced luncheon and weekend dinner buffets (see *Eating Out*). The huge lobby bar jumps every night with the sounds of a traditional jazz band. Besides a health club and pool, there are 11 meeting rooms, secretarial and concierge service, 24-hour room service, CNN, and express checkout. 614 Canal St. (phone: 525-6500 or 800-543-4300; fax: 586-1543). Expensive.

104 NEW ORLEANS / Best in Town

New Orleans Hilton – At the heart of the bustling Mississippi Riverfront, this 1,602-room resort offers a fine view and the *International Rivercenter,* an entertainment development that includes a cruise-ship terminal, a tennis club, and a luxury shopping mall. The property also has a pool, a health club, a sauna, and a garage. Pluses are *Kabby's* (see *Eating Out*), a creole restaurant that overlooks the Mississippi; the *Rainforest* nightclub; *Pete Fountain's* nightclub, featuring the famous jazz clarinetist; and *Le Café Bromeliad,* with its lively Sunday champagne brunch with rousing jazz and gospel accompaniment. Support services include a concierge desk, secretarial assistance, and express checkout. The 41 meeting rooms hold up to 3,600 people. Room service delivers around the clock, and there's CNN, too. 2 Poydras St. at the Mississippi River (phone: 561-0500 or 800-HILTONS; fax: 568-1721). Expensive.

New Orleans Marriott – Unabashedly glitzy, this 1,290-room hotel is tailor-made for those in search of Las Vegas–style ambience. Its spacious but low-ceilinged lobby houses a warren of casual eateries and lounges; and guestrooms are done up in lots of bright colors. On the top floor, the *River View* restaurant offers a pleasant panorama of the Mississippi, the French Quarter, and Canal Street. There's also a health club with Nautilus equipment and a pool. Convention facilities are more than adequate for larger meetings. Efficient, affable service is a plus. Canal and Chartres Sts. (phone: 581-1000 or 800-228-9290; fax: 523-6755). Expensive.

Omni Royal Orleans – Moderate in size and elegantly appointed, this was the first of the French Quarter's hotels to combine 19th-century atmosphere with modern, efficient facilities. It was completed in 1960 on the site of the old *St. Louis* hotel, a 19th-century showplace that is memorialized in a large wall painting at the center of the Italian-marble lobby. Most of the 350 rooms are elegantly furnished, and the Tennessee Williams Suite, lined with photographs and other memorabilia relating to the writer's career, overlooks a quaint French Quarter corner. The *Esplanade Lounge* is popular with the late-night crowd, as is the 3-level *Touché Bar.* The menu at the plush *Rib Room* includes meat and seafoods prepared on a giant rotisserie, as well as typical New Orleans dishes (see *Eating Out*). The outdoor rooftop *Riviera* restaurant, near the swimming pool, serves breakfast on balmy days. Amenities include a fitness center, shops, and a garage. Secretarial and concierge services are available, as well as 24-hour room service, and CNN. There are 6 meeting rooms for business tête-à-têtes. 621 St. Louis St. (phone: 529-5333 or 800-THE-OMNI; fax: 523-5076). Expensive.

Pontchartrain – With 100 tastefully decorated rooms, each done individually, and suites replete with French provincial antique furnishings, this is a favorite of celebrities and traveling dignitaries. There are two restaurants, the casual *Coffee Shop* and the lavishly appointed *Caribbean Room* (see *Eating Out*), which offers creole specialties. A jazz pianist performs nightly in the intimate *Bayou Bar.* Around-the-clock room service is offered, as well as a concierge desk, secretarial services, and CNN. A separate wing for business meetings was added a few years ago, with 2 rooms that can accommodate up to 300 for banquets and conferences. 2031 St. Charles Ave. (phone: 524-0581; fax: 524-1165). Expensive.

Royal Sonesta – Somewhere between glitzy and elegant, this swanky marble, crystal, and brocade-bedecked French Quarter establishment, with 500 rooms and 35 suites, is in the heart of brassy Bourbon Street — a good choice if you've come to New Orleans to experience its more hedonistic pleasures. The lobby is surprisingly quiet, as are the rooms overlooking the lush interior patio. Then again, there are also rooms with balconies overlooking that frenetic Bourbon Street nighttime revelry. *Begue's,* the hotel's prestigious restaurant, offers creole-continental food with occasional lighter, contemporary dishes (see *Eating Out*). Facilities include an outdoor pool, a concierge desk, convention facilities, and a garage. 300 Bourbon St. (phone: 586-0300 or 800-343-7170; fax: 586-0335). Expensive.

NEW ORLEANS / Best in Town 105

St. Louis – One of the many French Quarter hostelries designed to blend in with the surrounding 19th-century architecture, its modest size (69 rooms) and subtle elegance are proof that good things do come in small packages. All of the rooms open onto a handsome arcaded courtyard with a central fountain. The rather plain rooms may be a letdown after the classiness of the small, welcoming lobby. The handsomely decorated *Louis XVI* restaurant flanking the courtyard is one of the city's better purveyors of French-creole cooking (see *Eating Out*). 730 Bienville St. (phone: 581-7300 or 800-535-9111; fax: 524-8925). Expensive.

Sheraton New Orleans – Ideally located — right across from the French Quarter and a few blocks from the Mississippi — this 1,100-room, 49-story establishment has a comfortable multilevel lobby and offers the admirable service to its guests that the national chain is noted for. On the premises are the *Gazebo Lounge, Cafe Promenade,* and the *Creole Tomato* snack bar, a gift shop, a parking garage, and an outdoor pool with its own bar and grill. Business executives will find secretarial services, cellular phones for lease, and computers. Nonsmoking guestrooms are available. Video checkout. 500 Canal St. (phone: 525-2500 or 800-325-3535; fax: 561-0178). Expensive.

Westin–Canal Place – There are remarkable panoramic city views from the 11th-floor lobby of this establishment atop the *Canal Place* office-and-shopping complex, situated where the French Quarter, the Mississippi River, and Canal Street converge. It has 438 top-quality rooms and suites of varying sizes. The hotel's huge wood-and-marble lobby, one of the city's swankiest, offers spectacular views of the Mississippi River and the nearby French Quarter. The best place to enjoy the panorama is from a table at *Le Jardin,* a posh, very spacious restaurant that offers breakfast, lunch, and dinner (see *Eating Out*). Twenty-four-hour room service is available. Other features include a large lounge, a concierge desk, CNN, and 8 meeting rooms. 100 Iberville St. (phone: 566-7006 or 800-228-3000; fax: 523-2549). Expensive.

Windsor Court – Luxuriously British-style, this establishment, just steps from Canal Street and the Mississippi River, consistently appears on lists of the world's best hotels, including those of *Condé Nast Traveler* magazine and "Lifestyles of the Rich and Famous." Some of the reasons are evident in the public rooms, which are decorated with expensive 17th- to early-20th-century English art, fine carpets and tapestries, and exquisite antiques and bibelots such as museum-quality porcelains. Its 52 deluxe rooms and 256 suites (and 2 penthouses) are impeccably appointed, and service is extraordinarily good. The *Grill Room* (see *Eating Out*) and *Polo Lounge* are as luxurious as they come, and the food, part continental, part contemporary, has gotten raves from a legion of critics. Afternoon tea in *Le Salon,* just off the lobby, is rich in British tradition. Other amenities include an Olympic-size pool, a health club, and a parking garage. While certainly not inexpensive, the rates are surprisingly competitive. 300 Gravier St. (phone: 523-6000 or 800-262-2662; fax: 596-9513). Expensive.

Cornstalk – This old Victorian home is surrounded by a New Orleans landmark — an elaborate wrought-iron fence with a cornstalk and pumpkin-vine motif. The interior is something of a landmark, too — a grand entrance hall and lobby with antique mirrors and crystal chandeliers. The 14 rooms feature four-poster beds, and you can take continental breakfast there, in the front gallery, or on the patio. The staff can be less than friendly at times. 915 Royal St. (phone: 523-1515; fax: 525-6651). Expensive to moderate.

LaMothe House – Surrounded by moss-draped oaks on the Boulevard Esplanade at the edge of the French Quarter, this 150-year-old double townhouse exudes Old World charm with elaborate late Victorian furnishings and ambience. Careful attention to detail is the hallmark here. The 11 rooms and 9 suites are furnished with period antiques. Room service is available for breakfast only. Also see *New*

106 NEW ORLEANS / Best in Town

Orleans's Best Hotels, DIVERSIONS. 621 Esplanade Ave. (phone: 947-1161 or 800-367-5858; fax: 943-6436). Expensive to moderate.

Bourbon Orleans – On a quiet block of the French Quarter, this 210-room hotel incorporates what was, from 1815 to the late 19th century, a ballroom for Creole ladies and gentlemen. Today it is certainly more luxurious, with its Queen Anne furniture, canopied king-size beds, marble baths, and crystal and brocade accents. The interior courtyard is relaxing, as is the intimate lounge. An outdoor pool and secretarial services are other pluses. 717 Orleans St. (phone: 523-2222 or 800-521-5338; fax: 525-8166). Moderate.

Dauphine Orleans – Almost hidden along one of the French Quarter's more residential streets is this well-run, 109-room establishment that blends modern conveniences with a reasonable amount of creole charm. Across the street is the *Dauphine Patios,* a small annex, with pleasant rooms opening onto a courtyard. Services include a complimentary newspaper, a fitness room, free parking, continental breakfast, and a lending library. The hotel also operates its own complimentary open-air jitney to transport guests around the Quarter and Central Business District. 415 Dauphine St. (phone: 586-1800 or 800-521-7111; fax: 586-1409). Moderate.

Doubletree New Orleans – When the small Doubletree chain took over this modern property several years ago, it transformed the once glitzy lobby into a more intimate space and added French country accents to the 363 rooms and 15 suites. The *Chicory Rotisserie and Grill* serves continental fare, and the hotel's location — near the Mississippi River, the *New Orleans Convention Center,* and the French Quarter — adds to its appeal. 300 Canal St. (phone: 581-1300 or 800-528-0444; fax: 522-4100). Moderate.

Holiday Inn Château LeMoyne – The fancier of the French Quarter's two links in the Holiday Inn chain, it is decked out in traditional New Orleans fashion: period wallpaper, baroque accents in the lobby, a swimming pool, and a courtyard. The 175 comfortable rooms, however, have a run-of-the-mill look about them. 301 Dauphine St. (phone: 581-1303 or 800-HOLIDAY; fax: 523-5709). Moderate.

Holiday Inn Crowne Plaza – The image of this internationally known chain was elevated a notch or two when this sleek-looking member was added. Convenient to the *New Orleans Convention Center* and the office towers of Poydras Streets, its 440 rooms are designed for comfort and efficiency; businesspeople will find communications equipment easily available. A restaurant, swimming pool, CNN, room service, and an exercise room are offered, too. 333 Poydras St. (phone: 525-9444 or 800-522-6963; fax: 581-7179). Moderate.

Maison Dupuy – Off the French Quarter's beaten track is this modern, handsomely turned out 4-story hostelry with a spectacular courtyard and meticulously maintained public spaces. The 195 rooms and suites are decorated in pastels and floral motifs; some suites have 3 bedrooms. *Le Bon Creole,* a colorful, casual restaurant and lounge, offers updated creole standards. 1001 Toulouse St. (phone: 586-8000 or 800-535-9177; fax: 525-5334). Moderate.

Monteleone – At the gateway to the Vieux Carré, this 600-room property maintains a friendly atmosphere while offering the amenities of a larger operation. There are a rooftop pool and bar; revolving lounge; formal dining at *Steaks Unlimited; Le Café,* a lobby-level coffee shop; an oyster bar; and a garage. Amenities include 24-hour room service, 6 meeting rooms, CNN, and concierge and secretarial services. 214 Royal St. (phone: 523-3341; fax: 561-5803). Moderate.

Le Pavillon – Eighteenth-century France was the obvious inspiration for this recently refurbished Poydras Street place. A pair of 20-foot-high Greco-Roman statues flank the driveway, and the lobby is filled with a profusion of crystal chandeliers, marble, and brocades. As we went to press, some of the 200 rooms

NEW ORLEANS / Best in Town 107

were still being redecorated, so be sure to ask for one of the newer accommodations. A rooftop swimming pool, a restaurant serving steaks, seafood, and chicken, and communications equipment for businesspeople are part of the draw. 833 Poydras St. (phone: 581-3111 or 800-535-9095; fax: 522-5543). Moderate.

Place d'Armes – A few steps from Jackson Square, nestled among the St. Ann Street shops, this functional but tastefully decorated hostelry has a lovely courtyard with a pool, fountains, magnolia and banana trees, and outdoor tables. There are 79 rooms and 8 suites in five 18th-century renovated buildings. The lobby is diminutive, however, but the place is comfortable and clean, and some rooms have balconies overlooking the Chartres Street corner of Jackson Square. Room service delivers a complimentary continental breakfast only (there is no restaurant on the premises), and 1 small meeting room holds 30 people. 625 St. Ann St. (phone: 524-4531). Moderate.

De la Poste – A recent top-to-bottom renovation has brought some new sparkle to the 92 rooms in this attractive, well-maintained motel, located on the reasonably quiet Chartres Street. Much of the ground-floor space is taken up by *Bacco* (see *Eating Out*), a large, beautifully decorated Italian restaurant opened in late 1991 by the Brennan family of New Orleans restaurateurs. Off the drive-through carriageway is a spacious and simply landscaped courtyard with a pool. 316 Chartres St. (phone: 581-1200 or 800-448-4927). Moderate.

Radisson – While in a prime location for *New Orleans Convention Center* activities, it's otherwise rather isolated — unless you're planning to spend lots of time in the Warehouse District and on the Riverfront. Made up of 253 one-, two-, and three-bedroom suites, this starkly modern hotel has an airy feeling, thanks to the large, glass atrium that forms the lobby. There is a restaurant on the premises. 315 Julia St. (phone: 525-1993; fax: 515-1993, ext. 4109). Moderate.

Soniat House – This remarkable pair of townhouses in a quieter section of the French Quarter has been beautifully restored, and everything possible has been done to reinforce the feeling of a gracious New Orleans of 150 years ago. This place is one of our very favorites. Guests are pampered and the close attention to detail is obvious in everything from the homegrown strawberry preserves made especially for the hotel to the faint scent of potpourri on the pure-cotton sheets. Each of the 24 one-of-a-kind rooms and suites is filled with antiques — many include canopied beds and Victorian love seats. A continental breakfast of hot biscuits and coffee (for a small additional charge) is served on the shaded patio, but there is no restaurant. There are also intimate rooms available in the former slave quarters in the courtyard. Reserve as far in advance as possible. Also see *New Orleans's Best Hotels*, DIVERSIONS. 1133 Chartres St. (phone: 522-0570 or 800-544-8808; fax: 522-7208). Moderate.

Columns – One of the city's most elegant and evocative stopping places, this 19-room inn offers a taste of the 19th century. It was a private Garden District home in 1883, and the large, unique rooms are furnished with period antiques. Its grand, freestanding stairwell and touches of Honduras mahogany give an atmosphere of opulent splendor. An additional point of interest is that Louis Malle filmed the notorious movie *Pretty Baby* here. The bar, serving such local appetizers as jambalaya and gumbo during happy hour, is considered one of the best around. *Albertine's*, the hotel's restaurant, is available only for private dining; 48 hours' notice is required. A continental breakfast is included in the room rate. Also see *New Orleans's Best Hotels*, DIVERSIONS. 3811 St. Charles Ave. (phone: 899-9308 or 800-445-9308). Moderate to inexpensive.

Provincial – A personal touch is also evident throughout this well-designed establishment on lower Chartres Street. A French-country look characterizes the guestrooms, many of which have canopied beds, old armoires, and floral fabrics. The

108 NEW ORLEANS / Best in Town

small bar and moderately priced *Honfleur* restaurant are especially picturesque, decorated with unpretentious antiques and old prints. There is no charge for children sharing rooms with adults. Convenient to the *French Market,* Jackson Square, and Decatur Street. 1024 Chartres St. (phone: 581-4995 or 800-535-7922; fax: 581-1018). Moderate to inexpensive.

Holiday Inn Downtown-Superdome – The drawing card at this convenient location is its complete renovation of the 300 guestrooms. The *John James Audubon Room* restaurant serves standard New Orleans fare, and the rooftop Olympic pool is a great perch for watching sunsets. Amenities include room service until midnight, a concierge desk, secretarial services, CNN, and 4 meeting rooms that hold up to 250. 330 Loyola Ave. (phone: 581-1600; fax: 586-0833). Moderate to inexpensive.

Quality Inn–Maison St. Charles – A few blocks from Lee Circle, this pretty complex of renovated buildings with 121 rooms and 11 suites has a touch of old New Orleans charm combined with up-to-date efficiency. On the premises is *Patout's* restaurant (see *Eating Out*), serving authentic Cajun dishes in handsome surroundings near the pool. Nonsmoking rooms available. The French Quarter and business district are a short ride away on the *St. Charles Streetcar.* 1319 St. Charles Ave. (phone: 522-0187 or 800-831-1783; fax: 525-2218). Moderate to inexpensive.

Le Richelieu – This 69-room hostelry on the fringes of the French Quarter was the place former *Beatle* Paul McCartney hung his hat when he came to town. Fans may be surprised at his rather modest taste. Still, the place does have its charms, such as kitchenettes in the 17 suites and, in many of the rooms, such old-fashioned touches as brass ceiling fans and pull-down ironing boards. There is a pleasant little restaurant overlooking the pool, and cheerful, efficient service. 1234 Chartres St. (phone: 529-2492 or 800-535-9653; fax: 524-8179). Moderate to inexpensive.

Ste. Helene – A carefully preserved historic building, this guesthouse has a courtyard pool and 3 floors with 16 rooms, 7 with balconies overlooking the pool or busy Chartres Street. Conveniently located 2 blocks from Jackson Square and the popular *Napoleon House* bar/restaurant, it features reproductions of 19th-century antiques; each room has a full bath, color TV set (with CNN), central air conditioning, and telephone. Room service is available for breakfast only. Continental breakfast is served near the lobby. Rates run the gamut, depending on the season. 508 Chartres St. (phone: 522-5014; fax: 523-7140). Moderate to inexpensive.

Château Motor Hotel – In a quieter part of the French Quarter, this attractive, serviceable hotel is for the traveler seeking comfort and convenience with a minimum of frills. Access from the small lobby to the 37 rooms and 5 suites is through a carriageway and patio. While the rooms are not luxurious, they're well maintained and pleasantly decorated. There is also a small restaurant and bar. Jackson Square is a short walk away. 1001 Chartres St. (phone: 524-9636). Inexpensive.

French Quarter Maisonettes – A converted Vieux Carré townhouse with a flagstone carriageway and spacious patio in the French Quarter, the inn is a quaint and friendly place to stay, with few frills (there is no restaurant, for example). Pets are allowed, and the proprietor offers touring suggestions. While the 7 suites and 1 double room have no phones, all have private baths and TV sets. The 2- or 3-room suites are neat and comfortable. And the neighborhood, almost entirely residential, is always serene. No credit cards accepted. Reservations must be made between 11 AM and 7 PM central time; be persistent, as they are somewhat erratic about answering their phone. 1130 Chartres St. (phone: 524-9918). Inexpensive.

Prytania Inns – This one's for budget-minded travelers who enjoy a homey atmosphere. Although it's located in the Lower Garden District, away from the urban hubbub, it's easily accessible to downtown. Made up of three former residences, the property is operated much like a bed and breakfast establishment. The tastefully appointed bedrooms and sitting rooms reflect the turn-of-the-century architecture of the handsome old buildings. Traditional creole breakfasts are served, and streetcars and buses are a short walk away. 1415 Prytania St. (phone: 566-1515; fax: 566-1518). Inexpensive.

 EATING OUT: Almost every block in New Orleans has one or more places to eat. Many are good; some are truly excellent. The distinctive regional cuisine — creole cooking — has been shaped through the years by the cultures of France, Spain, America, the West Indies, Native Americans, and African Americans. Seafood is king in creole recipes, and the nearby waters are filled with crab, shrimp, red snapper, flounder, Gulf pompano, and trout. Vegetables in season, fowl, veal, and fresh herbs and seasonings are culinary staples that add to the regional style that many consider a culinary art form. The newer restaurants are adding a multitude of variations to the traditional creole food canon, and are offering lighter dishes in keeping with contemporary preferences. The city's reputation as a trencherman's delight is strong, not only with out-of-towners but also with locals; for generations of New Orleanians, a couple of visits a week to a full-service eatery has been almost considered a birthright, whether the restaurant is one of the fancy creole palaces, the trendy contemporary bistros, or the neighborhood red-beans-and-rice joints. Expect to pay $80 or more for two at the places we've noted as expensive; between $50 and $80, moderate; and $50 or under, inexpensive. Prices include tax and tips, but not drinks or wine. Except where noted, *reservations are advised;* it is best to call ahead to confirm. All telephone numbers are in the 504 area code. Jackets for men are advised for many of the more expensive restaurants.

Andrea's – Italian regional cooking gets a classy continental veneer in this sprawling suburban dining place. Crystal, gilt, and plush carpets define the rather traditional atmosphere in a series of low-ceilinged dining rooms. Ingredients, especially the seafoods and pasta, are first class; and presentation usually is far above average. Favorites include fresh gulf fish baked in aromatic vegetables, and the quail, rabbit, and veal dishes, all done with chef Andrea Apuzzo's native Italian flair. Open daily. Major credit cards accepted. 3100 19th St., Metairie (phone: 834-8583). Expensive.

Antoine's – With a menu that reaches back more than 100 years, and a maze of rooms filled with enough memorabilia for two or three small museums, this place defines the classical creole style in New Orleans. The delicate butter sauces that grace the fish and shellfish are consistently satisfying. The recipe for oysters Rockefeller was invented here, and the presentation of the dish is still excellent. Other good bets are the cool and spicy shrimp rémoulade, crabmeat *ravigote* (crabmeat in a cold, spicy mayonaise), crawfish étouffée tournedos of beef, broiled pompano (a gulf fish similar to flounder) topped with sautéed lump crabmeat, and baked Alaska emblazoned with the date of the restaurant's founding — 1840. The quintessential French Quarter atmosphere is enchanting. Closed Mondays. Major credit cards accepted. 713 St. Louis St. (phone: 581-4422). Expensive.

Arnaud's – Old-style creole elegance fairly oozes from this glittery French Quarter establishment. An entire wall of the sparkling main dining room is made of antique glass, etched and leaded, reflecting the light from the delicate chandeliers hanging from the soaring ceiling. A profusion of other rooms, many used for banquets, fills the several buildings forming the large restaurant. Lunch is an especially good time to visit, since this is when the kitchen becomes more imaginative. At dinner, the reliable dishes include shrimp Arnaud (a superb version of rémoulade), oysters in cream, sautéed fish in various seasoned butter sauces, the airiest of soufflé potatoes, and bread pudding. *Café brûlot,* a creole version of coffee flambéed with brandy, orange, lemon, and spices, is prepared tableside for a showy finale. Open daily. Major credit cards accepted. 813 Bienville St. (phone: 523-5433). Expensive.

Begue's – Romantic and elegant, with a view of a lovely courtyard, this hotel dining

110 NEW ORLEANS / Best in Town

spot presents classic versions of creole and French fare. Appetizers include gulf shrimp rémoulade, Louisiana crabcakes, and smoked Norwegian salmon; entrées feature lobster (in season), steaks, roast guinea hen, and rack of lamb. Live piano music plays in the background Thursday, Friday, and Saturday evenings and during brunch on Sundays. Jacket required for dinner. Open daily. Major credit cards accepted. *Royal Sonesta Hotel,* 300 Bourbon St. (phone: 553-2278). Expensive.

Bella Luna – One of the most relaxing views of the Mississippi River you'll find in a New Orleans restaurant is from the dining room of this posh, second-floor establishment couched inside the *French Market* just steps from Jackson Square. Deep carpets and soothing gray walls define the mood in the main dining room, while the second one, surrounded by French doors and fan windows, takes on the look of a Viennese ballroom. While traditional Italian cooking is the principal inspiration for the menu, you'll also find flourishes of regional American, continental, and creole cooking in many of the dishes. The osso buco is a standout, as are the pasta, creative salads, and luscious desserts. Open Mondays through Saturdays for dinner only; brunch on Sundays. Major credit cards accepted. In the *French Market* complex near the corner of Decatur and Dumaine Sts. (phone: 529-1583). Expensive.

Brennan's – Fancy and festive breakfasts and brunches with a creole lavishness are what put this picturesque French Quarter restaurant on the map. Many of the luxurious dining rooms, in a beautiful, early-19th-century building, are done up in the high style of the period. Good views of the pretty, Spanish-colonial courtyard can be had from most of the tables. The bill of fare sticks fairly closely to classic creole with a fine gumbo, good fish dishes, and a profusion of butter and cream sauces. Poached eggs with elaborate and numerous embellishments can be ordered from morning to near midnight. *Brennan's* is not for the budget-minded at any hour, however. Open daily. Major credit cards accepted. 417 Royal St. (phone: 525-9711). Expensive.

Broussard's – Crystal and damask define the mood in this big, plush "old-line creole" establishment, whose menu combines French and New Orleans cooking. The main dining room, elegantly decorated in maroon and beige, is reminiscent of a European hotel dining room. Other rooms flanking the garden patio are more colorful, and just as fancy. Augmenting the traditional creole dishes are such comparatively nouvelle creations as a carpaccio of tuna with herbs, a seafood terrine, seared salmon with a gazpacho-like salsa, and fried eggplant topped with fried oysters in a rémoulade sauce. Also featured are such classic fare as turtle soup, oysters Rockefeller, and trout meunière. Open daily. Major credit cards accepted. 819 Conti St. (phone: 581-3866). Expensive.

Caribbean Room – The *Pontchartrain* hotel's exceptional dining room serves French and creole dishes. The menu is imaginative, and specialties are beautifully presented — trout Véronique (poached and topped with green grapes and hollandaise sauce), crabmeat Biarritz (lump crabmeat with whipped cream dressing and topped with caviar), and, if you can go the distance, Mile-High Ice Cream Pie for dessert. An elegant brunch is served Sunday mornings. Open weekdays for lunch; daily for dinner. Major credit cards accepted. 2031 St. Charles Ave. (phone: 524-0581). Expensive.

Commander's Palace – Few restaurants in the city can match this Garden District dining institution for combining the richness of mainstream creole cuisine, a festive atmosphere, and first-rate service. While the large menu concentrates on traditional New Orleans cooking, it also contains enough innovation to rival the most forward-looking of the city's restaurants. Among the headliners here are a definitive turtle soup, excellent rémoulades and gumbos, as well as very imaginative fish,

NEW ORLEANS / Best in Town   111

shellfish, and game dishes. The fried soft-shell crab is superb, as are the sautéed trout with pecans and the bread pudding soufflé. There are several dining rooms in this late-19th-century frame mansion, including the beautiful glass-walled, second-floor Garden Room overlooking the venerable oak trees in the garden below. Reservations necessary a week in advance for dinner. Open daily. Major credit cards accepted. 1403 Washington Ave. (phone: 899-8221). Expensive.

Emeril's – Almost from the night chef Emeril Lagasse opened this vibrant and original creole-American restaurant in the trendy Warehouse District, it has been one of the hottest tickets in town. The principal reason is the food — unusual combinations of ingredients and innovative preparation that enhance the deep flavors of the south Louisiana cuisine. Among the main attractions are an excellent version of New Orleans–style barbecue shrimp, an étouffée of duck with wild mushrooms, wonderful soups and salads, and belt-busting desserts that on some nights number more than a dozen. Since hard surfaces predominate in the decidedly contemporary-looking dining room (of brick, glass, and hard woods), the acoustics leave much to be desired. Reservations necessary a week in advance for dinner. Closed Sundays. Major credit cards accepted. 800 Tchoupitoulas St. (phone: 528-9393). Expensive.

Grill Room – Everything about this palatial restaurant — from the Lalique crystal table that stands in the entry to the fresh Japanese oysters — bespeaks money freely spent. The three dining rooms here are decorated with expensive English art, dramatic bronzes, rich fabrics, and more plush than you thought possible. But somehow it's not nearly as intimidating as you'd expect, even with the most precise service in town. And the menu, which changes daily at lunch and dinner, challenges the decor for refinement; a simple but excellent salad of lump crabmeat contrasts with seared foie gras, a glorious shrimp bisque, and Mediterranean rouget in a pesto sauce. And desserts are as spectacular in appearance as they are rewarding in taste. Open daily. Major credit cards accepted. *Windsor Court Hotel,* 300 Gravier St. (phone: 522-1992). Expensive.

Le Jardin – In a spacious setting 11 floors above the Mississippi River, this posh hotel dining room often fills up at midday on Sundays. The draw is a very generous brunch buffet, accompanied by a jazz combo, at a reasonable fixed price. The terrific view of the French Quarter and the river is another plus. At lunch and dinner, look for a wide array of top-of-the-line ingredients prepared with lots of finesse. Much of the food is a blend of the traditional and the contemporary. Seasonal dishes include grilled fish in a spicy butter sauce, a bisque of wild mushrooms with crabmeat, and soft-shell crabs fried in a batter spiked with Dixie beer, a local brew. Open daily. Major credit cards accepted. *Westin–Canal Place Hotel,* 100 Iberville St. (phone: 568-0155). Expensive.

K-Paul's Louisiana Kitchen – Chances are you'll have to cool your heels outside the door for an hour or more at dinnertime for a sampling of trailblazer Paul Prudhomme's creative Cajun dishes. Once inside the rather rudimentary dining room, you also may have to share a table with strangers. Still, legions of out-of-towners keep coming back for the Cajun guru's earthy gumbos, peppery étouffées, and fish — the ones that started the blackening craze almost a decade ago. Wiser customers come at lunch, when the line is shorter, the prices are lower, and the food is much the same as it is at dinner. Closed Saturdays and Sundays. No reservations. American Express only. 416 Chartres St. (phone: 942-7500). Expensive.

Kabby's – For a big hotel dining room, it does an above-average job of putting out authentic creole-style food, ranging from such down-home fare as po-boys (hearty French-bread sandwiches made with a variety of local ingredients) to more elaborate and upscale dishes like oysters Rockefeller and sautéed shrimp in anisette

112   NEW ORLEANS / Best in Town

liqueur. The crabmeat rémoulade, gumbos, and warm, fluffy bread pudding have valid New Orleans birth certificates, too. A big draw here is the close-up view of the Mississippi River; excursion boats and other craft often tie up in front of the place, just yards away from the window tables. Open daily. Major credit cards accepted. In the *New Orleans Hilton*'s Riverside complex, Poydras St. at the Mississippi River (phone: 584-3880). Expensive.

Louis XVI – French classicism reigns in these soft, elegant spaces flanking the exceptionally pleasant courtyard of a French Quarter hotel. Typical creations are shellfish in puff pastry with cream sauce, beefsteak in wine sauce with mushrooms, Caesar salad, and baroque desserts. The cream soups are especially good. Banks of arched windows and a warm color scheme add to the ambience. The service is very attentive, and there is a first class wine list. Open daily. Major credit cards accepted. *St. Louis Hotel,* 730 Bienville St. (phone: 581-7000). Expensive.

Pascal's Manale – While this Italian-creole eatery in the Uptown section is beginning to fray at the edges, it still pulls 'em in with a handful of signature dishes that first made its reputation. First among these is barbecued shrimp, baked in their shells with an herbal, spicy butter sauce. Pasta dishes are popular, too, especially those with seafood. The wait for a table is spent in a convivial oyster bar festooned with photos, posters, pennants, and memorabilia. Closed Sundays. Major credit cards accepted. 1838 Napoleon Ave. (phone: 895-4877). Expensive.

Rib Room – Lunch hour usually finds clusters of local business and professional types in this hotel dining room in the heart of the French Quarter. The lofty, brick-lined spaces are brightened considerably by a row of large fan windows along Royal Street. Offered here are familiar creole dishes, along with excellent roast beef, lamb, and pork cooked on a large, open rotisserie. Cuddly banquettes and fully cushioned armchairs make this an especially comfortable oasis from the Quarter's noise and bustle. Open daily. Major credit cards accepted. *Omni Royal Orleans Hotel,* 621 St. Louis St. (phone: 529-7045). Expensive.

Ruth's Chris Steak House – What makes this comfortable no-nonsense restaurant the city's leading purveyor of steaks is the quality of the beef, the exemplary charbroiling, and a distinctive seasoned butter that arrives sizzling on the plate. The formula has paid off in a chain of *Ruth's Chris* branches from Honolulu to Washington, DC. Hearty seafood appetizers, two-fisted salads, and excellent desserts are offered, too. Politicians pack the place almost nightly, but the dark-wooded dining rooms, lined with soothing paintings, are spacious. Service is far above average. Open daily. Major credit cards accepted. 711 N. Broad St. (phone: 486-0810). Expensive.

Sazerac – With a dining room as frilly as a dozen wedding cakes, this very upscale hotel restaurant is just the place for a romantic — if expensive — evening. White lace covers the red tablecloths, and a dramatic burst of flowers crowns a central cluster of red-velvet banquettes. A harpist plays as historical Louisiana personages gaze down from nearly life-size oil portraits lining the off-white walls. The menu, which seems to undergo a complete overhaul annually, is a combination of French, south Louisiana, and regional American cuisines. Foie gras, turtle soup, and fancied-up creole dishes are the mainstays, however. Open daily. Major credit cards accepted. *Fairmont Hotel,* University Pl. (phone: 529-4733). Expensive.

Veranda – On the second level of the *Inter-Continental* hotel, this meticulously maintained restaurant, decorated to resemble the dining rooms of elegant antebellum mansions, has a lush tropical garden within a glass-canopied atrium. Frequently on the lunch and dinner menus are seafood in imaginative sauces and top-quality meat done with flair. The braised veal shank and sautéed fish are especially good. Weekday lunches and fixed-priced Sunday brunch buffets are good buys for the quality and selection. Open daily. Major credit cards accepted. *Inter-Continental Hotel,* 444 St. Charles Ave. (phone: 525-5566). Expensive.

NEW ORLEANS / Best in Town   113

Versailles – Located on the fringe of the Garden District, proprietor/chef Gunter Preuss pairs European refinement and creole classicism. The main dining room overlooking St. Charles Avenue is plush. Meat and seafoods are of impeccable quality, and service is a pleasant combination of European precision and Southern congeniality. Among the signature dishes are a light but deep-flavored bouillabaisse, veal medallions in a rich brown sauce, a superb fillet of salmon Argenteuil, and a grand array of fancy desserts. While the atmosphere has a touch of the baroque, the mood is usually convivial. Closed Sundays. Major credit cards accepted. 2100 St. Charles Ave. (phone: 524-2535). Expensive.

Alex Patout's – Part creole, part Cajun, this upscale eatery on upper Royal Street is a good place to get familiar with south Louisiana's mainstream cuisine. You'll find rich gumbos, buttery seafood dishes, and robust duck and pork dishes on chef Alex Patout's bill of fare. The ambience in the deep, narrow dining room is upscale but very welcoming. Open daily. Major credit cards accepted. 221 Royal St. (phone: 525-7788). Expensive to moderate.

Bacco – Italian cooking was late in coming to New Orleans. This bright, beautifully decorated restaurant, the brainchild of the owners of *Mr. B's Bistro* (see below), fills the bill. The menu is ambitious, with dozens of choices among antipasti, pizza, pasta, and entrées including *papardelle* with a rabbit ragout, roasted pork loin in a rosemary sauce, hickory-smoked swordfish in a Mediterranean-style tomato sauce. Leave room for the chestnut dessert crêpes filled with ricotta cheese and topped with a chocolate cream. Decorative accents in the four dining rooms and bar were inspired by several eras, from the Gothic to the contemporary. Open daily. Major credit cards accepted. *Hotel de la Poste,* 310 Chartres St. (phone: 522-2426). Expensive to moderate.

Bayona – The setting is an ancient stucco cottage on a quiet French Quarter street, shaded by banana fronds and magnolia in a rear patio. The food, which combines Mediterranean robustness with contemporary American sophistication, is some of the best in town. The creative spirit behind it all is chef Susan Spicer, who calls her cooking "New World" cuisine. That's as good a term as any for such creations as small but thick medallions of lamb in a five-pepper brown sauce, fried oysters tossed with fresh spinach in a rosemary vinaigrette, or a casserole of artichoke hearts, polenta, and cream. The intimate, handsomely decorated dining rooms are similarly eclectic, with murals and photos depicting lush Mediterranean landscapes and gardens. Closed Sundays. Major credit cards accepted. 430 Dauphine St. (phone: 525-4455). Expensive to moderate.

Brigtsen's – After a couple of centuries south Louisiana cooking is still evolving, and chef Frank Brigtsen adds his brilliant improvisations to the school in this small and unpretentious restaurant in the Carrollton section. You'll find any number of offbeat ingredients in the food here, but everything retains the characteristic richness and depth of creole-Cajun flavor. Roasted, boned duck in pecan gravy is a tour de force, and the blackened tuna elevates that cooking process to new heights. The cream of oysters Rockefeller soup is better than the dish that inspired it. And the fresh ice creams and bread puddings are unsurpassed anywhere in the city. The setting is a small frame cottage just a few yards from the Mississippi River, where the mood is informal and friendly. Closed Sundays and Mondays. Major credit cards accepted. 723 Dante St. (phone: 861-7610). Expensive to moderate.

Christian's – The fact that a restaurant with this name inhabits a church building is purely happenstance. And there is nothing gimmicky about the food, which puts several new spins on the French-creole repertory. Seafood entrées, especially the bouillabaisse and sautéed fish, are standouts. A smoked soft-shell crab preparation adds a whole new dimension to this Louisiana delicacy. Even the beef filet, swathed in a winey and peppery brown sauce, is stuffed with oysters. Many of the dishes —

114 NEW ORLEANS / Best in Town

such as oysters *en brochette,* crabmeat *maison* and lamb chops béarnaise — are carbon copies of those at *Galatoire's* in the French Quarter (the proprietor is a member of the same family). Elbow room is at a minimum in the hyperactive dining room, designed with banquettes lining the walls, stained glass windows, and contemporary lighting fixtures hanging from the vaulted ceiling. Closed Sundays. Major credit cards accepted. 3835 Iberville St. (phone: 482-4924). Expensive to moderate.

Galatoire's – It's been around for almost 100 years, but this classic creole bistro has lost none of its glitter and spunk. Everything is in place in the single narrow dining room: snowy linen tablecloths, bentwood chairs, wraparound mirror panels, gleaming brass coat hooks, and chandeliers. Fitting right in are the definitively cool and spicy shrimp rémoulade, soul-warming eggplant stuffed with shrimp and crab, tender and subtle pompano with a sprinkle of crab lumps, lamb chops drenched in bearnaise sauce, and a huge array of other creole classics. Tuxedoed waiters dart around the narrow aisles, adding to the conviviality. Ask what's fresh and you'll dine royally. Drop in at off-hours and you may not have to wait outside for a table. Closed Mondays. No reservations or credit cards accepted. 209 Bourbon St. (phone: 525-2021). Expensive to moderate.

Gautreau's – There is a high level of sophistication in both food and atmosphere in this bistro situated in a tree-shaded residential Uptown neighborhood. The creative force behind the menu is chef Larkin Selman, who puts a New York spin on such familiar local ingredients as shrimp, crab, and crawfish. The season's menu might contain a terrific reinterpretation of seafood gumbo, along with succulent slices of guinea hen in sage sauce served with a prune-flavored risotto, and Key lime pie spiked with tequila. Crunchy soft-shell crab arrives under a canopy of matchstick potatoes, and salads are always as good as they are adventurous. The downstairs dining room, with its oxblood walls and drugstore-tile floors, is favored by locals. But the brighter, quieter room upstairs is recommended for those who prefer more elegant surroundings. Closed Sundays. Major credit cards accepted. 1728 Soniat St. (phone: 899-7397). Expensive to moderate.

Mike's on the Avenue – "Fusion cooking" (dishes influenced by a blend of many different cultures) has been around for years now, but chef-owner Michael Fennelly takes the concept to its limits in his smartly minimal restaurant in a revitalized old hotel on the edge of the Warehouse District. Fennelly draws inspiration from Japan, Thailand, China, the American Southwest, New Orleans, and any other part of the culinary map that strikes his fancy. The results on the plate are such concoctions as spring rolls filled with crawfish, a black-bean dip spiked with Cajun seasonings, a casserole of shrimp, mussels, and Cajun sausage, and sautéed cakes of crab and scallops with three sauces zapped with chilies. Somehow, it all works deliciously in the spare but beautiful, whitewashed dining rooms, bathed with light from wide glass walls and hung with the chef's own abstract-expressionist paintings. Reservations necessary a week in advance for dinner. Closed Sundays. Major credit cards accepted. *Lafayette Hotel,* 628 St. Charles Ave. (phone: 523-1709). Expensive to moderate.

Mr. B's Bistro – The pace is quick, but the style is laid-back in this classy contemporary bistro at the corner of Royal and Iberville Streets. The menu doesn't lack excitement, either, thanks to chef Gerard Maras's ceaseless improvising. There are terrific versions of gumbo, barbecue shrimp, bread pudding, and other creole standbys, plus less familiar fare — grilled fish in extraordinary sauces, imaginative pasta and pizza, hearty quail and rabbit dishes, and unusual salads. The low-ceilinged rooms, divided with wood and glass partitions, are rather dark, but the place has an energy about it. Service is excellently organized and affable. Open daily. Major credit cards accepted. 201 Royal St. (phone: 523-2078). Expensive to moderate.

NEW ORLEANS / Best in Town 115

Palace Café – Canal Street's restaurant scene got a powerful shot in the arm with the appearance of this sparkling new 2-level "grand café" in a building that once served as New Orleans's biggest music store. A carpeted mezzanine, brightened with a large mural depicting the city's legendary musicians, is reached by a central staircase. Both levels are lively during peak hours, when the bar fills up and things start to sizzle in the open kitchen. "Clever Creole" is the kitchen's style: rabbit ravioli in a Louisiana-style sauce piquante, a red-bean dip with the kitchen's own potato chips, a creamy "napoleon" of seafood, and a yummy white-chocolate bread pudding. Marble tabletops and stained-wood booths warm up the ambience. Open daily. Major credit cards accepted. 605 Canal St. (phone: 523-1661). Expensive to moderate.

Pelican Club – Innovative New Orleans cooking rose a couple of notches a couple of years ago with the appearance of this crisply stylish dining place located in a stately French Quarter townhouse. Proprietor/chef Richard Hughes's food combines New York dash with lots of Louisiana robustness. Examples are the appetizer of artichoke leaves filled with seared scallops in seasoned butter, a refreshingly simple salad of shellfish, unusual treatments of trout and gulf fish, and a seafood-and-rice creation that is part Louisiana jambalaya and part Spanish paella. Each of the three dining rooms has its own mood, from the clubby, wood-paneled room in the back to the warm, elegant space overlooking Bienville Street. Closed Sundays. Major credit cards accepted. 312 Exchange Alley at Bienville St. (phone: 523-1504). Expensive to moderate.

La Riviera – Many New Orleanians got their first taste of northern Italian cooking from this kitchen in suburban Metairie, where chef Goffredo Fraccaro still turns out soul-warming pasta in cream sauce, a delicately seasoned artichoke soup, imaginative fish dishes, and even spaghetti with meatballs in tomato sauce. The atmosphere is a pleasant combination of suburban American and colorful Italian. A horde of locals regularly fills the place, but the staff is equally attentive to out-of-towners. Closed Sundays. Major credit cards accepted. 4506 Shores Dr., Metairie (phone: 888-6238). Expensive to moderate.

Bayou Ridge Cafe – With more than a touch of the West Coast in its food, this sleekly handsome spot on the city's edge draws a legion of regulars. The biggest lure is a combination of lightness and flavor: Pasta and pizza are creative without being silly; a wood-burning stone oven produces succulent roasted salmon and chicken moistened with zesty vegetable sauces; the grilled shrimp rémoulade is a winner, as are the spinach-feta pizza and *crème brûlée*. The angular design of the dining rooms borders on the minimal, with mirrored panels, large framed photographs, and art on consignment adding a cheerful note. Closed Sundays. Major credit cards accepted. 5080 Pontchartrain Blvd. (phone: 486-0788). Moderate.

Bistro at Maison de Ville – This French Quarter spot continues to attract local and out-of-town regulars for its imaginative culinary approach, a blend of modern American and lusty Mediterranean. While the menu changes almost weekly, some things remain predictable — among them the light and herbal seafood soups, beef tournedos with boursin cheese in a subtle wine sauce, unusual pasta dishes, and first-rate *crème brûlée*. The tiny dining room, with lustrous wood paneling and a full-length maroon banquette, holds 40; the charming little courtyard out back is used in pleasant weather, too. Open daily; no lunch on Sundays. Major credit cards accepted. *Maison de Ville,* 733 Toulouse St. (phone: 528-9206). Moderate.

Bon Ton Café – A strong traditional streak runs through the menu in this rather old-fashioned, but always humming, creole-Cajun bistro at the Central Business District's core. Crawfish is perhaps the biggest seller, and the crawfish étouffée bisque, and jambalaya are well seasoned. Other popular dishes are the oyster omelette, bounteous cold crab salad, shrimp rémoulade, and dense, intense gumbos. Space is at a premium in the brick-lined dining room, with checkered table-

116 NEW ORLEANS / Best in Town

cloths and a cadre of energetic waitresses who keep things moving. Closed Saturdays and Sundays. Major credit cards accepted. 401 Magazine St. (phone: 524-3386). Moderate.

Chez Daniel – Add a dash of elegance to home-style French cooking and you have something akin to the menu offered at this lively and informal spot that's just a short drive across the city limits in Metairie. French-trained chef Daniel Bonnot has won over a small army of followers from the oak-shaded neighborhoods nearby. They come for his garlicky snails, endive salad, steak *au poivre,* grilled fish with fennel in *beurre blanc,* and *crème brûlée.* A large mural, inspired by the Belle Epoque, adds to the gaiety. Closed Sundays and Mondays. Major credit cards accepted. 2037 Metairie Rd., Metairie (phone: 837-6900). Moderate.

Chez Helene – This is the restaurant that inspired the "Frank's Place" TV series a few years ago. The resemblances, however, are minimal. The real thing is a small, crowded eatery, plain but proud, in a working class neighborhood off the beaten track. Fried chicken is a staple here, as are the meaty gumbos, creamy red beans and rice, collard greens, and corn bread. Snapshots and posters are the main decorative elements in the wood-paneled dining rooms, and the jukebox hardly ever rests. Open daily. Major credit cards accepted. 1540 N. Robertston St. (phone: 945-0444). Moderate.

Clancy's – If you're tired of the tourist track, consider this likable contemporary bistro deep within an Uptown residential section near the river. It has tuxedoed waiters, very good food, and a decor so simple it's almost nonexistent. The crab bisque and shrimp rémoulade are superb. Almost as good are the sautéed fish in cream sauce, sweetbreads with lemon and capers, lamb chops in béarnaise sauce, and home-style lemon icebox pie. There is a good wine list and the steward is exceptionally informed. Closed Sundays. Major credit cards accepted. 6100 Annunciation St. (phone: 895-1111). Moderate.

Dooky Chase's – The spirited cooking in this beautifully appointed establishment is traditional creole with a dash of Southern-style soul, the kind of nutrition that has fueled generations of New Orleanians. Chef Leah Chase's okra with tomatoes is definitive, as are her veal grillades, pork chops smothered with onions, crab soup, and bread pudding. The weekday luncheon buffets are justifiably popular. Just minutes from the French Quarter by taxi, the restaurant is handsomely done up with good-quality paintings and prints by local black artists. Service is exemplary. Open daily. Major credit cards accepted. 2301 Orleans Ave. (phone: 821-2294). Moderate.

Flagons – Oenophiles usually find a bounty of new releases with which to wash down the zesty contemporary dishes in this stylish Uptown wine bar and bistro. Gray walls, accented with maroon, and the latest paintings and prints by local artists define the ambience. Deftly grilled fish are one of the menu's strengths; others are pasta topped with shellfish in boldly seasoned sauces. Good desserts are the chocolate St. Emilion cake and *crème caramel.* Closed Sundays. Major credit cards accepted. 3222 Magazine St. (phone: 895-6471). Moderate.

G&E Courtyard Grill – The mood in this very pleasant place on bustling lower Decatur Street is always relaxed yet lively, thanks to the updated creole-Italian dishes and an atmosphere that combines old-fashioned Italian warmth with modern-day elegance. Proprietor/chef Michael Uddo's specialties include cream of oysters Rockefeller soup, zesty antipasto of crudités and cold cuts, grilled shrimp, and hearty pasta. In good weather, try for a table in the canopied courtyard, with its bubbly fountain, profusion of potted herbs, and always-sizzling outdoor rotisserie. Open daily; no dinner on Mondays. Major credit cards accepted. 1115 Decatur St. (phone: 528-9376). Moderate.

La Gauloise – Turn-of-the-century Paris is re-created at this cozy hotel dining room.

NEW ORLEANS / Best in Town   117

The menu includes traditional Gallic fare with a touch of local creole. The very reasonable fixed-price buffets at lunchtime and at night on weekends are popular with locals. The Sunday jazz buffet is especially pleasant. Open daily. Major credit cards accepted. *Meridien Hotel,* 614 Canal St. (phone: 527-6712). Moderate.

Kelsey's – Paul Prudhomme's kitchen has spawned any number of ambitious young chefs. One is Randy Barlow, who in mid-1991 opened this unassuming but attractive second-floor spot in Algiers, just across the Mississippi from central New Orleans. Barlow carves his own earthy, bold south Louisiana style with excellent gumbos, a superb shrimp stew, a terrific all-meat jambalaya, and any number of other creole-Cajun classics. The orange-poppyseed cheesecake is addictive, as are the bread pudding and other desserts. The pleasant dining spaces, with ample natural lighting from wraparound windows, are perked up with attractive paintings. Closed Sundays and Mondays; no lunch on Saturdays. Major credit cards accepted. 3920 Gen. DeGaulle Dr., Algiers (phone: 366-6722). Moderate.

Little Greek – Greek restaurants are mainstays in most port cities, but New Orleans · is the exception, with only this suburban establishment worthy of note. The deftly prepared food here is a real treat: The spreads and dips, especially *taramasalata* and *skordalia,* are deliciously authentic. Original creations include garlic sautéed fish in buttery phyllo dough and shrimp baked with olive oil, sherry, garlic, and lemon in a paprika sauce. Appropriately, the two colorful dining rooms and bar are hung with every sort of eastern Mediterranean artifact; the service is welcoming and efficient. Closed Mondays. Major credit cards accepted. 2051 Metairie Rd., Metairie (phone: 831-9470). Moderate.

Mandich's – What it lacks in chic it makes up for with an unusually good array of home-style classics, augmented with such upscale dishes as filet mignon and oysters Rockefeller, along with more basic fare such as white beans and rice, fried oysters with garlic butter, and buttery sautéed trout. About a 15-minute drive from the downtown hotels, its hours are quirky — lunch Tuesdays through Fridays and dinner Saturdays and Sundays. MasterCard accepted. 3200 St. Claude Ave. (phone: 947-9553). Moderate.

Mosca's – Not all of New Orleans's best restaurants are located inside the city limits. About a half hour's drive to the West Bank across the Mississippi River, via the Huey P. Long Bridge, this highway roadhouse in a rudimentary clapboard building serves the heartiest Italian-creole cuisine in the area. Everything on the moderate-size menu is a classic, but the most popular dishes are the baked oysters Mosca, Italian shrimp, roasted chicken with rosemary and garlic, and roasted sausage with potatoes. Closed Sundays and Mondays. No credit cards accepted. 4137 US Hwy. 90, Waggaman (phone: 436-9942). Moderate.

Patout's – The frilly look of this place may be a surprise since it is, after all, a Cajun-style restaurant. But the Patout family, originally from the bayou country, knows how to spice up the atmosphere with deep-flavored étouffées, robust game dishes, and all sorts of seafood concoctions. Among the better bets are the crab and corn bisque, crawfish étouffée, sauteed shrimp, and roasted duck. If supersweet desserts are your cup of tea, try the bountiful bread pudding. Open daily. Major credit cards accepted. In the *Quality Inn,* 1319 St. Charles Ave. (phone: 524-4054). Moderate.

La Provence – Another unprepossessing roadhouse, this one nestled in the piney woods of Lacombe, Louisiana, across Lake Pontchartrain, is the provence of Marseilles-born chef Chris Kerageogiu, who turns out exceptional, earthy Provençal dishes using local and regional ingredients. His quail gumbo, *jambalaya des gourmands,* rack of lamb, leg of rabbit, and fish dishes are among the best in the region. The atmosphere is reminiscent of a French country inn. Reservations advised. Closed Mondays and Tuesdays. Major credit cards accepted. About 35

118 NEW ORLEANS / Best in Town

miles from central New Orleans, on the north shore of Lake Pontchartrain on US Hwy. 190, Lacombe (phone: 626-7662). Moderate.

Upperline – In an unpretentious frame building in the Uptown section, chef Tom Cowman builds on a solid creole foundation with such novel, yet sensible, variations as crawfish tamales, sautéed gulf fish with pecans and garlic, a marvelously creamy hors d'oeuvre of trout mousse, and baked oysters topped with heavenly sauces. Salads, especially the endive and orange in ginger vinaigrette, are consistently good, as are the desserts. The latter include a fine Barbados rum trifle, coconut-banana cake, and silky lemon mousse. Closed Sundays. Major credit cards accepted. 1413 Upperline St. (phone: 891-9822). Moderate.

L'Economie – A short walk from the Warehouse District's cluster of art galleries, this place serves light fare with a distinctive French twist. A cement floor, white and dark green paint, and an occasional oil painting or houseplant sets the style. Proprietor/chef Hubert Sandot's culinary creations arrive on oversize white plates. The short, seasonal menu might offer hydroponically grown lettuce dabbed with lumps of crab in vinaigrette, subtly flavored shrimp with pasta, or a luscious salad of crawfish flavored with aniseed. No butter or cream is needed to enhance the natural flavors of the dishes. Closed Sundays. MasterCard and Visa accepted. 325 Girod St. (phone: 524-7405). Moderate to inexpensive.

Ralph & Kacoo's – Even with several locations in the French Quarter and in the suburbs, the tables fill up fast at this casual and very popular Cajun eatery. The Cajun theme is carried out with a full-size fishing boat in the bar and a jumble of nostalgic artifacts strewn everywhere. Freshness and consistency mark the extensive menu, with such dishes as a fine crab gumbo, trout meunière, fried shrimp or oysters, and good renderings of sautéed fish. No reservations. Open daily. Major credit cards accepted. 519 Toulouse St. (phone: 522-5226) and 601 Veterans Blvd., Metairie (phone: 831-3177). Moderate to inexpensive.

Alberto's – Slightly Bohemian and full of energetic pizzazz, this upstairs spot, a few blocks from the French Quarter, unusually good Italian food at reasonable prices. Any of the several cannelloni, especially the one with crawfish, is a good way to start. Shrimp with Pernod cream and fettuccine is fresh and flavorful, as are the sautéed soft-shell crab, and veal *panée*, a kind of breaded cutlet. The chef makes his own pasta, and it is all excellent. The decor is colorful and the mood is spontaneous. Dinner only. Closed Sundays. No reservations or credit cards accepted. 611 Frenchmen St. (phone: 949-5952). Inexpensive.

Bozo's – Dozens of neighborhood-style seafood restaurants around the city are run by Yugoslav Americans whose ancestors came to the city for the bountiful fishing. One of the best is this rather frenetic but very satisfying spot in the commercial heart of suburban Metairie. Oysters on the half shell are impeccable, and the fried oyster and shrimp po-boys have the right taste and crunch. Virtually everything else — stuffed crab, chopped steaks with onions, chicken gumbo, and cheesecake — is equally first-rate. Expect a wait for a table on weekend nights, and dress down. Reservations not accepted on Friday nights. Closed Sundays. Mastercard and Visa accepted. 3117 21st St., Metairie (phone: 831-8666). Inexpensive.

Casamento's – Cleanliness is an obsession in this legendary oyster house on upper Magazine Street. In fact, the gleaming white tiles give the two small dining spaces the look of a large bathroom. Oysters are the stars here, either fried and served without a trace of grease, freshly shucked and served up on the half shell, or served in a homey stew with milk and scallions. The shrimp and oyster "loaves," made with scooped-out white bread, are delicious. The rest of the menu is unimpressive. Closed Mondays. No reservations or credit cards accepted. 4330 Magazine St. (phone: 895-9761). Inexpensive.

Central Grocery Company – Its grocery store has been here since 1906 and still

NEW ORLEANS / Best in Town 119

stocks flour, beans, and other staples in barrels to sell by the pound. More popular, however, are the great take-out Italian sandwiches, cheeses, and salads. Open daily. No reservations or credit cards accepted. 923 Decatur St. (phone: 523-1620). Inexpensive.

China Blossom – Good Chinese-American restaurants are a rarity in New Orleans. This one, tucked away in a small shopping mall across the river, may be the best in town. Chef Paul Fung does a great job with shrimp and oysters, grilling or sautéeing them before adding marvelous piquant sauces. The pan-Chinese menu covers all the bases from egg rolls to fortune cookies, and it's all reliably good. Closed Mondàys. Reservations advised on weekends. Major credit cards accepted. 1801 Stumpf Blvd., Gretna (phone: 361-4598). Inexpensive.

Croissant D'Or – This small nook makes an excellent morning stop. Fresh French pastries are baked on the premises and are served with mugs of thick café au lait. Open daily. No reservations or credit cards accepted. 617 Ursulines St. (phone: 524-4663). Inexpensive.

Kung's Dynasty – A Greek Revival mansion in the Lower Garden District wouldn't be the first place you'd look for good Chinese food. But you'll find it here. Mandarin, Szechuan, and Cantonese cooking are all represented, in competently prepared dishes that sometimes show some originality. The atmosphere inside the lofty double parlors is unusually nice. Open daily. Reservations unnecessary. Major credit cards accepted. 1912 St. Charles Ave. (phone: 525-6669). Inexpensive.

Mandina's – Once upon a time, every New Orleans neighborhood had its own purveyor of po-boys, red beans, and spaghetti, with a room out back for family gatherings. Still thriving in the farther reaches of Canal Street, this place carries on the tradition faithfully. After a wait at the stand-up bar, sit at a Formica-topped table and dig into very good po-boys, garlicky cracked crab claws, butter-drenched trout meunière, or a creditable gumbo. Open daily. No reservations. No credit cards accepted. 3800 Canal St. (phone: 482-9179). Inexpensive.

Praline Connection – A couple of blocks beyond Esplanade Avenue near the Mississippi docks is this bright and bustling specialist in down-to-earth creole home cooking. Neat as a pin and always packed, the dining room, with an adjacent confectionery shop, is a fun place to sample first-rate versions of fried chicken, meat-stuffed peppers, corn bread, sweet potato pie, beans and rice, and a wide selection of other dishes deeply rooted in the city's food culture. After the succulent pork chops or grand chicken stew, try some of the authentic and luscious pecan pralines. Open daily. No reservations. Major credit cards accepted. 542 Frenchmen St. (phone: 943-3934). Inexpensive.

Taqueria Corona – Aficionados of tacos, nachos, and burritos will find exceptionally good renditions here. The state-of-the-art tortillas, either flour or corn, are filled with marinated meat or shrimp and the usual garnishes. But everything has fine flavor. Try the "tacocado" salad, a fried tortilla filled with guacamole, meat, lettuce, olives, and cheese. Seating is at both the counter and tables. Service is make-do. Open daily. No reservations or credit cards accepted. 857 Fulton St. and 5932 Magazine St. (phone: 897-3974 for both locations). Inexpensive.

■**BIG EASY FOOD FACTS:** Gumbo, a culinary essential of Louisiana life, is a thick, spicy soup based on seafood, poultry, sausage, duck, or any combination of these. No two cooks make it exactly alike. You'll find several especially good versions of it at three restaurants listed above: *K-Paul's Louisiana Kitchen* (416 Chartres St.; phone: 942-7500); the extra-thick "gumbo ya ya," with chicken and sausage, at *Mr. B's Bistro* (201 Royal St.; phone 523-2078); and seafood gumbo with okra in a light, well-seasoned broth at *Galatoire's* (209 Bourbon St.; phone: 525-2021).

120 NEW ORLEANS / Best in Town

Filé, a powder made by grinding sassafras leaves, is often used in gumbos as a thickener. *Gumbo filé* is difficult to find in New Orleans, but *Eddie's at Krauss* on the second floor of *Krauss* department store (1201 Canal St.; phone: 523-3311) and *Dooky Chase's* (2301 Orleans Ave.; phone: 821-2294) both serve good versions of it.

A traditional Acadian-creole dish served all over town is étouffée ("smothered" in French), a thick stew that was once made exclusively with crawfish but now sometimes features shrimp or other seafood cooked in a covered black iron pot. Some good places to sample it are *Alex Patout's* (221 Royal St.; phone: 525-7788), *K-Paul's Louisiana Kitchen* (416 Chartres St.; phone: 942-7500), and *Patout's* (1319 St. Charles Ave.; phone: 524-4054).

Po-boys, two-fisted sandwiches of thick French bread, slit open and filled with meat, seafood, and vegetables, is a New Orleans staple. Fried shrimp or oysters, ham, hot roast beef with gravy, and meatballs and tomato sauce are just some of the variations. Order your po-boy "dressed" and it'll come with lettuce, tomato, and mayonnaise. Best bets are the fried shrimp po-boy at *Acme Seafood and Oyster House* (724 Iberville St.; phone: 522-5973); roast beef or ham po-boy at *Mother's* (401 Poydras St.; phone: 523-9656); and the fried-oyster "loaf" at *Casamento's* (4330 Magazine St.; phone: 895-9761).

Another hearty sandwich is the muffuletta — round, crusty bread stuffed with ham, salami, mozzarrella, and salad of pickled green olive and pimentoes. The best and most authentic, for about $4 or $5 a quarter loaf, are found at *Progress Grocery* (915 Decatur St.; phone: 525-6627) and *Central Grocery* (923 Decatur St.; phone: 523-1620).

And last, but far from least, beignets, those sweet, square-shaped doughnuts, sprinkled with powdered sugar, are the perfect complement to New Orleans–style chicory coffee. Get the best of both at *Café du Monde* (813 Decatur St.; phone: 581-2914) and *Café Beignet* (620 Decatur St.; phone: 566-1225).

DIVERSIONS

For the Experience

Quintessential New Orleans

Romance, mystery, and an almost palpable sense of the past constantly converge in New Orleans. Peek through the wrought-iron gate of a French Quarter carriageway, beyond the cobblestones and into the verdant courtyard, and imagine what plots might have been hatched or what loves might have been consummated 100 years ago. From a table at *Antoine's,* watch a couple walk through the cavernous, neo-Gothic dining room into a labyrinth of inner sanctums. Who are they? What might they be up to? In New Orleans, the possibilities are endless. With such a beautiful and timeless setting, your imagination is stimulated at every turn, heightened by the sound of a jazz trumpet coming from who knows where, the perfume of blossoming sweet olive in the early spring, the pungent taste of a creole remoulade sauce, the arresting beauty of a black iron-lace balcony against tarnished stucco. If all of this seems unreal, that's as it should be — in New Orleans, reality is always put on hold until the final song is sung and the last drop of wine consumed.

MARDI GRAS: When you think New Orleans, you think *Mardi Gras.* Choreographed parades and well-planned, fancy balls are the raison d'être of this celebration, but what makes *Mardi Gras* truly great happens spontaneously, unpredictably, and wildly — serendipitous moments that are the real magic of this more-than-a-century-old celebration. On one corner of the French Quarter, a high school linebacker and a primly dressed woman, probably old enough to be his grandmother, strangers only seconds ago, dance a makeshift jitterbug; down the block, a family of four dressed as clowns try to catch beaded necklaces being thrown from a balcony by some outrageously cross-dressed transvestites; on St. Charles Avenue, a senior partner in a Denver law firm finds himself scrambling on a curb in a good-humored contest with a 12-year-old kid for a 10¢ trinket tossed from a parade float. Meanwhile, on Canal Street, Pete Fountain's celebrated clarinet calls the tune as his *Half-Fast* (and half-sober) *Marching Club* wends its way through a hip-to-haunch crowd without missing a beat. Multiply such vignettes by about 50,000 and the product is *Mardi Gras,* a magical day when reason sleeps and the real ties that bind are forged moment by moment. It's the day when an accountant from Akron can be Sir Lancelot, and a waitress from Seattle can fulfill her lifelong dream to be Marilyn Monroe, if only for a few hours. It's a day that reaffirms, finally, that underneath the costumes and greasepaint, all of us are the same. (For more information on the festivities, see "Mardi Gras Madness" in *For the Mind.*)

JAZZFEST: No single event captures the essence of New Orleans as vibrantly as does the *New Orleans Jazz and Heritage Festival.* Held each year in late April and early May, *Jazzfest* celebrates the city's two great obsessions — music and food. Outdoors, indoors, on water and on land, more than 4,000 musicians and hundreds of cooks and artisans ply their musical, culinary, and artistic genius. Several concerts a night take place in music halls and nightclubs and on riverboats. The real blowout comes on the 3-day weekends that begin and end the festival. Almost filling the huge inner green-

124 DIVERSIONS / Quintessential New Orleans

sward of the *New Orleans Fair Grounds* racetrack, on a dozen bandstands and in oversize tents, jazz and folk musicians from New Orleans and around the country and the world make music from morning to sunset. There are scores of booths offering soul-warming jambalaya, alligator sauce piquante, po-boy sandwiches, and other Big Easy specialties. Regional artisans display a colorful variety of carvings, pottery, textiles, and paintings. Festivalgoers sprawl on whatever slice of turf they can find and down spicy crawfish étouffée while taking in every note of a down-and-dirty blues band, an African folk troupe, or a group of Swedes delivering hot Dixieland licks. The huge Gospel Tent throbs nonstop with the wails and shouts of local church choirs. Happily, the sound of *Jazzfest* will linger with you long after you leave here. Just listen to a recording of Louis Armstrong playing "The Birth of the Blues"; you can recapture the experience — and perhaps make plans to return next year.

AND ALL THAT JAZZ: Veteran banjoist Danny Barker claims that jazz sounds best in New Orleans because the city's pervasive high humidity endows the music with unique acoustical qualities. Sit for an hour or two in the *Palm Court Jazz Café* on Decatur Street listening to Barker play in his vintage style and you're not likely to argue the point. Or amble up a few blocks to the ramshackle *Preservation Hall,* take in a set by the *Olympia Brass Band,* and you might begin to wonder if mildewed old brick produces a similar effect on the quality of the music. Jazz has traveled the world many times over, but this is its hometown and remains its natural habitat. Where else but on the seedy edge of the New Orleans waterfront could a place like *Tipitina's* exist? Born many decades ago as a neighborhood restaurant and bar, its creaky wood frame now throbs every night till the wee hours with wailing, tooting, and plunking, priming the dance floor and urging the assembled crowd into a near-frenzy. Singer and percussionist Aaron Neville frequently appears here with his brothers, along with blues divas Irma Thomas and Marva Wright — not to mention any good band passing through town. Cooler heads prevail at *Snug Harbor,* in the Faubourg Marigny, a couple of blocks from the French Quarter. In a cramped, unadorned room out back, such masters of the "New Orleans Sound" as singers Charmaine Neville and Germaine Bazzle perform. Another regular is Ellis Marsalis, the most inventive contemporary jazz pianist the city has seen in decades and patriarch of the wondrous, musical Marsalis family (see "Nightclubs and Nightlife," THE CITY, for all of the above). Some say the special sound of New Orleans jazz is created by the city's incredibly high humidity — but we think incredible talent has something to do with it, too.

BEIGNETS AND COFFEE AT CAFÉ DU MONDE: Everybody comes to the *Café du Monde* — hard-core partygoers at dawn trying to sober up for the drive home; well-dressed matrons giving their feet a midday rest; a family from the Midwest, rosy-cheeked and sleepy-eyed at mid-morning, here to find out what a beignet is and how to pronounce it (ben-*yay*). A puffed-up square of rather chewy fried dough that you sprinkle with powdered sugar from the shaker on the table, it's also the ideal accompaniment to a steamy cup or two of café au lait New Orleans–style — half hot milk, half jet-black coffee brewed with a tad of ground, roasted chicory root. With stunning views of Jackson Square, Decatur Street, and the pavilion overlooking the Mississippi River framed by huge stucco arches, this is the best place to relax and watch the world go by. On cold days, dark-green vertical awnings are raised and the inside room fills up fast. The café is the gateway to the old *French Market,* made up of ancient colonnaded buildings extending several blocks along the river. Even though it is open 24 hours a day, every day except *Christmas,* getting a seat at one of the café's dozens of rudimentary tables usually involves a wait — but the unabashedly old-fashioned charm of the place is worth every minute.

PRALINES: Pralines (pronounced *prah*-leen, not *pray*-leen) are almost as old as New Orleans itself. Aproned women once peddled them from huge baskets all over town. Today they're sold in more than a dozen shops in the French Quarter. As sweet

DIVERSIONS / Quintessential New Orleans 125

confections go, the traditional creole praline is the soul of simplicity: Sugar is cooked down with butter, sometimes with a tad of milk and a sprinkle of the native pecan, to become a crisp candy wafer. Purists insist that they be eaten as soon as possible after cooling and disdain the recent additions of such things as vanilla, chocolate, coconut, and food coloring. For a taste of the real thing, begin at the *Old Town Praline Shop* (627 Royal St.; phone: 504-525-1413), where these down-home, slightly buttery candies have been sold for decades. Wrapped in old-fashioned waxed paper, they can be bought one at a time for a quick snack on the little patio just outside or packed in quaint little boxes, which can be shipped anywhere you wish. *Aunt Sally's Original Creole Pralines* in the *French Market* (810 Decatur St.; phone: 504-524-5107) adds a touch of vanilla to the pecan flavor of the basic praline. Just outside the Quarter, on the other side of Esplanade Avenue, is the *Praline Connection* (542 Frenchmen St.; phone: 504-943-3934), a restaurant and confectionery that specializes in all kinds of pralines, from traditional sugar-and-pecan blend to chocolate and coconut varieties, as well as a delicious praline cookie. In the adjoining dining room, you can get a slice of cheesecake with praline sauce poured on top. Yum!

BOURBON STREET: Synonymous with boisterous, bawdy exploits, it's 8 blocks crammed with strip joints, naughty novelty shops, jazz clubs, and emporia offering transvestite shows and pornographic paraphernalia. The elegant buildings here, once inhabited by aristocratic Creole families, now house raunchy activities that would make their ghosts blush. Bourbon Street began its evolution into the Bible Belt equivalent of Sodom and Gomorrah in 1917, not long after the federal government shut down the legendary bordellos of Storyville, just a few blocks away. Everything happens here — street performers dance to the music pouring from the nightclubs and hustle dollar bills; barkers hawk the feminine charms of the performers inside (sometimes failing to mention that the star's real name is Ralph). If you think Bourbon Street is just another Tenderloin district, check it out after a football game in the *Superdome,* when half the fans are indulging in some postgame high jinks. Since it's legal to drink on the streets of New Orleans if you use plastic containers, parties can pop up anywhere. Both sides of the block are crammed with places where you can get any kind of cocktail imaginable (don't forget that New Orleans's bartenders invented a couple themselves — the Hurricane and the Absinthe Frappe), all designed to put you in a merry mood as you stroll down one of the arteries of the fun-loving Big Easy. But with all the activity, real life does go on here — keep an eye out for couples pushing babies in perambulators, and don't forget to tip your hat at the house with the pale blue shutters in the 600 block, the full-time residence of retired Congresswoman Lindy Boggs, hardly the typical denizen of this naughty neighborhood.

JAZZ BRUNCH AT COMMANDER'S PALACE: A late-morning feast on a Saturday or Sunday, accompanied by a small jazz ensemble playing favorite tunes as it weaves its way around the tables, has become a New Orleans ritual. Every major restaurant does it, but Ella and Dick Brennan, proprietors of *Commander's Palace* in the Garden District, do it better than anybody else. The several settings in the big frame mansion are ideal — in the understated main dining room, brightly colored balloons sprout from the tables like bouquets as waiters weave their way around table-hopping locals catching up on the latest gossip. Upstairs in the Garden Room, floor-to-ceiling windows on both sides look out over gigantic old oaks. The bright green and yellow walls and cushioned garden furniture give the sense of eternal spring. If the appropriate gods aren't angry, the day will be balmy enough to get a seat outside in the pavilion hung with lush tropical plants and shaded by giant oaks. Truth be known, the food suffers by comparison to the more sumptuous fare served at dinner (brunch prices are geared to filling the seats), but it's still good. The starter of sautéed shrimp with mushrooms is wonderful; the elaborate poached-egg dishes, drenched in buttery sauces, are nothing to be ashamed of. And the bread pudding soufflé is addictive. In any case, an icily invigorating milk punch or Bloody Mary can endow eggs with the flavor of nectar and transform a simple tune like "Do You Know What It Means to Miss New Orleans" into a piece worthy of Mozart. Don't be surprised if the waiters occasionally gather around a table and sing "Happy Birthday." Schmaltzy? Certainly. Cheering? You bet. The infectious conviviality of a *Commander's* jazz brunch just may convince you it's your birthday, too.

THE GARDEN DISTRICT: This neighborhood, a sterling example of Protestant sobriety and tranquil beauty located within the same square mile as the wild, hedonistic Bourbon Street, presents yet another face of New Orleans. Unlike the French Quarter, the Garden District is not at all a "people place." Walk in the cooling shade of its majestic oaks, the sidewalks buckling above the trees' unyielding roots, and you're not likely to encounter many strollers. This is a place much more suited to contemplation than celebration, unless it's to revel in the incredible lushness of its vegetation and its 19th-century domestic architecture. The houses in this residential neighborhood come in a stunning array of styles — imposing Greek Revival, intricate neo-Gothic, and any other hybrid that struck the fancy of the local architects of the time. The neighborhood's integrity has remained remarkably intact. Take away the parked automobiles and the asphalt under them and you have an upper class town of the mid-19th century — which is precisely what the Garden District was. The town fathers were enterprising merchants, shippers, and lawyers, mostly of English and Scottish descent, whose wealth accumulated quickly in the glory days of New Orleans's river commerce. The air that lingers there today combines the seductive aromas of jasmine and magnolia with the faint scent of old money.

The area is especially beautiful in early spring, when the profusion of fuchsias and pink azaleas seem to make the stately white houses seem even more pristine, and the majestic trees and well-tended lawns even greener. The effect is much like strolling through an aristocratic old European colony on a Caribbean island — only better.

NEW ORLEANS NOEL: Celebrating *Christmas* in the romantic, historic French Quarter is yet another of New Orleans's delightful happenings. In early December, the city dresses up in all its finery; garlands of pine and holly tied with big red bows make their appearance on the iron-lace balconies along Royal and Chartres Streets, as this old historic district, with its elegant creole houses, gets ready to celebrate *Creole Christmas,* an annual festival organized by the *French Quarter Festival* (phone: 504-522-5730) that recaptures the holiday season as it was celebrated by the Creoles in the 19th century. For several weeks, historic homes like the Hermann-Grima House and Gallier House are decked out in heirloom decorations, and traditional creole delicacies are served in period porcelain and crystal serving dishes in elegant dining rooms. Carols are sung in Jackson Square, where the annual tree lighting takes place. More than a score of restaurants in the Quarter offer fixed-price menus replicating the *reveillons,* the elaborate feasts held by the early French inhabitants when they returned from midnight mass at St. Louis Cathedral. Tours of private homes decorated in the style of the 19th century are given. *Joyeux Noël!*

New Orleans's Best Hotels

What distinguishes the best hotels from the merely adequate in New Orleans is not only the quality of the service or the lavishness of the decor, but a sense of style. Most hoteliers try to bring a feel for the city's culture and its love of beauty to their establishments, and those that succeed do so subtly and gracefully. Food served in hotel dining rooms, for instance, must pay tribute to the city's proud culinary heritage; service should not be just efficient, but should reflect the

DIVERSIONS / Best Hotels   127

best traditions of Southern hospitality. The atmosphere should be elegant but not intimidating. All of these qualities help to distinguish the hotels in the list below.

COLUMNS: Listed on the National Register of Historic Places, the unusual 19-room hotel where director Louis Malle filmed Brooke Shields's notorious film *Pretty Baby* has become no less than one of New Orleans's most evocative stopping places. In the Garden District, with the *St. Charles* streetcar passing its front door, it started out in 1883 as a wealthy tobacco merchant's home, became a boardinghouse in 1914, and was transformed into a hotel in the 1940s. Now it has a kind of luscious decadent splendor, from its Victorian lounge and ballroom-restaurant to its grand, freestanding stairwell and its abundant touches of Honduras mahogany; its bar is considered one of the city's best. Information: *Columns Hotel,* 3811 St. Charles Ave., New Orleans, LA 70115 (phone: 504-899-9308 or 800-445-9308).

INTER-CONTINENTAL: Though this very modern and efficient establishment caters most specifically to business executives, it draws all those who appreciate all-around quality. The lustrous wood-paneled mezzanine lobby is decorated with striking works by contemporary New Orleans artists, and is further brightened by the fresh flowers lining the 'escalator leading from the driveway to the registration desk. *Veranda,* a dramatic dining room with a lofty glass ceiling and lush greenery, serves continental fare created by celebrated New Orleans chef Willy Coln. Among the 482 guestrooms are several suites luxuriously decorated in 19th-century Louisiana style with antique furniture, canopied beds, and prints and fabrics reflecting that bygone era. Even the standard rooms are well appointed, featuring peach or sea foam–green walls and pastel floral fabrics. The rooms are equipped with mini-bars and dressing alcoves containing telephones and small TV sets. There is butler service on the executive floor and 24-hour room service; on the top floor are a health club and pool. Located at the corner of St. Charles Avenue and Poydras Street, it is steps away from both the business district and the Mississippi Riverfront. During *Carnival,* guests are treated to an ideal view of the pageantry as many parades pass by. Information: *Hotel Inter-Continental,* 444 St. Charles Ave., New Orleans, LA 70130-3171 (phone: 504-525-5566 or 800-327-0200).

LaMOTHE HOUSE: Built in the early 1800s by a successful planter named Jean LaMothe, this exquisite early New Orleans townhouse is a delightful place to call home while visiting the Big Easy. From the stately foyer to the lushly planted courtyard and throughout the elegantly antiques-furnished establishment, you can't help but find yourself transported to the city's earlier, gentler days. But you won't find the discomforts: All of the 20 rooms and suites are air conditioned, and each has a private bath, a color TV set, and a phone. Continental breakfast, the only meal served, is always an event: Everyone sits at a long banquet table and lingers over chicory coffee. The inn is in the French Quarter, very close to the jazz, good food, and intriguing shops. Information: *LaMothe House,* 621 Esplanade Ave., New Orleans, LA 70116 (phone: 504-947-1161 or 800-367-5858).

MAISON DE VILLE: This gem of a hotel in the heart of the French Quarter offers a choice of accommodations: In the maison — where Tennessee Williams did his final draft of *Streetcar* — there are 16 magnificent antiques-furnished rooms and suites with balconies and street or courtyard views; out back, there are the remodeled slave quarters (ca. 1742). And then, a stroll away on Dauphine Street, are the 7 delightful *Audubon Cottages,* where John James Audubon lived and worked in 1821. Built in the creole brick-and-post style (something like the old European half-timbered buildings), the cottages have perhaps the most elegant rooms of all, with luxuriously furnished bedrooms, kitchens with stocked refrigerators, and private gardens. The entire *maison* stands out, however, for the service: Tables in restaurants and space on sightseeing tours are booked by an omniscient concierge; shoes left outside your door are shined; a classic French breakfast is served on a silver tray, along with copies of *USA Today*

128 DIVERSIONS / Best Hotels

and the *Wall Street Journal* — and a rose. And when you return after a night on the town, you find a chocolate on your pillow. Enjoy casual dining and conversation at *The Bistro.* Information: *Maison de Ville,* 727 Toulouse St., New Orleans, LA 70130 (phone: 504-561-5858 or 800-634-1600).

LE MERIDIEN: This classy, sleek member of the French chain has become a major presence on Canal Street's hotel row. The plush, marble lobby is dominated by a spectacular geometrically shaped chandelier that casts a soft glow on the muted tones of the carpeting, walls, and comfortable furniture. Beyond the lobby, *Jazz Meridien* is a marble-and-wood bar where traditional jazz bands play nightly, adding a sassy energy to the atmosphere. *La Gauloise,* a bistro-style restaurant, borrows the look of turn-of-the-century Paris and serves excellent buffets featuring creole and French dishes. Chic understatement characterizes the look of the 497 guestrooms and 5 bi-level suites, all tastefully decorated in either beige, green, or pink. An entire floor is reserved for nonsmokers. To soothe travel-weary muscles, guests can order a massage in the fully equipped penthouse health club. The impressive services for businesspeople include translators and a full communications setup. Information: *Le Meridien,* 614 Canal St., New Orleans, LA 70130 (phone: 504-525-6500 or 800-543-4300).

NEW ORLEANS HILTON: The Mississippi River is almost at the doorstep of this immense and impressive link in the Hilton chain that seems to have something for everyone. The immense and lavish multilevel lobby, which connects directly to the *Riverwalk* shopping mall, is lavish and luxuriously appointed, with lustrous marble floors and polished wood walls decorated with paintings by some of the country's most respected artists. Located here is *Pete Fountain's,* a nightclub where some of the city's top musicians perform, including Fountain himself, and gospel singer Marva Wright holds forth during the Sunday jazz brunch buffet in the *Café Bromeliad.* At *Kabby's,* diners get not only a dramatic, close-up view of the Mississippi, but also the authentic creole-Cajun cookery of native chef Stanley Jackson. The 41 meeting rooms contain 127,000 square feet of space for conferences and exhibitions. The state-of-the-art *Racquet and Health Club* has 11 tennis courts — 8 indoor and 3 outdoor — as well as 2 squash courts and 1 basketball court. All of the 1,602 guestrooms are soundproofed, and children occupying their parents' room stay free. Information: *New Orleans Hilton,* 2 Poydras St., New Orleans, LA 70140 (phone: 504-561-0500 or 800-HILTONS).

SONIAT HOUSE: No hostelry in New Orleans captures the city's romantic charm and Old Southern gentility quite like this place. Proprietors Rodney and Frances Smith refurbished 2 balconied, early-19th-century creole townhouses in the tranquil lower French Quarter and furnished them with stunning period antiques and exquisite paintings and objets d'art. Each of the 16 elegant and comfortable rooms and 8 suites in the main houses and rear slave quarters is unique, with canopied beds in the larger rooms. A breakfast of orange juice, biscuits with homemade strawberry preserves, and New Orleans chicory coffee is served in the inner courtyard, shaded by aromatic tropical trees and plants. Service has a distinctly personal touch: In the downstairs sitting room a home-style bar operates on the honor system — guests who return after-hours can pour their own drinks and leave a check at the desk; umbrellas are available on request; and the Smiths, avid restaurant patrons, can recommend dining spots tailored to individual preferences. No wonder many guests feel as though they're visiting friends who happen to live in one of the city's most tasteful old residences. Information: *Soniat House,* 1133 Chartres St., New Orleans, LA 70116 (phone: 504-522-0570 or 800-544-8808).

WESTIN–CANAL PLACE: Although the entrance may be unassuming, this hotel located near the French Quarter, Canal Street, and the Mississippi River is as modern and plush as they come. What makes it unique is the view from its 11th-floor lobby — a panorama that takes in the French Quarter and the river as it begins forming its famous crescent. The vast pale wood–and–marble lobby is richly decorated with cushy

DIVERSIONS / Best Eats 129

armchairs, antiques, and thick rugs. The glistening marble bar off the lobby — known simply as the *Bar* — is a wonderful place to stop for a drink. Beyond the lobby proper is *Le Jardin,* an elegant restaurant and bar, which offers contemporary creole cuisine; it's also an ideal setting for either coffee and croissants in the morning or a cognac after dinner. Most of the 438 spacious rooms and suites, decorated in pastels and accented with prints of the French Quarter, have views of the river. All contain mini-bars and such extras as Caswell & Massey soaps and toiletries. There are special nonsmoking rooms and rooms equipped for the handicapped. Information: *Westin–Canal Place Hotel,* 100 Iberville St., New Orleans, LA 70130 (phone: 504-566-7006 or 800-228-3000).

WINDSOR COURT: The handsome, secluded driveway is an indication of the pleasures that lie within, and indeed this impeccably furnished hotel doesn't disappoint. Delicate Oriental figurines rest in glistening antique cases, sprays of cymbidium orchids crown massive marble tables, and 4 centuries of art — oil paintings, sculpture, tapestries, and antique furniture — decorate the ground-floor lobby and public rooms. Of the 310 rooms, about 250 are suites with separate living rooms, dressing rooms, and kitchenettes or wet bars. All of the guestrooms have private balconies or bay windows, Italian marble bathrooms, and three telephones equipped with two incoming lines. The spacious rooms are decorated with luxurious fabrics in traditional prints, dark-stained traditional furniture, and thick carpeting. There are 55 2-bedroom suites and 2 spectacular penthouse suites on the 22nd floor, each of which includes a library and a large, landscaped terrace overlooking the Mississippi; the hotel also has 15 rooms equipped for the handicapped. In *Le Salon,* a string quartet plays as guests sit among the palms and munch on scones and cucumber sandwiches served at afternoon tea. The elegant *Grill Room* features such delicacies as fresh oysters on the half shell flown in from Japan, Breton sardines, or Sonoma lamb. As you'd expect, there is 24-hour room service, a multilingual staff, secretarial services, an Olympic-size pool, and a fully equipped health club. The location, near Canal Street and the Mississippi Riverfront, is another plus. Information: *Windsor Court Hotel,* 300 Gravier St., New Orleans, LA 70140 (phone: 504-523-6000 or 800-262-2662).

Big Easy's Best Eats

The natives of this city have always looked on good food as a birthright, whether the matter at hand be a delicately composed cream sauce, a hearty dish of ham-flavored red beans and rice, or the newest variation on jambalaya to come out of a trendy bistro. Gastronomy is embedded in the New Orleans consciousness, and some of the more traditional dishes — like gumbo and jambalaya — date back almost 2 centuries. Creole cookery is a sophisticated, ever-evolving cross-fertilization of many cultural styles and tastes. The city's earliest French, Spanish, African, and Caribbean cooks created unique dishes by using their own techniques and spices to prepare the region's rich supply of seafood, game, and produce. Throw in Acadian (also known as Cajun) cooking, the boldly flavored peasant-style dishes developed by people from the backwater region of southern Louisiana, and it's easy to see why the food in this city is a passion and a constant source of inspiration to the scores of celebrated chefs who practice their art here today.

Choosing New Orleans's best restaurant, therefore, is akin to choosing the most spectacular diamond from Tiffany's — there simply are too many gems. The city is now in the midst of a restaurant revolution of sorts, thanks to a cadre of very creative chefs who are forging a bold new contemporary cuisine founded on the bedrock principles of creole and Acadian (or Cajun) cooking. The more traditional places meanwhile

130 DIVERSIONS / Best Eats

continue to thrive, so the spectrum of cooking styles is wider than ever. Consider the list below a representative one, possibly the start of a flawless culinary discovery.

BAYONA: Even though it is located in a quaint, 150-year-old cottage in the French Quarter, this restaurant is no shrine to New Orleans's past. Warm terra cotta colors, boldly striped chair cushions, flower-filled urns, and strikingly modern photographs define the decor, and chef Susan Spicer's fertile imagination defines the menu. Calling her cooking "New World," she combines an innovative use of herbs with diverse inspirations — Mediterranean, Oriental, Californian, and, occasionally, creole. Try the tiny medallions of lamb tenderloin in a pinot noir wine sauce with fennel seed, rosemary, and three types of peppercorns; a gratinéed casserole of polenta and thin crescents of artichoke in an Italian cheese sauce of fontina, grana padano, and crescenza; or a tart with ricotta blended with cream cheese, lemon juice, molasses, and a tinge of vanilla. Wines are carefully selected to accompany the chef's earthy style, and service is informed and energetic. Dining in the lush, candlelit courtyard is a decidedly romantic experience, with the magnolia, banana, wax legustrum, and ginger casting shadows on the white linen tablecloths. Information: *Bayona,* 430 Dauphine St. (phone: 504-525-4455).

BRIGTSEN'S: Homey curtains and simple mantels in a small and unpretentious cottage is the setting for chef Frank Brigtsen's dazzling food, which is rooted in southern Louisiana bayou country but is full of fresh approaches. Try the delicately flavored fish brushed with light butter sauces seasoned with roasted garlic, sun-dried tomatoes, and thyme; roast duck with pecan gravy and "dirty rice" (a traditional Cajun side dish of rice with ground giblets, beef, vegetables, and spices), or a creamy and rich oysters Rockefeller soup. The pecan pie and bread puddings are close to perfect, as are the banana ice cream and double-chocolate cake. The three dining rooms are small, and service is informal, but efficient. Though the wine list is short, the selections complement the deep, rich flavors of the dishes. Only dinner is served, and tables are hard to come by on weekends, so book early. Information: *Brigtsen's,* 723 Dante St. (phone: 504-861-7610).

COMMANDER'S PALACE: This big, festive — yet undeniably elegant — restaurant in a handsome late-19th-century Garden District mansion is cast in the rich, traditional creole mold. The menu ranges from familiar classics to innovative dishes. You'll find what is arguably the world's best turtle soup here, as well as fresh fish such as trout or grouper prepared in a zesty horseradish crust with a saffron cream sauce. Among other winners are a thick, bracing creole bouillabaisse loaded with shellfish, finny fare, and seafood sausage, and fried oysters wrapped in bacon inside a crunchy batter and served on a piquant jelly of sweet and hot peppers. There's no better finale to all this than the celebrated bread pudding soufflé. There are two dining rooms, both overlooking the oak-shaded courtyard; the upper Garden Room, with its exposed view of the sinuous oak trees that makes you feel as if you are dining in an elegant treehouse, is the more celebrated. The wine cellar holds a bounty of premium California chardonnays and cabernets, and service is impeccable. Reserve as early as possible, and wear your best duds; jackets are required for men. Information: *Commander's Palace,* 1403 Washington Ave. (phone: 504-899-8221).

EMERIL'S: Since its opening in 1990, this dining spot has become a haven for serious eaters looking for modern New Orleans cooking. Owner-chef Emeril Lagasse uses creole, Acadian, and "New American" influences to create an array of unique dishes. The duck and mushroom étouffée has all the lustiness of the bayou gastronomy that inspired it; the pan-roasted salmon in herb crust is a new approach to a seafood dish often misunderstood by other New Orleans chefs. The culinary repertoire is impressive: On any given evening, as many as 15 desserts will be offered, including a luscious chocolate bread pudding and mouth-watering coconut cream and peanut butter pies. The wines, primarily Californian, have been chosen for their novelty and quality. The

DIVERSIONS / Best Eats 131

lofty dining room has a geometric, post-modern look with its persimmon-pink textured walls, exposed brick, black metal bar stools, and modern furniture — which fits right into its trendy Warehouse District neighborhood. It's noisy, though — not the place for intimate conversation. Information: *Emeril's,* 800 Tchoupitoulas St. (phone: 504-528-9393).

GALATOIRE'S: A visit to this classic old French-creole bistro in the French Quarter is a necessity if you want to understand the foundations of New Orleans gastronomy. While it adheres to some unbending rules — no reservations or credit cards, no pasta, and no obscure ingredients — it has retained a vitality untarnished since its founding in 1905. The mood is convivial, especially on weekend nights, when spiffily dressed locals squeeze into the deep, narrow dining room that's more functional than fussy. Mirrors run the length of the room, multiplying the image of the antique brass chandeliers, gleaming brass coat hooks, white linen–draped tables, and bentwood chairs. The menu reads like a museum catalogue, and it can lead to an exceptional meal. *Galatoire's* remains at heart an upscale seafood house, thanks to a number of seafood dishes such as shrimp remoulade (the best in New Orleans) and fried oysters with bacon *en brochette.* Everything served here is seasonal, and if delicate, buttery pompano (a flounder-like Gulf fish) is in the kitchen, order it grilled or broiled with a sprinkle of crabmeat sautéed in butter and green seasonings. Or dig into a simple cold appetizer of crab lumps tossed with mayonnaise and a bit of onion. Some regulars swear by the lamb or veal chops in a rich, herbal bearnaise sauce. Desserts are perfunctory. The best way to order is to discuss your preferences with one of the tuxedoed waiters and follow his advice. Wines are similarly dealt with, since the printed list is basically generic. Avoid the usual long lines outside by planning to dine early. Information: *Galatoire's,* 209 Bourbon St. (phone: 504-525-2021).

GAUTREAU'S: Nestled among the oak trees in a quiet Uptown neighborhood, this is an elegant bistro where a single dish might contain shrimp from the Louisiana wetlands, greens grown in southern California, herbs from the Orient, and a Mediterranean garlic mayonnaise. The creator of this polished, urban cooking style is Larkin Selman, a New Orleans native and an alumnus of New York City's *Gotham Bar & Grill.* There is a superb, light seafood gumbo on the menu, along with the moistest, most delicate crab cakes in town. The breast of guinea hen in a luscious sage sauce, accompanied by prune-flavored risotto, is another winner. Salads and soups are as imaginative as they are delicious, and desserts are good, especially the sweet, refreshing tequila Key lime pie with coconut whipped cream, orange *crème brûlée,* and dark-chocolate terrine spiked with Bailey's Irish Cream. There is something on the eclectic wine list for both the connoisseur and the novice. The original downstairs dining room, with its handsome antique drugstore display case set against the deep burgundy walls, is charming but sometimes noisy. The pale yellow room upstairs is more tranquil most nights. The place is rather small, so book early. Information: *Gautreau's,* 1728 Soniat St. (phone: 504-899-7397).

GRILL ROOM: For its visual splendor alone, the *Windsor Court* hotel's dining room has few rivals. Turn-of-the-century oil portraits of members of the English aristocracy grace a sumptuous room rich in tufted damask banquettes and expensive crystal and porcelain; waiters tread unobtrusively from table to table; and the menu, choreographed by the executive chef, Kevin Graham, changes daily, depending on which fresh ingredients are available. One evening you might be tasting thick, pink slices of duck foie gras, the edges seared to a crisp brown, with shiitake mushrooms, reed-thin green beans, and a tarragon sauce. Another day might bring smoked blue marlin with zucchini ribbons. The creamy seafood bisque with a touch of saffron is excellent, vibrant with deep, rich creole flavors. Desserts are similarly rich: a crisp *tuile* of gingersnap dough filled with fresh berries and sorbets, served atop a white-wine gelatin; and a little cup and saucer made of cookie dough and filled with espresso ice cream. The number and quality of wines are stunning, too — ask for the wine list and you'll get an inch-thick tome listing an eye-popping collection of some of the best Bordeaux vintages of the century, along with hundreds of other excellent choices. Service is stopwatch precise. Information: *The Grill Room, Windsor Court Hotel*, 300 Gravier St. (phone: 504-522-1992).

MR. B'S BISTRO: The convivial atmosphere at this stylish bistro is underscored by a piano accompaniment during dinner; its informal, low-ceilinged dining room is made more intimate by wood and glass screens separating the tables. Chef Gerard Maras's handiwork includes appetizers of various types of fish cooked on a wood-fired grill and served with a number of herb and vegetable sauces; Louisiana oysters, hickory-smoked with garlic, rosemary, and olive oil and served with little kernels of orzo, are appealing entrées, as are the house-cured salmon and smoked sable in a dill-caper dressing. Shrimp remoulade, a creole staple, is done here with a twist — roasted sweet pepper is added to the thick and peppery vinaigrette and ladled onto cool, spicy shellfish. Desserts are heartily delicious: a fluffy lemon cassata; bread pudding with Irish whiskey sauce; and spice cake with apples and walnuts under a nutmeg double-cream. Forget the diet — you won't regret it. Information: *Mr. B's Bistro,* 201 Royal St. (phone: 504-523-2078).

UPPERLINE: With three dining rooms located in an old frame building, this smart-looking Uptown bistro, with its pale-gray walls, colorful paintings and prints, bursts of flowers, Art Deco–style floor lamps, and streamlined bar, offers a menu as sophisticated as its setting. Chef Tom Cowman mixes the familiar and the innovative. The trout mousse, redolent of dill and lemon, is a grand way to begin a meal. What follows might be a knockout version of New Orleans–style barbecue shrimp, or robust-tasting tamales with crawfish tails and andouille sausage, or a glorious vichyssoise of roasted sweet pepper, or a well-prepared lamb curry. Cowman is that rare chef who can produce all of these, as well as four different gumbos faithful to the deep, distinctive flavors of true creole cuisine. Grilled fish is a specialty, and it's served with any of several salsas. For dessert, try the scrumptious coconut-banana cake. The small but selective wine list contains solid labels at easy-to-swallow prices, just as the menu offers several fixed-price bargains. Service is efficient, too. Information: *Upperline,* 1413 Upperline St. (phone: 504-891-9822).

VERSAILLES: Overlooking St. Charles Avenue, with a picturesque view of streetcars passing by under the oak trees, this comfortable restaurant, with its body-hugging chairs, slightly Old World atmosphere, and European service, is classy without being cloying. Although cast in the continental mode, the dishes are decidedly lavish, though not overwrought, just as the decor is plush without being intimidating. The baroque accents and warm colors make a good setting for the food that owner/chef Gunter Preuss and his wife, Evelyn, serve — and it's the food that brings locals back time and again. They come for the salmon Argenteuil, perhaps the best preparation of this dish in the city, or the grill of scallops wrapped in filets of pompano, each little roulade with a jumbo shrimp, and set in a classic cream sauce tinged with mustard and capers. The elegant bouillabaisse and the superb mignonette of beef périgourdine in a truffled sauce with port are also favorites. Among the outstanding desserts are pears poached in red wine and stuffed with pecans, a fine *creme brûlée,* and a cookie tulip filled with hazelnut mousse. Information: *Versailles,* 2100 St. Charles Ave. (phone: 504-524-2535).

A French Quarter Shopping Spree

Nestled among the French Quarter's profusion of tacky souvenir boutiques and T-shirt emporia are dozens of shops offering unusual — and often unique — merchandise. The resourceful shopper may well stumble upon a kitchen gadget he's wanted for years, or an out-of-print book, or the perfect

DIVERSIONS / Shopping Spree   133

anniversary gift. The shops and galleries below were chosen because they offer things you may not find at home.

The Acorn – This little treasure house of exotica has crowded display cases filled with such diverse items as glittering malachite pillboxes, Oriental textiles, and unusual jewelry. 736 Royal St. (phone: 504-525-7110).

Brass Menagerie – If it's made of brass, this place almost certainly stocks it. The choices range from faucets to fire screens to everything in between — coat hooks, drawer handles, you name it. 524 St. Louis St. (phone: 504-524-0921).

Coghlan Gallery – Specializing in hand-crafted copper fountains (they can be used indoors, too) and garden ornaments in a variety of styles and sizes. The shop also stocks odds and ends to perk up your garden or terrace. 710 Toulouse St. (phone: 504-525-8550).

Cuisine Classique – After a few minutes here, you're more than likely to leave with something for your kitchen you didn't know you needed — an oversize stockpot, perhaps, or an apple corer, or a lemon zester. Aside from a vast array of cooking tools there is also a selection of local cookbooks that is especially good. 439 Decatur St. (phone: 504-524-0068).

Dansk Factory Outlet – Prices are deeply discounted on all sorts of Scandinavian-designed dishes, glasses, pots, and other household items. 541 Royal St. (phone: 504-522-0482).

DeVille Books & Prints – Several outlets of this store offer offbeat, esoteric, hard-to-find titles, as well as lavishly illustrated books on painting, architecture, photography, and other arts. *Jackson Brewery,* at Decatur and St. Ann Sts. (phone: 504-525-4508). Also at One Shell Sq., Poydras at St. Charles Ave. (phone: 504-525-1846), and *Riverwalk Mall,* One Poydras St. (phone: 504-595-8916).

French Market – Couched among the ancient colonnades beginning at the *Café du Monde* near Jackson Square and extending 6 blocks along the Mississippi is the famous *French Market.* All sorts of items are sold here — souvenirs, confectioneries, toys, candles, pralines, spices, and funky clothes, just to name a few. Beginning at the corner of Decatur and Gov. Nicholls Streets, stalls are set up offering a cornucopia of fruits and vegetables, some of the more exotic being raw sugarcane, branches of fresh bay leaves, seasonal "creole" tomatoes, mirlitons (a species of vegetable pear, also known as *chayote*), and oranges from the fertile soil south of the city. Beyond the *Farmers' Market* is the *Community Flea Market.* T-shirts abound here, but you'll also find lots of bric-a-brac, old books and records, tropical plants, and a hodgepodge of creole and Cajun spices. There are also fish vendors here who can package fresh shellfish for you to take home. *French Market,* Decatur St., between St. Ann and Barracks Sts.

A Gallery for Fine Photography – One of the finest photo galleries we've seen, its fascinating collection ranges from 19th-century portraits of native Americans to the latest work of Annie Leibovitz and Helmut Newton. Many first-rank national and international photographers are represented on 2 floors of exhibition space. 322 Royal St. (phone: 504-568-1313).

Hayes Antiques – This quaint little shop holds a remarkable selection of items, with an emphasis on early-20th-century bibelots, prints, and photographs. 828 Chartres St. (phone: 504-529-4221).

Hove Parfumeur – Perfumes, colognes, and soaps are produced on the premises of this charming boutique, operated by the same New Orleans family for generations. Dried aromatic herbs such as vetiver are sold, too. 824 Royal St. (phone: 504-525-7827).

The Idea Factory – The variety of hand-crafted wood objects — all made in the workshop in the back — is amazing. All kinds of whimsical creations, as well as handsome marquetry boxes and practical objects, fill the shelves. 838 Chartres St. (phone: 504-524-5195).

Merrill B. Domas American Indian Art – The work of the best weavers, potters,

134 DIVERSIONS / Antiques

and painters from the Southwest is on display in this beautifully designed gallery. Other items include handsome rings, necklaces, and bracelets in silver and gemstones by some of Santa Fe's leading artisans. 824 Chartres St. (phone: 504-586-0479).

Mignon Faget Ltd. – New Orleans's premier jewelry designer offers elegant pieces inspired by nature in precious metals and stones. Familiar regional icons, such as shellfish, are prominent motifs in the bracelets, brooches, necklaces, and cuff links. *Canal Place Mall,* 333 Canal St. (phone: 504-524-2973), 710 Dublin St. (phone: 504-865-7361), and 8220 Maple St.; phone: 504-865-1107).

Le Petit Soldier Shop – Collector or not, you're apt to be charmed by the hundreds of exquisitely crafted and painted lead soldiers sold in this museum-cum-shop. There also are all sorts of antique military memorabilia. 528 Royal St. (phone: 504-523-7741).

Serendipitous – There is an abundance of shops offering masks in the French Quarter, but this one is original — the diversity and colors are spectacular. 831 Decatur St. (phone: 504-522-9158).

Victoria's Designer Discount Shoes – From simple pumps to glittery evening shoes, produced by some of the fashion world's most noted designers of women's footwear. And they are priced to sell. 532 Chartres St. (phone: 504-568-9990).

William Norris Ltd. – Antique and contemporary cast-iron ornaments are shown in this one-of-a-kind shop, which also stocks such diverse items as glass-top tables, side chairs, and even beds — all strikingly original. 1029 Royal St. (phone: 504-524-1010).

Antiques: New Orleans's Best Hunting Grounds

In the South, New Orleans is the place to go for antiques. The fascination New Orleanians have for period antiques is understandable — it's part of their preoccupation with the past. In addition, the large number of 19th-century homes that are still occupied call for the types of furnishings that would complement their graceful high-ceilinged parlors and rooms. In the early 19th century, the French-educated creole aristocracy furnished their elegant homes with furniture, objets d'art, and tapestries bought in France. During the 1830s to 1850s, with the arrival of the Anglo-Saxons, there was an influx of 19th-century English furniture. When the plantation culture fell apart after the Civil War, most of what was left of the furnishings from all over the South found their way to New Orleans. Today, there are over 200 antiques shops and auction houses, as well as over 30 restoration and reproduction concerns that service the industry. The range of the kinds of antiques one could find here is extraordinary — everything from an 18th-century French ormolu clock to antique Oriental rugs to an American art glass pitcher from the turn of the century. The city's antiques shops are concentrated in two areas: Royal and Chartres Streets between Iberville and St. Philip Streets in the French Quarter contain most of the finer merchandise from England, France, and the Orient. The other district is Uptown on Magazine Street, beginning approximately at Jackson Avenue and extending almost to Audubon Park. The offerings here are eclectic — some shops specialize in local or regional furniture valued more for its nostalgic qualities; others limit their inventory to luxurious 19th-century English or 18th-century French pieces. Many of the French Quarter shops display only a part of their inventory and maintain large warehouses in other parts of the city. The biggest bargains, however, are found at the auction houses, where excellent pieces often go for a fraction of what they could fetch in New York or on the West Coast. What follows is the tip of the iceberg.

DIVERSIONS / Antiques 135

FRENCH QUARTER: *Henry Stern Antiques* is a long-established dealer in fine English furniture and paintings from the late 18th and early 19th centuries (329-31 Royal St.; phone: 504-522-8687). *Lucullus* is delightfully crowded with French and English dining room furniture, crystal, porcelain, and decorative objects relating to food and wine (610 Chartres St.; phone: 504-528-9620). A browser's paradise, *M.S. Rau Inc.* has 2 large floors packed to the rafters with everything from art glass to antique music boxes, and more crystal and porcelain than you may have thought existed (630 Royal St.; phone: 504-523-5660). *Waldhorn Co. Inc.* is for connoisseurs of English and French furniture (343 Royal St.; phone: 504-581-6379). *Hayes Antiques* (828 Chartres St.; phone: 504-529-4221) is a quaint shop filled with a remarkably good selection of early-20th-century bibelots, prints, and photographs.

MAGAZINE STREET: *Stan Levy Imports* (1028 Louisiana Ave. near Magazine St.; phone: 504-899-6384) is a good source, not only of European pieces, but also Southern armoires, 19th-century Louisiana furniture, and objects from the region of more recent vintage; the items are affordable, too. More modest treasures are found at *Bep's Antiques,* where you just might discover that indispensible objet d'art among the hundreds of old bottles, homey Victorian washstands, and charming little side tables (2051 Magazine St.; phone: 504-525-7726). *Jon Antiques* has an especially good selection of English and French porcelains, as well as furniture, from the 18th and 19th centuries (4605 Magazine St.; phone: 504-899-4482). *Ditto 19th Century Antiques* specializes in clocks, cut-glass, and above-average bric-a-brac (4838 Magazine St.; phone: 504-891-4845).

AUCTION HOUSES: One sign of the great bargains to be had at New Orleans auction houses is the many local and national antiques and art dealers present. Auctions are usually held on Saturdays, and illustrated catalogues are published for the major ones. The principal houses are *Morton M. Goldberg Auction Galleries Inc.* (547 Baronne St.; phone: 504-592-2300), *Neal Auction Galleries Inc.* (4139 Magazine St.; phone: 504-899-5329), and *New Orleans Auction House* (801 Magazine St.; phone: 504-566-1849).

For the Body

Goin' Fishing

New Orleans's location on the central Gulf Coast makes it ideal for fresh- and saltwater sport fishing year-round. The Gulf of Mexico, about 100 miles south of the city, teems with hundreds of species of sport and food fish, including tarpon, tuna, blue marlin, wahoo, ling, cobia, and dolphinfish. Full-day excursions from New Orleans to Venice, near the mouth of the Mississippi River, are easily arranged for groups of 2 to 20. Lakes, bays, inlets, and marshes, less than an hour's drive from the center of town, are filled with redfish, largemouth bass, catfish, and freshwater drum. In the very heart of town, City Park's lagoons are pleasant places to drop a line on a balmy afternoon. Temporary state licenses are required for non-state residents — saltwater and freshwater licenses cost $8.50 for 2 days — and are available at the Louisiana Department of Wildlife and Fisheries office in the French Quarter (400 Chartres St.; phone: 504-568-5636). Their hours are 8 AM to 4 PM Mondays through Fridays. Be sure to inquire about seasonal regulations, too. What follows is a brief guide to the area's most fertile fishing waters.

GULF OF MEXICO: About a 90-minute drive from New Orleans is the Venice Marina, the gateway to some of the best deep-sea fishing in the nation. All sorts of guided charter boats are available, for groups from two people to a dozen or more. Costs range from about $100 to about $600 a day for 12 or more passengers. Information: *Venice Marina,* PO Box 990, Venice, LA 70091 (phone: 504-534-9357).

PASS RIGOLETS AND LAKE BORGNE: Less than an hour's drive from the French Quarter, this is one of the most prolific inshore saltwater fishing areas in America. Boats can be rented. Information: *Rigolets Marina,* US Hwy. 90 E., New Orleans, LA 70127 (phone: 504-662-5666).

MISSISSIPPI RIVER GULF OUTLET: This channel was dug as an alternate commercial route from New Orleans to the Gulf of Mexico, bypassing the Mississippi. Locals also find it fertile fishing grounds. About 20 miles from the city, on Paris Road in Chalmette, 15-foot flat-bottomed skiffs with motors can be rented at the *Gulf Outlet Marina.* Information: *Gulf Outlet Marina,* 5353 Paris Rd., Chalmette, LA 70044 (phone: 504-277-8229).

CITY PARK: The tranquil lagoons inside City Park are where many local fisherfolk first discovered the joys of the sport. The ponds are regularly stocked, and acquiring a 1-day permit is simply a matter of inquiring at the park's Casino Building. Information: *Boating and Fishing Department,* City Park Administration Office, 1 Dreyfous Ave., New Orleans, LA 70124 (phone: 504-483-9371).

MISSISSIPPI RIVER: Many New Orleans residents don't know that it's still possible to fish the mighty river that courses through their city. But it can be done, once you've found a spot away from the wharves and floodwalls. The most easily accessible one is Uptown, where St. Charles and Carrollton Avenues meet near the River Road. Climb the grassy levee and you'll reach the small strip of land (the local name for it is the "batture") separating the levee from the river. Drop your line and wait: That's what fishing is all about, isn't it?

Tennis

New Orleans has not escaped the tennis fever that still grips the country. The tropical (summer) and mild (winter) climate is, after all, tailor-made for virtually every outdoor sport that doesn't require snow, ice, or mountains (although the August humidity can definitely put a damper on your backhand). Visiting tennis buffs will find good choice of public courts; and if you belong to a club back home, it's worth checking to see if it enjoys reciprocity with one of New Orleans's private clubs.

WISNER TENNIS CENTER: These well-maintained courts, nestled among the verdant spaces of City Park, are the most popular public venues in the city. A total of 39 outdoor courts, some asphalt, some clay, are available 7 days a week, beginning at 7 AM. All of them are lighted, permitting play until 10 PM if the weather cooperates. Private or group instruction and complete pro shop services, including racquet and string repair, are offered. Information: *Wisner Tennis Center,* 1 Dreyfous Ave., New Orleans, LA 70124 (phone: 504-483-9383).

AUDUBON PARK: In a place where summer can last 9 or 10 months, tennis enthusiasts are grateful for any pocket of cooler air they can find. Audubon Park's courts, just yards away from the tempering waters of the Mississippi River, may be a few degrees less torrid than the others in town. Ten new public courts with a clay-like surface are maintained in the rear of the park. They're not lighted, so don't plan on playing past sunset. Official hours are 8 AM to 6 PM on weekdays and 8 AM to 5 PM on Saturdays and Sundays. But, again, closing times are usually regulated by the sun. Information: *Audubon Tennis Center,* 6320 Tchoupitoulas St., New Orleans, LA 70118 (phone: 504-895-1042).

RIVERCENTER RACQUET AND HEALTH CLUB: If the thought of game, set, and match on a rooftop court overlooking the Mississippi River appeals to you, this club, adjacent to the *New Orleans Hilton,* offers the setting. The 8 indoor and 3 outdoor courts are beautifully maintained on top of the 5-story *Hilton* hotel's garage, with great views of the river below. They're open to *Hilton* guests for an $8 fee or non-guests for $10. There's a matchmaker service if you need a partner, as well as a complete pro shop, racquet rentals, and instruction by the resident pro. Court reservations may be made 3 days in advance. Operating hours Mondays through Thursdays, 6 AM to 10:30 PM; Fridays, 6 AM to 9 PM; Saturdays, 8 AM to 7 PM; and Sundays, 8 AM to 5:30 PM. Information: *Rivercenter Racquet and Health Club, New Orleans Hilton,* 2 Poydras St., New Orleans, LA 70140 (phone: 504-587-7242).

Jogging

The numerous green spaces scattered around New Orleans, a few within blocks of the major hotels, make jogging a simple matter of choosing the right park or path. Woldenberg Park, just beyond the *Aquarium of the Americas,* along the French Quarter riverfront, is one pleasurable spot. In the Uptown section, Audubon Park, between St. Charles Avenue and Magazine Street, contains a 2-mile jogging path circling the golf course — the oak trees and lagoons make for a scenic run. Just as pleasant are the grounds of City Park at the other end of town. Outside the commercial stretches of the Mississippi Riverfront, local joggers favor the river levee, accessible from the juncture of St. Charles Avenue and Carrollton Avenue Uptown.

Bicycling

While there are no designated bicycle paths in New Orleans, the tree-lined avenues that crisscross the city are unusually suitable for a bracing bicycle ride in almost any season. The flattened crest of the river levee in the Carrollton section is especially pleasant, offering a soothing view of the water; Wisner Boulevard along Bayou St. John, stretching from City Park to Lake Pontchartrain, is also a pleasant stretch. Audubon and City parks are especially practical in the summer, thanks to their cooling umbrellas of trees. Bicycles can be rented at *Bicycle Michael's* (618 Frenchmen St.; phone: 504-945-9505) and on Dreyfous Avenue in City Park (phone: 504-483-9371).

Big Easy Rambles

Most of New Orleans is situated several feet below sea level, so don't look for a hill higher than 3 or 4 feet. But the city is surrounded by wooded areas that are fine for communing with nature on long walks. Here are a couple of gambols worth taking.

JEAN LAFITTE NATIONAL HISTORICAL PARK: This unspoiled wild landscape on the West Bank of the Mississippi is a half-hour drive from the city center. Its several trails offer an invigorating way to explore Louisiana's fascinating topography, with some interesting archaeological sites along the way. Information: *Jean Lafitte National Historical Park, Barataria Unit,* 7400 Louisiana Hwy. 45, Marrero, LA 70072 (phone: 504-589-2330).

LOUISIANA NATURE AND SCIENCE CENTER: Located on the eastern edge of the city, this center maintains a short hiking trail in the woods; the center staff also plans hiking and backpacking excursions into areas outside the city proper. Information: *Louisiana Nature and Science Center,* 11000 Lake Forest Blvd., PO Box 870610, New Orleans, LA 70187-0610 (phone: 504-246-5672; 504-246-9381 for recorded information).

Sailing and Boating

Lake Pontchartrain's brisk breezes and typically calm waters make it ideal for Sunday sailors. And the bayous and lagoons that ring New Orleans provide for relaxing excursions along the water. Even if you forgot to tow your boat, there are still ways to take advantage of New Orleans's favorite offshore activity. From March through October, recreational craft can be rented on the New Orleans lakefront from *Sailboats South*. For lake boating, the choices include

DIVERSIONS / Sailing and Boating   139

monohulls, catamarans, sailboats, and powerboats, ranging in size from 9 to 36 feet. *Sailboats South* also rents rowing shells and skiffs for coasting along the nearby bayous and inlets. Information: *Sailboats South,* 300 Sapphire St. (phone: 504-288-7245). Less ambitious sailors can rent canoes, rowboats, and paddleboats by the hour for skimming along the lagoons of City Park. Information: *City Park,* 1 Dreyfous Ave., New Orleans, LA 70124 (phone: 504-483-9371).

CANOEING: The swamps and marshes within an hour's drive from the center of town, teeming with vegetation and wildlife, provide an exotic backdrop for explorations by canoe. *Canoe and Trail Outings* specializes in "sunset paddling" excursions to the Manchac Swamp, west of the city and the Honey Island Swamp to the east, among other places. The company rents all the necessary equipment. Information: *Canoe and Trail Outings,* 802 Chapelle St., New Orleans, LA 70124; phone: 504-283-9400).

CRUISING OL' MAN RIVER: The large sternwheeler *Natchez,* one of the five remaining steamboats on the Mississippi, departs the Toulouse Street Wharf (behind *Jax Brewery*) twice a day on 2-hour runs up and down the river. The scenic tour includes a narrated history of such landmarks as Jackson Square and the Chalmette Battlefield and, for an extra fee, a luncheon buffet of creole specialties. The company also offers an evening dinner/jazz cruise with live music by the *Crescent City Jazz Band.* Information: *New Orleans Steamboat Company,* Suite 1300, World Trade Center, New Orleans, LA 70130 (phone: 504-586-8777; for reservations, 800-233-BOAT).

For the Mind

All That Jazz

Musicologists still quibble over exactly how jazz, America's only truly original art form, actually evolved. There's no debate, however, on *where* it began — in the dance halls, bawdy houses, and back alleys of New Orleans, where black musicians took the hand-me-down rhythms of their African forebears and the vigorous hymns of their churches and created an entirely new musical species. To paraphrase Louis Armstrong, if you have to ask what jazz is, no explanation will suffice; you'll simply have to sample it for yourself. And New Orleans is the place to do that in style.

In New Orleans, escaping the sound of jazz is almost impossible. Gospel and blues singers hold forth in doorways along Royal Street; teenage horn players and impromptu bands play Jackson Square. At night, hardly a block of Bourbon Street is without a group of street musicians playing, a hat or open instrument case ready to receive a tip. This is jazz in its purest form — spontaneous, sincere, and totally unpretentious. Visitors shouldn't be surprised if a marching band suddenly appears from nowhere, since New Orleanians will seize almost any excuse to grab their horns and drums and take to the streets.

The whole spectrum — from gospel and blues, through "moldy fig" traditionalism, Dixieland, rhythm and blues, the most cerebral modern styles, and the latest hybrid, "New Orleans Sound" — is heard every night of the week. Cajun and "zydeco," the music of southwestern Louisiana's fun-loving inhabitants, have gained a foothold in the city's clubs, too, joining the happy mix.

Every year, all of them come together in the *New Orleans Jazz and Heritage Festival,* 2 weeks of almost uninterrupted jazz, folk, Cajun, and gospel music in late April and early May. Information: *New Orleans Jazz and Heritage Festival,* 1205 N. Rampart St., New Orleans, LA 70116 (phone: 504-522-4786). (Also see "Quintessential New Orleans" in *For the Experience*). At other times, you may be lucky enough to catch a set by some native New Orleans musicians: pianist-singer Harry Connick, Jr., or one of the horn-playing Marsalis brothers, Wynton and Branford. What follows is a basic rundown on jazz and its variations in its Big Easy birthplace.

"MOLDY FIG": A surprisingly large number of musicians who helped shape the jazz idiom are still active, passing on the ancient techniques to a whole new generation. The Humphrey brothers — clarinetist Willie and trumpeter Percy — are entering their 10th decade! Banjoist Danny Barker, not far behind in age, is showing no signs of slowing his strumming. The venerable *Olympia Brass Band,* whose members' ages range from youth to extreme old age, is still hopping. The ensemble, along with the *Preservation Hall Jazz Band,* can be heard nightly in the French Quarter at either *Preservation Hall* (726 St. Peter St.; phone: 504-522-2841) or the *Palm Court Jazz Café* (1204 Decatur St.; phone: 504-525-0200).

DIXIELAND: Purists disdain the term, but "Dixieland" is as good a name as any for

DIVERSIONS / All That Jazz 141

the brassy, syncopated jazz hybrid that emerged during the 1930s and 1940s. Its most celebrated present-day practitioners are clarinetist Pete Fountain and trumpeter Al Hirt, who have their own local nightclubs — respectively, *Pete Fountain's* in the *New Orleans Hilton* (2 Poydras St.; phone: 504-523-4374) and *Jelly Roll's* (501 Bourbon St.; phone: 504-568-0501); Fountain plays regularly at his club, and Hirt occasionally appears at his. Bourbon Street is filled with Dixieland nightspots. Among the better ones are the *Second Line* (216 Bourbon St.; phone: 504-523-2020), where ace saxophonist Sam Butera and his group play when he's home from Las Vegas. Other clubs on the street offering good Dixieland are the *Famous Door* (339 Bourbon St.; phone: 504-522-7626); *Lulu White's Mahogany Hall* (309 Bourbon St.; phone: 504-525-5595); and *Maison Bourbon* (641 Bourbon St.; phone: 504-522-8818). In a much more elegant setting, the toe-tapping music of the old riverboats is played once again in the *Louis Armstrong Foundation Jazz Club* in the huge lobby bar of the *Meridien* hotel (614 Canal St.; phone: 504-525-6500). The resident group is *Jacques Gauthé's Yerba Buena Creole Rice Jazz Band.* Another especially compatible setting for Dixieland is *Le-Moyne's Landing,* near the Plaza d'España and the *Riverwalk Mall* (Canal St. at the Mississippi River; phone: 504-524-4809).

BLUES: The blues tradition, one of the lifelines of jazz, and rhythm and blues, the forerunner of rock 'n' roll, have an honorable lineage in New Orleans. Some of the great names in R and B and the basic blues — Professor Longhair, Dr. John, and Fats Domino — have their musical roots in the city. That tradition still continues, thanks to such knock-'em-dead wailers as Irma Thomas, Ernie K-Doe, and Marva Wright. They and others regularly hold forth at *Tipitina's* (on the Uptown riverfront at 501 Napoleon Ave.; phone: 504-895-8477), the city's premier spot for every type of local music. Usually, Wright also can be found at *Muddy Waters* in Carrollton (8301 Oak St.; phone: 504-866-7174), and regularly performs for the Sunday jazz brunch at the *New Orleans Hilton*'s *Café Bromeliad* (2 Poydras St.; phone: 504-584-3840). Other clubs with regular blues bands and singers are *Rhythms* (227 Bourbon St.; phone: 504-523-3800) and *Benny's Bar* (Uptown at 938 Valence St.; phone: 504-895-9405).

THE NEW ORLEANS SOUND: While jazz continues to evolve, it also comes back to its roots in the newest form to emerge from the city's musical psyche. The "New Orleans Sound," as it's called, draws heavily on jazz's African roots, using unusual percussion instruments and a very basic rhythmic line. Its principal practitioners are the celebrated Aaron Neville and the *Neville Brothers,* singer Charmaine Neville (Aaron's niece), Allen Toussaint, George Porter and his band, singer Germaine Bazzle, and a duo of female singers going by the apt name of *Born Divas.* Some of the places where they appear regularly are *Snug Harbor* (626 Frenchmen St.; phone: 504-949-0696); *Tipitina's* (501 Napoleon Ave.; phone: 504-895-8477); *Muddy Waters* (8301 Oak St., Carrollton; phone: 504-866-7174); *Jimmy's* (8200 Willow St.; phone: 504-861-8200); the *Maple Leaf* (8316 Oak St.; phone: 504-866-9359); and the *New Orleans Entertainment Hall* in the Warehouse District (907 S. Peters St.; phone: 504-523-4311).

CONTEMPORARY JAZZ: As the Jacksons were to the Motown sound, the Marsalises are to contemporary New Orleans jazz. The first member of the family to make his mark was pianist Ellis Marsalis, and his sons Wynton, Branford, and Delfeayo have followed suit, carving out large niches of their own. Patriarch Ellis still plays frequently in New Orleans clubs, most often at *Snug Harbor* (626 Frenchmen St.; phone: 504-949-0696); Wynton and Branford perform their music all over the world (though Branford usually can be seen leading his band on the "Tonight Show"), but they do make occasional appearances in the Big Easy. Keep an eye on kid brother Delfeayo, who holds forth with his quintet nightly at the *Crescent City Brewhouse* (527 Decatur St.; phone: 504-522-0571).

CAJUN AND ZYDECO: While Cajun music has only the most tenuous connections to the jazz idiom, both are rooted in the same raw spirit of southern Louisiana. Raucous but charming zydeco (the term derives from the Acadian pronunciation and corruption of the French *les haricots rouges,* or "red beans") is Cajun music with a distinctively black style. Fiddles and accordions are the essential instruments in a Cajun or zydeco band, producing a folksy sound that is beginning to rival Cajun cuisine in popularity. The most familiar names among performers in New Orleans are Allen Fontenot, *Beausoleil,* Bruce Daigrepont, the *Breaux Bridge Playboys,* and Steve Cormier and the Cajun Sound. You'll find them rocking customers onto the dance floors at *Mulate's* (201 Julia St.; phone: 504-522-1492); *Michaul's* (701 Magazine St.; phone: 504-522-5517); and the *Cajun Cabin* (501 Bourbon St.; phone: 504-529-4256). Other clubs where Cajun groups often perform are *Tipitina's* (501 Napoleon Ave.; phone: 504-895-8477) and the *Maple Leaf* (8316 Oak St.; phone: 504-866-9359).

Mardi Gras Madness

Just as the medieval jousting of the *Palio* helps to define Siena, Italy, and *Fasching* annually reinvigorates Munich, Germany, the New Orleans *Carnival* is the ultimate reflection of the city's fun-loving communal spirit. The yearly celebration culminating on *Mardi Gras* (or *Fat Tuesday*) is a reminder that New Orleans is, culturally speaking, much closer to Rio de Janeiro or Nice than it is to Atlanta or Houston.

Words don't do justice to the pleasures that *Carnival* can generate: the remarkable sense of camaraderie shared on the streets with thousands of strangers, the spectacle of glittery floats rumbling through masses of humanity screaming for trinkets, the incredible variety and ingenuity of the costumes. All of the usual traits we use to define (and often divide) us — age, income level, gender, and race — crumble in the face of the indefinable *Mardi Gras* spirit.

What we now call *Carnival* began more than a century and a half ago as a quaint, spontaneous celebration. The local descendants of French and Spanish settlers, picking up on a southern European tradition dating back several millennia, began carousing on the final day before the pre-*Easter Lenten* season. The first instance of an organized revelry dates to 1857, when six men formed the *Mystick Krewe of Comus,* which established the still-operative tradition of secret membership and elaborate parades and balls on specific days. Also in 1857, another group formed the *Rex* organization to entertain the visiting Grand Duke Alexis Romanoff of Russia and chose an ad hoc monarch who was anointed the *King of Carnival,* a title recognized to this day. Over the decades, the number of *krewes* multiplied, covering virtually every socioeconomic stratum of the population.

Carnival season traditionally begins on the 12th night after *Christmas,* January 6. The date on which *Mardi Gras* itself falls depends on the date of *Easter,* which comes 46 days later (this year, it will be February 23). Balls are held throughout the city and suburbs in the preceding weeks. The first parade usually takes to the suburban streets about 3 weeks before *Mardi Gras;* the first in the city proper is held about 10 days before the big day, and the number accelerates toward the season's grand finale.

Although the balls are strictly private affairs (even the super-spectacular ones held in the *Louisiana Superdome* are by invitation only), the real fun of *Carnival* is available to everyone, as some 50 *krewes* parade day and night through the city and beyond. The number of floats per *krewe* varies from about 15 to 30, separated by marching bands and equestrians. The sizes and quality of the floats cover a wide range, too, the largest being more than 110 feet long, carrying 100-or-so masked riders, who energize the throng by tossing souvenir "doubloons" and cups, beaded necklaces, and a hodgepodge of other trinkets. The jostling for these trophies occasionally degenerates into a fracas, but in fact, *Carnival* remains surprisingly crime-free, considering that more than a

DIVERSIONS / Mardi Gras 143

million people throng the city's thoroughfares. What follows is offered to help bring order out of the potential chaos of spending *Carnival* time in "The City That Care Forgot." Information: *Greater New Orleans Tourist and Convention Commission,* 1520 Sugar Bowl Dr., New Orleans, LA 70116 (phone: 504-566-5011).

A DRESS REHEARSAL

First, a cautionary note: Though visiting New Orleans at the height of *Carnival* season can mean a once-in-a-lifetime experience, it also means no-vacancy signs in hotels, often-mediocre meals in the top restaurants, chaotic nightclubs, traffic nightmares, and overbooked flights. Those who want to appreciate the year-round assets of the city are advised to visit during the other 50 weeks of the year. But for those who've come to see what *Carnival* is all about, here are a few tips.

What to Bring – *Carnival* season and *Jazzfest* are not the times for pearl necklaces and three-piece suits. The most practical clothes are jeans, a good pair of walking shoes, and rain gear. Thanks to the humidity, February can be a very cold month in New Orleans, with daytime temperatures in the low 30s F not uncommon.

Hotels – Most hotels and bed and breakfast establishments require a minimum stay of 3, and sometimes 4, nights up to *Fat Tuesday* itself. (The same policy applies during the April *Jazzfest.*) Room rates also rise by as much as 30%. Reservations should be made at least 1 month in advance for most accommodations. Understandably, the hotels and bed and breakfast places fill up quickly, so planning ahead can mean the difference between a comfortable room in a centrally located hotel or a makeshift one in a roadside motel a half hour's drive from New Orleans proper. Inside the city, festivalgoers can expect to pay premium rates for accommodations.

Restaurants – The size of the crowds at *Carnival* and *Jazzfest* place unusual pressures on fine dining places. Most of them try to accommodate their customers, but the reality is that food and service quality generally suffer.

Transportation – The French Quarter, Canal Street, and many central thoroughfares in and around New Orleans are frequently closed to vehicular traffic at *Carnival* time, making automobiles more of a burden than a convenience. Those who must come by car should arrange in advance for a place to park it and take a taxi to their hotels or any other place they want to go.

CURTAIN UP

Parades and balls may form the framework for New Orleans's *Carnival,* but the nonstop partying in the streets is what really distinguishes it from other jamborees. Free-wheeling spontaneity is the order of the day — or night. In the French Quarter, the party begins about a week before *Mardi Gras* itself, as the crowds start arriving from virtually every state in the Union and from countries the world over. By Saturday night, a certain frenzy takes hold on Bourbon Street, spilling over to Jackson Square, Decatur Street, and the Mississippi Riverfront.

What's going on? Well, just about everything — most of it in good taste, some of it absolutely not. Inexorably, the momentum builds to Tuesday, when hardly a square foot of the French Quarter, Canal Street, and St. Charles Avenue isn't occupied by a masker, a marcher, or a gawker. Costume contests are always a good bet for entertainment. In the 600 block of Canal Street, in front of the *Meridien* hotel, the line of contestants waiting to take the stage evokes images of the bar scene in *Star Wars.* The most famous competition, however, is the one in the French Quarter at Burgundy and St. Ann Streets. Known locally as the "He-She Contest," it puts the spotlight on some of the cleverest and funniest transvestite getups imaginable. Everybody from Bo-Peep to Bo Derek is represented. Like everything else about *Mardi Gras,* the contests never start at the advertised time, so play it by ear. If you miss one zany fashion show, another one is sure to pop up.

Until the 1970s, many *Carnival* parades filed through the French Quarter, but as they

144 DIVERSIONS / Mardi Gras

grew in size and complexity, and the crowds multiplied, this became, at best, impractical. Canal Street and St. Charles Avenue are the principal routes of the major *krewes.* The exact routes are published in the daily *Times-Picayune* on the day of the parade. Note: Many of the *krewes* grew out of private social clubs with restrictive membership policies, a practice challenged in late 1991 by an antidiscrimination city ordinance. As a result of the ensuing debate, two of the oldest organizations — *Comus* and *Momus* — canceled their 1992 processions. As we went to press, city officials and *krewe* officers were negotiating possible compromises. The result may be alterations in some hallowed *Carnival* traditions this year, but no one doubts that its essential character will be retained.

THE PLAYERS

So now that you've made all the necessary arrangements and arrived at the festivities, what exactly can you expect to see? We'd like to introduce you to the cast of characters you'll find parading through the streets at *Carnival* time, as well as when they're likely to appear.

The Mystick Krewe of Comus – *Carnival* has always come to a close on *Mardi Gras* night with the appearance of *Comus,* who disdains all regal titles. He wears an ostrich-plumed cap rather than a crown and carries a wine cup in place of a scepter. The 17 floats he brings to the traditional St. Charles Avenue–Canal Street route are designed along strictly traditional lines, depicting flowers and exotic creatures. *Comus*'s procession, beginning at 6 PM, is one of only a few that are still illuminated by *flambeaux,* which are oil torches attached to long poles carried by prancing marchers.

Rex, King of Carnival – For many the personification of *Mardi Gras, Rex* reigns atop a glittery float draped in gold cloth edged with ermine, under a huge replica of a crown. True to tradition, the king's float leads the procession, followed by more than 25 others, all elaborately decorated according to the parade's theme, which might be taken from literature, history, mythology, nature, or the arts. The craftsmanship of the color-splashed carriages, many of them topped with gargantuan mobile figures, is exceptionally imaginative. *Rex,* always a local businessman, begins his parade at 10 AM on *Mardi Gras,* starting uptown near St. Charles and Napoleon Avenues and reaching Canal Street around noon.

King Zulu – An hour or two before *Rex's* appearance, *King Zulu,* potentate of the fiercest African tribe, rolls along basically the same route with his 30-float entourage, tossing golden coconuts and other appropriate trinkets to the crowds. Humor is the strong suit here. In 1949, Louis Armstrong was the monarch. Other whimsical noblemen of this *krewe* are Mr. Big Stuff, the Witch Doctor, Province Prince, and Big Shot. The best marching bands in the city play in the parade, which usually reaches its climax on Canal Street about 3 hours after it starts.

The Krewe of Proteus – *Mardi Gras* eve is the time for *Proteus* to shine. The *krewe* dates back to 1882, and its 20-odd floats are classically designed, usually subtly colored and revolving around themes of nature, history, or mythology. As shepherd of the ocean, *Proteus* rules from inside an immense seashell. The parade begins around sunset and traces a route along St. Charles Avenue to Poydras Street, where it makes a U-turn at the *Riverwalk Mall,* then returns to St. Charles Avenue and Canal Street.

The Krewe of Bacchus – Perhaps the most popular of all the *Carnival* parades, *Bacchus* takes to the streets on the Sunday night before *Mardi Gras* with 24 huge, elaborate, and animated floats. These riders are considered the most generous in all of *Carnival,* tossing thousands of doubloons, cups, and beads to the hundreds of thousands lining the curbs. *Bacchus* himself is invariably a show-biz celebrity. Among those chosen in years past were Bob Hope, Jackie Gleason, Charlton Heston, Kirk Douglas, and Dennis Quaid. After covering St. Charles Avenue and Canal Street, the *krewe* parades right into the vast *New Orleans Convention Center,* its floats providing the backdrop for a spectacular ball featuring prominent entertainers.

The Krewe of Endymion – *Bacchus*'s only rival for unfettered spectacle, *Endymion* brings out 27 "super-floats" carrying 1,325 members on the Saturday night before *Mardi Gras*. Each member of the royal court, garbed in stunningly intricate costumes, is granted an individual float. The parade begins at City Park, then stretches along Canal Street, effectively cutting off one-half of the city from the other. Famous entertainers such as trumpeter Doc Severinsen and singer Kenny Rogers have played prominent roles in past parades.

The Krewe of Hermes – The Friday night before *Fat Tuesday* belongs to *Hermes*, messenger of the gods. The *krewe* preserves a number of *Carnival* traditions — handheld torches, for instance — and the 20 floats are usually designed with traditional styles and colors. The float riders' costumes clearly fit the parade themes, an increasingly rare occurrence. After parading down St. Charles Avenue and Canal Street, the *krewe* files down North Rampart Street before disbanding at Armstrong Park.

The Knights of Momus – This *krewe*'s namesake is the god of mockery, which accounts for the boldly satirical themes it uses for its parades, held on the Thursday night before *Mardi Gras*. No one — especially the political establishment — escapes the barbs blazoned across the *krewe*'s 15 floats. And a court jester always sits at *Momus*'s knee as he proceeds, accompanied by several jazz bands, along St. Charles Avenue and Canal Street.

Memorable Museums

New Orleans's reputation as a festive, food- and jazz-obsessed city may sometimes overshadow its rich, multifaceted cultural and historical aspects. The city has always intrigued artists, scholars, and writers and is home to a thriving arts community and several impressive museums. These are the major ones.

NEW ORLEANS MUSEUM OF ART: Built in 1912 by local philanthropist Isaac Delgado, *NOMA* has since become an important American museum. Set in pastoral City Park, its permanent exhibits include examples of the major European and American art movements as well as specialized collections including Oriental porcelains and painting; late Gothic and early Renaissance painting from the Samuel H. Kress Collection; fine examples of French Impressionism and 20th-century European painting; a wide array of European and American decorative arts (including jewelry, ornamental pieces, exquisite *Easter* eggs, cigarette cases, and boxes created by Peter Carl Fabergé); contemporary photography; and pre-Columbian and African sculpture. Among the more unusual possessions is a portrait by French Impressionist Edgar Degas of his cousin, Estelle Musson; it was painted during the artist's extended 1873 visit to New Orleans, where his relatives were then residing. Open Tuesdays through Sundays from 10 AM to 5 PM. Admission charge. Information: *New Orleans Museum of Art,* City Park (phone: 504-488-2631).

LOUISIANA STATE MUSEUM: Together, the *Cabildo* and the *Presbytere,* the twin Spanish Colonial buildings flanking St. Louis Cathedral on Jackson Square, form the hub of the *Louisiana State Museum* network. They are filled with displays and exhibitions — documents, relics, portraits, costumes, and furniture — pertaining to the culture and history of the region. Built by the Spaniards in 1795, the *Cabildo* was the seat of the colonial governments of both Spain and France. In a large room on the second floor, documents were signed in 1803 that transferred the entire Louisiana Territory — stretching from the Gulf of Mexico to the Canadian border — from France to the United States. Among some of the more notable relics on display are a box compass, a spy glass, and other items believed to have been owned by the pirate Jean Lafitte, as

146 DIVERSIONS / Avant-Garde New Orleans

well as a bronze casting of Napoleon Bonaparte's death mask. Portraits of prominent past Louisianians are on display throughout the building. In 1988 the *Cabildo's* large attic (an addition in 1847) was destroyed by a fire; happily, the two main floors and their contents escaped serious damage. The *Presbytere,* once the offices of colonial church officials, is now devoted to temporary exhibitions relating to the history of New Orleans and Louisiana. There are many artifacts and information relating to Louisiana-born President Zachary Taylor; the early days of the shipping industry in New Orleans; and the history of Jefferson City, which is now the Garden District. Until the *Cabildo's* restoration (slated for completion later this year), only the *Presbytere* is open, from 10 AM to 5 PM Wednesdays through Sundays. Admission charge. Information: *Louisiana State Museum,* 751 Chartres St. (Jackson Square; phone: 504-568-6968).

HISTORIC NEW ORLEANS COLLECTION: In two handsomely restored, aristocratic French Quarter residences, the L. Kemper Williams Foundation has established one of the South's most impressive historical and cultural research centers. All of the materials, dating from the pre-colonial era to the present, relate to the history of New Orleans and Louisiana. They include maps, books, documents, photographs, and artwork that reflect the culture, economy, and politics of the city and the region, all catalogued and available to scholars and researchers by appointment. Among its recent acquisitions are thousands of negatives purchased from the estate of the celebrated New Orleans photographer Clarence John Laughlin. But this is no stodgy institution catering only to specialists. Tours of the house, furnished with exquisite antiques and decorative art, as well as of the courtyard and the archives, are given on a regular basis. And temporary exhibitions are mounted regularly in the ground-floor gallery on subjects ranging from maps predating the English colonization of America to a slide show on the spectacular costumes of the *Mardi Gras* "Indians," who parade every year during *Carnival.* Open from 10 AM to 4:45 PM Tuesdays through Saturdays. Admission charge for tours of the collection, but none for the ground-floor exhibit gallery. Information: *Historic New Orleans Collection,* 533 Royal St. (phone: 504-523-4662).

Avant-Garde New Orleans

In many ways, New Orleans is like the two-faced Roman god Janus, who looked to the past and the future at the same time. One of New Orleans's many ironies is this artful blend of reminiscence and anticipation. Nowhere is the contrast more striking than in the city's contemporary art galleries, where outrageously avant-garde paintings and sculpture often are housed in quaint, 150-year-old buildings. Below are some of the best.

CONTEMPORARY ARTS CENTER: This early-20th-century former drugstore and office building on the edge of the Warehouse District is now the headquarters of New Orleans's artistic avant-garde. Three floors have been converted into gallery space that features the latest trends in painting, sculpture, film, theater, and photography. The nonprofit *CAC* often spotlights local artists and writers, but talent from other areas of the country and the world also can be seen here. The range of activities presented includes such diverse offerings as a performance art piece by *Harlem's Urban Bush Women;* the big-band sound of Duke Ellington performed by local musicians; group shows by important up-and-coming regional artists such as George Dureau, George Dunbar, and Robert Tannen; and a multimedia event on the latest political crisis. The *CAC's* annual *Sweet Arts Ball,* held in mid-February, is one of the top social events of the year, with music, food from local restaurants, and special exhibitions created around a central theme. Open Wednesdays through Sundays from 11 AM to 5 PM.

DIVERSIONS / Historic Houses   147

Admission charge. Information: *Contemporary Arts Center,* 900 Camp St. (phone: 504-523-1216).

JULIA STREET: If the contemporary art scene has a nucleus, it is Julia Street in the Warehouse District, where a number of contemporary art galleries are located. Showcased are not only important regional artists, but emerging painters, sculptors, and photographers from around the country. Among the major galleries in this area are the *Galerie Simonne Stern* (518 Julia St.; phone: 504-529-1118), where abstract expressionist paintings and contemporary sculpture are showcased; *Arthur Roger Gallery* (432 Julia St.; phone: 504-522-1990), whose lavish exhibit spaces are given over to some of the more daring artists of the city and the region; *Gasperi Gallery* (320 Julia St.; phone: 504-524-9373), which specializes in contemporary folk art and works with strong ethnic connections; and *Still-Zinsel Contemporary Fine Art* (328 Julia St.; phone: 504-588-9999), which often introduces new painters and photographers who work in a variety of styles.

GALLERY FOR FINE PHOTOGRAPHY: Located in the French Quarter, this virtual treasure house of world class photographs is a must for photography buffs. The exhibits range from 19th-century daguerrotypes to original prints by such masters as Henri Cartier-Bresson, Margaret Cameron, Ansel Adams, Irving Penn, Helmut Newton, and Robert Doisneau. The collection contains dozens of excellent photographs relating to New Orleans's musical history as well. Open Mondays through Saturdays from 10 AM to 6 PM and Sundays from 11 AM to 5 PM. No admission charge. Information: *Gallery for Fine Photography,* 322 Royal St. (phone: 504-568-1313).

Historic Houses

The pride New Orleanians take in their past is evident in the many buildings and homes that have been carefully preserved and restored. Many of these homes are still private residences, but a few are open to the public.

HERMANN-GRIMA HOUSE: Of all the historic New Orleans homes open to public view, none conveys a better feel for the city's mid-19th century golden age than this elegant residence in the heart of the French Quarter. Samuel Hermann, a prosperous German immigrant, built the splendid Georgian-style mansion in 1831, and the rooms, kitchen, gardens, and stables have been faithfully restored in the style of that period. The 2 floors of gracefully proportioned rooms, some with wooden friezes and marble mantels, are furnished in fine rosewood and mahogany period pieces, antique English wool carpets, and silk damask draperies copied from 19th-century Italian designs. The scent of aromatic flowers and herbs fills the two inner courtyards. On special occasions, typical creole meals have been prepared on the large kitchen hearth. During December, the downstairs rooms are filled with garlands of fresh boxwood, apple topiaries, and a period-style *Christmas* tree; the table is festively set and laid with traditional foods. Open Mondays through Saturdays, 10 AM to 4 PM. Admission charge. Information: *Hermann-Grima House,* 820 St. Louis St. (phone: 504-525-5661).

LONGUE VUE HOUSE AND GARDENS: This stately home, reminiscent of an Edwardian estate in England, is an elegant world unto itself located just across the road from Metairie Cemetery on the city's edge. The modified Greek Revival house, exquisitely appointed with antique English furniture, also contains a stunning collection of 20th-century artworks by such masters as Arp, Miró, and Chagall. The rooms themselves are a virtual museum of English and American decorative art. The house and gardens are the former property of New Orleans philanthropists Edith and Edgar B. Stern, Jr., who donated it to the city. The view from the library of the formal 8-acre garden is stunning. Open Mondays through Saturdays, 10 AM to 4:30 PM, and Sundays from 1 to 5 PM. Admission charge. Information: *Longue Vue House and Gardens*, 7 Bamboo Rd. (phone: 504-488-5488).

A Shutterbug's New Orleans

Its remarkable architecture, ever-changing moods, and festive character make New Orleans a photographer's dream town. Think of the possibilities: brilliantly colored *Mardi Gras* floats lumbering through the streets, surrounded by thousands of masked revelers clamoring for trinkets from the float riders; an early misty morning on Jackson Square, when the ancient buildings appear in an almost ethereal light; a lush, tranquil courtyard shaded by sweet olive, banana, and magnolia trees; old sternwheelers churning along the Mississippi River; street musicians strumming and tooting under iron-lace balconies.

With backdrops like these, even a beginner can achieve remarkable results with a surprisingly basic set of lenses and filters. Equipment is, in fact, only as valuable as the imagination that puts it into use. (For further information on cameras and equipment, see *Cameras and Equipment* in GETTING READY TO GO.)

Don't be afraid to experiment. Use what knowledge you have to explore new possibilities. Don't limit yourself with preconceived ideas of what's hackneyed or corny. Because the Mississippi River has been photographed hundreds of times before doesn't make it any less worthy of your attention.

In New Orleans as elsewhere, spontaneity is one of the keys to good photography. Whether it's a paddlewheeler right out of Mark Twain chugging along the river or a funky street musician blowing cool jazz from a saxophone, don't hesitate to shoot if the moment is right. If photography is indeed capturing a moment and making it timeless, success lies in judging just when a moment worth capturing occurs.

A good picture reveals an eye for detail, whether it's a matter of lighting, positioning your subject, or taking time to frame a picture carefully. The better your grasp of the importance of details, the better your results will be photographically.

Patience is often necessary. Don't shoot a pastoral garden in the park if someone suddenly blocks your view of it. Reframe your image to eliminate obvious distractions. Are people walking toward a scene that would benefit from their presence? Wait until they're in position before you shoot. After the fact, many of the flaws will be self-evident. The trick is to be aware of the ideal and have the patience to allow it to happen. If you are part of a group, you may well have to trail behind a bit in order to shoot properly. Not only is group activity distracting, but bunches of people hovering nearby tend to stifle spontaneity and overwhelm potential subjects.

The camera provides an opportunity, not only to capture a city's charm, but to interpret it. What it takes is a sensitivity to the surroundings, a knowledge of the capabilities of your equipment, and a willingness to see things in new ways.

LANDSCAPES, RIVERSCAPES, AND CITYSCAPES: An especially good vantage point from which to photograph the French Quarter is one of its taller buildings or whatever elevation you can find. To capture Jackson Square's beautiful proportions, position yourself on the Moon Walk pavilion near the river or the *Jackson Brewery*'s terraces. The rooftop restaurant of the *Omni Royal Orleans* hotel on St. Louis Street is ideal for photographing Chartres Street's activity, as well as for a bird's-eye view of the Quarter's old buildings, which from here are silhouetted against the river. Panoramic views of the Quarter are especially good from the 11th-floor lobby of the *Westin–Canal Place* hotel on Iberville Street near the river. The Garden District and the city's public parks are the best places to capture New Orleans's natural aspects — its lush vegetation, majestic oaks, and profusion of flowers.

DIVERSIONS / Shutterbug's New Orleans   149

Color and form are the obvious ingredients here, and how you frame a picture can be as important as getting the proper exposure. Study the shapes, angles, and colors that make up the scene and create a composition that uses them to best advantage.

Lighting is a vital component in landscapes. Take advantage of the richer colors of early morning and late afternoon whenever possible. The overhead light of midday is often harsh and without the shadowing that can add to the drama of a scene. This is where a polarizer is used to best effect. Most polarizing filters come with a mark on the rotating ring. If you can aim at your subject and point that marker at the sun, the sun's rays are likely to be right for the polarizer to work properly. If not, stick to your skylight filter, underexposing slightly if the scene is particularly bright. Most light meters respond to an overall light balance, with the result that bright areas may appear burned out.

Although a standard 50mm to 55mm lens may work well in some landscape situations, most will benefit from a 20mm to 28mm wide-angle. Panoramic views taken of Jackson Square fit beautifully into a wide-angle format, allowing not only the overview, but the opportunity to include other points of interest in the foreground.

To isolate specific elements of any scene, use your telephoto lens. This is the best way to photograph the *Presbytere* or focus in on *Rex* sitting atop his float. The successful use of a telephoto means developing your eye for detail.

PEOPLE: As with taking pictures of people anywhere, there are going to be times in New Orleans when a camera is an intrusion. Your approach is the key: Consider your own reaction under similar circumstances, and you have an idea of what would make others comfortable enough to be willing subjects. People are often sensitive to having a camera pointed suddenly at them, and a polite request, while getting you a share of refusals, will also provide a chance to shoot some wonderful portraits that capture the spirit of the city as surely as the scenery does. For candid shots, an excellent lens is a zoom telephoto in the 70mm to 210mm range; it allows you to remain unobtrusive while the telephoto lens draws the subject closer. And for portraits, a telephoto lens can be effectively used as close as 2 or 3 feet.

Aim for shots that tell what's different about New Orleans. For authenticity and variety, select a place likely to produce interesting subjects. A *Carnival* parade is obviously ideal. But look for other places where people gather — the *Community Flea Market* in the *French Market,* at the sidewalk artists' easels on Jackson Square, at the *Audubon Zoo*'s exhibits (especially good for photographing children). Street musicians and performers are always around to add a human element to a shot of a historic building or a quaint piece of French Quarter architecture. Seek out vignettes — a cluster of tuxedoed waiters taking a break on the sidewalk outside *Antoine's,* perhaps, or a gardener at work among the shrubbery and flowers in the garden behind St. Louis Cathedral. In portraiture, there are several factors to keep in mind. Morning or afternoon light will add richness to skin tones. To avoid the harsh facial shadows cast by direct sunlight, shoot in the shade or in an area where the light is diffused. The only filter to use is a skylight.

SUNSETS: New Orleans's urban density challenges any photographer's ingenuity when it comes to capturing sunsets. So does its geographic position, which puts the western horizon opposite the most photogenic parts of town. The best bet is to find a vantage point that provides a wide-angle western view. Tall buildings are the obvious places.

When shooting sunsets, keep in mind that the brightness will distort meter readings. When composing a shot directly into the sun, frame the picture in the viewfinder so that only half of the sun is included. Read the meter, set, and shoot. Whenever there is this kind of unusual lighting, shoot a few frames in half-step increments, both over and under the meter reading. Bracketing, as this is called, can provide a range of images, the best of which may well be other than the one shot at the meter's recommended setting.

150 DIVERSIONS / Shutterbug's New Orleans

Use any lens for sunsets. A wide-angle is good when the sky is filled with color-streaked clouds, when the sun is partially hidden, or when you're close to an object that silhouettes dramatically against the sky.

Telephoto lenses also produce wonderful silhouettes, either with the sun as a backdrop or against the palette of a brilliant sunset sky. Bracket again here. For the best silhouettes, wait 10 to 15 minutes after sunset. Unless using a very fast film, a tripod is recommended.

Red and orange filters are often used to accentuate a sunset's picture potential. Orange will help turn even a gray sky into something approaching a photogenic finale to the day and can provide particularly beautiful shots linking the sky with the sun reflected on the water. If the sunset is already bold in hue, the orange may overwhelm the natural colors. A red filter will produce dramatic, highly unrealistic results.

NIGHT: If you think that picture possibilities end at sunset, you're presuming that night photography is the exclusive domain of the professional. If you've got a tripod, all you'll need is a cable release to attach to your camera to assure a steady exposure (which is often timed in minutes rather than fractions of a second).

For situations such as nighttime celebrations on the Mississippi River, a strobe does the trick; but beware: Flash units are often used improperly. You can't take a view of the skyline with a flash. It may reach out as far as 30 feet, but that's it. On the other hand, a flash used too close to a subject may result in overexposure, resulting in a "blown out" effect. With most cameras, strobes will work with a maximum shutter speed of 1/125 or 1/150 of a second. If you set the exposure properly and shoot within range, you should come up with pretty sharp results.

Below are some of the Big Easy's best views.

A SHORT PHOTOGRAPHIC TOUR

ROYAL STREET: With its iron-lace balconies and creole architecture, its antiques shops, restaurants, and street performers, this is the quintessential street to capture New Orleans's romantic spirit. To shoot antiques-shop windows, you'll need a polarizing filter to eliminate reflections, but no special equipment is needed to capture the picturesque architecture and street musicians. Royal Street's iron lace is the finest in the city. At 700 Royal Street is a superb example of the craft, a photogenic building with ironwork framed by a profusion of baskets of fern. The 3-tiered balcony of the Labranche House (at the corner of Royal and St. Peter Streets), with its unusual gray ironwork, is perhaps the most photographed in the entire Quarter. Farther down Royal (at No. 1100) are rows of connected balconies extending on one side of the street almost to the end of the block. Next door, at 1118-1132 Royal, is Gallier House, with its strikingly original balcony painted in bright "Paris green."

JACKSON SQUARE: Walk up Decatur Street to the broad pavilion that separates the square from the Mississippi River, and from any angle you'll get a good shot. First, there is Jackson Square itself, its beautifully symmetrical buildings and St. Louis Cathedral forming a backdrop for the equestrian statue of Andrew Jackson. Flanking the cathedral are the *Cabildo* and *Presbytere,* and the red brick Pontalba Apartments. As you're facing the cathedral, to the right is the *Café du Monde,* marking the beginning of the picturesque *French Market.* To the left are the landing docks for the steamboat *Natchez* and several other excursion boats, framed by the skyscrapers of the business district and the twin bridges that span the river. Then there's the river itself, with cargo ships, tugboats, barges, and excursion craft usually plowing by.

NATURE AND PARKS: Mild winters, a long growing season, and a profusion of evergreens make New Orleans's lush landscape ideal for nature photographers. Flowers of one kind or another are always in bloom. In the fall, look for geraniums and chrysanthemums hanging along balcony rails in the French Quarter. In late winter and early spring, azaleas, gardenias, and camellias accent the elegant homes in the Garden

DIVERSIONS / Shutterbug's New Orleans 151

District and along St. Charles Avenue. Trees and shrubbery — aspidistra, sweet olive, magnolia, and oak — are always around to lend their color, too. The best places to look for them are in the public parks, especially City Park, filled with moss-draped oaks dating back hundreds of years. Longue Vue Gardens is a rich source of flowering plants year-round, and any number of courtyards are decorated with bromeliads, jasmine, and ivy.

MARDI GRAS: Parades are not the only source of great photos during New Orleans's *Carnival* season. On *Fat Tuesday* itself, the French Quarter becomes a candid photographer's paradise. Thousands of people fill the streets, many of them in costumes exotic enough to rival the parade floats themselves for spectacle. Marching bands appear from nowhere, their members always garbed in glittery attire, and revelers fill the balconies, many of them more than happy to perform for the camera. Shutterbugs in search of the truly bizarre should head for the corner of St. Ann and Burgundy Streets, the site of an annual costume contest that attracts the most outrageous getups of all. The limits of taste are repeatedly challenged as gawdiness and bawdiness rule the day.

DIRECTIONS

Introduction

The streets and neighborhoods of New Orleans are ideal for walkers. This curiously intimate, sensual city begs to be seen up close; for it is only in this way that the visitor can fully absorb its sights and sounds in all their glorious details. Among the city's great assets for the pedestrian are its manageable scale, its profusion of trees and green spaces, its quiet, elegant neighborhoods, and the laid-back friendliness of its population.

There is probably no more congenial place to stroll than the French Quarter, to view its fascinating architecture with an impromptu band of street musicians providing the background music. Or what more refreshing atmosphere than that of an oak-shaded avenue lined with stately old mansions of classical proportions, or the cooling air drifting off the mighty Mississippi as it rushes past its banks toward the Gulf of Mexico?

New Orleanians are proud of them all, so feel free to ask advice from anyone who looks like a local, whether you're searching for a street address, a landmark, or a good place for gumbo. He or she will more than likely take the time to oblige with a minute or two of native expertise.

There's just one problem: When directions are the point of discussion, New Orleans becomes a city of contradictions. The points of the compass mean little or nothing in light of the crescent-shape street plan of the older parts of town. Instead, directions are determined by geographical features: One is Canal Street, which connects the city's two natural boundaries — the Mississippi River to the south and Lake Pontchartrain to the north. For most of the 19th century, Canal Street divided the original creole city (what is now essentially the French Quarter) from the "American Sector," where later citizens of other origins settled. Today, everything on the French Quarter (or eastern) side of Canal is "downtown," and everything on the "American" (or western) side of Canal is "uptown."

The other two directional points used by the natives are "riverside" (south) and "lake" (north). What forces the issue is the crescent formed by the Mississippi at New Orleans as it flows toward the Gulf of Mexico. Uptown streets are laid out in curves roughly paralleling the bend of the river, making a compass useless in navigating one's way from one street to another. For example, the city's rather prosperous neighborhood known as Uptown is not uptown, as its name implies, north of the Canal Street dividing line, but actually south of it.

So, when you're asking directions, don't be surprised to hear such explanations as "Magazine Street is on the river side of St. Charles Avenue." Likewise, be prepared to be told that a certain address is on the "uptown-lake corner" of the street.

Matters are further muddied by the fact that, because of its twisting route, the Mississippi at New Orleans actually flows from west to east. Yet the

156 DIRECTIONS

section across the river south of the city's core (the French Quarter, the Riverfront area, the Central Business District, for example) is known as the West Bank. The rationale behind this is that if the Mississippi flowed in a straight line, the communities across from the city proper would be west of the river. Confused? Don't despair: Read on; then follow our lead and all will be well.

In 1718, Jean-Baptiste le Moyne, Sieur de Bienville, chose this as the site for the new French royal colony of La Nouvelle Orleans mainly because it was the highest point on the riverbank. Most of the Quarter is at mean sea level — in other words, zero elevation. The remainder of the modern city remains below sea level, meaning rainwater must be pumped from an elaborate system of subterranean drains into Lake Pontchartrain. It's done with a model system of immense mechanical pumps built in the 1890s and still functioning efficiently today.

The boundaries of Bienville's original city (the French Quarter) remain in effect today. They are Iberville Street, 1 block from Canal and parallel to it; the Mississippi River; Esplanade Avenue; and North Rampart Street, formerly the Rue des Ramparts, where the original town's fortifications were set up. The Quarter covers a rectangle formed by 72 city blocks.

The oldest street names reflect the city's history, religious traditions, and folklore. The French creoles called the French Quarter Vieux Carré (meaning, roughly, "old squared-off area"). Because French royal families were in power at the time of city's founding, streets were given such names as Royale (from which the final "e" has since been dropped), Dauphine, Toulouse, Bourbon, and Du Maine (now contracted to "Dumaine").

Later, in other parts of town, the religious traditions of the mostly Catholic population were also echoed in the names of such streets as Conception, Ascension, Annunciation, and Piety. Almost a score of streets honor the Catholic saints, or the illustrious personages of the same name — St. Louis, St. Peter, St. Ann, and St. Philip in the original colony, and St. Roch, St. Charles, St. Andrew, and St. Mary, among others, in later eras.

In some neighborhoods, Greek mythology was the inspiration — Thalia, Erato, Homer, Coliseum, and Olympia. As the city expanded, literary figures were honored, too — among them Dante, Shakespeare, Milton, and Poe.

And though today's New Orleans also has its share of fast-food outlets, shopping and apartment complexes, and rubber-stamp architecture, happily, its essential, quaint character remains intact.

The ride on the *St. Charles* streetcar provides a special perspective of New Orleans. The six walks visit the historic French Quarter and majestic Royal Street, and take you on journeys through literary New Orleans, to the riverfront, to the art-filled Warehouse District, and last but certainly not least, to the splendid Garden District. The two drives are the Esplanade Avenue–City Park route, which meanders through and then out of town; and the plantation tour, which wanders even farther afield to a place magically frozen in time.

Some bits of information you'll likely need to get around comfortably: Outsiders still stumble over the pronunciation of many street names. Those who use their best college French will invariably miss the mark. For example, in New Orleans, Chartres is pronounced "*Char*-ters." The "gun" in Bur-

DIRECTIONS 157

gundy is stressed ("Bur-*gun*-dy"). Say "*Eye*-berville" when asking for directions to Iberville Street, and "Or-*leens*" when searching for Orleans Street. The biggest challenge of all may be Tchoupitoulas, pronounced "Chop-uh-*too*-luss." Also, the median dividing an avenue is called the "neutral ground," and a sidewalk is occasionally referred to as a "banquette" (pronounced "*bank*-et"), an old French word designating the banked walkways beside the roadbeds. Practice makes perfect.

Regardless of what they call their streets, one thing is certain: New Orleanians are notoriously bad drivers. Many of the streets are one-way, a fact sometimes ignored by certain of the local citizenry. When driving in the French Quarter, it's a good idea to approach corners slowly. Drivers on the Quarter streets between Canal and Esplanade have the right-of-way. On intersecting streets that extend from the river to North Rampart Street, stop signs are posted at each corner, but they are occasionally ignored or unseen by those unfamiliar with the Quarter's traffic system.

Aggravating the situation are missing traffic signs, as well as street signs that have been removed or turned around. In some parts of town, streets are identified by tiles imbedded in the cement at corners. On some French Quarter buildings, elaborately colored tiles identify the street names used during the Spanish colonial period; some of the names are no longer used, a possible source of confusion.

Another word of advice: As in most major American cities, street crime is a fact of life in New Orleans. Visitors should take the same precautions they would take in any big city. This is especially true along the quieter side streets of the lower French Quarter near Esplanade Avenue, as well as the mostly residential blocks near North Rampart Street. The city's old cemeteries are best visited in groups, the larger the better, and only during the daytime.

That said, stop for a beignet and a café au lait, and travel with us through a luxurious, lovely, laid-back, lusty, lilting day in the life of the Big Easy. We promise you, you won't forget it.

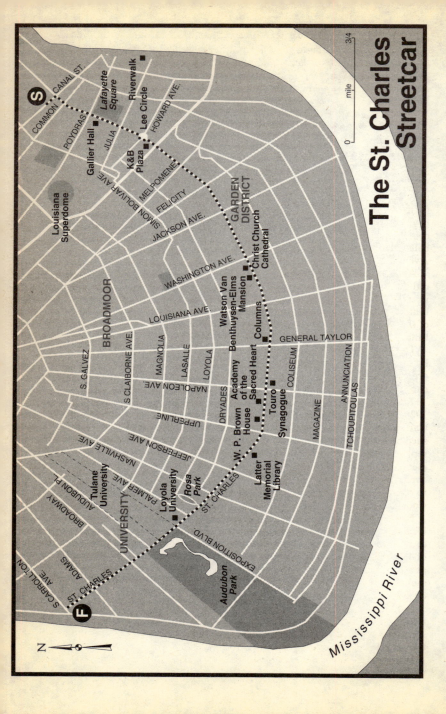

The St. Charles Streetcar

The *St. Charles* Streetcar, part of the oldest continuously operating muncipal railway system in America, journeys leisurely through one of the most beautiful urban residential areas in the country. The quaint, yet efficient, old coaches begin their journey of a little over 3 miles at Canal Street in the heart of the central business district, gently lurching their way uptown to the clanging of bells until they eventually reach the grassy median of oak-shaded St. Charles Avenue, a very tony thoroughfare.

Along the way, windows on both sides of the car afford views of elegant old mansions, as well as some of New Orleans's most noteworthy churches, its two largest universities, plantation-style houses, and numerous public buildings that are both architecturally and historically significant. For most of the trip, hundreds of oaks, most of them 100 years old or more, form a leafy tunnel along the 50 blocks of St. Charles Avenue.

The *St. Charles* streetcars aren't trolleys (a groups of connected cars pulled by some kind of locomotive), nor are they cable cars (which in San Francisco are mechanically operated with an elaborate system of underground pull-cables). Rather, they are powered electrically by overhead cables.

The 35 olive-green and russet cars operating today were built in 1923 and 1924 by the Perley A. Thomas Car Company, based in High Point, North Carolina. Over the years, they have undergone extensive renovations without succumbing to excess modernization. New mahogany window sashes have replaced the old ones; the roofs, once canvas-topped, now are lined with metal. Exact-change fare boxes and metal automatic doors were installed just over a decade ago to allow for one conductor, rather than the previous two, to operate the coach. But the seats are still made of hard, smooth, varnished wood, and there is no climate control system.

New Orleanians use the streetcars often, so they're likely to be jammed with local commuters traveling to and from work in the central business district or with students shuttling to and from school. The cars rarely exceed speeds of 15 or 20 miles an hour, so there's usually ample time for looking around at all the sights. Traffic signals and autos blocking the median as they await a chance to cross also provide some time to appreciate particular buildings or curiosities.

Ideally, the optimal way to see the various landmarks from the streetcar would be to take a round-trip journey, sitting on the left side one way, the right side going back. But we think this ride should be used as an introduction to New Orleans as a whole, since you'll be passing through many of the key points of interest in the individual walks in this section. As you ride, note

160 DIRECTIONS / St. Charles Streetcar

those attractions that especially intrigue you and plan to return later for closer study (see *Walk 4: The Riverfront; Walk 5: The Warehouse-Art District,* and *Walk 6: The Garden District,* as well as THE CITY).

The commentary that follows assumes you will board either at the corner of Carondelet and Canal Streets or at the corner of St. Charles Avenue and Common Street. Each description of a point of interest indicates whether it is on the right side or the left side when the coach is traveling *uptown* — that is, away from Canal Street and toward Carrollton. (Keep in mind that exact change is necessary for the fare, which at this writing is 90¢.)

The first major intersection after Canal and Carondelet Streets is Poydras Street, in the heart of the business district. A few blocks up on the left, notice the elaborate entrance to the *Riverwalk Mall,* on the Mississippi Riverfront (see also *Walk 4: The Riverfront*), and the *Louisiana Superdome,* visible between the office towers, on the right.

One block past Poydras Street on the right is Gallier Hall (543 St. Charles Ave.; phone: 504-565-7457), a momument-like Greek Revival temple named in honor of its designer, celebrated architect James Gallier, Sr. It functioned as the City Hall from 1853 until the 1950s; today, it is used for some of the city's official events (see also *Special Places* in THE CITY). Directly across from Gallier Hall on the left is Lafayette Square, a lush, lovely green space with the first of the many large oak trees that line the route. At the edge of the square, near the street, is a white granite pedestal with a life-size bust of 19th-century philanthropist John McDonough. He was a major benefactor of New Orleans public schools, and many of them still bear his name. The figures of a small boy and girl next to the bust are further examples of his generosity.

The next 4 blocks of St. Charles contain a hodgepodge of old and new commercial structures, forming one of the boundaries of the Warehouse District, an area of late-19th-century structures now being rehabilitated into apartment complexes, restaurants, galleries, and shops (see also *Walk 5: The Warehouse-Art District*).

The streetcar now turns right at Lee Circle. On the left, at the corner of Lee Circle and Howard Avenue, is the Howard Memorial Library (not open to the public). Dating to 1889, this fortress-like red stone building was designed by Henry Hobson Richardson, a Louisiana native who became one of the most respected American architects of the late 19th century. The building, no longer a library, is now the headquarters of a private foundation.

The streetcar next edges around Lee Circle, at the center of which, surrounded by a grassy mound of turf, is the Lee Monument. Supported by a 60-foot-high fluted column is a statue of Confederate General Robert E. Lee, arms folded as he gazes south (where else!).

At the end of this half circle, the ride continues toward K&B Plaza on the right. This is one of the first truly modern New Orleans office buildings, designed by the New York–based architectural firm Skidmore Owings Merrill. Placed around the pavilion surrounding the structure are sculptures by major contemporary artists, among them Henry Moore, Isamu Noguchi, and George Segal. They form part of the corporate collection of contemporary art assembled by the K&B regional drugstore chain. The ground-floor lobby contains dozens of other sculptures and paintings. (Also see *Walk 5: The Warehouse-Art District.*)

DIRECTIONS / St. Charles Streetcar 161

For the next dozen-odd blocks, the streetcar travels through the Lower Garden District, which 100 years ago was a tony neighborhood of graceful, galleried Greek Revival mansions. They now contain shops, restaurants, bars, and other businesses.

Watch for the canopied *Pontchartrain* hotel on the right, between St. Andrew and Josephine Streets. This small, elegant, white hostelry contains the famous *Caribbean Room* restaurant (see also *Eating Out* in THE CITY). Across the street from the *Pontchartrain* is the former *Restaurant de la Tour Eiffel,* a large, raised structure of geometric ironwork built in 1987 and inspired by the design of Paris's Eiffel Tower. It closed in 1990, and remains vacant at press time.

One block past the *Pontchartrain,* the far corner of Jackson Avenue marks the start of the Garden District. Filled with handsome 19th-century houses and lavish gardens, the district extends 5 blocks to the left from St. Charles Avenue (toward the Mississippi River) to Magazine Street and about another 13 blocks straight ahead to Louisiana Avenue. The streetcar stop at St. Charles and Jackson is a good starting point for a walking tour of the district, after which you can return to St. Charles Avenue and reboard the streetcar (it will cost you another fare) at any of several convenient stops (also see *Walk 6: The Garden District*).

On the right, 8 blocks past Jackson Avenue, look for the late-Gothic-styled Christ Church Cathedral, which dominates the 2900 block of St. Charles. Since its construction in 1887, the church has been the seat of the Episcopal Church in New Orleans. The complex of buildings owes its design to New York architect Lawrence Valk, who used traditional English elements for the interior.

The Watson Van Benthuysen–Elms mansion, at the corner of Seventh Street on the right (3029 St. Charles Ave.; phone: 504-895-5493), is the only one of the St. Charles mansions open to the public. The owners will occasionally permit tours of the house, by reservation only; there is an admission charge. The immense stone house, set on a grassy mound, was built in 1869 by Van Benthuysen, who was responsible for expanding the streetcar system beyond First Street and also served as the treasurer of the Confederate States of America. Each of the principal rooms is decorated in the style of a different period. The dining room, with Jacobean appointments, contains the original chandelier brought from Paris. In the Louis XVI drawing room are mirrors and consoles, also imported from France. A sitting room done in the French Empire style still has the house's original lavish wall covering. And the staircase — hand-carved, spiral, and freestanding — is a remarkable feat of engineering and design.

Eight blocks up, between Peniston and General Taylor Streets on the right, is the *Columns* hotel, built in 1883 as the home of Simon Hersheim, the well-to-do owner of a large cigar factory on Magazine Street. The building, set far back from the street, is notable for the massive pairs of white columns flanking its large verandah. French director Louis Malle filmed part of *Pretty Baby,* his movie about life in a Storyville bordello, in its elaborate Victorian interior.

Two blocks beyond the *Columns,* on the corner of Constantinople Street on the left, is the Sully House, a brick-and-wood residence built in 1890 in

162 DIRECTIONS / St. Charles Streetcar

the Queen Anne style by architect Thomas Sully for his family. His 25-year career, from 1880 to 1905, was enormously productive, as he designed some 35 homes along the avenue; alas, many of his creations are no longer standing.

Three blocks up on the left, at the corner of General Pershing Street and St. Charles Avenue, is Touro Synagogue, seat of one of the city's most important Reform Jewish congregations. Distinctly Middle Eastern in its use of geometric motifs, this 1909 building was named for Judah P. Touro, the son of a Rhode Island rabbi who came to the city as a young man and became one of its most generous philanthropists.

The next large intersection, Napoleon Avenue, is 1 block farther; another block past Napoleon on the right is the Academy of the Sacred Heart (4521 St. Charles Ave.), a Catholic girls' school. The impressive building, with its wraparound balconies and layers of shuttered and arched windows, is set on beautifully manicured lawns. Several of the streets near Napoleon Avenue were named for sites where the French emperor led his army into battle, such as Jena, Milan, and Constantinople. (General Pershing Street had been called Berlin Street, but the name was changed after World War I.)

Two streets past the school, at the corner of Bordeaux Street on the right, is W.P. Brown House (4717 St. Charles Ave.), the city's most majestic example of Romanesque Revival architecture. Designed by a disciple of Henry Hobson Richardson, this awesome residence was built from 1902 to 1905 and cost $250,000 (a princely sum in that era). The mass of ivy-covered stone rests on one of the best-maintained lawns in town. Brown, a rags-to-riches entrepreneur, began his career as a clerk in a Mississippi country store and wound up cornering the cotton market. He had the house constructed as a wedding gift to his bride.

Two more blocks up on the right, set back from the corner of Robert Street, is the *Orleans Club* (5005 St. Charles). Founded in 1925 as a private social and cultural club for women, the mansion (not open to the public) contains a library and reading room, meeting and lecture rooms, and a restaurant. Note the lacy, intricate ironwork on the columns, rails, balconies, and fence.

On the next block on the left is the Latter Memorial Library (5120 St. Charles; phone: 504-596-2625). Constructed in 1907 as a private home and occupied by a long list of affluent New Orleanians, it was donated to the city in 1948. The downstairs rooms, outfitted with several period pieces, make for opulent reading areas, and there is a glass-enclosed balcony overlooking the avenue. Open daily; no admission charge.

The next major intersection, 2 blocks up, is Jefferson Avenue, and the site of the starkly modern Jewish Community Center on the left. Danneel Park, a small playground, is on the right. Movie buffs are likely to recognize the stately building 2 blocks farther up, on the far right corner of Arabella Street: It is a replica of Tara, Scarlett O'Hara's homestead as depicted in the film version of *Gone With the Wind*. Copied in the 1940s from MGM Studios' movie set, the whitewashed brick exterior has the classic, clean lines, square columns, and graceful entryway of the Hollywood original. (Also see *Special Places* in THE CITY.)

One block past Tara, at the corner of Rosa Park on the right, is one of the most imposing and elaborate mansions on the avenue (5809 St. Charles Ave.).

DIRECTIONS / St. Charles Streetcar   163

It is one of the few remaining creations of architect Thomas Sully, whose 1896 2-story colonial-revival design includes double and triple columns, garlanded friezes, and fanciful finials. Notice the curvilinear dormers in the huge attic. Another Sully house is 2 blocks farther up on the left, at No. 6000. The house is distinctive for its swan's neck pediments, casement windows, and portico entrance designed with swags and garlands — all earmarks of the colonial revival style Sully helped to popularize in New Orleans.

Three blocks farther up is the *Round Table Club* (6330 St. Charles), at the corner of Exposition Boulevard on the left. The club is the male version of the *Orleans Club* you passed several blocks ago. Organized in 1898 by a group of men interested in literature, science, and art, the private club contains reading rooms, a billiard parlor, and a library.

Across the street on the right is the campus of Loyola University, a Catholic institution operated by the Society of Jesus. The red brick buildings facing St. Charles are in the Tudor-Gothic style. Today, the 14-acre campus has an enrollment of about 5,000. It was founded in 1911, evolving from Loyola Academy, a prep school established on the site in 1904.

Right next to Loyola is Tulane University, a private, non-sectarian institution that began in 1834 as the Medical College of Louisiana, became the University of Louisiana in 1847, and in 1883 adopted its present name following a bequest by philanthropist Paul Tulane. The neo-Romanesque buildings facing St. Charles were constructed from Bedford stone in 1894. Today, the 93-acre campus has an enrollment of about 10,000 students.

Across the avenue from Tulane on the left is Audubon Park, with picnic grounds, a bridle path, lagoons, a golf course, and a major zoo, occupying 340 acres extending to the Mississippi River. The park combines a former sugarcane plantation and part of the estate belonging to the city's first mayor, Etienne De Boré, who invented a way to granulate sugar in 1794. Purchased by the city in 1871 and dubbed "New City Park," the site was renamed in honor of 19th-century naturalist and artist John James Audubon, who spent several years studying and painting Louisiana flora and fauna. From 1884 through 1885, the *World's Industrial and Cotton Exposition* was held here to commemorate the 100th anniversary of the first shipment of cotton from Louisiana to a foreign port. Today the park is divided into three sections. The first fronts St. Charles Avenue and is a huge playground for golfers, horseback riders, tennis players, joggers, and bikers. Its green spaces are dotted with lagoons where ducks gather daily for handouts, and there is a beautiful tropical plant conservatory. The second section is the Audubon Zoo (6500 Magazine St.; phone: 504-861-2537), fronting Magazine Street, between the park and the Mississippi River. One of the country's finest, the 55-acre zoo has more than 1,500 species in re-creations of their natural habitats. The third sector is the riverside area between the zoo and the Mississippi, which has a tranquil and scenic walkway along the river. If you want to head back to town, the *John James Audubon* riverboat operates a shuttle between here and the *Aquarium of the Americas* and can take you back to the foot of Canal Street (see also *At-A-Glance* and *Special Places,* THE CITY).

Just past Audubon Park on the right is Audubon Place, a private street guarded by twin stone gatehouses. It dates back to the early 20th century,

164 DIRECTIONS / St. Charles Streetcar

when a Texas real estate magnate developed this parcel of land now shared by 28 homes.

A block away is the Broadway intersection, and 2 blocks farther up, on the corner of Millaudon Street on the left, is the curiously Moorish building that formerly was Dominican College (7214 St. Charles). Set at the end of a neat, well-maintained formal garden, the college was founded in 1860 by a group of Irish nuns. The liberal arts college for young women closed in the 1970s and is now owned by Loyola University, which uses the 1872 structure as a dormitory and for some administrative offices.

Past this point, the blocks along the avenue once were part of the town of Carrollton, an independent municipality until 1874. Carrollton was first a village, and later became a resort and railroad terminus. Although it was annexed to New Orleans more than a century ago, it still has its own unique character, with quiet, cozy side streets and modest houses, neighborhood bars, and bakeries.

St. Charles Avenue ends at the intersection of Carrollton Avenue, and while the streetcar makes a right turn on its tracks and continues along the median for several more blocks, the first stop after the turn is a good place to get off and take a breather. The grassy hill ahead of you is the river levee, a perfect vantage point for viewing the rolling Mississippi where it bends — a geographic phenomenon that gave this section of Carrollton the name Riverbend. This makes an ideal place to enjoy a picnic spread, but if you didn't bring one, the *Camellia Grill* across the street offers a tasty menu of casual fare (626 S. Carrollton; phone: 504-866-9573). Pull up a stool for some old-fashioned, gracious counter service of first-rate hamburgers, club sandwiches, pecan pie, and "freezes," icy, frothy drinks that can be made either with or without ice cream — a refreshing way to end your streetcar introduction to the Big Easy.

Walk 1: The French Quarter

New Orleans's French Quarter — or Vieux Carré, as it's sometimes called — has one of the most impressive concentrations of 18th- and 19th-century buildings in North America — and that's only a small part of its many charms.

Unlike colonial Williamsburg, Virginia, the French Quarter is not a manicured quasi-museum. Unlike Washington, DC's Mall, it is not a collection of austere public buildings. Rather, it remains a vibrant, integral, and constantly evolving part of the city it inhabits. Behind the façades of its buildings, some of them almost 200 years old, are myriad distinctive restaurants, elegant residences, churches, shops, striptease shows, museums, jazz bands, libraries, hotels — in other words, every component, and then some, of a modern American city. Neatly dressed residents go to and from their offices amid tourists and street performers, itinerant musicians in town for a gig, shopkeepers, daintily dressed Southern matrons doing their marketing, and sidewalk artists displaying their work.

Occupying a 90-square-block area in the heart of the modern city of New Orleans, the Quarter is diffused with a sense of history. Legends from its quirky, colorful past could — and do — fill volumes. To this day, it resounds with the exotic earthiness of its French, Spanish, and African origins, even as dozens of T-shirt shops, tacky souvenir emporia, and glitzy malls increasingly threaten the unique atmosphere of its streets and alleys.

The French Quarter manages somehow to remain the least "American" of America's urban neighborhoods. The Quarter's essential atmosphere owes more to the Mediterranean than it does to the Gulf of Mexico. Its quaintly distinctive architecture, constructed on a nearly ideal human scale, partly accounts for that, as does the sense of mystery conveyed by its shuttered windows, hidden interior patios, and aromatic gardens.

Once you've escaped the rank commercialism of Bourbon Street and the waterfront from Canal Street to Jackson Square, you can easily succumb to the seduction of its streets. They are tailor-made for strolling, with many stretches of sidewalk sheltered from the frequent showers and the tropical sun by overhead balconies. Royal and Bourbon Streets are daytime pedestrian malls, and three sides of Jackson Square are permanently closed to automobile traffic.

Depending on your penchant for lingering, a walking tour of the French Quarter's interior can be done in either a half or a full day. We have included points of interest from Jackson Square and its environs and continued away from the river and in the direction of North Rampart Street and Esplanade

The French Quarter

0 — mile — 1/4

BARRACKS

GOV. NICHOLLS

FRENCH MKT. PL.

N PETERS

Thierry House ■

Lalaurie House ■   ■ Clay House   French Quarter Maisonettes

Gallier House ■   ■ Soniat House   Ursuline Convent

URSULINES

Beauregard-Keyes House

ST. PHILIP

Lafitte's Blacksmith Shop

Cornstalk House ■

DUMAINE

■ Madame John's Legacy   MADISON

ST. ANN

Bourbon Orleans   Presbytere ■   St. Louis Cathedral   Pontalba Apartments

ORLEANS   PÈRE ANTOINE

PIRATES ■   **S** Jackson Square

St. Anthony's Garden   Labranche House ■■ Cabildo

ST. PETER

Maison LeMonnier ■   **F**   WILKINSON

TOULOUSE

DAUPHINE   BOURBON ST.   ROYAL   CHARTRES   DECATUR   N

ST. LOUIS

CONTI

N PETERS

BIENVILLE

DIRECTIONS / The French Quarter 167

Avenue. For a comprehensive look at all the French Quarter has to offer, this tour should be supplemented with three others: *Walk 2: Royal Street; Walk 3: A Literary Tour of New Orleans;* and the French Quarter sections of *Walk 4: The Riverfront (and Farmer's Market).*

The first task is to get your bearings. The official boundaries of the rectangularly shaped French Quarter district are Iberville Street, parallel to and 1 block from Canal Street; the Mississippi River; Esplanade Avenue, the divided boulevard beginning at the river; and North Rampart Street, site of the early colony's fortifications. They enclose 12 blocks between Iberville and Esplanade and approximately 5 blocks from the river to Rampart Street.

This walk begins at the Quarter's focal point: St. Louis Cathedral, on Chartres Street at Jackson Square between St. Peter and St. Ann Streets. While it is the oldest cathedral in the United States, the present-day building is actually the third to occupy the site. The first was the parish church erected by Jean-Baptiste Le Moyne Bienville soon after he founded the colony in 1718. Demolished 5 years later by a hurricane, the church was rebuilt in 1727, only to be destroyed in the great fire of 1788. In 1793 the parish church was proclaimed a cathedral and the seat of a diocese; a year later, the basic structure existing today was erected, with rounded Spanish-style steeples at the front. The present façade, with its columned entablature and three conical steeples, was constructed between 1849 and 1851 to the specifications of architect J.N.B. de Pouilly. Today the cathedral remains the paramount symbol of the city's traditionally strong ties to Roman Catholicism.

To the left of the cathedral is the *Cabildo,* the seat of Spanish rule in the late 18th century (*cabildo* was the Spanish term for "council"). Dating to 1795, it's the successor to earlier governmental headquarters on the site. In 1803, in the room at the front of the second floor, the Louisiana Purchase was signed, transferring the entire Louisiana Territory (stretching from the Gulf of Mexico to the Canadian border) from France to the United States. The historical museum inside is temporarily closed — the large attic, enclosed by a mansard-style roof with dormer windows, was destroyed by fire in 1988. As we went to press, a painstaking restoration was under way, scheduled for completion later this year.

The *Cabildo* and the *Presbytere,* its twin to the right of the cathedral, together contain the most important historical collections of the *Louisiana State Museum. The Presbytere* (phone: 504-568-6968) originally was the seat of the French and Spanish colony's church government, although it functioned primarily as a courthouse.

The *Cabildo*'s permanent collection contains such curiosities as a bronze casting of Napoleon Bonaparte's death mask and mementos of the pirate Jean Lafitte, whose ragtag band of thieves ruled the coastal waters leading to the city in the first years of the 19th century. Inside the *Presbytere* are permanent and temporary exhibitions relating to the arts, crafts, documents, and costumes of New Orleans and Louisiana (for more information on both sites, also see *Memorable Museums* in DIVERSIONS).

St. Louis Cathedral faces Jackson Square, laid out in 1721 as the Place d'Armes, a parade ground used for military drills and church and government functions. In 1848, still a dusty parade ground, it was rechristened to honor

168 DIRECTIONS / The French Quarter

General Andrew Jackson's 1815 victory over the British at the Battle of New Orleans during the War of 1812. The battle took place 6 miles from the square, downriver in the town of Chalmette. The statue of Jackson on his rearing horse, a casting of which appears in Washington, DC's Lafayette Square, was erected in 1856. The work of American sculptor Clark Mills, it's believed to be the first equestrian statue to have the horse with more than one hoof off the ground. Jackson Square divides the lower, more residential section of the quarter, beginning at St. Ann Street, from the upper, more commercial, section, extending from St. Peter Street up to Iberville.

The square's symmetry is completed with the two, 3-story brick buildings flanking it along St. Peter and the opposite street, St. Ann. They are the Pontalba Apartments, completed in 1850 from the plans by James Gallier, Sr., who designed them at the behest of Spanish Baroness Micaela Almonester y Pontalba, daughter of Don Andres Almonester y Roxas, the richest citizen to inhabit the Spanish colony a half century earlier.

The baroness was intent on stopping the shift of waterfront activity from the old district to the American sector on the other side of Canal Street. Toward that end, she had these twin buildings constructed, each extending a full block and containing eight row houses, with upper-level luxury apartments and street-level shops and offices. At the center of each cast-iron balcony rail, the baroness's monogram, with the intertwined letters A and P, is visible.

Today, the upper building on St. Peter Street is owned and administered by the city government, and the lower one on St. Ann Street by the state government in Baton Rouge. The apartments are private residences, as they have been for almost 150 years. After a look at the confectioneries, bakery, restaurants, and shops here, return to the corner of Chartres and St. Ann Streets and continue along Chartres, walking away from the cathedral. A half block away on the right is the 1-block-long Madison Street, which offers a fine perspective of the corridor of handsome old residences leading to a view of the *French Market*'s colonnades on Decatur Street.

Continuing along Chartres leads to the mostly residential Lower Quarter, considerably quieter and less traveled than the blocks on the other side of Jackson Square. Stroll and admire the occasional glimpse of a courtyard, visible through the wide, gated carriageways, and the balconies, casting curious shadows across the narrow street.

Continue on Chartres past the cross street, Dumaine, to 920 Chartres, on the right side, with a walkway leading to a 2-story outbuilding edged with giant banana plants. Across the street at 921 Chartres is the Contesta Apartments Building, with an especially large courtyard framed by a pair of arches at the end of the stone carriageway. On the sidewalk in front of the gate is a relic of the horse-and-buggy era, a row of alphabet tiles spelling out "Stalls for Rent."

Proceed past the intersection of St. Philip and Chartres to Ursulines Street. On the near left corner is a modest masonry cottage in the classic French-creole style, with an outbuilding at the rear. In the antebellum city, almost every house of any substance in the Old City was equipped with such auxiliary structures, which functioned as slave quarters; always narrow, simple homes

DIRECTIONS / The French Quarter 169

with brick ground floors and wooden upper ones, they usually also contained kitchens and storage rooms. Today they are popular with couples and single residents as modest-sized homes.

Visible from the corner of Ursulines and Chartres Streets are two of the Quarter's most important buildings — the Beauregard-Keyes House and Garden to the left and the old Ursuline Convent to the right.

Of the two attractions, only the Beauregard-Keyes House (1113 Chartres; phone: 504-523-7257) is open to the public. Before entering the house, take a peek through the grate at the beautifully landscaped, formal garden. Joseph Le Carpentier, a professional auctioneer, had it built in 1826, in the neo-classical style then beginning to appear in the old city. The site is on a portion of the 3 city blocks he purchased from the Ursuline nuns living across the street. Le Carpentier lived here with his daughter and her husband, attorney Aliens Morphy. (Although the house bears the name of the Confederate General Pierre Gustave Toutant Beauregard, he lived there for only 2 years in the 1860s.) During the 1940s and 1950s, it was owned by novelist Frances Parkinson Keyes, one of the many writers who chose the city as her creative home. The most famous of Keyes's romantic novels is *Dinner at Antoine's,* a reference to the historic restaurant on St. Louis Street a few blocks away (see also *Walk 3: A Literary Tour of New Orleans*).

The house has been painstakingly restored and contains many of the antique rugs and furniture owned by Mrs. Keyes, as well as her fascinating collection of dolls (also see *Special Places* in THE CITY).

Just across the street is the cream-colored masonry wall surrounding the old Ursuline Convent (at the corner of Chartres and Ursuline Sts.), one of the oldest buildings in the Mississippi Valley. Much of the present structure dates to 1749; even though the convent is not open to the public, the architecture of the 2 stories and attic that can be viewed from the outside shows many influences from the Louis XV style.

It was home to the Sisters of St. Ursula, who arrived in New Orleans from France in 1727. Isolated from the bustling center of the French colony, the Ursulines managed a military hospital and established an orphanage, and schools for the children of the colonists, as well as for the slaves and Native Americans. At different times during the 19th century, the convent building served other functions. It housed a Catholic school for boys in 1831, then the Louisiana Legislature from 1831 to 1834. From the late 1830s to 1899, it was the official residence of the Archbishop of New Orleans. Today it houses the archdiocesan archives.

The small church at the left of the convent wall is Our Lady of Victory, one of the oldest Catholic churches in New Orleans. It was originally the convent chapel. At the turn of the century, long after the Ursulines moved their headquarters, it became St. Mary's, the parish church of the Italian immigrants who settled in the French Quarter during the late 19th and early 20th centuries. Notice the ornamentation of raised cement work on the flat façade of stuccoed brick. On the frieze above the church's door frame, a pair of angels in flight carry a chalice between them. Under the cross on the gable, the papal coat of arms stands out in relief.

Next door, with a carriageway flanked by two charming iron horse heads,

170 DIRECTIONS / The French Quarter

is the *French Quarter Maisonettes* (1130 Chartres St.; phone: 504-524-9918), one of the oldest guesthouses operating in the district. Through the carriageway gate, there's a very pleasant courtyard.

Just across the street is *Soniat House* (1133 Chartres St.; phone: 504-522-0570), originally an 1829 townhouse built by Joseph Soniat du Fossat, a wealthy aristocratic planter. The townhouse, as well as the adjacent building on the right, was used as a guesthouse until the early 1980s, when it became a hotel with rooms decorated in period antiques and rugs (see also *New Orleans's Best Hotels* in DIVERSIONS).

Continue on Chartres to the corner of Gov. Nicholls Street. To the right is a row of five nearly identical Greek Revival buildings. In the mid-19th century, they were designed by J.N.B. de Pouilly, the architect of St. Louis Cathedral, as luxurious 2-story duplex houses.

Turn left and walk down Gov. Nicholls Street, one of the Quarter's most pleasant thoroughfares, with many small trees lining the sidewalk for several blocks. In the middle of the 600 block on the left is the handsomely proportioned Clay House (618-620 Gov. Nicholls St.), built as a residence in about 1828 by John Clay, brother of Henry Clay, the 19th-century American statesman. Although the house is not open to the public, the exterior is well worth a look. At each end of the long brick wall to the left of the house is a door pierced with peepholes. Peer through both of them for views of the spectacularly lush garden. At the garden's rear is a 2-story balconied building, added after 1871; in the 1890s it was used as a schoolhouse.

Proceed down Gov. Nicholls to the next corner, Royal Street. The building on the near left corner (1140 Royal) is the infamous Lalaurie House, also known as "The Haunted House." According to the oft-quoted legend, Delphine Lalaurie, who acquired the house from her father in 1831, was one of the town's most prominent hostesses. When a fire broke out one night in 1834, firemen and neighbors discovered in the attic seven starved, tortured slaves in chains. Word of the atrocity quickly spread, and an infuriated mob sacked the house. Delphine and her husband, Dr. Louis Lalaurie, escaped in a carriage. The couple fled to Mandeville across Lake Pontchartrain, then to Mobile, Alabama, and finally to Paris. Local folklore says that the slaves' ghosts still haunt the house's numerous private apartments and account for occasional disturbing noises such as groans, screams, the savage hissing of whips, and the clanking of chains.

From here, make a short detour across Royal Street to the 700 block of Gov. Nicholls Street. In the middle of the block on the left, at 716 Governor Nicholls, is a 2-story apartment house known as the Spanish Stables. In the 19th century, it served as a mews for the carriage horses of the neighborhood. Look through the wide central gate for a view of the excellently maintained garden at the center of the quadrangle.

Across the street at No. 721, behind a brick wall, is the Thierry House, built in 1814 for Jean-Baptiste Thierry, editor of the *Courrier de la Louisiane*, an early French-language daily newspaper. Though relatively modest in scale, the house is the earliest remaining example of the Greek Revival style that ultimately influenced much of Louisiana's architecture. Henry Latrobe, who designed the house at the tender age of 19, later became a nationally promi-

DIRECTIONS / The French Quarter 171

nent architect of the early 19th century. The small, pillared portico leading to the entry of the house was inspired by the temples of ancient Greece.

Backtrack to the corner of Royal and Gov. Nicholls and turn right down Royal. In the center of the block, on the left side, is the immediately recognizable bright-green balcony of the Gallier House (1118-1132 Royal St.; phone: 504-523-6722), a charming example of the French Quarter's elegant Victorian manses now open for public view. Before entering, be sure to look across Royal Street at the stunning vista of iron-lace balconies running the length of the block, one of the most impressive in the entire district.

The house was completed in 1857 by the respected architect James Gallier, Jr., for his own family. He followed the fashion of the day by using trompe l'oeil techniques to create the impression of exterior granite blocks on the plastered brick façade and the look of marble and beautifully grained wood in the interior. The color of the balcony, known as "Paris green," was meant to simulate the patina of oxidized copper or bronze.

Tours of the elegant house and garden, with a restored cistern, are given every hour or so, and end with coffee on the balcony (see also *Museums and Historic Houses* in THE CITY).

If you're ready for a break at this point, you're in luck. From Gallier House, turn left and continue along Royal to the corner of Ursulines and turn left again. A short distance down the block is the *Croissant d'Or* (617 Ursulines St.; phone: 504-524-4663), an excellent French bakery offering ten varieties of croissants, more than 20 different French pastries, and, at lunch, sandwiches, soups, and salads, all very reasonably priced. If the weather is pleasant, you can enjoy your snack in a picturesque little courtyard, complete with a fountain and chattering birds.

Turn right when leaving the bakery and return to Royal Street. Turn left and proceed 1 block to St. Philip Street. Another block to the right on St. Philip Street is Bourbon Street. At the far left corner of Bourbon and St. Philip is *Lafitte's Blacksmith Shop* (941 Bourbon; phone: 504-523-0066). Now a popular bar and lounge, this building, dating to 1772, has the oldest record of ownership of any private building in the city. Although the story has never been documented, local legend says it once was a smithy where the Lafitte brothers, the "hero pirates" of New Orleans, posed as blacksmiths while plundering cargo vessels near the mouth of the Mississippi River. They supposedly used the shop as a transfer point for stolen goods. Jean Lafitte and his band assisted General Andrew Jackson in defeating the British at the Battle of New Orleans. Visible behind the building's broken plaster are soft bricks and posts (known as *briquets-entre-poteaux*), a typical construction method of the time.

Retrace your steps back to Royal Street and turn right. Continue on the right side of Royal to the *Cornstalk House* hotel at 915 Royal. The tall, cast-iron fence with the pattern of intertwining stalks and ears of corn, erected circa 1850, is one of only a few in the city. It was cast in Philadelphia by the Wood & Perot Foundry and delivered to New Orleans by ship. The dark-green and yellow paint is a modern addition; black was the original color of all the iron fences of the period.

Across the street on the near left corner of Royal and Dumaine Streets are

172 DIRECTIONS / The French Quarter

the connecting Miltenberger Houses (900-910 Royal), built in 1838 by the widow Miltenberger for her three sons. Her great-granddaughter, Alice Heine, was one of New Orleans's social heroines (and the grandniece of Heinrich Heine, the German poet). In 1874, at the age of 16, Heine became a duchess by marrying the French Duc de Richelieu. After the duke's death in 1879, she went to Paris, where she met Albert, Prince of Monaco (the present Prince Rainier's great-grandfather). They hit it off royally, and she married him in 1889, becoming the Princess of Monaco.

At the corner of Royal and Dumaine Streets, turn left and walk a few yards. At No. 632, on the right side, is a simple, raised-frame cottage painted a neutral color. Dating to 1726, this unassuming building, known as Madame John's Legacy, is the oldest house in the Quarter, and one of the oldest in the Mississippi Valley. Its first owner was Jean Pascal, a sea captain from France's Provence region, who was given the site by La Compagnie des Indes, which controlled the French colony. Pascal lived here with his wife and daughter until he was slain in a 1729 massacre by the Natchez Indians. The structure was one of the few to survive the 1788 fire which nearly demolished the entire city. Its identity as Madame John's Legacy stems from a 19th-century novel, *Tite Poulette,* by Creole author George W. Cable. The book's hero, John, lived in this house with his parents until their deaths, and he bequeathed it to his mistress, known as Madame John, and her infant son.

The cottage and its simple, covered porch is an excellent example of the West Indies plantation architectural style. The ground floor is enclosed by thick brick walls and has an uneven rough brick floor; the upper floor is of wood. The building's porch, steeply pitched roof, and depth of only one room were design features that maximized air circulation during the steamy summers.

Return to Royal Street (on the right when facing Madame John's Legacy), turn left, and walk 1 block to St. Ann Street. At the corner, linger for a moment to enjoy the profusion of ironwork balconies. This is one of the most frequently photographed sites in all the interior Quarter, since it captures much of its architectural spirit. Look right along St. Ann Street for a view of the arched entrance to Louis Armstrong Park, developed in the 1970s to honor the city's illustrious jazz musician. Used primarily for local festivals, there are lagoons, bridges, and walkways throughout the park.

Continue down Royal Street for about a half block to the little garden at the rear of St. Louis Cathedral, bounded on one side by Père Antoine Alley and on the other by Pirates Alley, both running alongside the church and leading to Jackson Square. The little garden is one of the loveliest green spaces in the French Quarter. Although officially named Cathedral Garden, locals call it St. Anthony's Garden in memory of Antonio de Sedella, who came to New Orleans in 1779 and was affectionately known by the cathedral's Creole parishioners as Père Antoine.

Orleans Street is almost directly behind the garden. Walk down Orleans to the middle of the block; on the right is the *Bourbon Orleans* hotel (717 Orleans). In 1817, it debuted as the famed *Orleans Ballroom* (also known as the *Quadroon Ballroom*), where young Creole bachelors would come to meet and dance with elegantly dressed young women of European and African

DIRECTIONS / The French Quarter 173

descent, chaperoned by the Sisters of the Holy Family, an order of black nuns. The nuns acquired the site in 1881 and used it as a motherhouse and a school until 1964, when they sold the property to the developers of the hotel. It was created by John Davis, who would later operate the *Orleans Theater* and establish the first operatic performances in America in what was the old *French Opera House* (destroyed by fire in the 1920s) on the corner of Bourbon and Toulouse Streets. The famed ballroom, at the center of the second floor, is now a meeting room for local businesspeople.

Return to Royal Street; turn right and walk 1 block to the corner of St. Peter Street. On this corner, at the left, are two of the French Quarter's most remarkable buildings. The one on the near corner is Labranche House, with its triple tier of oak leaves and acorn-patterned cast-iron balconies. Across from Labranche House is Maison LeMonnier (640 Royal St.), a 3-story structure that is frequently referred to by locals as the "First Skyscraper," since it was easily the district's tallest building when it was erected in 1811 by Dr. Yves LeMonnier and a pharmacist, Francois Grandchamps. The doctor had a study on the third floor, and his monogram, "YLM," is still visible on the wrought-iron balconies.

By this time, it may be time for lunch or dinner; if you need some refreshment, the *Royal Café* (700 Royal St.; phone: 504-528-9086) isn't far from here. The breakfast, brunch, lunch, and dinner menus offer variations on many traditional creole dishes, and the view off the bustling street corner from the balcony offers some of the best street theater in town.

Royal Street

0 mile 1/8

MADISON

ST. ANN

PÈRE ANTOINE

St. Anthony's Garden

ORLEANS

PIRATES

St. Louis Cathedral

Jackson Square

F

ST. PETER

Labranche House

WILKINSON

■ M. S. Rau Inc.

Old Town Praline Shop ■

TOULOUSE

Historic New Orleans Collection ■

Gerald D. Katz Antiques ■

ST. LOUIS

ROYAL

Raymond Weill Co. ■

CONTI

Old Bank of Louisiana ■

A Gallery for Fine Photography ■

EXCHANGE ALLEY

CHARTRES

BOURBON ST.

BIENVILLE

Hanson Art ■ Galleries

French Antique ■ Shop

IBERVILLE

N

S

Walk 2: Royal Street

If the French Quarter has a Main Street, it is neither raw and boisterous Bourbon nor glitzy Decatur, but rather Royal Street.

Royal Street is to New Orleans what Fifth Avenue is to New York; though both streets may be less glamorous than in their heyday, they reflect the soul of their respective cities. Royal boasts the French Quarter's most remarkable concentration of commercial and residential creole architecture, as well as some of the district's best restaurants and shops.

The focus of this walking tour is on the shops, restaurants, and ambience found along the 5 blocks of Royal between Iberville and St. Peter Streets, the core of the street's commercial life. It can be taken as an adjunct to the more comprehensive French Quarter walking tour, which includes the blocks of Royal beyond St. Peter and focuses on historical and cultural landmarks (see *Walk 1: The French Quarter*).

Royal Street has been a daytime pedestrian mall for almost 2 decades, making it ideal for strolling, appreciating its elegant façades and fascinating antiques-shop windows, and people watching.

When the streets of the French Quarter were laid out in 1722, the arterial thoroughfare behind the little church (which later became St. Louis Cathedral) was named Royal-Bourbon, in honor of France's ruling family. Soon the name was changed to La Rue Royale (perhaps as a hedge against any future changes in the seat of power).

Today, the great majority of the street's balconied townhouses, modest creole-style masonry cottages, and imposing public buildings reflect the architecture of the early 19th century. This area of the city was largely destroyed by two devastating fires — one in 1788, the other in 1794; only a few of the French colonial buildings survived. Since the neighborhood was rebuilt during the Spanish domination of New Orleans, the damaged structures were replaced by Spanish colonial houses — two basic elements of which are the "iron lace" balconies and interior courtyards that set the standard for the city's architecture for years to come. Supposedly, one of the reasons the Spaniards built in this style was to protect themselves and their families from intruders from the streets. Closed and shuttered on street level, the houses had an inner courtyard which functioned as naturally air conditioned gathering places for friends and family. Many of the courtyards were connected with each other through a system of passageways, so residents could visit others on the block without ever having to step outside.

None of the Quarter's other streets can compare with Royal for examples of intricately patterned iron balconies. The 8-block corridor between St. Louis and Gov. Nicholls Streets is a virtual museum of elegant creole ironwork. The balconies were constructed with one of two types of ironwork: either hand-wrought into patterns and designs or produced from cast iron poured into

176 DIRECTIONS / Royal Street

molds. While wrought-iron work was introduced to New Orleans in the 1790s, its exorbitant expense curtailed its use. When the less expensive cast iron was introduced about 1830, it was an instant success and balconies were often added to existing structures. A good example of the look is the splendid LaBranche House at the corner of Royal and St. Peter Streets. The house — actually a series of connected townhouses — was built in 1840, but its wrap-around galleries framed in cast iron were added after 1850.

After the 1803 annexation of the Louisiana Territory "Americanized" New Orleans, the city grew wealthier, and so did its Royal Street shops. Although the emporia were cramped and cluttered, their merchandise was often comparable to items from such cosmopolitan capitals as London and Paris. The many French and English antiques dealers found on Royal Street today are the successors to those dealers who began setting up shop in the early 1800s, when the street was the center of the city's furniture trade. By the 1850s, Royal's profusion of such places prompted the *Daily Picayune* to observe that "Royal is hardly large enough for the daily growing furniture business."

But as the 19th century drew to a close, the street began to earn its share of criticism. Detractors painted Royal as being plagued with peddlers who flocked to the city during the cooler seasons and made nuisances of themselves, blocking traffic with their overflowing carts. By the 1880s, George W. Cable, one of the creole city's literary giants, described the neighborhood as "a region of architectural decrepitude where an ancient and foreign-seeming domestic life in second stories overhangs the ruins of a former commercial prosperity, and upon everything has settled a long Sabbath of decay."

But the street continued to prosper despite its critics, and its European veneer lent it an air of class and Old World respectability that it still retains. The architectural scale and style of its buildings are part of the reason; also, the majority of its shops have escaped the rubber-stamp, shopping-mall mentality that would have turned it into just another commerical strip. Royal Street is still the place to find New Orleans's finest French and English antiques shops; several of its galleries sell high-quality works by distinguished local and national artists; and a few of the restaurants on or near Royal are among the city's best. In some cases, the businesses on this street have been run by the same family for generations.

If you want to have lunch before beginning, one good restaurant is at Royal Street's very gateway, at the corner of Iberville: *Mr. B's Bistro* (201 Royal St.; phone: 504-523-2078). This bustling, laid-back dining room serves food that combines the spicy heartiness of creole cooking with contemporary treatments of hickory-grilled fish, cleverly created soups and salads, and first-rate desserts (also see *Big Easy's Best Eats* in DIVERSIONS). Another excellent nearby dining spot is *Alex Patout's Louisiana Restaurant* (221 Royal St.; phone: 504-525-7788). The eponymous proprietor-chef, born in Cajun country, specializes in spicy versions of roasted young pig, duck smothered in rich gravy, and a wide variety of seafoods and gumbos.

Start this walk at the corner of Royal and Iberville Streets by window shopping or browsing through the *French Antique Shop* (225 Royal St.; phone: 504-524-9861), the Granet family's glittery emporium of exquisitely crafted 18th- and 19th-century French furniture and objets d'art. Chandeliers

DIRECTIONS / Royal Street   177

of ormolu, brass, and other fine metals are a specialty. While the prices are not inexpensive, the lustrous wood cabinets and tables are the stuff of dreams.

The contrast in mood couldn't be sharper between the *French Antique Shop* and *Hanson Art Galleries* (229 Royal St.; phone: 504-566-0816), a few doors down. This shop is a showplace for the contemporary painting, graphics, and sculpture of such popular artists as Peter Max, Erté, and Leroy Neiman, as well as New Orleans native Adrian Deckbar.

The Far East is the focus at *Diane Genre Oriental Art and Antiques* (233 Royal St.; phone: 504-525-7270), an uncluttered showroom spotlighting beautifully crafted antique Chinese and Japanese lacquerwork, ornate vases, antique woodblock prints, and fine Oriental textiles.

For a leisurely stroll like this, the perfect accessory is a walking stick. You'll find an array of antique ones next door at the *Brass Monkey* (235 Royal St.; phone: 504-561-0688), along with a huge variety of French and English bibelots, vases, and other decorative objects.

The next stop is for more serious antiques collectors. *Dixon and Dixon of Royal* (237 Royal St.; phone: 504-524-0282) offers 10,000 square feet filled with 17th-, 18th-, and 19th-century antiques, estate jewelry, rugs, and a striking selection of old European oil paintings.

Rothschild's (at 241 and 321 Royal St.; phone for both: 504-523-5816) is the place to look for antique silver, estate and contemporary precious jewelry, chandeliers, porcelain, and furniture.

Continue to the 300 block of Royal, which is chockablock with more antiques shops. *Royal Antiques* (307-309 Royal St.; phone: 504-524-7033) has 17,000 square feet of showrooms filled with English and French country antique furniture, chandeliers, mirrors, porcelain, and jewelry.

For photography buffs, a feast awaits next door at *A Gallery for Fine Photography* (322 Royal St.; phone: 504-568-1313). The 2 floors of exhibition space hold a treasury of photographs spanning more than a century, including the finest original prints of such masters as Ansel Adams, Edward Curtis, Yousuf Karsh, and Henri Cartier-Bresson, along with a collection of great photography books. You'll also find many excellent shots of New Orleans musicians, street scenes, and portraits by the city's best photographers.

Farther down the street, *Waldhorn Antiques* (343 Royal; phone: 504-581-6379) specializes in antique silver, important old European jewelry, and fine 18th- and 19th-century English furniture. The building was erected circa 1800 during the Spanish colonial period and has been the headquarters for three different banks during its history. *Waldhorn* has occupied the building since 1880, when Moise Waldhorn first opened the business; the fourth generation of Waldhorns is now in charge.

Set back from the sidewalk, the imposing stucco building on the opposite side of Royal Street was the Old Bank of Louisiana; constructed in 1826, its columned portico was added in the 1840s. The design of the surrounding iron fence and gates were based on those at Lansdowne House in London. The building has served several functions in modern times — an American Legion hall, headquarters of the Greater New Orleans Tourist Commission, and, today, a district police station.

The antiques shop across Conti and Royal Streets is *Manheim Galleries*

178 DIRECTIONS / Royal Street

(409 Royal St.; phone: 504-568-1901), founded at this site in 1919 by Bernard Manheim. Constructed in 1820 as the Louisiana State Bank, its design was the final work of Benjamin Henry Latrobe, a major American architect of the period. Some aspects of the building recall his design of the Bank of Pennsylvania in Philadelphia. The gallery's specialties are Oriental porcelain, antique European furniture, and the realistic porcelain birds of Edward Boehm.

Nearby is *Raymond Weill Co.* (407 Royal St.; phone: 504-581-7373), one of the country's premier stamp dealers. Some of the most unusual and rare stamps in the world are here, bought at auction by the Weill brothers, Raymond and Roger, for hundreds of thousands of dollars.

Next door is *Moss Antiques* (411 Royal St.; phone: 504-522-3981), with a good selection of small silver items such as dresser bottles, pie servers, fish sets, and fruit knives, as well as large and small pieces of furniture.

If you've not had breakfast or lunch, *Brennan's* restaurant (417 Royal St.; phone: 504-525-9711) offers delectable food in a stunning atmosphere. Poached eggs in exquisite sauces are the specialty here, along with gumbo, trout, crab, and veal dishes. The old-fashioned rooms and large, lush patio are elegant and handsome.

The ornate, white marble building that occupies the entire block across the street was built in 1907 to house the Louisiana Supreme Court. To make room for the large edifice, the state demolished the entire block, including General Andrew Jackson's Royal Street headquarters during the Battle of New Orleans and the original site of Antoine Alciatore's 1840s boardinghouse, which preceded *Antoine's* restaurant. Currently, only a small part of the space is being used (a branch of the state Wildlife and Fisheries Department has offices here), but the legislature is considering returning the building to its original function.

From the corner of Royal and St. Louis Streets, continue along Royal to the 500 block. On the left, not far from the corner of St. Louis and Royal, is *Gerald D. Katz Antiques* (505 Royal St.; phone: 504-524-5050), one of the city's largest dealers in antique American and European jewelry.

Farther along (533 Royal) is the Merieult House. Its granite pilasters are typical of the simple French architectural style prevalent in 1792, when it was built for Jean-François Merieult. This is one of the few buildings in the area to escape the second of the devastating 18th-century fires that destroyed most of the French colonial buildings of the Quarter. It was bought in 1938 by the late General and Mrs. L. Kemper Williams, the city's leading collectors of historical materials relating to New Orleans, the lower Mississippi Valley, and the Gulf Coast. The documents and artifacts, comprising the most important collection in private or public hands, were bequeathed to a foundation that now maintains them as the *Historic New Orleans Collection* (phone: 504-523-4662). The Collection includes research libraries, exhibition spaces, and the Williamses' former living quarters. The central gallery on the ground floor shows temporary exhibits relating to the history of New Orleans and the region. The Williamses' former home, decorated with important French and English antiques, can be visited by inquiring at the gallery. Open Tuesdays through Saturdays from 10 AM to 4:45 PM.

At the corner of Royal and Toulouse Streets is the *Dansk Factory Outlet*

DIRECTIONS / Royal Street 179

(541 Royal St.; phone: 504-522-0482), an excellent source of practical and decorative kitchen equipment, dishes and glassware, all at discount prices. Some great bargains can be found here, but inspect everything carefully before buying, since some items are factory seconds or have design flaws.

Crossing Toulouse Street, and remaining on the left, continue on Royal to the *Old Town Praline Shop* (627 Royal St.; phone: 504-525-1413). Locals consider the creole pecan-praline candies sold here to be the real thing — crunchy, buttery, and fresh. They can be eaten on the premises, packaged to go, or shipped anywhere in the world. (Also see *Quintessential New Orleans* in DIVERSIONS.)

A couple of doors down, at 631 Royal, is a modest, early-1790s building, believed to be the second-oldest on the street. But it is famous for another reason. For several years during the 1860s it was the home of Adelina Patti, a legendary 19th-century opera singer who appeared in the title role of Bellini's *Lucia di Lammermoor* in the old *French Opera House;* the house stood at the corner of Bourbon and Toulouse Streets a couple of blocks away before being destroyed by fire in 1920.

Directly across from the Patti house is one of the city's most fascinating antiques shops, *M. S. Rau Inc.* (630 Royal St.; phone: 504-523-5660), with 2 floors overflowing with glassware, porcelain, garden ornaments, chandeliers, antique furniture, and a charming collection of huge, mechanical music boxes. For an excellent overhead view of Royal Street, climb the rear stairs to the second floor and walk to the balcony (the doors are usually open). This family institution was founded in 1912 by Mendel Rau and his wife, Fanny. Their sons, Joseph and Elias, took over shortly after Mrs. Rau's death in 1989. The Raus' emphasis on cut glass is believed to have helped revive a worldwide interest in the American Brilliant Period, which began about 1880 and lasted until 1910.

On leaving *M. S. Rau,* walk the few yards to the corner of Royal and St. Peter Streets. On the right is the Labranche House, dating from 1840 and perhaps the most photographed building in the French Quarter because of its three tiers of spectacular iron-lace balconies. The quaint pattern of the ironwork, with entwined oak leaves and acorns, is considered one of the finest in the district (see also *Walk 1: The French Quarter*).

Across from the Labranche House on Royal is the *A&P Food Store* (701 Royal St.; phone: 504-523-1353), an oft-overlooked source of creole cookery ingredients. Inside are many savory souvenirs — New Orleans coffee and chicory, all sorts of spices and sauces indigenous to the area, and myriad other creole foodstuffs.

At this point, you are a block away from the sights and bustle of Jackson Square, an ideal place either to begin another tour or to just sit back and relax.

Walk 3: A Literary Tour of New Orleans

New Orleans's mystique has long lured writers, and the French Quarter has been both a haven to and a source of inspiration for large numbers of them. Some have lived and worked here, others merely have passed through. Many, like Tennessee Williams, came and went frequently, and lived in a variety of places in the city he called his "spiritual home."

Truman Capote, who wrote his first novel, *Other Voices, Other Rooms,* in New Orleans, described his impressions of the city this way: "New Orleans streets have long, lonesome perspectives; in empty hours their atmosphere is like Chirico, and things innocent, ordinarily (a face behind the slanted light of shutters, nuns moving in the distance, a fat dark arm lolling lopsidedly out some window, a lonely black boy squatting in an alley, blowing soap bubbles and watching sadly as they rise to burst), acquire qualities of violence. . . . New Orleans is a secret place."

Capote was not alone in his fascination with the city. In the 1920s, a group of writers and artists would often gather in the home of Jackson Square resident (and Ohio expatriate) Sherwood Anderson, best known for *Winesburg, Ohio,* a collection of short stories. The French Quarter became the American counterpart to Paris's Left Bank; according to one of Anderson's friends, cartoonist Bill Spratling, "there were casual parties with wonderful conversation and with plenty of grand, or later to be grand, people. . . . Carl Van Doren and Carl Sandburg and John Dos Passos and many others were there from time to time and there was a constant stimulation of ideas."

One of those "later to be grand" people was a skinny young man from Oxford, Mississippi, who would eventually win the Nobel Prize and forever change the face of American literature — William Faulkner. In a foreword to a friend's privately published collection of caricatures, Faulkner wrote that the French Quarter "has a kind of ease, a kind of awareness of the unimportance of things that outlanders like myself . . . were taught to believe were important." Perhaps the mystique of the French Quarter and the city itself is best described by one of Tennessee Williams's most famous creations, the tragic Blanche DuBois, who remarks, "Don't you just love these long, rainy afternoons in New Orleans when an hour isn't just an hour — but a little piece of eternity dropped into your hands?"

Many of the landmarks on this literary walking tour are noteworthy for reasons other than their literary significance (see also *Walk 1: The French Quarter*). And though some of the sites are not extant, you can imagine such literary legends as Williams, Faulkner, and Gertrude Stein crisscrossing the Quarter, absorbing its earthy, often raucous, charm.

182   DIRECTIONS / Literary Tour

The French Quarter was where at least two famous pen names were born. As a riverboat captain, Samuel Langhorne Clemens stopped here between 1857 and 1861, contributing occasionally to the *Crescent,* a local literary journal in which Clemens's nom de plume, Mark Twain, first appeared. By 1882, his name now known nationwide, Clemens returned to New Orleans to write *Life on the Mississippi,* which includes ten chapters filled with his impressions of the city.

Later, in 1896, William Sidney Porter was writing for the *Item,* a local newspaper, when he ventured into a bar one night and mentioned he was scouting for a pen name for his short stories. As legend has it, a customer called to the bartender, "Oh, Henry, another of the same." We don't know if the fellow got his drink, but Porter got the message and signed the name "O. Henry" on his work thereafter.

Begin this literary stroll where a piece of Tennessee Williams folklore was spawned: the old, now-abandoned Second City Criminal Court Building (410 Chartres Street at the corner of Conti, next to *K-Paul's* restaurant). Williams was hauled into court one night as a witness against his landlady, who was accused of pouring water on a boisterous tenant hosting a noisy party. Trying to be as diplomatic as possible, Williams told the court, "I think it highly unlikely that a lady would do such a thing." The woman was fined $50 anyway, and she confronted Williams later about what she believed to be his damaging testimony. "Any fool could tell I'm not a lady," she chastised. A similar scene turns up in Williams's 1978 play, *Vieux Carré.*

A half block down Chartres, toward Jackson Square, at the corner of St. Louis Street is the *Napoleon House Bar* (500 Chartres St.; phone: 504-524-9752). Over the years, its patio has been a favorite meeting place for writers. The main bar, laden with yellowed prints and dusty busts of its namesake, is a good place to pull up a chair and soak up some of the ambience. If hunger strikes, try a muffuletta, the lusty Italian sandwich made with thick, crusty bread, ham, salami, and mozzarella cheese, and a briny salad of olives and pimientos.

Looming across Chartres Street from *Napoleon House* is the *Omni Royal Orleans* hotel (621 St. Louis; phone: 504-529-5333), a favorite lodging place for writers during the 1960s and 1970s. Williams often stayed here on his many visits to the city, as did Lillian Hellman and Truman Capote. When Williams died, his estate was valued at $10 million. But when visiting the *Royal Orleans* in 1969, he is said to have complained bitterly about the cost of the room. That didn't deter the hotel from naming a corner suite for him and decorating it with photographs of the author's many sojourns into the French Quarter.

From *Napoleon House,* cross Chartres and walk 1 block to Royal Street. Cross Royal to *Antoine's* (713 St. Louis St.; phone: 504-581-4422). Founded in 1840, the legendary French-creole restaurant has hosted hundreds of prominent authors, American and foreign. When William Faulkner was awarded the Legion of Honor, the highest decoration bestowed by the French government, he came to New Orleans to receive the medal at the French Consulate, then celebrated with a meal in one of the labyrinth of ancient rooms at *Antoine's.* Frances Parkinson Keyes, a popular novelist of the 1940s, paid the

DIRECTIONS / Literary Tour 183

restaurant the ultimate literary compliment, naming one of her romantic tales *Dinner at Antoine's*. (See also *Eating Out* in THE CITY.)

After leaving *Antoine's*, turn left and return to Royal Street; then turn right and walk 1 block to Conti Street. The imposing building on the corner of Royal and Conti surrounded by the railed black iron fence is now the New Orleans Police Department's Vieux Carré District headquarters. But in the 1920s, costume balls of the beaux-arts variety, a favorite event in the artistic community, were held here. At the time, William Faulkner lived in a small apartment a few blocks away, on Pirates Alley across from St. Louis Cathedral. He attended several of the balls, despite his shy, reclusive habits. A couple of decades later, Tennessee Williams was known to haunt the antiques shops along this stretch of Royal. Once, when he was making a purchase, a merchant asked him if he was the Tennessee Williams who wrote plays. He replied that he was the Tennessee Williams who wrote checks.

Continue up Royal, walking toward Canal Street for 2 blocks to Iberville Street. Turn right at Iberville and walk a block and a half. On the left side of Iberville was the rear entrance to the now-defunct *D.H. Holmes* department store, referred to in John Kennedy Toole's Pulizer Prize–winning novel, *A Confederacy of Dunces*. At the store's main entrance, around the corner on Canal Street, was the famous clock that was a favorite meeting place of New Orleanians, including Toole's hapless hero, Ignatius J. Reilly. A half block farther down Iberville is the rear of the *Maison Blanche* department store, referred to by name in two of Williams's plays — *Summer and Smoke* and *Sweet Bird of Youth.*

Return to Bourbon and turn left, remaining on the left side. In the middle of the block is *Galatoire's* (209 Bourbon; phone: 504-525-2021; see also *Big Easy's Best Eats* in DIVERSIONS), a setting that has inspired works of literature such as contemporary author Sheila Bosworth's novel *Almost Innocent,* and Eudora Welty's short story "No Place for You, My Love." It was to this restaurant that Stella and Blanche repair for a meal, leaving Stanley at home with a plate of cold food, in Williams's *A Streetcar Named Desire.* Across the street, the *Old Absinthe House* (240 Bourbon St.; phone: 504-523-5181) hosted an impressive list of writers over the years, among them Walt Whitman and Oscar Wilde (not together!). Passing through town on a lecture tour in 1883, Wilde is said to have quipped that when Southerners were complimented on their cities, they would always reply ruefully, "You should have seen it before the war." Today, the *Old Absinthe House* is occupied by *Tony Moran's,* an Italian restaurant on the second floor, and a lively bar and lounge at street level. The bar's patrons are mostly visitors to the city who leave their business cards stapled to the walls.

Walk up Bourbon and turn left on Conti to *Broussard's* restaurant (819 Conti St.; phone: 504-581-3866; see also *Eating Out* in THE CITY). Now a plush, crystal-laden eatery, this was an unpretentious creole bistro in the 1920s when Faulkner endowed it with some notoriety as the only restaurant mentioned by name in *Mosquitoes,* an early novel set in New Orleans.

Backtrack to Bourbon and Conti Streets, turn left, and walk 1 block down Bourbon (heading toward Esplanade); then turn left at St. Louis Street and walk to No. 820. This is the Hermann-Grima House (see also *Historic Houses*

184 DIRECTIONS / Literary Tour

in DIVERSIONS), which served as the model for the family home in the romantic novel *Feast of All Saints* by contemporary author Anne Rice, a native of New Orleans.

Returning once again to Bourbon, turn left. The handsomely designed, but now rather seedy-looking, building at 516 Bourbon is where Lafcadio Hearn lived during his stay of several years in New Orleans in the 1880s. Hearn, a newspaper writer at the time, wrote numerous feature pieces on New Orleans life, and compiled the first creole cookbook before traveling to Japan to write about that country's culture and lifestyle.

Continue down Bourbon to the next block, walking toward Esplanade Avenue. At 623 Bourbon is a stately townhouse sandwiched among the bars and nightclubs that fill much of Bourbon Street today. Behind the front door at 623, however, is a glamorous home with a lush courtyard; Thornton Wilder, author of *Our Town,* spent several months writing here in the 1940s. Continue down Bourbon to Toulouse and turn right. At 727 Toulouse is *Maison de Ville,* a small, quiet, and pricey hotel where Tennessee Williams occasionally stayed and labored over his typewriter (see also *New Orleans's Best Hotels* in DIVERSIONS). Williams always reserved Room No. 9, where he reportedly worked for about 5 hours a day. On one particularly productive day, when he was scheduled to check out, he kept a honeymooning couple waiting in the lobby for several hours until he had finished his work.

A few doors farther down Toulouse, walking toward Royal Street, is No. 719, home of the late Lord Bradford. Bradford, the former night city editor of the *Times-Picayune* newspaper, became one of Faulkner's patrons when he published the writer's early "New Orleans Sketches." Bradford had other noteworthy literary connections — novelists Sinclair Lewis and John Steinbeck were guests at his apartment, and his grandson, Richard Bradford, wrote the critically acclaimed novel *Red Sky at Morning.*

Across the street (at 722 Toulouse) are the administrative offices of the *Historic New Orleans Collection.* During the 1940s, the building was an apartment dwelling; Tennessee Williams lived on the third floor (his former apartment is identifiable by the dormer window, barely visible above the roofline).

Walk a few more doors down Toulouse. At the intersection of Royal and Toulouse Streets (741 Royal) is a 16-room, creole-style townhouse, which in the 1930s and 1940s was rented for $16 a month by the late Lyle Saxon, important for his lyrical depictions of New Orleans. His best-known works are *Father Mississippi, Fabulous New Orleans,* and *Children of Strangers.* Saxon is said to have employed an especially talented cook, who rustled up lunches and suppers at which the author entertained fellow writers.

Continue 1 block farther along Toulouse to the corner of Chartres. *Victor's Café,* a literary hangout until its demise in the 1960s, stood on the near left corner. In the 1920s, it was a favorite neighborhood dining spot for Faulkner and fellow Quarterite Sherwood Anderson. About 20 years later, a hypochondriacal Tennessee Williams was hard at work on a play that he first called *The Poker Night,* but later changed to *A Streetcar Named Desire.* In his memoirs, he credits *Victor's* as an integral part of the creative process: "I would work from early morning to late afternoon, and then, spent from the

DIRECTIONS / Literary Tour   185

rigors of creation, I would go around the corner to a bar called Victor's and revive myself with a marvelous drink called a Brandy Alexander, which was a specialty of the bar."

Turn left at the corner and continue on Chartres for a block toward Jackson Square. At the near left corner of Chartres and St. Peter Streets, where the square begins, is *Le Petit Théâtre du Vieux Carré,* a community theater founded in the 1920s that continues to present two seasons of amateur performances each year (see also *Theater* in THE CITY). The theater entrance is on St. Peter Street. One of the many stories surrounding "Little Theater," as it's locally known, concerns novelist Sinclair Lewis. In the 1940s Lewis visited the city with a woman he introduced as his niece and convinced the theater's management to cast her in a starring role — and in exchange, he would write the script. The reviews of this resultant travesty were far more complimentary to Lewis's writing than to his "niece's" acting.

Return to Chartres and walk the few steps to *La Marquise Pastry Shop* (635 Chartres St.; phone: 504-524-0420), a coffee-and-dessert spot with excellent croissants, pastries, and other snacks, as well as good coffees and teas. Should you decide to stop in for a refreshment, you'll be in what once was a private home where Faulkner and Anderson often visited friends, inspiring Anderson's short story "A Meeting South."

Afterward, return to St. Peter Street and Jackson Square. On the square, you may see a bizarre vending cart in the shape of a huge hot dog. This is one of the "Lucky Dog" carts, known to readers of John Kennedy Toole's *A Confederacy of Dunces* as "Paradise Vendors." Facing the square at St. Peter and Chartres, to the right are the Upper Pontalba Apartments, extending the full block from Chartres to Decatur Streets. Apartment 540-B on the second floor is where Anderson and his wife lived in the 1920s while he produced two impressionistic essays, "A New Testament" and "More Testament." The Andersons were known among New Orleans writers for their hospitality as well as their parties, often offering shelter to literary types who were down on their luck and needed a place to stay. Faulkner was one of them.

Jackson Square itself has a certain literary cachet. Tennessee Williams's poem "Morning on Bourbon Street" mentions the equestrian statue of General Andrew Jackson, and Blanche DuBois, the ill-fated romantic in *A Streetcar Named Desire,* refers to the sound of St. Louis Cathedral's bells as the only truly clear thing in life. In Lillian Hellman's autobiographical *An Unfinished Woman,* she recalls running away at the age of 14 from her aunts' home uptown to the French Quarter and hiding in the cathedral. In his novel *Mosquitoes,* Faulkner compared peering through the iron fence surrounding the square with gazing through an aquarium.

With the cathedral at your left, continue along Chartres, across St. Ann Street and 1 block to Madison Street. At the corner of Chartres and Madison is the *Librairie Book Shop* (823 Chartres St.; phone: 504-525-4837), which stocks a large selection of used books, especially hardcover fiction and reference volumes. It is owned by Gary Beckham, who also runs *Beckham's Book Shop* in the French Quarter (228 Decatur St.; phone: 504-522-9875), one of the largest used-book emporia in the city. After you've finished browsing,

186 DIRECTIONS / Literary Tour

walk down Madison for a short block toward the *French Market,* to Decatur Street. Truman Capote fondly reminisced about the famous market in "A Voice from a Cloud," an autobiographical essay: "I would walk through the humid, balconied streets, past St. Louis Cathedral and go on to the French Market, a square crammed in the early morning with the trucks of vegetable farmers, Gulf Coast fishermen, meat vendors, and flower growers. It smelled of earth, of herbs and exotic, gingery scents, and it rang, clanged, clogged the ears with the sounds of vivacious trading. I loved it." On the near left corner of Madison and Decatur Streets is *Tujague's* bar and restaurant (823 Decatur; phone: 504-525-8676). At the turn of the century, *Madame Begue's,* the most celebrated New Orleans restaurant of its era, existed in the building on the second floor; O. Henry dined there frequently. The expert weaver of tales had moved to New Orleans, where he wrote five stories, after a stint in a Texas prison.

Walk back down Madison to Chartres Street; turn right, and continue 1 block to Dumaine Street. Turn left on Dumaine and walk the few steps to No. 615. During the 1940s and 1950s William March Campbell, a shipping executive who wrote under the pen name William March, lived here and produced such respected novels as *Company K* and *The Bad Seed.* (The latter was adapted with great success for Broadway and Hollywood.) Across the street (632 Dumaine) is one of New Orleans's most legendary buildings, both in historical and literary terms. Dating to the mid-18th century, this is one of the oldest structures in the Mississippi Valley and the model for the house of Jean Pascal, or "Madame John's Legacy," a focal element in George Washington Cable's 19th-century novel, *Tite Poulette.* Cable masterfully depicted the everyday life of the creoles in New Orleans in the late 1800s (see also *Special Places* in THE CITY).

From Madame John's Legacy, walk a half block to Royal Street. Turn left on Royal and continue to the intersection of Royal and Orleans Streets. Turn right onto Orleans; in the middle of this block is *La Librairie d'Arcadie* (714 Orleans; phone: 504-523-4138), a bookshop specializing in French-language books and fine antique prints and engravings. Just across the street is the *Bourbon Orleans* hotel (717 Orleans St.; phone: 504-523-2222). Until the mid-20th century it functioned as a convent. The Quadroon Ballroom on the second floor figures in Faulkner's *Absalom, Absalom.* At the corner of Orleans and Royal (719 Royal) is yet another building in which Tennessee Williams lived, this one in the early 1940s following his theatrical success with *The Glass Menagerie.* Much of his later play *Camino Real* also was written here. He often told friends how much he enjoyed the view of the verdant garden behind St. Louis Cathedral from his balcony.

Now turn right onto Royal, walk 1 block to St. Peter, and turn left toward Jackson Square. In what is now the *Gumbo Shop* (630 St. Peter) was once the home of Oliver LaFarge, a New Orleans writer whose novel *Laughing Boy* won a Pulitzer Prize in 1930. Nearby, on the same side of the street (632 St. Peter), is where Williams lived while working on two of his most successful plays, *A Streetcar Named Desire* and *Summer and Smoke.* Williams often said that of all the Quarter places in which he lived, this was his favorite. He once wrote, "What I liked most about it was a long refectory table under a

DIRECTIONS / Literary Tour 187

skylight which provided me with ideal conditions for working in the mornings. I know of no city where it is better to have a skylight than New Orleans." Until the 1950s, streetcars rumbled along tracks in the French Quarter, and since Royal Street was on the *Desire* line, the playwright no doubt heard the dull clang of the streetcar's bell as it passed under his window.

The final stop on this literary stroll is one of the most important. Across from the *Gumbo Shop* is a short alley that runs parallel to the 600 block of St. Peter. Walk the few steps through it to Pirates Alley, which runs along the side of St. Louis Cathedral; on your immediate left is *Faulkner House* (624 Pirates Alley; phone: 504-581-3262). This elegantly appointed, beautifully organized bookshop, specializing in the works of Southern writers and rare volumes of all sorts, was William Faulkner's first permanent home in New Orleans. The author was working on one of his early novels, *Soldier's Pay;* today you can buy a copy of that book on the spot where much of it was composed.

Stop for refreshment at the charming *Coffee, Tea, or . . .* (630 St. Ann St.; phone: 504-522-0830), a good place to end this walk. From the *Faulkner House,* walk through Pirates Alley to Chartres, turn left, walk past the *Cabildo* and the *Presbytere* to St. Ann Street, and make a left. Open daily from 8 AM to 6 PM, the shop offers coffees, several kinds of teas, croissants, pastries, cookies, and homemade soups. If the weather is pleasant, you can enjoy your snack in the quiet, dimunitive Spanish courtyard out back, where, amid the banana plants and flowering shrubs, you can relax and read about the exploits of Stanley Kowalski and Blanche DuBois, Amanda Wingfield, Cady, Regina Fox, or the other casts of characters created by the imaginations of the writers who lived here.

Walk 4: The Riverfront (and Farmer's Market)

More than any other factor, it is the mighty Mississippi, that rambling, 2,350-mile-long river, subject of songs and sonnets, renowned the world over, that shaped New Orleans's destiny and its character from that day in 1718 when the city was founded. River commerce and international shipping always have been a mainstay of New Orleans's economy. Without the river, the city's piquant creole cuisine might never have existed, for it was the Mississippi that brought the confluence of French, Spanish, African, and Caribbean cultures that created this distinctive cooking style. Were it not for the river, jazz music might have have remained little more than a local curiosity, since the earliest jazz performers first began carrying their syncopated message to the world on riverboats shuttling between New Orleans and Chicago.

The sustenance New Orleans draws from the Mississippi is even more basic: The river has always been the source of the city's drinking water, and as long as it "keeps on rollin'," New Orleanians will never go thirsty. It is said that once you've tasted New Orleans's river water (it's purified before it's potable), you'll keep coming back for more.

Much of the city's growth, especially before the advent of air travel, has been due principally to its position near the mouth of the Mississippi, about 100 miles south of the city at the Gulf of Mexico. It began with the flatboats that plied the waters between New Orleans and the American heartland, carrying every sort of cargo, both human and otherwise. Then came the big, legendary steamboats of the late 19th and early 20th centuries, laden with hundreds of tons of cotton, grain, merchandise, and foodstuffs on trips between New Orleans and the Midwest. This was the era when the city's port was the terminus of the immense transportation network formed by the Mississippi and its many tributaries.

Today every manner of vessel can be spotted gliding on the muddy water, lugging grain, coal, petroleum products, sand, gravel, salt, sulfur, and chemicals.

The Mississippi has the third-largest drainage basin in the world, exceeded in size only by the watersheds of the Amazon and Nile rivers. When joined with the 300 rivers that empty into it, the Mississippi's total length becomes 3,484 miles. Waters from as far east as New York and as far west as Montana flow into the lower river.

There is a certain Latin fatalism that New Orleanians have had about the river for the past 3 centuries — it has been a frequent blessing and an occasional curse. All but a small part of New Orleans's soggy land mass is at or below sea level. One result is flooding in the spring, when the mid-continent's

190 DIRECTIONS / The Riverfront

snows to the north melt into the tributaries, funneling billions of gallons of new water into the Mississippi. The floods were an annual event until the late 1920s, when immense mounds of earth, called levees, were raised along both of the river's banks to hold back the swelling waters.

Mark Twain, the Mississippi River's biographer, summed up his subject as "not a commonplace river, but on the contrary . . . in all ways remarkable." More than 100 years later, Twain's description still holds; in fact, the river is more vital to the city's landscape and character today than it was in his day.

For most of New Orleans's existence, city dwellers were cut off from the river because of a barrier of connected wharves and warehouses that extended from one end of town to the other. But in the 1970s, New Orleans port officials began removing the outdated, deteriorating sheds and pilings from the banks at either side of Canal Street. Grass-roots support for a design of parks and other public "people" spaces to replace the wharves and pilings took hold. The result was a strip of open riverbank stretching about 30 blocks along the French Quarter, Canal Street, and the Warehouse District.

The Mississippi Riverfront, as it's now called, is a prime source of entertainment as well as enterprise, and a perfect area for a leisurely stroll. A convenient starting point is in the Warehouse District (see *Walk 5: Warehouse-Art District*) at the corner of Convention Center Boulevard (which parallels the river) and Thalia Street. At this point you are standing almost directly under the pair of river bridges known as the Crescent City Connection, the principal links between New Orleans's east and west banks.

As you face the water, the span farther to the right is the Greater New Orleans Bridge, completed in 1958. It was the first bridge connecting central New Orleans to Algiers, the only section of the West Bank within the city limits. The Crescent City Connection's second, wider span, parallel with the first, was completed in 1988. At night, this newer bridge's superstructure is outlined in lights, adding considerable sparkle to the nocturnal waterfront views.

With the river to the right, proceed down Convention Center Boulevard to the mammoth *New Orleans Convention Center,* which has undergone two expansions since it opened shortly after the *1984 World's Fair.* Although the fair ended in bankruptcy, it is credited with helping to resuscitate many of the warehouses and small factory buildings along the New Orleans waterfront; in the early 1900s the area bustled with small port-related industries and offices. The *Convention Center* is the country's third-largest, with 700,000 square feet of contiguous exhibition space, 43 large meeting rooms, and a 35,000-square-foot ballroom. Nearby, many of the multi-story buildings that once housed light industrial operations have been converted into posh, contemporary apartment complexes.

At the end of Convention Center Boulevard, turn right and take the canopied path leading to yet another result of the *World's Fair* — the *Riverwalk Shopping Mall,* with 2 levels of shops, cafés, restaurants, and fast-food stands extending a quarter mile along the riverbank. Originally the International Pavilion of the 1984 *World's Fair, Riverwalk* was developed in 1986 as a mall by the Rouse Company, designers and developers of several similar projects

DIRECTIONS / The Riverfront   191

in other American cities. Many of *Riverwalk's* upper-level eateries have tables with sweeping views of the Mississippi. Among the shops, you'll find tropical cottons with that safari look at *Banana Republic,* clever gifts, clothing, and sporting goods at *Abercrombie & Fitch,* and the latest in electronic gadgetry at *A Sharper Image.* At the dozens of other shops and restaurants, the merchandise ranges from *Christmas* ornaments to kitchenware, and the food from po-boys to lasagna. *Riverwalk's* second level has railed pedestrian walkways that offer close-up views of cargo vessels, tugs, and excursion boats skimming along the river.

Outside the mall's main exit is the Plaza d'España, an open area with an expanse of geometric red, white, and black Spanish tiles and a large circular fountain. A jazz or rock group will more than likely be tooting and plucking away at the open-air bandstand. If your own whistle needs whetting at this point, there's a good selection of drinks, plus sandwiches and hot food, at *LeMoyne's Landing* (on the plaza near the Algiers ferry landing; phone: 504-524-4809); you can sit at the bar inside or at one of the tables outside. At the river's edge, there will probably be a docked paddlewheeler, excursion boat, or other pleasure craft pulling up to load or unload passengers. (For information on some of the boats and their sightseeing routes, see *Sources and Resources* in THE CITY.)

Before continuing along the waterfront, there is an optional but worthwhile detour to another interesting open space, the Piazza d'Italia. Go to the *New Orleans Hilton* hotel's main entrance, just behind *Riverwalk,* at the end of Poydras Street. Walk 4 short blocks along Poydras; on the left corner of Poydras and Tchoupitoulas Streets is a striking, contemporary tower, a postmodern interpretation of the ancient campaniles (freestanding church bell towers) so visible in the ancient squares of many Italian towns. Tucked behind it to the left is Piazza d'Italia, built with money raised by New Orleans's large Italian-American community. The tower and the whimsical post-modern rendition of a Roman ruin were created in 1979 by the nationally recognized architect Charles Moore, in cooperation with the local architectural firm of August Perez and Associates. There is a fountain and Roman arches with a humorous frieze of Roman-style masks that depict some of the modern-day local citizens who had a hand in the building of the piazza (one of those depicted is Moore himself). Note that the shape of the fountain's pool is that of the Italian peninsula. Unfortunately, the piazza and its fountain have not been well maintained — it was to be the focal point of a real estate development that did not materialize.

If you've taken this detour, return now to the Plaza d'España. From the central fountain, walk diagonally to the right down a slight incline to Canal Street. Before you is the large, modern *Rivergate Exhibition Center,* used for conventions and trade shows. For a pleasant, water-based interlude, taking a ride on the Canal Street ferry (to the right) is one of the most fun free things to do in the whole city. The refreshing, interesting trip across the mighty Mississippi takes between 10 and 20 minutes round trip, depending on the river traffic. The ferry operates daily from 6 AM to 9 PM.

The large, pleasant outdoor observation deck on the ferryboat's pedestrian level provides a panoramic view of the busy riverfront, beginning at the left

192   DIRECTIONS / The Riverfront

with the twin river bridges, then *Riverwalk Mall* and Plaza d'España, the high-rise buildings on and around Canal Street, the *Aquarium of the Americas,* Woldenberg Park, Jackson Square, and part of the *French Market.*

When the ferry docks at Algiers Point, you can either stay aboard or disembark and head for the river levee (to the left as you leave the ferry house). The grassy levee in Algiers is another good spot for a grand vista of the city's riverfront profile.

On returning to the east bank, just after exiting the ferry house at Canal Street, look to the immediate left. The sleek, angular high-rise building across from the *Rivergate Exhibition Center* is the World Trade Center (2 Canal St.). Enter the lobby and take the elevator 33 floors up to the *Top of the Mart* restaurant (phone: 504-522-9795), a plush, comfortable, glass-enclosed lounge that makes a complete revolution every 90 minutes. Have a snack and take in the spectacular bird's-eye views of the city, the Mississippi, and miles and miles beyond.

Exit the World Trade Center and turn right, past the Canal Street ferry and across the traffic intersection, to the fascinating *Aquarium of the Americas* (1 Canal St.; phone: 504-861-2537). Notice the row of playful abstract sculptures in hot, tropical colors as you pass. The aquarium's strikingly contemporary building, completed in 1990, houses 10,000 specimens of fish, birds, and reptiles, displayed in their natural habitats in more than a dozen major exhibits. You can see part of the walk-through Amazon rain forest exhibit from the outside of the building — inside, this exhibit features a wide array of equatorial plants, flowers, fish, and other animals. Another highlight is the immense 2-story tank that holds sharks and other species indigenous to the Gulf of Mexico. The Caribbean Reef exhibit is another walk-through tank filled with brightly colored fish and their even more exotic relatives. The aquarium contains a large cafeteria on the second floor, a bright pleasant place for a light meal or sandwich. (For more information, see *Special Places* in THE CITY.)

When leaving the aquarium, walk to the left along the river to Woldenberg Park, a large, grassy, tree-filled oasis with comfortable benches. The herringbone brick path leads past handsome outdoor sculptures by some of New Orleans's leading contemporary artists. If you're lucky, you'll happen on a band playing on the little bandstand, or one of the frequent ethnic food-and-crafts festivals; held in the park on weekends, they're sponsored by one of the diverse cultural groups in the city.

At the end of Woldenberg Park, turn left (away from the river) and walk the short distance to North Peters Street. This will put you at the *Marketplace,* an extensive 2-story complex of shops and restaurants, including *Tower Records* (408 N. Peters St.; phone: 504-529-4411), with the most colossal collection of compact discs and cassettes outside of New York City; *Bookstar* (414 N. Peters St.; phone: 504-523-6411), its 2 floors filled with thousands of recently published volumes in every category; and the *Hard Rock Café* (440 N. Peters St.; phone: 504-529-5617), with the chain's trademark rock-music memorabilia, high-decibel speakers, and menu of hamburgers, chili, and other all-American fare.

Starting at the *Marketplace,* North Peters Street temporarily becomes

DIRECTIONS / The Riverfront   193

Decatur Street. Walk to the waterfront just behind the large parking lot to the landing dock of the *Natchez,* a sternwheeler built in the 1920s with a steam engine that functions excellently to this day. The engine's steam drives not only the boat's paddlewheel but also the authentic old calliope on the top deck. Its toots and squawks often can be heard for blocks. The *Natchez* makes two daily excursions up and down the river, each about 2 hours long (for more information, see *Sailing and Boating* in DIVERSIONS).

Just beyond the *Natchez* dock, at Decatur and Toulouse Streets, is *Jackson Brewery,* a shopping and restaurant complex composed of two connected 5-story buildings — the Millhouse, completed in 1988, and the Brewhouse, opened in 1985, which replaced the original old *Jax Brewery.* Inside is a profusion of gift and souvenir shops, confectioneries, bookstores, restaurants, and an eclectic assortment of other retail outlets.

The Moon Walk begins where the *Jackson Brewery* ends (at the corner of Decatur and St. Peter Streets, just across the extension of St. Peter leading to the river). No, it has nothing to do with space suits and rocket boosters (or Michael Jackson, for that matter). The Moon Walk gets its name from Moon Landrieu, New Orleans's mayor from 1970 to 1978, who spearheaded the development of the French Quarter as a tourist attraction. Across Decatur Street from Jackson Square, the river levee is pleasantly landscaped, with a row of rustic lampposts that are lit at night and wide, wooden stairs that lead right to the muddy water of the Mississippi. From the Moon Walk, look across the river to the left. That nearly hairpin turn in the river is Algiers Landing, the deepest spot — recorded at 192 feet — in the Mississippi (the river's average depth from source to mouth is about 12 feet).

Walk down the Moon Walk's shoreside steps and cross the railroad tracks to the large pavilion overlooking Jackson Square. The view from here is splendid. At center stage is St. Louis Cathedral, fronted by the lush garden of the square itself. Flanking it are the handsome, stuccoed *Cabildo* and *Presbytere,* and forming the square's other two sides are the elegant, red brick Pontalba Apartments, built in the 1850s by a Spanish noblewoman and often advertised as the first true apartment buildings in the United States.

Facing the square, take the pavilion steps to the right to the *Café du Monde,* the gateway to the *French Market* and a delightful spot to relax with New Orleans–style café au lait (chicory-flavored coffee with hot milk) and the puffs of fried, sugar-topped fritters known as beignets (pronounced ben-*yays*). If the weather is pleasant, wait for a table on the terrace and enjoy one of the city's most picturesque spots, with its view of Jackson Square and Decatur Street's never-ending bustle. (Also see *Quintessential New Orleans* in DIVERSIONS.)

Housed in a building once known as the *Butcher's Market,* the café marks the beginning of the *French Market,* the colonnaded arcade that stretches along the riverfront for several more blocks.

The *French Market* is the oldest established marketplace in the Mississippi Valley, and although the five main buildings were erected between 1813 and the end of the 19th century, the market's history dates back much farther. Even before the French explorers arrived in 1718, the site was a trading post used by the local Choctaw Indians. For more than 2 centuries after that, it was the "belly" of New Orleans, lined with stalls crammed with not only

194   DIRECTIONS / The Riverfront

fruits, vegetables, poultry, fish, herbs, game, and other meats, but also such nonedible merchandise as clothing and hardware.

Documents of the early 1800s describe Indians selling freshly butchered rabbits, women hawking rice cakes, river boatmen stocking up for the trip back home, and an endless parade of merchants dealing in dry goods, trinkets, poultry, and pralines. While the French were content to have their market outdoors on the levee, the Spanish built the first structures to provide sanitary conditions for marketing meat. Over the years the buildings and merchandise have changed, but much of the heady atmosphere of exchange remains.

Farther down Decatur Street is a hodgepodge of boutiques selling home-made quilts, creole foodstuffs, toys, pralines, and ice cream.

Walk along the river 1 block away from Jackson Square to Decatur and Dumaine Streets; here is the *Bazaar,* where clothes, fabrics, cooking utensils, and every sort of household goods were once sold. It is one of several river-front structures designed in mid-1800s by New Orleans architect Joseph Abeilard, one of the scores of "freemen of color" who, as professionals and craftsmen, contributed greatly to the French Quarter's architecture. The *Bazaar* was destroyed by a hurricane in the 1930s, and was rebuilt shortly afterward with money from the federal Public Works Administration. Today, it houses a number of specialty shops selling apparel and accessories. Behind the *Bazaar,* in the *French Market,* is *Bella Luna* (near the corner of Decatur and Dumaine Sts.; phone: 504-529-1583), a contemporary-creole and Italian restaurant with stunning, second-floor views of the river (see also *Eating Out* in THE CITY). This might be a good spot to stop for lunch or dinner, depending on the hour. The kitchen specializes in such traditional dishes as fettuc-cine with cream, gumbo, and bread pudding, as well as mesquite-smoked gulf fish and shrimp.

Go back to the river and continue walking straight ahead (downriver) to the 1000 block of Decatur Street, intersecting Ursulines Street, to the old *Vegetable Market.* At the turn of the century, the market was jammed with Sicilan-American fruit and vegetable vendors. Today, beneath the colonnaded arches are cafés, restaurants, and crafts shops. On a typical weekend, street musicians and performers are usually adding their glides and strums to the scene.

With the river to the right, continue across Gov. Nicholls Street to the *Farmer's Market,* a large, roofed shed built in 1936 to allow retailers, whole-salers, and farmers from nearby parishes to sell fruits, vegetables, herbs, and spices. The market, which is open 24 hours, still holds a wide assortment of produce — notably tomatoes, sweet potatoes, mirlitons (the pale-green, pear-shape squash known in Mexico as *chayote*), pumpkins, watermelons, and in the early summer, sticks of raw sugarcane (whittle off the tough peel, cut the hard pulp into strips, and chew). But don't look for real bargains here.

The *Farmer's Market* leads right into the *Community Flea Market,* where scores of tables overflow from the sheltered walkway onto the open space known as French Market Place. Weekends are the best times to scavenge among the dozens of stalls, piled high with everything from T-shirts and used jeans to handmade furniture and antique-glass butter dishes. Filling the air is the scent of piquant spices and fresh shrimp, gulf fish, and crabs wafting

DIRECTIONS / The Riverfront   195

from the shops along this arcade which specialize in all sorts of local and regional foodstuffs. The massive, terra cotta–colored building in the background is the Old US Mint, home of the *New Orleans Jazz and Mardi Gras Museum* (see *Drive 1: Esplanade Avenue–City Park*).

We've saved the best of this walking tour for last: a fascinating ride back to the center of town along the riverfront on one of the vintage streetcars known as the *Ladies in Red*. Facing the river at the intersection of Esplanade and N. Peters Street, walk the few yards to the streetcar tracks and the car stop, where you can board the streetcar. The cars travel a delightful 1.9-mile rail route all the way to Julia Street in the Warehouse District, with many convenient stops along the way. The ride amounts to a series of second looks at many or all of the New Orleans riverfront's stunningly diverse sights.

Walk 5: The Warehouse-Art District

In their preoccupation with New Orleans's history and traditions, most people find it easy to forget that the city also has a modern, avant-garde side. The Warehouse District, a part of town near the Mississippi Riverfront that once bustled with the commerce and business of a flourishing port, has been completely refurbished and redesigned; it is at the center of the city's avant-garde nature.

Less than 15 years ago, this area was known mostly for its skid row and the abandoned buildings bearing mute testimony to a bygone era of shipping. But then the *1984 World's Fair* came to town, and the city rediscovered that the dozens of old office buildings, wholesalers' warehouses, small factories, and assorted other structures were a hidden, underdeveloped treasure. Now the district has evolved into the New Orleans equivalent of New York's Soho.

There are more than 100 art galleries throughout New Orleans, but most of those with fine regional or national reputations are clustered around the Julia Street area in the Warehouse District. The handsome, excellently proportioned rooms in these buildings are ideal for showcasing paintings, sculpture, ceramics, glass, and photographs. At any particular time, one Warehouse District gallery might display the shockingly original mixed-media work of an up-and-coming local artist while its neighbor features the subtle, abstract-expressionist oils of a nationally recognized painter. The energy and enterprise of the *Contemporary Arts Center,* a quasi-clubhouse and showcase for artists, spearheaded this movement, and their spirit is echoed throughout the thriving art scene here.

The emphasis of this walking tour through 12 square blocks of the Warehouse District will be on its function as a center for the city's contemporary art scene. But appreciation for its artistic contribution should not eclipse the historical and architectural value of its buildings. Anyone who wants to get a deeper understanding of the area's renovation and architectural significance need look no farther than the *Preservation Resource Center (PRC;* 604 Julia St.; phone: 504-581-7032). A nonprofit advocacy group seeking to preserve and restore the landmarks of the Warehouse District and other historic neighborhoods, the *PRC* was responsible for Julia Row's rejuvenation. Given the least bit of prodding, an enthusiastic *PRC* member will be happy to give you a fistful of brochures and a crash course in local architecture.

The most suitable place to begin an artistic tour of the district is the *Contemporary Arts Center (CAC),* just off Lee Circle (900 Camp St.; phone: 504-523-1216). Founded in 1976, the *CAC* is the center of the city's lively cultural community, acting as a showplace for the work of up-and-coming

198 DIRECTIONS / Warehouse District

local painters, sculptors, musicians, playwrights, and actors whose talents might otherwise be overlooked. It is housed in a renovated 1920s-vintage brick building that was the former headquarters of the local *Katz & Besthoff* drugstore chain. Each year, more than 200 exhibitions and other events in the visual arts, cinema, video, children's education, theater, dance, performance art, and music take place in this bilevel, 6,500-square-foot space. There are also two theaters, classrooms, and a screening room for films and videos. Call ahead to get a list of upcoming shows.

The contrast between the boldly avant-garde *Contemporary Arts Center* and the traditional *Confederate Museum* just across the street (929 Camp St.; phone: 504-523-4522) couldn't be more striking. Entering this storehouse of Confederate memorabilia is like journeying back in time about 150 years. The *Confederate Museum,* a late Romanesque edifice of earth-colored stone with a cavernous interior of dark, reddish cypress, has a significance all its own. Images of the Civil War (some diehard rebels still refer to it as "The War of Northern Aggression") are evoked by tattered flags and battle standards, ungainly rifles and cannonballs, and reams of yellowed documents.

Established in 1891, the museum houses such historic items as the uniform, sword, hats, and epaulets belonging to Confederate General Pierre Gustave Toutant Beauregard, the New Orleanian who began the Civil War by ordering the first shot at Fort Sumter, South Carolina, to be fired. He was one of the museum's founding fathers. One section is devoted to the clothing and books belonging to Jefferson Davis, president of the short-lived Confederate States of America. If you like, you can take a piece of the Confederacy home with you; a small gift shop features such souvenirs as Confederate banknotes circa 1864, books, and limited-edition prints of war scenes by artists of the period.

Outside, more Confederate memorabilia — on a somewhat larger scale — awaits. From the *Confederate Museum,* take a right and walk a half block to the corner of Howard Avenue. Turn right on Howard and continue 1 block to Lee Circle, a lovely knoll of green space that surrounds a 3½-ton, 16½-foot bronze statue of Confederate General Robert E. Lee, gazing southward. The memorial was dedicated in 1884, with many of Lee's family and friends present.

Continue left for about a quarter of the circle to the broad expanse of St. Charles Avenue. You might see the *St. Charles* Streetcar pass as you cross St. Charles to K&B Plaza (1055 St. Charles Ave.; phone: 504-586-1234), a thoroughly modern office building ringed by an especially fine collection of 20th-century sculpture — bronze figures, aluminum mobiles, and a mounted, stylized crescent. Inside the lobby (open during weekday business hours) are sculpted pieces by such noted artists as Isamu Noguchi, Henry Moore, George Segal, and Jacques Lipschitz, along with fine examples of late-20th-century painting. (By the way, if you're wondering why that woman sitting on a bench near the elevators is so immobile, the explanation is simple — she's one of sculptor Duane Hanson's strikingly realistic creations.)

The next area is the hub of the gallery scene — Julia Street. After leaving K&B Plaza, recross St. Charles Avenue, go right for a quarter of Lee Circle until you get back to Howard Avenue; turn left and walk on Howard for 1

DIRECTIONS / Warehouse District   199

block to Camp Street; turn left, and walk along Camp, crossing St. Joseph. On the way, pop into the *Galerie de Jumonville* (866 Camp St.; phone: 504-524-0082), one of the newest of the Warehouse District's galleries. It's on the ground floor of one of the nine connected townhouses that form Gasquet Row, constructed between 1838 and 1843.

Walk another block on Camp to Julia Street and turn right. Within the next 4 blocks of Julia are almost a dozen of the city's finest art galleries, ensconced in several renovated 19th-century shopfronts, offices, and former private homes. *Galerie Simonne Stern* (518 Julia St.; phone: 504-529-1118) specializes in fine contemporary paintings (most notably abstract expressionism), sculpture, photography, and master prints. Represented are artists with local, national, or international reputations. Continue on Julia to the *Arthur Roger Gallery* (432 Julia St.; phone: 504-522-1990), which boasts the most lavish exhibit spaces in New Orleans. Previous shows have focused on such artists as New York photographer Herb Ritts, New Orleans figure painter George Dureau, and Louisiana landscapist Elmore Morgan. On the next corner, at Julia and Constance Streets, the *Louisiana Children's Museum* (428 Julia St.; phone: 504-523-1357) is a lively place where children can romp through a series of ingenious educational installations — they can push a small grocery cart through a mini-supermarket, its shelves stocked with "products," then check them out on a real cash register; or they can tool around in an authentic TV studio and anchor the evening news while watching themselves on monitors.

From the museum, continue another block on the same side of the street and in the same direction to the *Downtown Gallery* (420 Julia St.; phone: 504-524-1988), which spotlights many Louisiana-born masters who worked between 1900 and 1950, along with samples of Art Deco, Art Nouveau, and Primitivism. A short distance nearer the river is the *Sylvia Schmidt Gallery* (400-A Julia St.; phone: 504-522-2000), which concentrates on works of contemporary realism and abstract expressionism.

On the next block of Julia, intersecting with Tchoupitoulas Street, is the Rotunda, a former grocery warehouse and an excellent example of the innovative refurbishing of the Warehouse District. If you're hungry for lunch, you couldn't have picked a better time, since the Rotunda houses *Emeril's* (800 Tchoupitoulas St.; phone: 504-528-9393), one of the city's most popular restaurants. Owner-chef Emeril Lagasse is a widely acknowledged master at blending deep, traditional flavors of creole cooking with new American ingredients — crab and corn in puff pastry with creole corn sauce; spicy, New Orleans–style barbecued shrimp with fresh-baked biscuits; and banana cream pie (see also *Big Easy's Best Eats* in DIVERSIONS).

The Rotunda also is home to a trio of art galleries, just around the corner from *Emeril's* on Julia Street. *LeMieux Galleries* (332 Julia St.; phone: 504-565-5354) showcases "Third Coast" artists (natives of various towns along Louisiana's gulf coastline). Next door, *Still-Zinsel Contemporary Fine Art* (328 Julia St.; phone: 504-588-9999) has more contemporary paintings, sculpture, and photography, along with drawings and paintings on paper. The *Gasperi Gallery* (320 Julia St.; phone: 504-524-9373) displays a colorful variety of Southern primitive and folk art.

200 DIRECTIONS / Warehouse District

If you didn't stop for lunch (or even if you did), at this point, a good cup of coffee is only a few steps away. Continue on Julia Street toward the river for 2 blocks, to the corner of Fulton Street. Here, *True Brew Coffee House* (200 Julia St.; phone: 504-524-8441) serves cappuccino, espresso, mochaccino (hot chocolate with a shot of espresso and topped with whipped cream), or *café crème,* a frothy concoction in hot or frozen versions combining 8 ounces of milk, a hazelnut fudge-coffee concentrate, and brown sugar. Like any self-respecting coffeehouse in an art district, *True Brew* is frequented by artists, actors, and writers, but it's also popular with doctors, lawyers, and office workers infiltrating from the adjacent business district. Wall space is reserved for local artists' works, and the intimate 60-seat theater on the premises often features works by local playwrights.

From here, cross Julia, turn left, and amble back the 2 short blocks past the intersection of South Peters Street to *Christopher Maier Furniture Design* (329 Julia St.; phone: 504-586-9079). This is a working studio and showroom for Maier's classically proportioned, custom-designed wood furniture, influenced by Greco-Roman forms and shapes, and featuring inlay work and exotic materials.

Walk to the right along Julia for a block and a half to the corner of Tchoupitoulas Street. Turn right onto Tchoupitoulas and walk the half block to No. 746, site of the Julia Place apartment building and *3 D's* restaurant (phone: 504-566-7255). In the Warehouse District's industrial days, this building was a factory that produced burlap bags for the tons of coffee beans that passed through the port daily. The restaurant, with its slightly arched windows and dramatic, black slate floors, offers such dishes as hot artichoke dip and a "suburban pâté" of chicken breast. Like other Warehouse District dining spots, *3 D's* doubles as gallery space, with revolving shows of local artists and occasional poetry readings.

From *3 D's,* return to Julia, turn right, and walk a half block to *Ariodante* (535 Julia St.; phone: 504-524-3233), where you can browse through one-of-a-kind furniture, glass, ceramics, jewelry, and decorative objects created by a variety of artisans. From the gallery, walk to the right a half block to the corner of Julia and Magazine Streets, cross Magazine, and turn right. A half block up Magazine is the *New Orleans School of Glassworks and Gallery* (727 Magazine St.; phone: 504-529-7277). In the rear studio, among the white-hot kilns, you can watch teachers and students shaping and blowing blobs of molten glass into beautiful vases, sculptures, and bibelots.

From here, turn right and walk the half block back to Julia. Turn right and walk up Julia to Camp Street. A few steps from the corner is *Wyndy Morehead Fine Arts* (603 Julia St.; phone: 504-568-9754), where an eclectic assortment of artworks is showcased against the dark gray walls. A hidden courtyard in the back doubles as a sculpture garden. Outside this gallery is a perfect vantage point from which to admire Julia Row, the beautiful brick structure across the street. This series of 13 connected brick townhouses in the Greek Revival style was called "The 13 Sisters" when they were built in 1832 by a company speculating in real estate. Each unit contains commercial space on the ground floor and apartments on the two balconied upper floors. In the mid-1800s, these were among the most fashionable addresses in town for

DIRECTIONS / Warehouse District   201

newly arrived non-creole immigrants (Creoles had claimed the French Quarter as their own). The houses, which offered such architectural novelties as ornamented doorways and high ceilings, were efficiently designed with elegantly proportioned rooms. But by the turn of the century, the neighborhood had begun to deteriorate, and it remained rather seedy until its revival in the early 1980s.

Continue along Julia to St. Charles Avenue, turn right, walk 1 long block to Girod Street, then turn left on Girod. Baronne Street intersects Girod 2 blocks later; turn right and head for No. 636. A pair of galleries on the street level is worth a visit. Inside the door and to the right is *Marguerite Oestreicher Fine Art,* which features figurative artwork; to the left and up a few steps, *Bronwen White* specializes in contemporary painting from Great Britain, Scandinavia, and Latin America (phone: 504-581-9253 for both galleries). A few doors down, *Estudio Gallery* (630 Baronne; phone: 504-524-7982 or 504-947-9651) is the working studio and exhibition space of local artists Zella Funck and Martin LaBorde. A visitor might find the couple hard at work on a silkscreen or other printmaking project. Next door, *Ya/Ya Inc.* (628-630 Baronne; phone: 504-529-3306) is the showplace of artist Jana K. Napoli and her young, inner-city protégés, who are becoming well known for creating colorful, whimsically painted furniture.

The end of this walk is a convenient location for visiting other parts of the city as well. To get to the French Quarter, turn right from *Ya/Ya Inc.* and walk 5½ blocks to Canal and Baronne Streets; to reach the riverfront area, walk 1½ blocks to the right to Poydras Street, then turn right and continue 6 blocks to the river.

The Garden District

0   mile   1/8

BARONNE

CARONDELET

ST. CHARLES AVE.

S

Louise S.
McGehee
School

Rink Shopping
Center

PRYTANIA

Lafayette
Cemetery
†

Toby -
Westfeldt
House

COLISEUM

F Commander's
Palace

CHESTNUT

PHILIP

Warwick
Mansion

CAMP

6TH

WASHINGTON AVE.

4TH

3RD

2ND

1ST

Forsyth -
Payne
Residence

MAGAZINE

N

CONSTANCE

Walk 6: The Garden District

Some years, spring comes to New Orleans as early as the end of February, when the city's numerous trees, flowering plants, and shrubs begin to bloom. Early spring is the best time to appreciate the simple, natural pleasures of the city's Garden District, a lushly verdant residential oasis less than a mile from the urban center. If the previous winter was mild (as often happens), azaleas spring onto the scene in February and March, their bright pinks and fuchsias blanketing much of the area surrounding the Garden District's graceful old houses. Camellias, in pure whites, delicate pinks, and soft reds, show up at about the same time. By mid-March, the air becomes fairly saturated with a dizzying blend of the perfumes given off by the blossoming shrubs and trees — snowy gardenia, pungent ginger and magnolia, and luscious-smelling jasmine, sweet olive, wax legustrum, and roses. Many of the district's bushes and trees were planted more than 150 years ago, after being brought from France, the Caribbean, or the huge sugarcane, cotton, and indigo plantations that once lined the Mississippi River's banks north of the city.

The mid-19th century was the Garden District's golden age, when one stately house after another, in a profusion of romantic architectural styles, sprouted among the hundreds of oak trees lining the then makeshift thoroughfares. In the antebellum period of the 1840s and 1850s, New Orleans was a culturally divided city, with the creole descendants of French, African, and Spanish colonists ensconced in the Vieux Carré and the newly arrived American entrepreneurs (mostly Scotch, Irish, and English merchants, manufacturers, shippers, and planters) settling uptown, in the sections beyond what is now Canal Street. The factors dividing the two groups were language (French was still the lingua franca of the Creoles) and religion (the Protestantism practiced by most of the American newcomers was virtually unknown in the older, Roman Catholic part of town). Therefore, not long after their arrival, the more prosperous of the new citizenry set about developing their own genteel, close-knit community, in a section not far from the uptown riverfront, then known as Lafayette City.

That sense of separateness lingers even today. Stroll through the Garden District and it's easy to feel you've entered another country — and traveled through the past to another era as well. The boundaries of this self-contained, aristocratic little world are not officially defined, but the term "Garden District" is commonly understood to embrace the 65 square blocks within the rectangle formed by St. Charles Avenue, Jackson Avenue, Magazine Street, and Louisiana Avenue.

The elegantly proportioned houses, mostly imposing mansions of white-

204 DIRECTIONS / Garden District

washed cypress or stuccoed brick in soft, neutral tones, come in a cavalcade of mid- to late-19th-century architectural styles — principally Greek Revival, Second Empire, Italianate, and "Victorian Ornamental."

Collectively, the buildings share a number of distinctive characteristics. Large front verandahs (also called "galleries") stretch from one end of the house to the other; massive or delicate columns extend from the gallery floors to ornate friezes; and delicate, frilly ironwork usually frames the galleries. Some homes were built in the old Louisiana style, with the main floor set upon a high masonry foundation, an architectural feature designed to protect the dwellings from the frequent floods that predated the construction of retaining levees along the Mississippi River. The houses contain as many as 20 or 30 rooms, and most have been carefully preserved. Some are even inhabited by descendants of the original owners.

The first owners spared little expense in the design and construction of their homes, which were built to withstand the ravages of the heat and dampness of the city's 9-month-long summers. An indication of the quality of their construction is the pristine condition they are in today.

Inside, hand-painted murals decorate some of the ceilings, and many of the houses contain sweeping staircases with hand-carved mahogany banisters and newel posts. The finest Italian marble was used to construct the mantels, and the fabrics, furniture, and rugs were almost always European imports.

Some of the Garden District mansions have not survived the onslaught of time. They were either neglected and allowed to deteriorate or sold and converted into apartment or commercial buildings. Those that survived intact are still private residences, so none are open for public inspection. However, the beauty and history of their architecture can be appreciated quite well even from a distance.

The best starting point on a walking tour of the Garden District is the corner of St. Charles Avenue and First Street — 2 blocks past Jackson Avenue if you're traveling on the *St. Charles* Streetcar from the central business district. This tour can be combined with the *St. Charles* Streetcar tour (see *The St. Charles Streetcar*).

From St. Charles, walk 1 block toward the river to Prytania Street, where, on the near left corner of First and Prytania Streets, is the Louise S. McGehee School (2343 Prytania). Once one of the Garden District's residential showplaces, now it is a girls' private elementary and high school. Designed in the "Free Renaissance" style of the early 1870s by James Freret, a prominent local architect, it features a wide front porch with wraparound railings separated by pairs of fluted Corinthian columns. The house is remarkable for its fully finished basement, an element rarely used in New Orleans, since the water table lies just a few feet belowground.

Across Prytania Street is the Toby-Westfeldt House (2340 Prytania), perhaps the most admired of the Garden District's structures; surrounded by an unpretentious white picket fence, its simple, austere lines are not unlike the plantation houses upriver from the city (see *Drive 2: Plantations Tour)*. The house is believed to be the oldest in the district, built around 1838 by Thomas Toby, a native Philadelphian and manager of the large plantation that once surrounded the house. Its popular name is "Toby's Corner," a holdover from

DIRECTIONS / Garden District 205

its earliest days when the corner was the terminus of the city bus line. The house underwent extensive improvements in 1855, but its basic design and character remain intact.

Continue down First Street to the 1300 block, considered by many to be the most beautiful strip in the neighborhood. Walk down First Street for a block and a half past the intersection of Coliseum Street to the home at 1331 First, dating to 1869 and distinguished by its monumental floor-to-ceiling windows, fine stucco work, dental molding, side projections, and lavish ironwork. Although No. 1315, the house across the street, may be somewhat less magnificent, its sweeping, inviting entrance is also noteworthy. This is also one of the few Garden District homes that retains its original accessory buildings, lush garden, and stately oaks.

Continuing down the next block of First, examine the decorative fence at No. 1239, distinctive for its woven iron wire, a patented process in which the iron rods were pulled, rather than cast or wrought. Designed in 1857 by architect James Calrow, a temporary resident of New Orleans whose work is well represented throughout the Garden District, the house was built at a cost of $13,000. At 1236 First is another fine house built in the Greek Revival style, completed in 1847. Inside, the home is embellished with black marble mantels and elaborate plaster ceiling medallions from which hang period crystal chandeliers.

On the next block of First, past the intersection of Camp Street, is the Forsyth-Payne residence (1134 First St.), one of the district's most important historical sites. In 1889 Jefferson Davis, former President of the Confederate States of America, died in the left rear first-floor guestroom while visiting a friend, Judge Charles Erasmus Fenner. The 2-story Greek Revival building, constructed of cement-covered brick, has the clean, simple lines of Greek Revival style, with wide front galleries extending across both floors, supported by six Ionic columns. Built from 1849 to 1850, the house was commissioned by J. N. Payne, the judge's father-in-law.

Return to the corner of First and Camp and turn left on Camp. A few yards away is the Warwick Mansion (2427 Camp St.). Originally a residence, it later served as a private school for children of the Garden District's affluent citizens. Continue 1 block along Camp to Third Street. Turn right on Third, to No. 1206. Inside this house, designed with an eclectic mix of architectural styles and erected before the Civil War, Confederate General John B. Hood and two members of his family died in 1879, victims of the devastating yellow-fever epidemic of 1878. Across the street, at 1213 Third, is one of the city's best examples of the 19th-century "Italianate Villa" school of architecture. The style — typified by curved façades and porches, slightly arched windows with rounded lintels, and elaborate friezes lining the roof — was popular on the East Coast at the time, but was not commonly used in New Orleans. The original owner was Archibald Montgomery, a Dublin native who employed James Gallier, Jr., the city's leading architect of the time, to design the residence for him.

Continue down Third Street for 1 block to 1331 Third, a house of special interest to art buffs because of its association with French Impressionist painter Edgar Degas. It was built for Michael Musson, a successful cotton

206 DIRECTIONS / Garden District

merchant who also was the city's postmaster. Musson's sister (who was Degas's mother) was born in New Orleans, and when the painter visited here, he stayed with other relatives who lived on Esplanade Avenue near the French Quarter. Degas's letters home reflect his positive impressions of the pretty Creole women, the buildings of painted wood (an extreme rarity in France), and the steamboats on the river. During one visit to the city, Degas depicted a moment in the New Orleans Cotton Exchange in a painting that today hangs in the municipal museum at Pau, in the French Pyrenées.

From here, continue down Third, past Coliseum Street, to the monumental structure at 1415 Third, one of the largest houses in the Garden District. Among its striking features are the sweeping curved portico and upper gallery that extends the full width of the façade, lofty Ionic columns, ornate dental moldings, and the center parapet above the roof line. Built in 1865 for Walter G. Robinson, a genteel Virginian, the home is said to have had the city's first indoor plumbing. The elaborate ceiling frescoes in the large parlor and dining room are the work of Domenico Canova.

The building next door (1417 Third St.) is a noteworthy example of the "carriage house," a New Orleans version of the small, quaint stables for carriage horses found in the narrow alleys of London.

Continue along Third Street in the same direction and turn left onto Prytania Street. No. 2605 is the only example of the Gothic Revival style in the Garden District — and one of the few in the entire city. Both the main house and its matching guest cottage are made of stuccoed brick. Notice that the pointed arches above the windows and doors are repeated in the balcony's ironwork motif.

Backtrack across Third Street to No. 2520, built in 1853; its asymmetrical design is a blend of the Greek Revival and Italianate architectural styles. The balcony is distinguished by its delicate finial ornaments and is supported by cast-iron lower railings. On the same block, at No. 2504, is a home built in 1859 and currently owned by the *Women's Opera Guild.* While the interior is decorated in Victorian style, the exterior is a hybrid of Italianate and Greek Revival styles. Across the street is No. 2507, an early-1850s building that was inhabited by Joseph H. Maddox, owner of the *New Orleans Daily Crescent,* an important newspaper of the period. The fireplace in this house is decorated with original hand-painted tiles that depict a bayou scene.

Continue along Prytania to Second Street; turn right and continue to Coliseum Street. At the corner, note the house at 1410 Second, with its Corinthian columns and stucco façade. Like most of New Orleans's 19th-century homes with brick exteriors, this one was painted or stuccoed and then repainted to resemble stone.

Turn right on Coliseum, and walk a block and a half to 2627 Coliseum Street, where the gingerbread-like trim and elaborate ironwork lend a story-book aspect to the red brick mansion, built during the post–Civil War Reconstruction period. It was originally inhabited by James Eustis, an American ambassador to France.

Facing this house, turn right, go to Fourth Street, and turn right again. In front of this house built in the Italianate Villa style (1448 Fourth St.) is a cast-iron fence with a cornstalk motif, similar to the celebrated one surround-

DIRECTIONS / Garden District   207

ing *Cornstalk House* in the 900 block of Royal Street (see also *Walk 1: The French Quarter*). History places the cost of construction at $23,750, no small sum in 1859, when the house was built. Inside, the double parlor's measurements are a palatial 43 feet by 26 feet.

This lavishly landscaped mansion dominates the 1400 block of Fourth Street and is a prime example of how much money was freely spent in constructing these elaborate Garden District houses. The 2-story antebellum house, surrounded by giant magnolias, elms, and palms, as well as prodigious shrubbery, contains 15 large, high-ceilinged rooms and features verandahs with wrought-iron railings lining three sides of the exterior.

Continue down Fourth Street and turn left at Prytania. Walk 1 block along Prytania and turn left onto Washington Avenue. To the right, this 1600 block of Washington forms a boundary of Lafayette Cemetery, which was laid out in 1833 by the original residents of the town of Jefferson, the precursor to the Garden District. Like other New Orleans cemeteries, Lafayette is filled with aboveground tombs, with mausoleums resembling stone and marble cottages, each used as the final resting place for generations of the same family. The cemetery gates usually are open, but strolling around the tombs is not always safe.

Now that your architectural appetite has been satisfied, you may be hungry for food and drink. Two dining options are just a few steps away from here. For a snack of fresh pastries accompanied by any one of several varieties of coffees and teas, try *La Tazza,* a little café in the *Rink Shopping Center* on the corner of Washington and Prytania (2727 Prytania; phone: 504-891-6968). If you want to indulge in a lavish lunch or dinner, however, you couldn't do much better than *Commander's Palace,* on the opposite corner at Washington Avenue and Coliseum Street (1403 Washington Ave.; phone: 504-899-8221). This establishment is consistently ranked among New Orleans's most creative creole restaurants. Specialties include sautéed shrimp with mushrooms, trout in pecan crust, fried soft-shell crabs, and bread pudding soufflé. Reservations are always advised, and men are required to wear jackets (see also *Big Easy's Best Eats* in DIVERSIONS).

To return downtown by streetcar, walk 2½ blocks along Washington Avenue to St. Charles and board the car on the Garden District side of the median. To go uptown toward Carrollton Street, the stop is on the Washington Avenue side of the median. Another option is to call a taxi from a public telephone at the *Rink Shopping Center;* the fastest and most reliable service is *United Cabs* (phone: 504-522-9771).

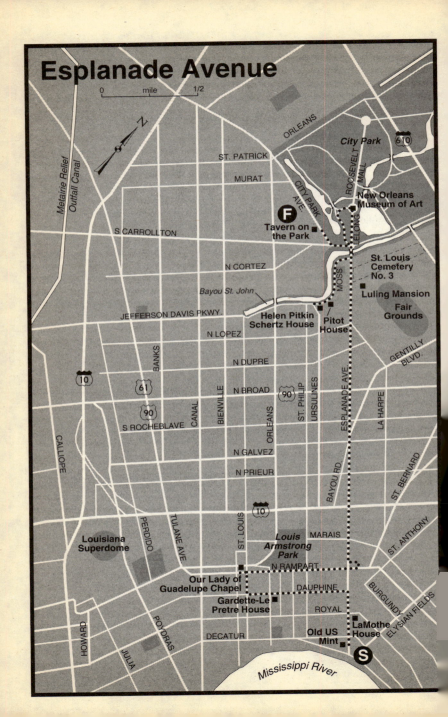

Drive 1: Esplanade Avenue–City Park

Readers of old maps and documents are often surprised to learn that Esplanade Avenue, the tree-lined boulevard that forms one of the French Quarter's boundary lines, was often referred to as Esplanade Ridge. In the topography of New Orleans, most of which is below sea level, a hill is defined as any mound of earth more than 8 or 10 feet high, and a "ridge" is nothing more than a strip of sloping terrain.

The founding fathers' "Ridge" was a slight exaggeration; there is absolutely no sense of elevation as you walk or drive this avenue. Parallel to central Canal Street, Esplanade Avenue (or Ridge, if you will) extends more than a mile beginning at the Mississippi River; for 10 blocks it forms the dividing line between the French Quarter and the ancient "suburb" of Faubourg Marigny. It then stretches more than a mile toward Lake Pontchartrain, ending at Bayou St. John and the entrance to City Park.

In the very earliest decades of New Orleans's existence, Esplanade had no name; it was little more than a strip of terrain between the colonial town now known as the French Quarter and the plantations and small farms of Faubourg Marigny. The then-nameless strip marked the beginning of the trade route from the center of town to Bayou St. John, which connects with Lake Pontchartrain, a coastal bay along the Gulf of Mexico.

During the city's boom era of the 1830s, Esplanade became a very desirable residential area, known as La Promenade Publique. Well-to-do French Creoles built stately frame houses amid lavish gardens, with oak, magnolia, elm, and palm trees. Although most of the houses survive today, in various states of repair and disrepair, few remain the elegant single-family dwellings they once were.

A sense of Esplanade Avenue's former splendor remains, however, thanks to the many restorations of its ancient mansions, and the giant oaks and flowering shrubs lining the curbs and the broad, grassy medians.

Taking in Esplanade's sights on foot is pleasant, though somewhat more strenuous than our other walks; going by car allows for an extended look beyond the avenue, along tranquil Bayou St. John, with its numerous old raised cottages on its banks, as well as bosky City Park. One of the last stops on this tour, City Park is an ideal spot for a picnic lunch.

The logical starting point is at Esplanade and the Mississippi River, in front of the *Old US Mint* (400 Esplanade Ave.; phone: 504-568-6968), which houses two museums and a historical research library. Entered on Esplanade Avenue, the huge granite structure is the oldest federal mint building still standing, and occupies the entire block bounded by Esplanade Avenue and

210 DIRECTIONS / Esplanade Avenue

Barracks, North Peters, and Decatur Streets. Designed in the Federalist style by William Strickland, it was completed in 1838. Between that year and the early 20th century, nearly $300 million in silver dollars and other coins were minted out. In 1861, at the outbreak of the Civil War, Louisiana's state government took possession of the building. (It reverted to federal ownership afterward, and eventually was used as a prison and a military barracks.) Today, legendary New Orleans jazzman Louis Armstrong's first trumpet rests in one of the *Jazz Museum*'s display cases, along with resplendent costumes worn in the hundreds of *Carnival* parades and balls that precede New Orleans's world-famous *Mardi Gras* celebration (see also *Mardi Gras Madness* in DIVERSIONS).

On leaving the Mint, cross Decatur Street at the Esplanade intersection traffic signal and travel 1 block up, away from the river, to the corner of Chartres Street. On the near right corner, at 524 Esplanade, is what may be the boulevard's oldest remaining structure. This 2-story residence, with an oversize attic, was built in 1810 for Gaspar Cusachs, a local historian, who embellished the ceilings with florid paintings and intricate moldings and medallions. Rooms in the house were used as sets for *Blaze*, the 1989 movie biography of former Louisiana Governor Earl K. Long. Unfortunately, the house is not open to the public.

Continue up 1 more block — pausing to note *LaMothe House* at 621 Esplanade, a 150-year-old double townhouse, surrounded by moss-draped oaks, that's now a hotel (also see *New Orleans's Best Hotels,* DIVERSIONS) — to 704 Esplanade, the towering stucco building with the large side courtyard on the far right corner — one of the largest and most flamboyant of all the residences on the avenue. Built in 1856 by John Gauche, a wealthy Creole, the intricate iron balconies that extend around three sides of the building are said to have been cast in Saarbrücken, Germany, from a design by the German Renaissance engraver Albrecht Dürer.

Continue 2 blocks up Esplanade to Dauphine Street, turn left, and drive 7 blocks to Orleans Street. The lofty structure on the far left corner (716 Dauphine) is the Gardette–Le Pretre House, dating from 1836. In June 1861, Confederate General Pierre G.T. Beauregard is said to have sent part of the captured flagstaff from his victory at Fort Sumter, South Carolina, here; it was presented to the Orleans Guards, who were part of the local militia.

Continue up Dauphine Street for 3 more blocks to St. Louis Street, then turn right on St. Louis for 2 blocks to the divided thoroughfare, North Rampart Street. Turn left and go 1 block to Conti Street. At the corner of Conti and North Rampart Streets is Our Lady of Guadalupe Chapel (411 N. Rampart St.), built in 1826 to serve as a "burial chapel" for the two nearby cemeteries, St. Louis Nos. 1 and 2. Funerals were frequent at that time, since the city was gripped by a virulent yellow-fever epidemic, which eventually took thousands of lives. The chapel was used exclusively for funerals until 1860, since it was believed that using the main cathedral would unnecessarily expose the general population to the highly contagious disease, transmitted by the mosquitoes that infested the city from spring to fall. To the right of the building is the grotto-like, and rather bizarre, Shrine of St. Jude, "the patron saint of lost causes." The shrine's stone-like walls are festooned with

DIRECTIONS / Esplanade Avenue   211

crutches and other objects signifying the cures, as well as little plaques engraved with a simple "Merci," expressions of thanks for favors granted. In the rear of the chapel proper is a statue of St. Expedite, the saint who never existed. In fact, the saint was "created" by the unknown parishioners who, seeing only the word "Expedite" on the shipping crate that the Italian-made statue arrived in, mistook it for his name. To this day, two-line ads regularly appear in the "Personals" column of the the *Times-Picayune* classifieds that read, "Thanks to St. Expedite for favors granted."

From Our Lady of Guadalupe, make a U-turn on Conti and return via North Rampart Street about 8 blocks to Esplanade Avenue. Since no left turns are permitted here, drive 1 block farther, make a U-turn, and drive 1 block back to Esplanade; then turn right. About a mile up this road is Leda Court, home to Luling Mansion, one of the great architectural treasures of New Orleans, now an apartment building.

On the way to Leda Court, 6 blocks up Esplanade Avenue, is an intersection with Bayou Road, which once led to Bayou Sauvage; 8 blocks farther, past the traffic signal at North Broad Street, is another diagonal intersection at Grand Route St. John, which is the site of the ancient thoroughfare that once linked Bayou Sauvage to the east and Bayou St. John to the west.

Another 5 five blocks up Esplanade on the right is Leda Court, a very short street nestled in a lush neighborhood just behind the *Fair Grounds* racetrack. At No. 1438, almost obscured by trees and shrubs, is the splendiferous, neo-Romanesque Luling Mansion, dating to 1848. It once sat on an 80-acre estate, 10 acres for the house and gardens, the remainder mostly woods. In 1865, James Gallier, Sr., the leading New Orleans architect of the time, designed and built the 4-story, 22-room mansion from a crude sketch by its owner, Florenz Luling, a cotton merchant exiled from Germany during the Revolution of 1848. During the Reconstruction period after the Civil War, Luling's economic difficulties forced him to sell parcels of the estate. In 1880 the house of cement-covered brick, with balconies encircling the 3 upper floors, became the *Louisiana Jockey Club*. Since the 1920s it has been an apartment house.

Backtrack to Esplanade Avenue and turn right to St. Louis Cemetery No. 3 (3421 Esplanade Ave.). Installed in 1856, its original gates remain, a relic of the time when the old Bayou Cemetery was taken over by the Roman Catholic Archdiocese of New Orleans and given its present, numerical name. Priests and nuns were traditionally entombed here. (Bishops and archbishops were buried beneath the altar of St. Louis Cathedral on Jackson Square.) James Gallier, Sr., architect of the Luling Mansion, the old City Hall (now Gallier Hall) in the Central Business District, and numerous other major 19th-century public buildings, was buried here with his wife after they lost their lives in a shipwreck in 1866. Other tombs house the remains of Father Adrien Rouquette (1813–1887), a poet and missionary to the Choctow Indians, and the black philanthropist Thomy Lafon (1811–1893).

One block farther up Esplanade is Moss Street, which runs along the bank of Bayou St. John. The bayou, extending from Lafitte Avenue to Lake Pontchartrain, was a key factor in Jean-Baptiste le Moyne Sieur de Bienville's decision to select New Orleans as the site of the royal French colony in 1718.

212 DIRECTIONS / Esplanade Avenue

The local Indians and early settlers used the bayou to move wares to and from the town on the Mississippi River, and its connection to Lake Pontchartrain provided access to the Gulf of Mexico beyond. In the 1790s, the Carondelet Canal was dug near the ramparts at Toulouse Street in the French Quarter to connect Bayou St. John with the town itself. In 1927, the canal was filled in, ending the bayou's commercial function and making it in effect a decorative waterway for the plantation houses and weekend cottages along the banks.

Turn left onto Moss Street and go the dozen-or-so blocks to the Pitot House, also known as the Ducayet House (1440 Moss St.; phone: 504-482-0312). Designed in the traditional West Indies style, featuring 2 stories topped by a high-pitched, gently tapering roof and functional rooms on the ground floor, this small plantation house was originally a country home for the aristocratic Ducayet family, who retreated to the cool edge of Bayou St. John on weekend getaways from their French Quarter cottage. Later, it was the home of the family of James Pitot, who served from 1804 to 1805 as the first mayor of the newly incorporated city. The outer wall construction is of *briquets-entre-poteaux* ("bricks between posts") covered with stucco; the interior has been furnished by the Louisiana Landmarks Society with Louisiana and American antique furniture, fabrics, and bibelots reminiscent of the early 1800s. (For more information, see *Special Places* in THE CITY.)

At the end of the next block is the Helen Pitkin Schertz House (1300 Moss St.), constructed about 1784, the same time as the Pitot House. It was known long ago as the Spanish Custom House because of its reputation as a storage place for booty confiscated by the numerous pirates who ran their boats up the bayou. Also done in the West Indies style, the house's broad galleries are supported by Pompeiian brick columns, a design feature that helped promote air circulation throughout the rooms. The galleries and the roof are of wood, while the first floor is of plastered brick. The two dormer windows in the American colonial style were a later addition, as was the rear room. Unfortunately, this house is a private residence and not open to the public.

Backtrack now to Esplanade Avenue, turn right, and cross Bayou St. John. The equestrian statue dominating the circle you see before you is of New Orleans–born Confederate General Pierre G.T. Beauregard, veteran of the battles of Fort Sumter, Bull Run, and Shiloh. The sculptor is Alexander Doyle, creator of the monumental bronze of Beauregard's commander, Confederate General Robert E. Lee, at Lee Circle in the city's center (see also *Walk 5: The Warehouse-Art District*).

Halfway around the circle is Lelong Avenue, a broad alley that leads to the *New Orleans Museum of Art* (open Tuesdays through Sundays, 10 AM to 5 PM; phone: 504-488-2631); it's worth a visit for its superb collections of painting, sculpture, decorative art, and photography that range from pre-Christian Oriental and Mediterranean works through to the major contemporary American and European periods. The original neo-classical building, dating to 1912, has been expanded over the years to permit more exhibition and educational space (see also *Memorable Museums* in DIVERSIONS).

The museum is located in City Park, the perfect place to stop and enjoy a picnic. This onetime sugar plantation is one of the largest urban parks in

DIRECTIONS / Esplanade Avenue   213

the country, and includes 1,500 acres of picnic grounds, an amusement park, tennis courts, lagoons, flower-filled gardens, and some 22,000 sprawling oaks, some of which are said to be 800 years old. The 8 miles of lagoons, filled with swans and ducks, can best be appreciated by renting one of the self-propelled paddleboats or canoes. The amusement park has a child-scale locomotive that winds through the grounds, a restored 19th-century carousel, and a fantasy village called *Storyland,* inhabited by larger-than-life Mother Goose characters. For the sports-minded, there are 4 golf courses and 39 tennis courts, along with volleyball and baseball fields (see also *Special Places* in THE CITY).

If you haven't brought a picnic, and want a bite to eat, the nearby *Tavern on the Park* restaurant (900 City Park Ave.; phone: 504-486-3333) is a good choice. Go to the left side of the museum (as you're facing the building), turn right, continue for about 50 yards, and, at the first fork in the road, keep left. Drive along the edge of the lagoon to reach the wide, divided City Park Avenue. Continue a few blocks; the restaurant is on the left. Across the avenue, note the cluster of magnificent oak trees. Under their branches, Creole gentlemen of the 19th century settled affairs of honor with pistols or swords, giving the trees the name Dueling Oaks. The imposing, 2-story building that houses the restaurant was opened in 1860 as a coffeehouse, and later evolved into a restaurant for park visitors. At other points in its history it also was a bordello and, most recently, a raucous neighborhood sports bar. The current incarnation is a comfortably elegant dining place, with Siena marble floor tiles, a lustrous mahogany bar, and excellent views of the oaks through the row of large glass windows. The menu of steaks, seafood, and chops is moderately priced, and dishes are competently prepared. Especially good are the oysters Rockefeller, shrimp rémoulade, fried oysters, and New York strip steaks with cracked pepper. Don't worry about the calories: You'll burn them off after you park your car.

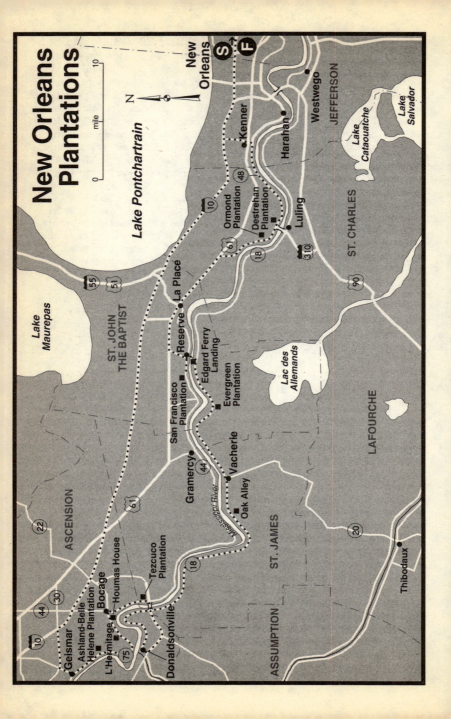

Drive 2: New Orleans Plantations

During much of the 19th century, the elaborate plantation culture flourished along the banks of the Mississippi River. The wealthy families who built the plantations were mostly Creole, descendants of the region's early French and Spanish colonists. The agriculture that attracted and supported their lavish lifestyles dates back to the early 1700s, when the territory was a French colony. In an effort to further populate the area and develop the swampland, France began recruiting from its prisons and slums, transporting people to the fertile Louisiana territory. When that strategy failed, the country began to offer large tracts of land to anyone who could bring in tenants to work it. The lure worked, but it promoted the slave trade and it benefited only those who were able to accumulate a sufficient number of slaves to do the work.

By the early 19th century, it was technology that ensured the long-term economic future of the aristocratic planter society, even after Louisiana became a part of the United States in 1803. First, a Creole planter named Etienne de Boré discovered a method to granulate sugar. Then, Eli Whitney invented the cotton gin, which removed seeds that were tightly entangled within the tough fibers of cotton bolls. And, finally, Robert Fulton designed the steam-driven engine that could help move crops and cargoes up and down the Mississippi. These momentous technological advances spawned a scramble for land along the river — land that had suddenly become valuable.

In the northern half of Louisiana, cotton became king; up to 2 million acres were used to grow the crop in the 1830s. In the rich, black soil of the southern half of the state, sugarcane accounted for another 250,000 acres. The number of slaves grew accordingly: By 1840, Louisiana's slave population was about 140,000 (about 15% of the total in the US). At the outbreak of the Civil War in 1861, an average of 50 slaves lived and worked on each of Louisiana's 1,500 plantations.

The Emancipation Proclamation and the resultant Civil War threw a wrench into the machinery of the South's plantation economy. With the burning and looting that accompanied the military battles, most of the plantations were destroyed. Of the few antebellum plantation houses that survived, many have been painstakingly restored. Some homes were preserved by descendants of the original owners, but most were restored through the contributions of individuals, corporations, and nonprofit foundations. Today, some 20 plantations still stand less than 100 miles upriver from New Orleans. Some are either closed to the public entirely or open only by special appointment, but others offer short guided tours, and a few have been converted into comfortable, even elegant bed and breakfast establishments.

216 DIRECTIONS / Plantations

The plantation designs of the early 19th century were inspired by the tropical architecture of the West Indies. But as the planters prospered, the monumental Greek Revival architectural style, with a large number of variations, became widely used. The houses, designed for the region's damp, subtropical climate, were also planned to simplify the comings and goings of large numbers of relatives, friends, and workers. They served not only as residences, but also as centers of self-contained communities living, working, and trading on the land. Usually, the houses were built off the ground as a protection from the Mississippi River's frequent spring floods. In order to capture cross breezes, the ground floor of most houses was split into only 4 large rooms with a minimum of interior walls. Ceilings, windows, and doors were high, and most rooms opened onto porches that could extend around three or all four sides. Steeply sloped roofs carried off the frequent rains and extended out over the porches, known as "galleries," to block heat and glare.

Of the ten plantations on this driving tour, six offer guided tours lasting about an hour, and two of these serve meals and offer overnight accommodations. The other four are completely private and can be viewed only from the roadside. Although it's possible to visit them all in a single (very busy) day, spending 2 days touring is a better idea.

The method behind this driving tour is to save time by first traveling from New Orleans directly to the farthest plantation upriver, then making stops at the various sites on the return trip to the city.

The trip upriver is a 55-mile drive on Interstate 10 West. More than 10 miles of this preparatory drive are on an elevated roadbed cutting through a serenely beautiful coastal marshland. The muddy pools, grassy expanses, and moss-hung cypress trees vibrant with such wildlife as flocks of snowy egrets and other water birds, as well as turtles, make this drive an especially pleasant one. The Bonnet Carré Spillway, a dam-like device stretching about 2 miles through the swampy terrain from the Mississippi River at the left to Lake Pontchartrain at the right, is about 20 miles from the city. The spillway acts like a huge trapdoor, holding back river water from the marshland leading to the lake. When the river swells in the spring to the point of flooding, the spillway's immense bays can be opened, releasing the overflow into the marsh and the brackish lake.

About 35 miles past the spillway, take Exit 177 and turn left on Louisiana Highway 30. After about 1 mile, follow the sign for Ashland–Belle Helene Plantation. At Geismar, located at the junction of Highways 30 and 75, turn left onto Highway 75. This strip, which runs on either side of the river parallel to the levee, is also known as River Road, but its name changes as different state highways merge with it. Throughout this driving tour, you'll be traveling on or near this road; although its name changes, it is easily identifiable because of its position next to the riverbank. At this point of the tour, River Road cuts through part of the state's "chemical corridor" between New Orleans and Baton Rouge, the state capital, with petrochemical plants and refineries silhouetted against the sky in poignant counterpoint to the flat sugarcane fields surrounding them.

From the junction of Highways 30 and 75, continue on River Road for 3½ miles to Ashland–Belle Helene Plantation (phone: 504-473-1328). The 1842

DIRECTIONS / Plantations   217

Greek Revival mansion silently eulogizes the demise of its glorious era. The first impression conveyed by its aging outer layer of stucco and the random arrangement of the grounds' plants and shrubbery is of forlorn abandonment. Even with its architectural bones partly exposed, there is much evidence that it may have been the most splendid of all the homes along the Lower Mississippi.

The house is much taller than its 2-story design would indicate, thanks to unusually high ceilings. Its exterior walls are surrounded by 28 square, massive brick columns soaring 30 feet to the frieze below the roofline. The interior spaces are in various states of renovation and are still in the process of being furnished. Central halls on both floors provide access to large, airy rooms that in turn open onto wide galleries via step-through "guillotine" windows extending from the floors almost to the ceilings. At the rear, a magnificent spiral staircase links the ground floors to the attic, where wooden pegs and mortise joints hold the beams to the slightly pitched roof. Parts of the plantation's house and grounds have appeared in three movies: *The Beguiled, Mandingo,* and television's "The Autobiography of Miss Jane Pittman."

Originally called simply Ashland, it was built in 1842 for Duncan Kenner, who practiced law and served in the state legislature when he wasn't occupied with his duties as a planter. Kenner also served in the Confederate government in several capacities. The horses grazing on the front lawn serve as a reminder that Kenner was an inveterate horseman; he maintained his own racetrack on the grounds of the plantation. Its name was changed to Belle Helene by a subsequent owner in 1889. The house is open daily from 9 AM to 5 PM; admission charge.

From Ashland–Belle Helene, return to the River Road; turn left, then continue for about 7 miles. On the way, look for l'Hermitage on the left. It's considered the state's oldest surviving Greek Revival plantation house. Though the house is not open to the public, the calm, simple beauty of its setting, its steeply pitched roof punctuated by two dormer windows, and its handsomely proportioned, galleried façade can be admired from the road. Marius Pons Bringier built it in 1814 as a wedding gift for his son, Michel. Sugarcane was its principal crop, although indigo and tobacco were also cultivated.

Continue downriver 1 mile to Bocage, which means "Shady Retreat" in French, another of Marius Pons Bringier's wedding gifts to his children. He built this stately, 2-story manse in 1801 for his daughter, Françoise, who was 15 years old when she married. Remodeled in the 1840s, the house is fronted with six wide and two narrow wooden columns. The entablature extending above the roofline partly obscures the gently sloping roof. This house is also closed to the public, but its charms are apparent even from a distance.

A mile farther up River Road is the town of Burnside, and Houmas House (phone: 504-473-7841 or 504-522-2262 in New Orleans), which sits in one of the prettiest grounds of all the plantation houses in the vicinity. In the 1790s, nearly a half century before the house was built and named for the Indian tribe of the surrounding area, another house sat on this lot. The earlier, smaller one was built by Alexander Latil in early colonial style on land he had purchased from the Houmas. Latil's building was preserved and incorpo-

218 DIRECTIONS / Plantations

rated into the new plans via a gated, arched carriageway when Colonel John Smith Preston of North Carolina constructed Houmas House. Preston had come to Louisiana to assume control of the land, which had become the property of his father-in-law, General Preston Wade, a veteran of the Revolutionary War. Once installed in their new home, the Prestons apparently were homesick for the Eastern shore, since some design elements recall the colonial homes of New England and the Carolinas, such as the belvedere (a glassed-in cupola crowning the roof).

In 1858, the plantation was acquired by John Burnside, an Irish immigrant who expanded the sugar acreage to 20,000 and gave his name to the nearby town. Thanks to him, Houmas House escaped pillage by Union troops during the Civil War (Burnside claimed neutrality as a British citizen). But the house nevertheless fell into disrepair in later years and languished until 1940, when it was bought by Dr. George B. Crozat of New Orleans and rescued from years of decay.

The spacious grounds are partly shaded by huge, moss-draped oaks. Crepe myrtle trees and a rather formal garden of boxwood hedges add interesting touches to the landscaping. At each side of the house is a small, 2-story hexagonal building called a *garçonnière,* which was where the young men of the family (*garçon* is French for "boy") lived before they married.

Inside the house itself, note the exceptionally fine spiral staircase, the collection of 22 large armoires, all made in Louisiana, the original marble mantels, and the beautiful 19th-century English and American antiques. (An additional point of interest is that many of the scenes in *Hush . . . Hush, Sweet Charlotte,* a 1965 movie starring Bette Davis and Olivia de Havilland, were filmed here.)

Hour-long guided tours are given about every half hour. The house is open daily except *Thanksgiving, Christmas,* and *New Years's Day.* Hours are 10 AM to 5 PM from February through October, and 10 AM to 4 PM from November through January.

If you want to grab a bite of lunch or a snack at this point, a good restaurant is a short distance from Houmas House. Drive downriver along River Road about a half mile and turn left on Highway 44. At the intersection with Highway 22 (about 1 mile farther), turn left to find the four rudimentary frame cottages that make up *The Cabin* restaurant (phone: 504-473-3007). The buildings were created out of ten former slave quarters, each about 140 years old, taken from surrounding plantations. The rustic motif extends to the high-ceilinged, hexagonal dining room decorated with antique-looking farm implements. On the menu are sandwiches, crawfish étouffée, a gumbo thick with sausage and crawfish, black-eyed peas, red beans and rice, cornbread, and buttermilk pie. Open daily; no dinner Mondays through Wednesdays. (However, you may want to save your appetite for the fancier fare available at *Lafitte's Landing,* near Donaldsonville and the Tezcuco Plantation; read on.)

If you've detoured to the *Cabin,* return to Highway 44; turn right, and drive 2 miles downriver to the next stop. Tezcuco Plantation (phone: 504-562-3929), framed by beautiful oak and magnolia trees, was completed in 1855 after 5 years of meticulous construction. The spacious cottage, a creole varia-

DIRECTIONS / Plantations 219

tion on the Greek Revival theme, has 25-foot-square front bedrooms and 15-foot ceilings. The plantation was designed by 19th-century New Orleans architect James Gallier, Jr., for Benjamin Tureaud, a veteran of the Mexican War. The raised cottage's name is a variation of Lake Texcoco, where, according to legend, a divine eagle carrying a snake in its beak came to rest on a nearby cactus, which the Aztecs took as a sign to develop their empire on this spot (the present-day Mexico City).

The house is furnished with period antiques by such prominent Louisiana furniture makers as Mallard and Signoret. The rooms include a warming pantry, an office, a foyer, a parlor, a formal dining room, and three bedrooms. Antique dolls, Art Nouveau pottery, and Civil War memorabilia are also on display. In the carriage house at the rear of the main building is a 23-foot-long torpedo boat used during the Civil War.

Tezcuco Plantation offers both a moderately priced restaurant with a regional menu and pleasantly decorated and comfortable rooms in restored slave cabins. The price of the accommodations (from $60 to $95 per night) includes a tour, breakfast, and a bottle of wine. The house is open daily except *Thanksgiving, Christmas,* and *New Year's Day.* Guided tours are given every 25 to 30 minutes between 9 AM and 5 PM; admission charge.

At this point, if you've opted to wait to eat, return to the River Road; turn left, and proceed 1 mile to the Sunshine Bridge across the Mississippi River (there's a $1 toll) to Donaldsonville. The bridge was built in the 1950s during the administration of Governor Jimmie H. Davis, composer of the popular 1930s country-and-western tune "You Are My Sunshine." Cross the bridge to the west bank of the river and prepare to turn left at the first opportunity, less than an eighth of a mile, at the St. James–Vacherie sign. Continue along the riverbank to the large raised cottage now known as *Lafitte's Landing* (phone: 504-473-1232).

The restaurant is housed in an Acadian residence dating to 1797, which was moved in 1978 to its present site from farther inland. The building once served as the headquarters of Viala plantation; legend has it that the notorious pirate Jean Lafitte, who plundered in southern Louisiana's waters during the early 19th century, occasionally used the site as a stopping-off point.

But from this moment on, history takes a back seat to gastronomy. *Lafitte's Landing* is where celebrated Acadian (also known as "Cajun") chef John Folse first established his national reputation; he continues to supervise the menu when he's not making national TV appearances or traveling to some world capital to preach the gospel of Acadian cuisine. Risks are few when ordering here, but expect boldly seasoned butter sauces on almost everything, from the beautifully sautéed fish to the hearty venison and lamb dishes. The gumbos, crawfish dishes, and jambalaya are exceptionally good, as are the crunchy, meaty soft-shell crab and shrimp dishes. Open daily; no dinner on Mondays.

From the restaurant, return to the entrance at the service road, turn right, and drive the short distance to River Road. Turn right on River Road for a 15½-mile drive through the heart of Louisiana's sugarcane country, with tall, grassy stalks rising as far as the eye can see on both sides of the road.

At a bend in the river just off the road between Lagan and Vacherie is a

220 DIRECTIONS / Plantations

magnificent stand of oak trees marking the entrance to Oak Alley (phone: 504-265-2151; or 504-523-4351 in New Orleans). The majestic setting is one of the best among the River Road plantations. While great houses are normally built first and landscaped later, Oak Alley's classically proportioned, Greek Revival mansion was designed as the finale to the vast, leafy canopy formed by 2 parallel rows of oaks, 14 on each side. Some of the trees are 6 feet or more in diameter and 300 or more years old. They are placed 40 feet apart along the grassy, 80-foot-wide path, which narrows slightly as it extends to the house. The trees, valued by the Louisiana Forestry Commission at $2.5 million, are protected during electrical storms by lightning rods. Now they partially obscure the columned façade of the house at the end of the "alley," constructed in 1837 for Jacques T. Roman III and his bride.

Originally christened "Bon Sejour" (which roughly translates to "Pleasant Sojourn"), the mansion received its present name from riverboat travelers awed by the sight of this tunnel of oaks.

Spared during the Civil War, Oak Alley was more fortunate than its owners, whose financial problems had deteriorated to a point where the plantation was sold at auction in 1866 for $32,000. Afterward, several owners occupied the galleried mansion, its façade now painted a soft pink, and its columns a soothing cream. In 1925 the property was bought by Andrew and Josephine Stewart, who lived here for more than 3 decades. Today the house has a lived-in look much as it did when the state acquired it from the Stewarts in the 1970s, and tours are still conducted by the family's original service staff.

Restaurant meals and overnight accommodations in apartments or cottages are available. The restaurant's menu contains typical regional fare; the gumbo of chicken and sausage is especially good.

From Oak Alley, continue downriver for approximately 10 miles to Evergreen Plantation, a private home that is still a working sugarcane plantation. From the short driveway at the fence, the excellently proportioned, Greek Revival house can be seen in all its understated splendor. Set into the sloping roof are three dormer windows, just below the crowning "widow's walk," a name recalling the wives who sometimes stood watch there, scanning the river for the sight of a returning husband or other family member. Evergreen's most distinctive feature, its exterior front stairway, gracefully sweeping from the ground to the second-floor verandah, is a 20th-century addition.

Now continue along the River Road another 5½ miles or so to return to the river's east bank via the Edgard Ferry, which departs every half hour. You'll need to make a U-turn just past the St. John the Baptist Catholic Church onto the paved ramp that leads up the levee and ferry landing. The 15-minute boat ride is an enjoyable excursion on its own, often punctuated with views of cargo vessels, oil tankers, and barge-pushing tugs.

Once you disembark from the ferry, follow the landing road to the base of the levee and turn left at the stoplight. Proceed upriver along River Road for about 3 miles, to the town of Reserve and the sharp bend in the road dominated by San Francisco Plantation (phone: 504-535-2341).

The mansion's intricate, almost lacy detail and bright colors are a stunning contrast to the clean, uncluttered design of the Greek Revival houses previously encountered. The outer color scheme is a rainbow of bright blue, peach, and pale green, made even more striking by its profusion of finials, spindles,

DIRECTIONS / Plantations 221

and friezes. The flamboyant, detailed style is known as "Steamboat Gothic," a reference to both the decorative designs found on turn-of-the-century paddlewheelers and the monumentality of the basic architectural form.

Fittingly, a nautical motif is repeated in a few of the 3-story home's distinctive features: The two wide galleries resemble twin decks of a ship, and the peak of an observatory above the roofline looks like a crow's nest.

The interior architectural features are based on room plans of the creole houses in New Orleans, unusual for a plantation house: Rooms connect by doorways instead of the hallways found in other plantation houses, for example. Among the visual treats waiting inside are five ceiling frescoes, a floor painted to resemble a colorful rug, *faux-marbre* and *faux-bois* walls and doors (painted to resemble marble and unusually grained wood), as well as scrollwork, fluted pillars, and rococo grillwork in many of the rooms.

Edward B. Marmillion had the house built in 1856. His son, Antoine Valsin Marmillion, furnished it lavishly, then named it "Sans Fruscin," a French phrase loosely translated as "Without a Farthing" (apparently a lighthearted acknowledgment that his urge to outfit the place opulently had left him nearly penniless). Later owners anglicized "Sans Fruscin" to "San Francisco." In the 1970s, Marathon Oil Company, which owns the nearby refinery, purchased the plantation and financed a painstaking restoration of the house, furnishings, and grounds. Open daily except federal holidays from 10 AM to 4 PM.

From San Francisco Plantation, continue downriver to the traffic signal at the ferry landing. Take a left at Highway 53 and continue a little over 1½ miles to US Highway 61 (Airline Highway). At this intersection, turn right and drive just over 15 miles to the traffic signal at Ormond Boulevard. Turn right again and drive 3 miles farther, returning to River Road. Two-tenths of a mile down River Road is Ormond Plantation, another private residence that can be appreciated only for its exterior. There is just enough road shoulder to allow for a quick peek at the house's colonial style, typical of the era in which it was built, the late 1790s. The original owner was Pierre Trapagnier, owner of a huge tract between the Mississippi River and Lake Pontchartrain. The house's simplicity is also true to its period, with an unadorned, sloping roof leading to a railed gallery that is divided by seven narrow columns.

Another 3 miles down River Road is a plantation house that scholars claim is the oldest surviving one in the lower Mississippi Valley: Destrehan Plantation (phone: 504-764-9315), built in 1787 for Roger Antoine Robin de Logny by Charles Pacquet, a free black man. In return, Pacquet received "one brute Negro," one cow and her calf, 100 bushels of corn in husk, 100 bushels of rice in chaff, and $100 in cash.

The house's design conforms to the West Indies style, 2 stories topped by a high-pitched, gently tapering roof, functional rooms on the brick ground floor, and seven columns across the front, dividing the railed verandah. Records show that symmetrical wings on either side of the building were added some 20 years after the completion of the home. Another change was the replacement of the original wooden columns in 1840 with massive columns of cemented brick in the classic Doric style.

De Logny's daughter and son-in-law, Jean Noel Destrehan de Beaupre,

222 DIRECTIONS / Plantations

inherited the home in 1802. Here they reared 14 children and entertained lavishly. Legend has it that among their guests were the pirate Jean Lafitte and the Duc d'Orléans, who in 1830 became France's King Louis-Philippe. The house contains a bathtub of solid marble, believed to have been a gift to Destrehan from Napoleon.

Destrehan de Beaupre's descendants occupied the house until 1910. The house was deteriorating badly until the River Road Historical Society took control of it in 1972 and began to restore it. It now contains a collection of European and early American antiques and paintings. Open daily, except major holidays, from 9:30 AM to 4 PM.

To return to the city from Destrehan Plantation, continue downriver on River Road through St. Charles Parish and into Kenner in Jefferson Parish. Turn left on Williams Boulevard and drive 2½ miles to the intersection of Williams Boulevard and I-10. At this junction, turn right and continue about 13 miles into New Orleans.

Index

Academy of the Sacred Heart, 87, 162
Accommodations
  bed and breakfast establishments, 49, 102
  See also Hotels
Advance Purchase Excursion (APEX) fares, 11, 12–13
Airline clubs, 19
Airplane travel, 10–26
  cancellations due to personal and/or family emergencies, 64–65
  charter flights, 20–22
    bookings, 21–22
  with children, 53–54
  consumer protection, 26
  discount travel sources, 22–26
    bartered travel sources, 25–26
    consolidators and bucket shops, 22–24
    generic air travel, 25
    last-minute travel clubs, 24–25
    net fare sources, 22
  flight insurance, 40
  hints for handicapped travelers, 45
  meals on, 17–18
  scheduled flights, 10–20
    airline clubs, 18–19
    baggage, 18
    delays and cancellations, 19–20
    fares, 10–14
    frequent flyers, 14–15
    getting bumped, 19
    low-fare airlines, 15
    meals, 17–18
    reservations, 15–16
    seating, 16–17
    smoking, 17
    taxes and other fees, 15
    tickets, 10
  transportation from airport to city, 26–27
  trip cancellation and interruption insurance, 39
Alcoholic beverages, 65
  See also Nightclubs and nightlife
Antiques, 134–35, 176–79

Aquarium of the Americas, 55, 76, 83, 192
Armstrong, Louis, Park, 172
Art galleries, 199–201
Audubon Park, 87, 163
Audubon Place, 87, 163–64
Audubon Zoological Gardens, 55, 86–87, 163
Automatic teller machines (ATMs), 58–59
Automobile insurance, 29, 40

Baggage, 18
  insurance for personal effects and, 38
Banking hours, 59
Bankruptcy and/or default insurance, 39–40
Bartered travel sources, 25–26
Bayou Cabaret Theater, 100
Bayou St. John, 88, 211–12
Beauregard-Keyes House, 81–82, 169
Bed and breakfast establishments, 49, 102
Bicycling, 98, 138
Black Heritage Festival, 10, 92
Boats, 98, 138–39, 150, 191–93
Books, 68–69
  See also Publications
Bourbon Street, 82–83, 125
Bucket shops and consolidators, 22–24
Buses, 79, 91
Business hours, 59

Cabildo, 76, 81, 145–46, 150, 167, 193
Café du Monde, 81, 120, 124, 150, 193
Cameras and equipment, 70–71
Canal Street and the Central Business District, 84–85, 191–92
Carnaval Latino, 10, 92–93
Carnival. *See* Mardi Gras
Car rental, 27–29, 91
  costs, 28–29
  hints for handicapped travelers, 46
  insurance, 29, 40
  requirements, 28
Carriage rides, 79
Cash machines (ATMs), 58–59

224 INDEX

Celebration in the Oaks, 93
Cemeteries, 83, 86, 89, 207, 211
Children, traveling with, 52–55
  accommodations and meals, 54
  airplane travel, 53–54
  planning, 52–53
Christ Church Cathedral, 161
Cinema, 100
City Park, 77, 87, 88, 93, 98, 136
Climate, 9
Coliseum Square, 86
Colleges and universities, 94, 163
Commander's Palace, 125–26
Community Flea Market, 194–95
Computer services, 69–70
Confederate Museum, 10, 93, 198
Consolidators and bucket shops, 22–24
Contemporary Arts Center, 10, 84, 99,
  146–47, 197–98
Costs, calculating, 34
  car rental, 28–29
Credit cards, 57–58
  telephone calls with, 60, 61
Creole Christmas, 10, 93, 126
Cultural events, 9–10
Custom House, 85

Dashiki Theatre, 99
Default and/or bankruptcy insurance,
  39–40
Destrehan Plantation, 90, 221–22
Dixon Performing Arts Center, 100
Drinking, 65
Driving tours
  Esplanade Avenue-City Park, 208–13
    map, 208
  plantations, 214–22
    map, 214
Drugs
  illegal, 65–66
  prescription, 63

1850 House, 93
Electricity, 61
Emergency medical treatment, 62–63, 91
Esplanade Avenue-City Park, driving
  tour of, 208–13
  map, 208

Fair Grounds racetrack, 211
Farmer's Market, 194
Festa d'Italia, 93
Festivals, 10, 92–93

Fiesta Latina, 93
First aid, 62
  See also Health care
Fishing, 98, 136–37
Fitness centers, 98–99
Food
  on airplanes, 17–18
  Creole cookery, 77, 120, 124–25
  See also Restaurants
Football, 85, 92, 99
Freeport-McMoRan Daily Living Sci-
  ence Center, 94
French Market, 76, 81, 150, 193–94
French Market Tomato Festival, 93
French Quarter (Vieux Carré), 76, 80–83
  literary sites in, 181–82
  shopping in, 132–34
  walking tour, 165–73
    map, 166
French Quarter Festival, 10, 92, 126
French Quarter Maisonettes, 170
Frequent flyers, 14–15

Gallery for Fine Photography, 147
Gallier Hall, 85, 160
Gallier House, 93, 171
Garden District, 76–77, 85–86, 126
  walking tour, 202–7
  map, 202
Golf, 99
Great French Market Tomato Festival,
  10, 93
Gumbo Festival, 10, 93

Handicapped travelers, hints for, 41–47
  airplane travel, 45
  ground transportation, 45–46
  package tours, 46–47
  planning, 41–44
Health care, 61–65
  first aid, 62
  food and water, 62
  local services, 91
  medical assistance, 62–63
  pharmacies and prescription drugs, 63,
    91
  planning, 61–62
  publications, 64
Hermann-Grima House, 93, 147, 183–84
l'Hermitage, 217
Historical houses, 81–82, 84, 85–86, 88,
    89, 93–94, 147–48, 169, 170–72,
    173, 183–84, 203–7, 210, 211, 212

INDEX 225

Historical Pharmacy Museum, 93
Historic New Orleans Collection, 82, 146, 178, 184
Horseback riding, 99
Horse racing, 99
Hotels, 102–109, 126–29
  surcharges for telephone calls in, 61
  tipping, 66
  See also Accommodations
Houmas House, 90, 217–18

Insurance, 37–41
  automobile, 29, 40
  baggage and personal effects, 38
  combination policies, 40–41
  default and/or bankruptcy, 39–40
  flight, 40
  personal accident and sickness, 38–39
  trip cancellation and interruption, 20–21, 39
ITX fares, 13

Jackson Square, 76, 80, 150, 167–68, 185
Jazz and Heritage Festival, 77–78
Jazzfest, 123–24
Jazz Museum, 210
Jogging, 99, 137–38
Julia Row, 84, 200–1
Julia Street, 147, 197–201

K&B Plaza, 84, 160, 198
Kiefer UNO Lakefront Arena, 100

Lafayette Cemetery, 86, 207
Lafayette Square, 85, 160
La Fête, 10, 93
Lafitte, Jean, National Historical Park, 89, 138
Lakefront, 87–89
Lake Pontchartrain Causeway, 89
Lakeshore Drive, 89
Last-minute travel clubs, 24–25
Latino Festival, 10, 92–93
Latter Memorial Library, 87, 162
Legal aid, 65
Le Petit Théâtre du Vieux Carré, 9, 99, 185
Literary, walking tour, 180–87
  map, 180
Local services, 91–92
Longue Vue House and Gardens, 89, 147–48

Louis Armstrong Foundation Jazz Club, 101, 102
Louisiana Children's Museum, 93–94, 199
Louisiana Nature and Science Center, 94, 138
Louisiana Philharmonic Orchestra, 9, 100
Louisiana State Museum, 82, 145–46, 167
Louisiana Superdome, 85, 92, 99, 100
Louisiana Swamp, 86–87
Louisiana Toy Train Museum, 94
Louisiana Wildlife and Fisheries Museum, 94
Lower Depths Theatre, 100
Low-fare airlines, 15
Loyola University, 94, 163

Madame John's Legacy, 82, 172
Magazines, 69
  See also Publications
Mail, 59–60, 92
Maps, 4–5, 158, 166, 174, 180, 188, 196, 202, 208, 214
Mardi Gras, 9, 10, 77, 78, 92, 123, 142–45, 151
Mardi Gras Fountains, 89
McGehee, Louise S., School, 86, 204
Medical assistance. *See* Health care
Metairie Cemetery, 89
Mississippi River, 136–37, 216
  cruising, 139
  touring, 189–95
Money
  cash machines, 58–59
  sending, 58
  See also Credit cards; Traveler's checks
Moon walk, 81, 193
Musée Conti Wax Museum, 94
Museums, 88, 93–94, 145–46, 212–13
Music, 77–78, 82–83, 92, 100–1, 124, 140–42

Natchez, 139, 150, 193
New Orleans City Ballet, 100
New Orleans Convention Center, 84, 190
New Orleans Fair Grounds, 92, 124
New Orleans Jazz and Heritage Festival, 10, 92, 102, 123–24, 140
New Orleans Museum of Art, 9–10, 88, 145, 212–13

226 INDEX

New Orleans Opera Association, 9, 100
New Orleans Saints, 85, 99
New Orleans School of Glassworks and Gallery, 200
New Orleans Symphony Orchestra, 100
New Rose Dinner Playhouse, 100
Newsletters, 69
   See also Publications
Nightclubs and nightlife, 101–02
NORD Theater, 99–100

Oak Alley, 90, 220
Older travelers, hints for, 49–52
   discounts and packages, 50–52
   health care, 50, 61
   planning, 49–50
Old Mint, 10, 78, 82, 209–10
Orleans Ballroom, 172–73
Orleans Club, 87, 162
Our Lady of Guadalupe Chapel, 210–11
Our Lady of Victory, 169

Package tours, 29–33
   for handicapped travelers, 46–47
   for older travelers, 50–52
   for single travelers, 30–31, 48–49
   See also Tours
Palm Court Jazz Café, 101, 124
Parks, 150–51
Personal accident and sickness insurance, 38–39
Pharmacies and prescription drugs, 63, 91
Photographing New Orleans, 148–51
Piazza d'Italia, 191
Pitot House, 88, 212
Planning the trip
   health care, 61–62
   hints for handicapped travelers, 41–44
   hints for older travelers, 49–50
   hints for single travelers, 47–49
   hints for traveling with children, 52–53
Plantations, 87, 89–90
   driving tour, 214–22
   map, 214
Plaza d'España, 76, 84, 191
Pontalba Apartments, 76, 81, 93, 168
Pralines, 124–25
Presbytere, 76, 81, 146, 150, 167, 193
Preservation Hall, 9, 78, 82, 101, 124

Preservation Resource Center, 84, 197
Prytaneum, 86
Publications
   books, 185–86
   for handicapped travelers, 43–44, 45
   health care, 64
   magazines, 69
   newsletters, 69
   for older travelers, 50
   for single travelers, 49
   for traveling with children, 53, 54
Public transportation, 26–27, 91

Religion, 67
Restaurants, 109–20
   best in city, 129–32
   tipping, 66
Riverbend, 164
Riverfront and farmer's market, walking tour of, 188–95
   map, 188
Riverfront/Warehouse District, 83–84
Rivergate Exhibition Center, 191, 192
River tours, 79
Rivertown, 94
Riverwalk, 76, 83, 190–91
Roger, Arthur, Gallery, 199
Round Table Club, 163
Roussel Performance Hall, 100
Royal Street, 82, 150
   literary sites on, 183
   walking tour of, 174–79
   map, 174

Saenger Performing Arts Center, 9, 99, 100
Sailing, 99, 138–39
   See also Boats
Saints Hall of Fame Museum, 94
St. Charles Streetcar, 159–64, 204
   map, 158
St. Joseph's Day, 92
St. Louis Cathedral, 76, 80–81, 167, 185, 193
St. Louis Cemetery, 78, 83, 211
St. Patrick's Day, 92
Shopping, 95–98
   antiques, 134–35, 176–79
   books, 185–86
   in French Quarter, 132–34
   hours, 59

INDEX 227

Riverwalk, 76, 83, 190–91
 on Royal Street, 82, 175–79
Single travelers, hints for, 47–49
 package tours, 30–31, 48–49
 planning, 47–48
Snug Harbor, 102, 124, 141
Southern Repertory Theater, 99
Southern Yacht Club, 89
Spanish Stables, 170
Special events, 10, 77–78, 92–93
Sports and fitness, 98–99, 136–39
 bicycling, 98, 138
 boating, 98, 138–39
 fishing, 98, 136–37
 fitness centers, 98–99
 football, 99
 golf, 99
 hiking, 137
 horseback riding, 99
 horse racing, 99
 jogging, 99, 137–38
 sailing, 99, 138–39
 tennis, 99, 137
Spring Fiesta, 92
Storyland Theme Park, 88, 213
Streetcars, 79–80, 91, 195, 204
Sugar Bowl Classic, 92
Summer Lyric Theater, 100
Sweet Arts Ball, 146

Tara, 87, 162
Tavern on the Park, 88
Taxes
 airplane travel, 15
Taxis, 91
Telephone, 60–61, 90
 hotel surcharges, 61
Tennis, 99, 137
Theater, 99–100
Theater Marigny, 100
Theatre for the Performing Arts, 9, 100
1300 Block of First Street, 86
Time zone, 59
Tipitina's, 101–02, 124
Tipping, 66–67
Toby House, 86
Toulouse Theatre, 100
Tourist information, 68–71, 90
Touro Synagogue, 162

Tours, 79–80
 See also Driving tours; Package tours;
  Walking tours
Transportation
 from airport to city, 26–27
 local, 91
 See also Airplane travel; Buses; Car
  rental
Travel agents, how to use, 15, 36–37
Traveler's checks, 56–57
Trip cancellation and interruption insur-
  ance, 20–21, 39
Tulane University, 94, 163

University of New Orleans, 94, 100
Uptown—University Section, 86–87
Ursuline Convent, 81, 169

Venice Marina, 98
Vieux Carré. *See* French Quarter
Voodoo, 78
 tours, 80
Voodoo Museum, 10, 94

Walking tours
 French Quarter, 165–73
  map, 166
 Garden District, 202–7
  map, 202
 literary tour, 180–87
  map, 180
 Riverfront and farmer's market,
  188–95
  map, 188
 Royal Street, 174–79
  map, 174
 warehouse-art district, 196–201
  map, 196
Warehouse-Art District, 190
 walking tour, 196–201
 map, 196
Water, drinking, 62
Weather, 9
Williams Literary Festival, Tennessee, 9
Williams Residence, 94
Woldenberg Park, 84, 192
Women's Opera Guild, 206

Zoo, 86–87, 163